The African Christian and Islam demystifies the mutual ignorance that is often common amongst African Christians and Muslims, thus building a vital bridge towards interreligious epistemology. The edited book provides a complex historiography of Africa's religious tapestry, underscoring its robustness, spiritual and confessional variegatedness and unity, but also mutual dependence in growth, development and impact. While its main thrust is Christian critical reflections on the nature and manifestation of the particular 'faces' of Islam within African contexts; the book poses crucial challenges for a conscious articulation of a specifically African approach and engagement with Islam and Muslims. It also rejuvenates theological, missiological and existential import of Christian-Muslim relations. Such painstaking, non-essentialist reflections by scholars and religious practitioners based on varied regional contexts in Africa evince an indubitable backlash and corresponding challenge for an African Muslims' critical reflection on Christianity. Not only on their encounter and engagement with Christians in the African context, but also for Christians and Muslims alike, to reflect on indigenous traditions that form the triad of Africa's religious heritage. The urgency of such a book cannot be overstated at an increasingly insecure time in which the global arena is awash with incessant interreligious tensions, conflicts and violence. The book is a must-read for scholars, students and religious and political entrepreneurs who are genuinely committed to interreligious understanding and coexistence in Africa and globally.

Dr. Afe Adogame
World Christianity & Religious Studies
University of Edinburgh, UK

John Azumah is to be commended not only for his vision of, but also for bringing about the first conference of its kind on African Christian perspectives of Islam. A number of conferences have taken place on various aspects of Islam in Africa, but none has been as comprehensive or dedicated to the African Christian perspectives of Islam.

The stimulating papers from the conference contained in this volume have laid the foundation for African Christians to consider their relation to Muslims and Islam in the African context. They offer a basis for the development of critical biblical and theological obligations to engage with Muslims within the overall African context. Particularly valuable is the underlying approach of the papers. On the one hand they offer an overview of historical facts as well as insights into the contemporary nature of Islam in African. On the other hand they raise questions at various levels about the Christian obligation to relate meaningfully to fellow African Muslims.

The combination of theoretical context, empirical information and thoughtful analysis makes this volume an ideal text not just for theological students and pastors but to "rank and file" Christians and Muslims seeking to live and work together for peace and harmony in Africa and beyond.

Dr. Sigvard von Sicard
Department of Theology and Religion
University of Birmingham, UK

The African Christian and Islam

edited by
John Azumah
Lamin Sanneh

MONOGRAPHS

© 2013 by John Azumah and Lamin Sanneh

Published 2013 by Langham Monographs
an imprint of Langham Creative Projects

Langham Partnership
PO Box 296, Carlisle, Cumbria CA3 9WZ, UK
www.langham.org

ISBNs:
978-1-907713-972 Print
978-1-907713-965 Mobi
978-1-907713-958 ePub

John Azumah and Lamin Sanneh have asserted their right under the Copyright, Designs and Patents Act, 1988 to be identified as the Author of this work.

All rights reserved. No part of this publication may be reproduced, stored in a retrieval system or transmitted, in any form or by any means, electronic, mechanical, photocopying, recording or otherwise, without the prior written permission of the publisher or the Copyright Licensing Agency.

Scriptures taken from the Holy Bible, New International Version®, NIV®. Copyright © 1973, 1978, 1984, 2011 by Biblica, Inc.™

Scriptures also taken from the New Revised Standard Version Bible, copyright 1989, Division of Christian Education of the National Council of the Churches of Christ in the United States of America. Used by permission. All rights reserved.

British Library Cataloguing in Publication Data
A catalogue record for this book is available from the British Library.

Cover & Book Design: projectluz.com

Langham Partnership actively supports theological dialogue and a scholars right to publish but does not necessarily endorse the views and opinions set forth, and works referenced within this publication or guarantee its technical and grammatical correctness. Langham Partnership does not accept any responsibility or liability to persons or property as a consequence of the reading, use or interpretation of its published content.

Contents

Acknowledgments ix
Introduction xi

PART ONE: A HISTORICAL SURVEY

Chapter 1 1
The African Christian and Islam: Historical and Religious Dimensions
Lamin Sanneh

Chapter 2 41
Patterns of Christian-Muslim Encounters in Africa
John Azumah

Chapter 3 65
Hermeneutical and Theological Resources in African Traditional Religions for Christian-Muslim Relations in Africa
Abraham A. Akrong & John Azumah

Chapter 4 85
The African Christian and Islam: Insights from the Colonial Period
Elom Dovlo

Chapter 5 103
The African Christian and Islam: The Roman Catholic Perspective
John Onaiyekan

PART TWO: A THEMATIC ASSESSMENT

Chapter 6 125
Fault Lines in African Christian Responses to Islam
John Azumah

Chapter 7 147
Competition and Conflict:
Pentecostals' and Charismatics' Engagement with Islam in Nigeria
Matthews A. Ojo

Chapter 8 177
The African Christian and Ideological Islam
Josiah Idowu-Fearon

Chapter 9 193
    The African Christian and Muslim Militancy
    Moussa Bongoyok

Chapter 10 219
    The African Christian and Islamic Da'wah and Polemics
    John Chesworth

Chapter 11 251
    The African Christian and Islamic Mysticism: Folk Islam
    David W. Shenk

PART THREE: COUNTRY STUDIES

Chapter 12 273
    Egypt
    Tharwat Wahba

Chapter 13 289
    Ethiopia
    F. Peter Ford, Jr.

Chapter 14 303
    Ghana
    Rahman Yakubu

Chapter 15 317
    Kenya
    Stephen Mutuku Sesi

Chapter 16 341
    Nigeria
    Matthew Hassan Kukah

Chapter 17 363
    Senegal
    Daniel Gomis

Chapter 18 375
    South Africa
    Manfred Jung

Chapter 19 391
    Sudan
    James B. Obwonyo

Chapter 20 407
> *Tanzania*
> William Andrew Kopwe

PART FOUR: BIBLE REFLECTIONS

Chapter 21 427
> *Encountering the Other: A Study of Mark 7:24–30 and Matthew 15:21–28*
> Mercy Amba Oduyoye

Chapter 22 437
> *Bible Reflection: Luke 7:1–10, Healing the Centurion's Slave*
> Serge Traore

Chapter 23 449
> *Thinking Biblically About Islam and Muslims: Christian Attitudes toward Muslim Women and Seclusion*
> Josephine Katile Mutuku Sesi

Contributors 461

Acknowledgments

We want to express our deepest gratitude and appreciation to the following organisations, ministries, institutions, churches, and individuals for their invaluable contributions which made the conference and subsequent publication of this book possible: Michael Glerup and Joel Elowsky of the Centre for Early African Christianity; Jeff Ritchie and The Outreach Foundation; Caryl Weinberg and the Mission Council of First Presbyterian Church, Evanston; The PCUSA Africa Area and Evangelism offices; First Fruits, Inc; Chris Wright and Langham Partnership; Dan McVey for his personal friendship and support; Solomon Sule-Saa, then Director of the Presbyterian Interfaith Research and Resource Centre, Accra.

Introduction

This book is a collection of papers presented at an academic conference on the African Christian and Islam which took place in Accra, Ghana, from 6th to 10th July 2010. The conference, the first of its kind in Africa, was the initiative of John Azumah, then Director for the Centre of Islamic Studies, London School of Theology. It was convened in partnership with the Centre of Early African Christianity, Eastern University. There was a total of 52 participants from 27 countries across Africa representing 12 Christian traditions including Catholics, mainline Protestants, Evangelicals and Pentecostals. The Catholic Archbishop of Abuja, Archbishop John Olorunfemi Onaiyekan, chaired the conference which was attended by the General Secretary of the Association of Evangelicals in Africa (AEA). Prof Lamin Sanneh, who is the D. Willis James Professor of Missions and World Christianity at Yale University, gave the key note lecture.

There were lecturers from leading theological seminaries as well as practitioners and development workers such as the director for Pioneers Africa, three national directors of World Vision International and a number of others involved in various ministries in Muslim contexts. Key African Christian Islamicists and up and coming scholars, mainly PhD candidates in the field of Islam and Christian-Muslim Relations in Africa, presented very stimulating papers that generated lively discussions. The presentations were made up of main papers around the theme of the conference, 'The African Christian and Islam', and nine country studies. The purpose was to balance academic presentations with real situation Muslim-Christian encounters across Africa.

The main aim of the conference was for African Christians to articulate a specifically African approach to Islam as a resource for theological students and pastors and as an African contribution to the global discourse in the post 9/11 world. The subject matter of this book is therefore not about Islam in Africa per se, neither is it about Christian-Muslim relations as such. Rather it is an attempt at a critical African Christian reflection on Islam in a quest for a balanced theological and biblical engagement with Muslims in light of Africa, the collective African experience and heritage. For the purpose, five faces or manifestations of Islam were identified for reflection: 1) the radical or militant face of Islam, 2) the political/ideological face of Islam in the form of Islamists conceptions of an Islamic State and implementation of Islamic law, 3) Islamic missions or *da'wah*, 4) lived or folk Islam and Islamic mysticism, *tassawuf*, and 5) the progressive or 'moderate', self-critical face of Islam.

The different faces of Islam are identified to make the point that Islam, like Christianity, is not monolithic and its manifestations in Africa differ from context to context. These different manifestations impact Christian-Muslim relations in different ways in different parts of Africa. The main papers which form the first two parts of the book focus on the nature and manifestation of the particular 'faces' of Islam, with references to historical and contemporary examples within particular African contexts. Attempts are then made at shedding light on theological, missiological and existential questions and challenges Islam raises for African Christians and their witness in an Islamic context. In this regards, attempts are also made to provide scriptural and theological reflections for Christians in their engagement with the different faces of Islam.

By way of background, the first two parts of the book address general relevant themes in the encounter between African Christians and Muslims. In the first chapter, Lamin Sanneh explores the theme of reform and revival in Islam and Christianity in African hands and the role of religious experience, and concludes that inter-religious encounter is valid even if differences persist about the nature of truth and of our obligation. In chapter 3 Akrong and Azumah examine the common heritage of the primal worldview and its potential in building bridges between Muslim and Christian Africans, while Dovlo's chapter 4 surveys models of African Christian encounters with Islam during and against the backdrop of the missionary enterprise and colonial rule. In chapter 5 Onaiyekan gives an account of the official Roman Catholic perspectives on inter-religious engagement and its outworking within the African context, while Ojo looks at prevailing attitudes towards Islam and Muslims within the Pentecostal/charismatic traditions in chapter 7.

The country studies in the third part of the book cover nine carefully selected countries: Egypt, Ethiopia, Ghana, Kenya, Nigeria, Senegal, South Africa, Sudan and Tanzania. A brief historical survey is undertaken on the arrival and spread of Islam and Christianity in each country, as well as major divisions and denominations within Islam and Christianity in those countries. Where available, demographics based on national population census, including major ethnic and regional compositions of the two faiths, are provided. An account of the ways in which Christians of different denominational persuasion engage with Muslims in the particular country is surveyed.

The fourth part is biblical reflections which started each day of the conference. These reflections are offered as examples of Christians reading the Bible in the context of Islam. As indicated, the intended audience of the book is African theological students and pastors as well as academics interested in Christian reflections on Islam in the African context.

John Azumah

Part One: A Historical Survey

CHAPTER 1

The African Christian and Islam: Historical and Religious Dimensions[1]

Lamin Sanneh

Christianity and Islam have developed a deep connection with African values and practises, which has enabled them to establish an important and permanent place in society. Islam and Christianity have remained prominent on the continent, because the search for God has been reinforced as a perennial theme in the lives of African peoples. In good times and bad, Africans have turned to God as a present reality; a God who is too close to be overlooked and too unique to be commonplace.

Few factors are more important than religion in influencing how persons and communities understand and identify themselves. The fundamental search for who we are and what we are here for clamours for a religious response consistent with issues of personal security and a sense of possibility. We get a sense of the scope of religion when we contemplate its salience in such a wide range of activities. These include the personal names people bear; the descriptions people give to relationships; the calendar system and its festivals; the terms used for the natural environment and cycles of the seasons; rites of passage, including mortuary rituals; and ideas of our own humanity. From the cradle to the grave and in between religion dominates.

---

[1]. I am grateful to Michael Glerup and Joel Elowsky of the Centre for Early African Christianity for their help in making this lecture possible. They or the CEAC, however, bear no responsibility for the opinions expressed here; the responsibility lies solely with me.

As we shall see, Africa's bruising encounter with colonial rule, and therefore with the modern West, has merely heightened people's sense of urgency and thus deepened their need of religion.

The importance of Christianity and Islam in Africa is not often acknowledged by writers on the subject. I hope it is not just my African sensitivity that makes me uneasy with the oversight, but experience tells me that neglect of Africa's rich religious heritage is more widespread than can be justified and has contributed to a distortion in the picture of how Christians and Muslims have related to each other in the recent past. This chapter is an attempt to help redress that neglect.

Three major themes serve as a guide for our reflection: First, the role of Muslim and Christian religious experience in reform movements and in effecting radical social change. The second theme is an evaluation of the role of religious experience, including the places of dreams and visions, in its historical and social setting. The final theme is religious experience as the basis of social action and of individual self-discovery. In its concluding observation, this essay makes the point that inter-religious encounter is valid even if differences persist about the nature of truth and of our obligation.

Islam, Christianity, and Radical Reform and Social Change

Both Muslims and Christians had historical movements that influenced religious reform and social change in Africa. Both had reform movements in which their leaders were willing to repudiate prevailing customs and attitudes and for whom religious experiences such as ritual seclusion, visions, and dreams played an important role.

This chapter examines the role of religion in reform movements as personified by two Muslims, Abd al-Karim al-Maghili al-Tilimsani in Songay and north Nigerian Islamic reformer Uthman dan Fodio, and the Prophet William Wade Harris, a Christian in the Ivory Coast.

Muslim Reform Movements

Millenarian ideas about a coming radical change in society had a significant influence on Muslim reform movements in Africa. One of the earliest references to millenarian ideas in West Africa is contained in a report of one of the greatest medieval Arab travellers, Ibn Battuta (1304–1377). While on a visit to the West African kingdom of Mali in 1353, he saw what appeared to be a highly developed ritual for incubating millenarian expectancy in tropical Africa. The group was identified as a Shiite settlement in the tradition of *hijrah* (migration) communities set up to tend the flame of expectancy. The Shiite reference indicates that millenarian thought had strong roots in Shiite doctrine, though it was subsequently embraced by the wider Sunni tradition. Ibn Battuta wrote a rare eyewitness account of the ritual:

> The inhabitants of this city are all of them *imamis* [Shiite] of the Twelvers sect . . . Near the principal bazaar in this town there is a mosque, over the door of which a silk curtain is suspended. They call this the 'Sanctuary of the Master of the Age'. It is one of their customs that every evening a hundred of the townsmen come out, carrying arms and with drawn swords in their hands, and go to the governor of the city after the afternoon prayer; they receive from him a horse or a mule, saddled and bridled, and (with this they go in procession) beating drums and playing fifes and trumpets in front of this animal. Fifty of them march ahead of it and the same number behind it, while others walk to right and left, and so they come to the Sanctuary of the Master of the Age. Then they stand at the door and say 'In the name of God, O Master of the Age, in the name of God come forth! Corruption is abroad and tyranny is rife! This is the hour for thy advent, that by thee God may divide the true from the false.' They continue to call in this way, sounding the trumpets and drums and fifes, until the hour of the sunset prayer; for they assert that Muhammad b. al-Hasan al-ʿAskari entered this mosque and disappeared

from sight in it, and that he will emerge from it since he is, in their view, the 'Expected Imam' (1957: 324–325).

Abd al-Karim al-Maghili al-Tilimsani—Manifesto for Jihad

The doctrinal import of Ibn Battuta's account acquires a particularly sharp ideological tone in the account of another North African Muslim whose pronouncement has come to assume the status of a manifesto of Muslim African *jihad* movements. The fifteenth-century North African scholar and firebrand, 'Abd al-Karim al-Maghili al-Tilimsani (d.1506), who was visiting the West African Muslim state of Songhay, wrote in 1492 to the king, Askiya al-Hajj Muhammad Ture, to the effect that the Muslim world in their day was poised on a defining threshold. He wrote that devout believers like themselves should hasten the onset of the new age. The words of al-Maghili have reverberated in Muslim millenarian movements across the centuries:

> Thus it is related that at the beginning of every century God sends (people) a scholar who regenerates their religion for them. There is no doubt that the conduct of this scholar in every century in enjoining what is right and forbidding what is wrong, and setting aright (the) people's affairs, establishing justice among them and supporting truth against falsehood and the oppressed against the oppressor, will be in contrast to the conduct of scholars of his age. For this reason he will be an odd man out among them on account of his being the only man of such pure conduct and on account of the small number of men like him. Then it will be plain and clear that he is one of the reformers (*al-muslihin*) and that who so opposes him and acts hostilely towards so as to turn people away from him is but one of the miscreants, because of the saying of the Prophet, may God bless him and grant him peace: 'Islam started as an odd man out (*gharib*) and thus will it end up, so God bless the odd men out.' Someone said, 'And who are they, O Messenger of God?' He said, 'Those who set matters aright in evil times.' That is one of the clearest signs of the people of

the Reminder (*ahl al-dhikr*) through whom God regenerates for people their religion (Hunwick 1985: 66–67).

Al-Maghili's own marginal position, his 'separation from native land, friends and familiar things,' as Suhrawardi describes it, increased his receptivity to the text on reform. He was thus set to draw Songhay tightly into that ideological net. Three elements combine in al-Maghilii to thrust Muslims into the millenarian age: the prescriptive courage of a scholarly minority, the centennial hope induced by the religious calendar (a hundred-year rite of passage, if you will), and, with the backing of the Songhay state, a resolute will to recast the larger society in the image of the righteous few. These three elements conform nearly exactly to Turner's existential communitas, normative communitas and ideological communitas (1969). What is more, they stamp duration with the rhythm of revolutionary social change.

Hijrah Communities and Use of Ritual

From the fifteenth to the early decades of the twentieth century, the reform movements in Muslim Africa spawned a tradition of moral enclavement where cumulative pressures increase and finally erupt in reform movements. In such movements, Muslims are led by those able and willing to repudiate prevailing customs and attitudes and to place the trustworthy few at the head of affairs.

In principle the hijrah community transcends the limitations and inequalities of life, allowing free and equal access to goods and services. It inculcates a common ethical code among its members and a shared sense of moral exceptionalism that opposes the unjust and oppressive structures of the world. In this form of religious globalization, symbolic marginality is compressed into a boisterous moral ideal. It is, to cite Turner, 'the units of space and time in which behaviour and symbolism are momentarily enfranchised from the norms and values that govern the public lives of incumbents of structural positions' (1969: 166). What is conceived and nurtured in this special environment has the seal of virtue upon it that will, in turn, expose corrupt structures and institutions for the lie they are.

The hijrah community is the ultimate in millenarian enclaves. In hijrah they observe with unusual intensity and mindfulness the obligatory rituals of purification, prayer, fasting and dietary regulations. They peruse the code and the manuals and adhere with punctilious faithfulness to the letter and spirit of the law. With fastidious care and detail, they water the seeds of rebellion and keep the mainstream structures and institutions to which they object in view. Now and then they take a rest from these activities by maintaining ties with their world, recruiting newcomers and fitting out sympathizers to keep up the pressure.

The heightened attention to ritual observance helps to elevate ordinary *salat* into a special incubatory, millenarian rite. The washing of ablution that is done before the prayers becomes a ritual act of separation, of a turning from an indifferent, inattentive life to one of serious purpose. The entry into the mosque for salat becomes an act of transition, while the salat itself becomes a symbol of participation and incorporation into the ranks of the chosen few. All this intensifies the feeling of chosenness, of millenarian exceptionalism, and, if conditions are right, opens the way for judgment and action.

Leaders of hijrah have typically used the salat rite to cultivate an acute form of ritual withdrawal, called *salat al-istikharah*, consisting of ritual exclusion for a period of, say, forty days, during which time the cleric seeks guidance from God about a course of action. All contact with the outside world is cut off, and at the conclusion of the forty days the cleric is rewarded with a mandate for action, normally in the form of a clear dream or vision. What comes out of istikharah is deemed safe from contamination and corruption of this world, since it emerges from the pristine womb of faith and devotion and is protected against temporal compromise or defect. In the phrase of the masters, the istikharah vessel drips with what fills it (al-Ghazali quoted by Macdonald 1985: 222–223).

Istikharah brings the ritual imperative of revolutionary action to a concentrated point and it intensifies the motivation for making a moral change at a particular point in time, thus birthing religious change. Istikharah prescribes the rubric for personal and social transformation. It uses moral shortfalls between structures and injunctions to construct a fresh order that discredits the old and dramatizes moral opposition to the status quo of the majority. The moral vocation is a minority calling.

Salat al-istikharah exists in an abbreviated version as *khalwah*, a form of ritual seclusion and preparation undertaken for about a week or so by secular clerics. Some clerics undertake khalwah for a fee at the request of a client seeking healing, safe travel, marriage, a job, advancement or a prophylactic. Khalwah, however, is a risky procedure, fraught with dangers for the over-eager cleric. It may bring ill-prepared clerics to spiritual grief by reducing them to gibberish, unable to give words to their thoughts. The demand for khalwah reveals a social recognition that symbolic retreat may be endowed with rare social power. Even where it goes wrong, khalwah may appeal as a last resort against apathy and disenchantment. Those who resort to it demonstrate dissatisfaction with things and conditions as they are. Khalwah is their hope of thrusting aside the inhibitions and constraints of the status quo and improving their station in life.

Uthman dan Fodio—Use of Spiritual Techniques

The north Nigerian Islamic reformer, Uthman dan Fodio [Uthman ibn Fudii] (1754–1817), illustrates well the effects that istikharah and similar spiritual techniques may produce, and what that does in influencing millenarian claims to time and space. These special rites can have an exceptionally clarifying effect on what William James calls the will to believe and the resolve to bring change to pass.

Dan Fodio, who was also known as *Shehu* (Hausa for sheikh), described a vision that occurred in 1794, which was wrought in ritual gravitas, crystallizing the sublime proofs of a liminal charter for action. From it, Dan Fodio received the orders to embark on revolution, an idea he had long cultivated independent of heavenly visitation, but now could carry out with the added weight of divine approval. In his meticulous account, he begins by stating his age precisely in years, months and even days, wishing us to see symbolic meaning in that threefold division of time.

> When I reached forty years, five months and some days, God drew me to him, and I found the Lord of djinns and men, our Lord Muhammad—may God bless him and give him peace. With him were the Companions, and the prophets, and the saints. Then they welcomed me, and sat me down in

their midst. Then the Saviour of djinns and men, our Lord 'Abd al-Qadir al-Jilani, brought a green robe embroidered with the words, 'There is no god but God; Muhammad is the Messenger of God'—May God bless him and give him peace—and a turban embroidered with the words, 'He is God, the One.' He handed them to the Messenger of God—may God bless him and give him peace—and the Messenger of God clasped them to his bosom for a time; then he handed them to Abu Bakr al-Siddiq, and he handed them to 'Umar al-Faruq, and he handed them to Uthman Dhu 'l-Nurain, and he handed them to 'Ali—may God ennoble his face—and then to Yusuf—upon whom be peace—and Yusuf gave them back to my Lord 'Abd al-Qadir al-Jilani; and they appointed him to act on their behalf, and said, 'Dress him and enturban him, and name him with a name that shall be attributed exclusively to him.' He sat me down, and clothed me and enturbaned me. Then he addressed me as 'imam of the saints' and commanded me to do what is approved of and forbade me to do what is disapproved of; and he girded me with the Sword of Truth, to unsheath it against the enemies of God. Then they commanded me with what they commanded me; and at the same time gave me leave to make this litany that is written upon my ribs widely known, and promised me that whoever adhered to it, God would intercede for every one of his disciples (cited in Hiskett 1973: 66).

Dan Fodio felt that in the approaching apocalyptic time, the old enemy structures would be brought down. To hasten this he adopted the path of no compromise toward lax and prevaricating Muslims and the corrupt political leadership that had built its career on short-term cynical expediency to stroll unchallenged around the commandments of God. Reform and renewal would bring religious profession from the shadows of compromise and make public virtue of it. In the process, the contrast with the alternative African heritage would be made sharper.

Three years later, in 1797, the Shehu firmly set on that militant course and making preparations to arm his followers and set them up for jihad. He told his followers that preparing for jihad, as he directed them, was a *sunnah*, a prescribed norm of the prophet himself. During months of feverish activity, the Shehu used the prayer ritual to bolster the ardour of his disciples. His brother, 'Abdallah dan Fodio, records that the Shehu 'began to pray to God that he should show him the sovereignty of Islam in this country of the Sudan, and he set this to verse in his vernacular ode, *al-Qadiriyya* ['The Qadirite Ode'], and I put it into Arabic in verses' (Hiskett 1973: 67).

The Shehu coupled this millenarian stance with a decision to emigrate from where he was living in Gobir to Gudu. It was a symbolic act of giving public birth to his movement as well as an act of political defiance: Gobir had been hostile to him and to his disciples, and repudiating it would taint it with the stigma of infidelity and enmity towards God. This is the *territorial passage,* primed with ritual force, which van Gennep described as crucial to the liminal breakthrough (1960: 192). The Shehu insisted on the territorial passage, the hijrah, as a prerequisite of sound faith, especially where it entailed accepted personal deprivation:

> O brethren, it is incumbent upon you to emigrate from the lands of unbelief to the lands of Islam that you may attain Paradise and be companions of your ancestor Abraham, and your Prophet Muhammad, on account of the prophet's saying, 'Whoever flees with his religion from one land to another, be it [merely the distance of] the span of a hand, will attain to Paradise and be the companion of Abraham and his Prophet Muhammad' (dan Fodio 1978: 52).

Dan Fodio's phrase the 'span of a hand' stands for the pivotal millenarian shift of perspective, one in which the repudiation of worldly structures is very different from the ascetic call for worldly and carnal renunciation. The Shehu and his followers intended no flight from world conquest, no abatement of human passion, merely a tactical move to prepare the better for victory. Mystical discipline would scrape away the rust of corruption from truth, tone the muscles for action and rally the faithful by refining their motives and directing them to lawful ends. As a result, in the 1804 Muslim revolution of north Nigeria *Mahdist* (messianic) ideas circulated freely, though it is uncertain whether the leaders meant to suggest that the *Mahdi* had arrived and was one of them.

The *hadith* of Abu Dawud (d. 888), 'Surely God will raise up for this Community, at the beginning of every century, one who will reform their religion,' was widely attributed to the supreme *mujahid*, the Shehu himself. Although he rejected such Mahdist claims, the Shehu nevertheless claimed to be the portend, the Mahdist precursor or forerunner. He told his followers that the jihad dispensation being established would last until the Mahdi came. The apocalyptic teaching galvanized the jihad movement and led to mass conversions.[2]

Millenarian Drawbacks

Millennialism can also have a negative impact on a community. It reeks too much of uncertainty and the unknown to be entirely dependable for an established community raised on the orderly warrants of collective observance and obedience. Thus the Shehu's community faced serious disruption as the faithful prepared for mass exodus to meet the impending end. The road from Adamawa leading east, for example, was kept open to allow for unimpeded mass passage to Mecca. But the exodus threatened to become a ragged stampede, and forced the leaders to retract their advice to prevent people from leaving, apparently with little effect. The power to work miracles that was attributed to the Shehu and his companions soon deteriorated into apocalyptic confusion. Still, the Shehu's religious training and his teaching activity culminated in a mandate for change, in contrast to the former situation where he had choice forced on him.

Revolutionary incubation, as a stage of millennial preparation, can miss its moment. It is, for example, possible to undergo the rigours of ritual and physical seclusion and persist beyond the point of available resources and slip into stagnation. If that should happen the group fragments in disarray

---

2. For a discussion of this Mahdist theme in Dan Fodio's career see M.A. Al-Hajj (1967: 100–115).

and must either reset the calendar or they became mired in inertia. Under the right historical conditions, what remains of them can be gathered and recycled and used as fodder for new initiatives. The ideals of reform retain still an element of the combustible, waiting for the spark of opportunity and grievance to set them off.[3]

One example from African Islam shows the promise and the perils of millenarian adventurism. In the nineteenth century a mass popular movement, called the *Hubbubé*, arose in Futa Jallon (in what is now Guinea). Its members repudiated constituted authority and created in the countryside, outside the centres of power, a hijrah community called Boketo. They were led by Abal Juhe, the son and heir of the movement's charismatic founder, Mamadou Juhe, who charged that the inheritors of the utopian ideals of Karamokho Alfa, the Muslim reformer of 1727, had allowed standards to slip for the sake of personal gain. Specifically, the slavery had got out of hand when the Fulbe *mawubé*, the political elite, tried to squeeze increased revenue out of an already impoverished slave peasantry, and then resorted to plunder to increase the size of slave holdings.

The overburdened slave populations became increasingly restive and found a leader in Mamadou Juhe, a daring and cunning figure who knew well how to organize the scattered discontent of the countryside. He used Islam to amplify the grievances of his motley followers. The disenchanted, the overtaxed, the impoverished, and the rootless hailed the messianic dispensation, which shook the countryside. One scholar described the miscellaneous social composition of the Hubbubé as being caught up in the fervour of throwing off their chains and scarcely instructed by a vision of what to build.

Former slaves constituted a major component of the ranks of the Hubbubé, showing how the marginality of inferiority and economic

---

3. Hannah Arendt, commenting on the phenomenon of the Boer sense of isolation as 'the first European group to become completely alienated from the pride which Western man felt in living in a world created and fabricated by himself' argues that rootlessness is characteristic of race organisation, of the hatred of territorial limitation. Rootlessness inspired in this instance 'an activistic faith in one's divine chosenness.' (Arendt 1964: 194, 196–197).

deprivation can be exploited to boost the fortunes of prescriptive marginality and serve the end of real agents.

> The Hubbu movement mobilized and attracted to the periphery of Futa Jallon the oppressed; the jungle Fulbe, that is, Fulbe of inferior status and extraction who were liable to taxation and to forced labour without mitigation; descendants of pastoral Fulbe recently converted to Islam; certain unassimilated Jallonke; and thousands of slaves concentrated in the *rima'ibé* (slave camps) (Boubacar n.d.: 14–15).

The Boketo community conformed to the exaggerated features of hijrah, of revolutionary incubation. When Abal took over the leadership of the movement, he intensified his father's reform programme. He abolished slavery in the movement and issued a call to all slaves elsewhere to repudiate the bonds of servitude and to come to Boketo, the privileged enclave of egalitarian virtue. There the Hubbubé infused from a heady dose of millennial righteousness, turning that intoxicating fervour against the country's discredited mawubé.

They scoffed at conventional rules, flouted norms of established conduct and took to loot and general lawlessness. Virtue suddenly turned wild and impetuous.

The Hubbubé became the scourge of the countryside, a ragged band of disoriented malcontents who disdained lawful enterprise and made bold to live from plunder and violent sequestration. However, cut off from other centres of renewal and without an agenda to launch a sequel, the Hubbubé became sitting targets, or else aimless refugees. Blyden describes their painful demise in these words:

> The Hooboos, those renegade Foulahs, who for thirty years have been a terror to caravans passing through the districts which they infested, have been scattered by the military energy of Samudu [Samori], Mandingo chieftain from the Konia country, due east of Liberia. Abal, the chief of the Hooboos,

has been captured and banished to a distant region (Blyden 1967: 206).

In the end Samori's forces dealt brutally with Abal Juhe, his *disjecta membra* being put on public display as a show of triumph.

Dr Edward Blyden (1832–1912), the most influential Black intellectual of his day, visited Futa Jallon in 1872 and left an account of what he found of the rump of the Hubbubé movement.

> The Hoobos (he writes) are renegade Fulbe in revolt against the king of Timbo. Twenty years ago, on account of the exactions imposed by the Almamy Umaru, they rose in revolt and with their families removed themselves to come and settle the grazing lands between Futa Jallon and Solima country. They are called Hoobos or Hubus because following their departure from their homes they were chanting in chorus a verse from the Coran in which the word Hubu appeared twice. It says this: 'Nihibu [Nuhibbu] Rusul [Rasul] Allah Huban [Hubban] Wahidan', which means those who love the Envoy of God [without compromise] (Blyden 1967).

However, the fate of the Hubbubé is by no means characteristic of what happens to spent millenarian movements. Many are left to lie dormant until their vital substance can be absorbed by their successors. Thus have certain key elements of traditional African rites survived and become incorporated into viable forms of local Muslim practise.

Christian Wind of Change[4]

During a period of charismatic renewal on the coast of West Africa, the career of Prophet William Wadé Harris of the Ivory Coast peaked. His call to conversion represents one of the most spectacular examples of resurgence

---
4. Portions of this section have been adapted from Sanneh, L.O. 2008.

in the history of the Christian movement. As with the Muslim reform movements, religious experience played a prominent role in Harris's ethical change and in his reform movement, which also contributed to social change. Facing the accelerating machinery of colonial takeover, Harris set Christianity on a collision course with Western hegemony and gave the African response a popular religious outlet during a period of anti-colonial insurgency. His approach and achievements challenged Western norms about Christianity.

African Prophet

Harris was born in 1860 in Liberia. In 1892 Harris was employed by the American Episcopal Mission in Liberia as a schoolteacher and catechist before he became embroiled in politics and sought liberation for Africans from Western rule. Because of his role in a failed coup, he was arrested in 1909, tried, and sentenced to imprisonment and fined $500. He was subsequently placed on parole.

Arrested again for his part in the Glebo War of 1910, he was imprisoned for the second time. While in jail, he reported having a spiritual experience in which the angel Gabriel appeared to him and commissioned him to be a prophet, commanding him to preach repentance, abolish fetish worship and baptize converts. After being released later in 1910, Harris began a preaching tour in Liberia; in 1913 he went eastward along the coastal belt of the Ivory Coast and further on to Axim in western Ghana.

In the Ivory Coast, Harris presented a challenge to French colonial efforts to take the country and obtain the prompt and orderly submission of Africans. Between 1910 and 1913, under the lieutenant governor Gabriel Angoulvant, the back of Ivory Coast's anti-colonial insurgency had been broken through a programme that military officers euphemistically called 'pacification'. Angoulvant had the local rulers disarmed and interned, villages destroyed, and people regrouped into newly constructed settlements. He also imposed a poll tax and, to help pay for the tax, instituted the *corvée*, or forced labour. The French realised that they needed to expropriate Harris' moral capital lest Africans be emboldened by it to question colonial legitimacy. Christianity as an uncontrolled moral capital was a flammable ideology in the hands of Africans. The French arrested Harris in December 1914 and expelled him in January 1915, with an armed embargo clamped upon his followers.

In his eighteen months of public preaching in Ivory Coast, Harris had converted some 200,000 people, who at first embraced his lean iconoclastic message. Unable to return to the Ivory Coast, he continued preaching in Liberia and made three trips to Sierra Leone, continuing to make converts. He suffered a stroke in 1925 and died in 1929 in poverty (Akyeampong & Gates).

The intimate details we have of the Harris movement come from eyewitness accounts and contemporary reports. Some of them sound a bit incredulous—how could an unauthorized native presume to Christianize his heathen brethren?—yet much of the information is so careful and faithful. Acting under official instructions from the colonial administration, Fr. J. Hartz, the superior of *Missions Africaines* in the Ivory Coast, took notes at a meeting with Harris. Hartz described Harris as a man in his forties, with a long graying beard, a flowing white robe with broad sleeves, sandals and a white turban. He carried a wooden cross and a small calabash containing seeds slung in a net decorated with cowrie shells and carried a Bible which he had obtained from the Wesleyans. He claimed to be the envoy of Christ, a new John the Baptist, who came to convert fetish worshippers. His followers included several women, like him clothed in white.

Hartz said that Harris 'expounded the purpose of his visit to me in that pure and correct English which does such credit to Great Britain.' Here is part of Harris' testimony to Hartz:

> I am a prophet. Above all religions and beyond the control of men, I draw my authority from God alone, through the mediation of the angel Gabriel. Four years ago I was suddenly wakened in the night. I saw the guardian Angel in visible form above my bed. Three times he struck the crown of my head and said to me: 'I demand from you the sacrifice of your wife. She will die, but I will give you others who will help you in the work which you must undertake. Before she dies

your wife will give you six shillings; this will be your fortune; you will never need any more. With these six shillings, you will go everywhere. They will never fail you. I will go with you everywhere and reveal to you the mission for which you are destined by God, Master of the Universe, whom men no longer respect.'

After this revelation the Angel appeared on other occasions, and is gradually initiating me into my mission as the prophet of modern times, of the Age of Peace of which Saint John speaks in the twentieth chapter of the Book of Revelation: the Peace of a thousand years, whose coming is nigh. In fact my wife died soon afterwards, she too having learned of my Mission from the Angel. Before leaving me she foretold the difficulties of succeeding in my Mission. I was a Wesleyan teacher, and preacher, in the minister's absence. I now prepared for my prophetic ministry by prayer, and by reading and studying the Bible.

The Angel taught me of things to come: the actions of Gog and Magog, the wiles of the great dragon . . . which is to be found for a thousand years . . . I am sent by Christ, and nothing shall prevent me from accomplishing the deeds to which he calls me. I am going through this country, driven by inspiration from On High. I must bring back the lost nations to Christ, and to do so must threaten them with worse punishments, so that they may allow themselves to be baptized and instructed by Men of God, both Catholic and Protestant. I must bring men to honour the Natural Law and the divine precepts, and especially the observance of Sunday, which is so much neglected. I am coming to speak for all the people of this country, White or Black. No abuse of alcohol. Respect for Authority. I tolerate polygamy, but I forbid adultery. Thunder will speak, and the Angels will punish the World if it does not hear my words, which interpret the Word of God (cited in Hargreaves 1969: 249–250).

From these interviews, Harris emerges as a full-blown charismatic figure doing miracles, prophecies and healing powers to stir to life a largely peasant backwoods society scattered in villages and homesteads.

Pierre Benoît's detailed portrait of Harris draws attention to his physical stature, saying Harris talked animatedly, with vehemence; his chin pointing forward with a gleam in his big eyes as they rolled in their sockets. Harris had a strong, well-preserved body; his broad shoulders carrying a proud and expressive head. His muscular arms and strong legs were those of an athlete. He weighed about eighty-five kilograms. Harris fidgeted a lot, finding it difficult to sit still, changing his seat several times and nervously pacing up and down the room. He seemed agitated, a sign, perhaps, of suppressed spiritual energy (Shank 1997: 72ff). With rising urgency Harris warned repeatedly of the approaching denouement. He cut a striking apocalyptic figure, mitigated somewhat by his advice to build and organize churches for his converts. His followers had for the moment to tarry on earth rather than risk the cause in a final messianic gamble.

One missionary eyewitness noted Harris' strong monotheist emphasis and his demand for people to abandon their idols, to turn in faith to the one true God of Scripture and to observe the Sabbath. That testimony is echoed by yet another eyewitness account about Harris' religious message. According to this source, Harris:

> ... wanted no money, only the repentance of the people. ...
> He preached by interpretation to ten different tribes. He, too, demanded the destruction of the lower religious symbols of magic and witchcraft in the search for God. His movement achieved astounding success, until in 1915 it was calculated by the French Government officials that one hundred thousand people had accepted allegiance to Harris. These folk burned their superstitious symbols, built small churches, said prayers, and paid nearby African clerks from other colonies to teach them hymns. But they had no teachers, no translated Bible, little or no knowledge. Then, again, unworthy 'minor prophets' arose to make money out of the credulity and earnestness of these simple pagans, and, fearing disturbance

in war-time, the government asked Harris to leave the Ivory Coast. 'Wait and pray,' he told his people. 'Build churches, and one day missionaries will come to teach you the Way.' In this remarkable movement we see African prophetism at its best, for its leader brought the people to the very door of the Christian Church (Platt 1935: 87).

According to contemporary witnesses Harris' religious message made an astonishing impact because Harris spoke simply, directly, and persuasively to people's needs. His achievement seemed to fly in the face of the accepted ways of doing mission in Africa in which political and economic improvement was given more attention than Christianity was given. An astonished and an appreciative missionary declared:

The wandering preacher disappeared as suddenly as he came. His ministry covered only a period of three months, and then he passed into French territory, when, in the midst of similar scenes, he was arrested by the authorities and imprisoned, and finally expatriated as a disturber of the peace' (Armstrong 1920: 39–40).

In spite of his arrest, Harris had the last word and helped to change the face of African Christianity as well as the nature of mission itself. His open face showed that he had unmasked the spirits and looked into the face of angels. Everything about Harris suggested urgency, movement, liveliness, economy, brevity, lightness, poise and alertness. The common thoroughfare, not the walled manse and its guarded doors, seemed eminently suitable as his stage. He made Christianity a religion of the open road, a religion without borders, and left Catholic and Protestant missions equally in his debt.

Challenge to Western Assumptions

In the wider context of Christianity, Harris challenged Western assumptions about Africans and about the nature of Christianity, and so contributed to a gathering crisis that would engulf the land and cause wholesale social dislocation. The Catholic ambivalence toward Harris and the ensuing ambivalence of Protestant missions showed that a two-faced Christianity had entered the field. It compromised not only establishment Christianity, but also the European claim to being the religion's indispensable promoters, in both cases, with deference to Africans. In 1910 when Harris started his mission, there was a famous meeting of mission and church leaders called the World Missionary Conference, generally referred to as Edinburgh 1910. No one at that conference gave Christianity a chance in Africa, certainly not at the hands of Africans themselves. The mood was one of paternalist distrust at Edinburgh and those at the conference held the standard view that mission remained the child of the West. In that analysis Western civilization was indispensable to extending the kingdom of God in the world beyond the West.

In the meantime, the work of evangelisation that Harris was carrying out was in diametric opposition to the civilizing mandate of Europe, and Harris' converts appreciated for themselves this crucial distinction between gospel and civilization; they were willing to embrace Christianity but resisted the drive to bring their lands under colonial control. For these converts who had little exposure to the West, Christianity was a revealed religion, and it was only an accident of history that it became associated with European civilization. After all, there had been Christians in Asia and Africa before there were Christians in most of Europe. It made sense that Whites embrace a religion like Christianity that brought heaven and earth together in singular testimony to the power of God. At any rate, for Africans belief in God was a deeply rooted and was not something of foreign vintage lest that made God into little more than a piece of foreign costume. The God of history is the ally especially of remote and threatened populations, Harris proclaimed.

Given that religious fact, Africans asked whether apostolic witness required civilization as an accoutrement, and whether it was credible for the West to claim to be exclusive host of the things of God. Could one be Christian without the cultural scheme of the West? Peter was the Rock, but was instructional stonewalling a justified or necessary obstacle? Had Catholics squandered an opportunity of solidarity in faith with the Africans at a critical point of the colonial enterprise? Should John Calvin and John Wesley be the litmus test of Christian conversion? Was Albert Schweitzer justified in his view that high Christology was the prerequisite of being a Christian, making it necessary for Africans to defer becoming followers of Jesus in order to protect Christianity from heathen naïveté?

Additionally, colonial and missionary officials gave little merit to the culture of illiterate Africans. As far as they were concerned there was no such thing as illiterate Christianity; the milieu of African oral tradition was deemed foreign to the religion's civilizing nature. Europe's was considered a superior civilization, and the compromise of Africa would be a setback for the Christian and Western order. For officials of such persuasion:

> the idea that the interests of an assortment of barbaric, idealless and untutored tribesmen, clothed in sheep's fat, castor oil or rancid butter—men who smelt out witches, drank blood warm from the throats of living cattle and believed that rainfall depended on an arrangement of a goat's intestines—should be exalted above those of the educated European would have seemed to them fantastic (Cited in Murray-Brown 1972: 61).

Even as late as 1998 Episcopal Bishop John Shelby Spong of New Jersey wrote in the *New York Times* about Christian Africans in uncompromising terms (Spong 1998). In his view Whites who took a pro-African view were guilty of weakness, and earned the derogatory sobriquet of 'flannelfoot' (gullible liberal). Sir Richard Burton, for one, blamed pro-African views on the missionary movement, saying missions impeded the machinery of colonial hegemony by transfusing its muscular agenda with 'homoeopathic doses of scientific political economy' (Burton 1863, vol 2 p. 48). He referred to mission-educated Africans in the 'pejorative singular' as the half-reclaimed, semi-clad tribesman stained by the defects of the species (Burton 1863, vol 1 p. 217; vol 2 pp. 72–73).[5]

For Christian Africans the Christian faith was universal in scope, local in character, indigenous in agency and global only under metropolitan

---

5. The phrase 'pejorative singular' occurs in O'Brien (1962: 161).

colonial presumptions, presumptions that lurked in the designation of global Christianity. As Roland Allen pointed out with respect to China, many people enjoyed the benefits of Western civilization without in the least being predisposed toward Christianity, and many others enjoyed the blessings of Christianity while being adversely impacted by the effects of Western civilization.

Missionary Jealousy

Harris changed the face of African Christianity by giving religious experience a double foundation in personal faith and social renewal and turning it against colonial subjugation. Missionary jealousy stands to explain a good deal of the ambivalence toward Harris. The intruding colonial ascendancy makes the missionary jealousy easy to understand what with the circumstances of military defeat tempting them to extol the power and efficacy of Western technology against local superstition. Yet, Harris's teaching on prayer, healing and the power of God gave his converts a more grounded Christian faith than did the missionary teaching. A leader of the Harrist church reported how Harris offered a replacement for the power of fetishes:

> at the bidding of the Whites our ancestors buried or burned their fetishes, or threw them into the sea, but then they had nothing with which to replace them. Then they took their fetishes back. They thought that because they had no more fetishes, they had no strength and nothing worked well. They brought back their fetishes and with them they found their strength and freedom again. Each time the Whites told them to get rid of their fetishes, they tried to, but they received no replacement. Then Harris came (Walker 1983: 40).

Africans had heard the same message from Harris but with a vital difference. Harris promised to replace the old emblems of religion with the unrivalled power of the Christian baptism. 'Harris said once you are baptized, the fetishes will have no more power over you. Baptism will change your life. You should build a temple and worship God.'

Unlike the missionaries, Harris preached a threshold message, saying God would intercede in situations of personal crisis and that faith was necessary to effect meaningful change. Missionaries condemned traditional healing practises and divination as magical superstition and forbade their converts to practise them. Instead, missionaries prescribed the taking of pills for remedy of ailments and in so doing severed illness and its remedy from any religious underpinning, Christian or primal.

When Harris dismissed traditional healing as powerless, his converts asked him for an alternative. 'His reply was, in effect, take native medicine if you have to; but while you gather the leaves, pray to God; while you prepare the medicine, pray to God; when you take it, pray to God' (Walls 1989: 18). The pill bottle was the functional equivalent of traditional medicine, but was it, like fetishes, disconnected from faith? Missionaries believed so, but Harris' people did not agree. For support, the people could turn to the testimony of Scripture about the tree of life on either side of the river, whose leaves were for the healing of the nations (Revelation 22:2).

A Harrist follower, Alphonse Aké, argued that traditional healers looked for short cuts to retain the faith of their patients, thus opening the way for manipulation and abuse. Aké's critique recognized the need for Christianity to contest the ground with traditional healers by making the patient a conscious partner in the healing process. The goal was to shift the patient's trust in merely human means to God as the source of life and health. Here is Aké's exposé of the local herbalist:

> Thus, in the case of the fight against this or that sickness, the herbalists first crush the leaves, seeds, or roots of plants which are considered capable of treating the sickness before giving it to the patient for treatment. In this way, the patient is never able to know the origin of this plant, and finds himself obliged to trust his herbalist once more'.[6]

---

6. Translated from the original: 'Ainsi, en cas de lutte contre telle ou telle maladie, ils écrasaient d'abord les feuilles, les écorces ou les racines des plantes susceptibles de guérir le

For Harris, faith in an invincible God was the all-purpose cure for the soul and for the suffering and needy; that message stuck, in contrast to the preaching of the missionaries.

Harrist converts retained a lively sense that healing is part of religion, and religion part of healing; an attitude that allowed Harris to add the related idea of faith healing. Since God was the author of life and of well-being, and since evil forces worked to bring about death and misfortune, believers should choose God for their needs against the evil powers. Prayer was a request for healing, whether of body or spirit made no difference. In the battle between good and evil, medicine was not neutral. There was good medicine and bad medicine. Good medicine was God's gift and thus could heal, while bad medicine was the work of evil powers and wrought harm. Both kinds of medicine worked, and both belonged to the world of hidden causes. Thus, good doctors were also good agents and allies in God's work of healing and salvation, while bad doctors harmed their patients. 'Thou shall do no harm' of the Hippocratic oath is commensurate with God's mission of healing the broken hearted and binding wounds (Psalm 147:3). Instead of denigrating this work, missionaries should have welcomed and celebrated it.

The Harris resurgence also contributed to a challenge to colonial ascendency. Accordingly, the dramatic thrust of French power in the country, exacerbated by the forces unleashed by a market economy, upset the established order and threatened old assurances. An unsettling generation gap opened, pitting a rootless, restless group of young people against the older generation. The lines between the sexes were scrambled. The priests of the Mando cult and other diviners, for example, frequently poisoned young men, and accusations of witchcraft became rampant, requiring draconian measures to establish guilt and to punish offenders. Some of the ethnic groups, such as the Agnis of Sanwi, used the Harris movement as justification for defying French colonial intrusion. The Dida people refused to pay taxes and plotted for ways to resist French claims over their country.

---

malade avant de les lui confier pour le traitement. De cette manière, le malade ne pouvait jamais connaitre l'origine de cette plante, et se trouvait dans l'obligation de se confier à son féticheur une autre fois' (Aké 1980: 7).

Many more groups believed the popular mobilization resulting from the Harrist resurgence would help them escape the colonial subjugation that they regarded as intolerable.

This was all evidence of a festering collective insecurity and of a general strain on the traditional value system. Crisis ruled the day, and the people felt the need to make a radical choice involving the old and new. The work of Prophet Harris, as of his peers, has to be seen in that light. 'Harris had told his converts that they must become Christian or face certain destruction' (Walker 1983: 168). What Harris accomplished and the methods and means he employed suggest a telling revamping of Christianity's civilizational prerequisites in order to resolve new challenges without incurring the liability of the old sanctions. Missionaries seemed largely ineffectual in responding to the challenge of reinvesting the call to discipleship in a new idiom, held captive as they seemed to be by the prescriptions of the Western catechism. This would explain why missionaries looked to colonisation to bring about the outcome they wanted. Colonisation demonstrated that Africans were helpless and dependent on the West, whatever the achievements of Harris or others like him. Missionaries readily held up the benefits of Western control as being what Africans really needed, something Harris could not compete with because Europeans had the advantages of power and material resources. The missionary attitude was no insignificant factor in complicating the choices Africans faced. Missionary Christianity was a very different from African Christianity: the demands of one were incompatible with the demands of the other.

The issue was resolved by a paradox. The considerable advantages Europeans enjoyed also imposed a limitation on their ability to operate effectively in primal societies. The religion of primal societies was not a matter simply of bureaucratic organisation, external institutions, once-a-week church attendance, and official nomenclature, but a matter of the spirit, of the unseen, of protection from evil spirits, and of belief in a supernatural reality. Power and authority alone or together could not impede or pursue the spirit through its elusive and multifarious manifestations.

Africans could find in Christianity a system of ideas they could connect to the old venerable framework. A chief wrote to a missionary informing him that the chief and his people had already received Christianity but felt in need of instruction. His main motivation in requesting help was to use Christianity as a defence against the devil. The chief feared that the return of the devil was imminent. 'To avoid the devil visiting us any more, we pray that your church supplies our need by sending a teacher here before the close of the month' (Armstrong 1920: 41).

Evil, like healing, was a major preoccupation, and the new charismatic leaders paid it close attention. A leader of the new Pentecostal movement in Ghana named Apostle Opoku Onyinah produced a handbook on the subject, *Ancestral Curses*. In it he scanned the Bible, assembling materials and dividing them into appropriate subject matters in order to diagnose and prescribe remedies for affliction. He offered Christianity as the power to render curses null and void, saying faith in Christ dissolved the potency of the undeserved curse, citing Proverbs to that effect: 'Like a fluttering sparrow or a darting swallow, an undeserved curse does not come to rest' (Proverbs 26:2).

Apostle Onyinah stressed that a curse was the result of disobedience to God, and the remedy was obedience to God, the very God who made provision in Scripture for his people, Israel, to avert the consequences of the curse. The fruit of the curse was death, while the fruit of obedience was life. On that point, Onyinah cited Paul: 'Just as sin entered the world through one man, and death through sin, and in this way death came to all people, because all sinned' (Romans 5:12). Onyinah elaborated:

> Without the fall of Adam, no other curse would have occurred. It is the root cause of all man's problems. The fallen nature is an enemy of God and seeks to do its own [thing]. The attempt to do one's own thing without God is disobedience, which is the basic cause of a curse (Onyinah 1994: 27).

To remove the tree of affliction, Onyinah dug under the root.

Believers acquired a new status, having not only been cleansed of evil but also having assumed the role of moral agents. Onyinah cited the gospel: 'For by your words you will be acquitted, and by your words you will be condemned' (Matthew 12:37).[7] The redeemed in Christ held in their hands the key to their own well-being as well as to their own affliction. Submission to God stemmed from the same source as disobedience to God—the moral will. However, not all misfortune was the result of a curse. Onyinah pointed out that Jesus attributed the chronic affliction of a man born blind from birth not to the man himself or to his parents but to God so that his works might be displayed in the man's life (John 9).

Onyinah stressed that Christians were not exempt from suffering. 'I must say positively that the Scripture also speaks about Christians suffering' (Onyinah 1994: 37). This view of affliction represented a fundamental alteration in traditional systems of explanation because it introduced into the equation, for the first time, a God of salvation. Onyinah described the culmination of the entire kerygmatic process begun by Abraham by citing Scripture:

> Christ redeemed us from the curse of the law by becoming a curse for us, for it is written: 'Cursed is everyone who is hung on a tree.' He redeemed us in order that the blessing given to Abraham might come to the Gentiles through Christ Jesus, so that by faith we might receive the promise of the Spirit (Galatians 3:13–14).

Christianity was the solution for overcoming demons, Onyinah claimed in a study (Onyinah 1995).

For much of the time, this theological reflection has eclipsed issues of rank and social status (although it contained an implicit critique of social and physical deprivation by addressing social and physical need as part and parcel of the answer Christianity offered to all and sundry). The verdict of E. Bolaji-Idowu, one of Africa's most influential theologians, is pertinent here. Bolaji-Idowu argued that Christianity enlarged the people's vision, freed their minds from the shackles of superstition and the irrational, and liberated their spirits from besetting fears (1962: 209). For him, the idea

---

7. This verse echoes another one: 'The righteous one shall live by his fidelity' (Hebrews 2:4).

of divine transcendence did not mean divine remoteness or indifference; it meant transcendent solutions for spiritual and social problems. In the face of life's enigmas, God was dependable, and that fact drained the universe of its bogeys and jinxes.

By the same token, divine omnipotence meant simply that God's power was greater than the aggressive colonial version that was entering the land, for political control lacked the potency and permanence of faith in God. Africans remembered that administrators were dismissive of religion while they were bent on extending their unwelcome power. Yet for Africans, material authority could not prevail over the effects of hidden, more potent, causes. In any case, Apostle Onyinah assured his followers that both were evidence of God's undivided sovereignty. Africans were aggrieved that missions did not share a view of God's work as something greater than the claims of colonial subjugation and scientific superiority, work that made little moral distinction among levels of economic, intellectual or cultural attainment. For the missionaries, Christianity was religion without irrational elements.

Missionaries could have recalled the sentiments expressed by Lactantius, the fourth century North African theologian who brokered the Christian faith to its cultured despisers of the age. Lactantius spoke about the one God who gave being and life to all, who wished us all to be equal, and to be alike in our moral dignity as we are in our moral inadequacies. Human beings had the same terms of life and an equal longing for eternal fellowship. No one was excluded from the benefits of heaven or from a place in the daylight. It was the one power that nurtured the earth for the benefit of all and sustained us, not as slave or master, but as free and worthy. Within the divine providence, no one was exempt from the obligations of the moral life or from its privileges. The salvific benefits of Christ made no invidious distinction or grudging concession, as the Gentile experience showed. The apostolic practise in that regard laid down the precept that, where it was necessary, Christians must violate the taboo of cultural exclusion in order to fulfil the promises God first made to the Jewish nation and subsequently to the Gentiles: 'If you are Christ's, then you are Abraham's offspring, heirs according to promise' (Gal. 3:29 ESV).

For his part, Harris summoned Africans to make Christianity their own by rejecting foreign domination without discounting foreign support. In the process, he eschewed force and violence. This call to faith and forbearance is underscored in the standard Harris catechism by asking whether we should help and love our enemies. The catechism responds that we should, for only God reserves the right to judge and avenge wrong, stressing the fact that even though he was manhandled and insulted by the authorities, 'Harris lifted not a finger' (*Premièr Livret* 1956: 10). We should recognize the scale of this achievement for its local potential. Post-Western Christianity has been remarkable for its forbearance in the face of overwhelming power and suffering and for instilling hope and trust in people. Christianity banished the demons of fear and vengeance.

Equally striking is that Harris did not take a flight into utopian idealism. The suffering and dilemmas of existence did not ask for a flight from the world or, equally significantly, for a judgmental attitude towards others. Theological nitpicking was foreign to the leaders, allowing them, in the depths of affliction and the mystery of life, to cultivate a spirit of charity and forgiveness among their followers.[8] Beyond the West, the Christian awakening had in Harris a spectacular instance of large-scale social recomposition and profound personal transformation.

---

8. In this respect, the tragedy of the 1994 Rwanda genocide still defies explanation. Perhaps the failure to institute in African Christianity a post-Western idiom in the form of the mother tongue for Scripture and worship left official Christianity beholden to political and economic stratification. As such, civilization got in the way of the gospel, and also in the way of the African appropriation of the Gospel and the transformation of ethnic identity that goes with it. It happens that the warring Tutsi and Hutu share the same culture and language, their differentiation being the result of Belgian policy in the 1920s to favour the taller, cattle-owning Tutsi over the stockier, peasant Hutu cultivators. The height criterion gave Tutsi access to education while excluding the Hutu. Social stratification reinforced invidious distinctions, as did official Christianity's dogma that it was entitled to reproduce itself in its European forms among non-European races. Africans could not engage or confront themselves credibly as Africans in someone else's idiom. This left few safeguards in Rwanda against the politics of suspicion, retribution, and getting even. For a field report on the genocide see Nancy Gibbs, "The Killing Fields of Rwanda," *Time*, 16th May 16.

Evaluation of Religious Experience

As the previous sections reveal, religious experience can play a positive role for Christians and Muslims. Yet some would make sweeping generalizations to the effect that all religious experience is flawed because it is subjective. That experience is a slippery subject needs no emphasizing, but it is very different from saying we should never recognize the spiritual life as worthy of attention, even if we have to scrutinize it with critical alertness. Spiritual experience, especially where it has been conditioned by well and tried practises, may express enough of the nobility of spirit to command appreciation of its unique merit.

Religious experience can act as a facilitator and a criterion, not as the subverter of the canon. The intensely subjective character of the experience is counterbalanced by the objective rules of the code by which it is constrained, not adding to or taking away an iota of the law. Admittedly, there are many complex features in religious experience, including the extreme outlandish type in which seeming delirium is embellished with pious ascriptions, and its converse, where the mundane is taken out of context and turned into an elaborate source of the fantastic. In a milieu of credulity, events that may be striking for their external coarseness, including fables and other imaginative inventions, are dragged into reality and dogmatically predicated of reality, with the eclectic appetite feeding the penchant for marvel. Fortunately, much of that, though heaven knows not all of it, dissolves with historical exposure. Time has, accordingly, exposed many an impostor.

The African Muslim Commissioned

Two elements in the Shehu's (Dan Fodio) religious experiences are relevant for our consideration. One is that the religious experience may commission the person having it for the work of renewing the religion and securing greater adherence to religious teachings. In other words, there would be a convergence between experience and action. The second is that at a deeper level religious experience may correct or confirm the doubtful import of another religious experience: the message one receives in a dream or vision is unclear or represents too radical a departure from the norm not to require a retake, thus prompting a second visitation.

In the first case, the Shehu recounted what is essentially a vision of commissioning for vocation. He said at the age of forty 'God drew me to him' (precisely how is not clear) and brought him into the company of the Apostle, the *ashab*, the prophets and the saints who 'welcomed me, and sat me down in their midst.' Then 'Abd al-Qadir al-Jilani brought a green robe marked with the words of the *kalimah*, and a turban with the words, 'He is God, the One', which he handed to the Apostle who clasped them to his bosom before handing them over to Abuu Bakr al-Siddiq, and so on down the line to 'Ali to Yusuf and finally back to 'Abd al-Qadir al-Jilani whom they appointed to act on their behalf.

Connected to a chain of transmission, the Shehu's experience is concerned with mobilizing the Qadiriyah *tariqah* as a reforming and renewing vehicle in Muslim Africa. It is designed to bring to the surface tendencies and attitudes of Islamic identity that hitherto occurred in a vague, imperfect pattern. Thus vetted and affirmed, the experience becomes the orthodox flagship.

The second element of religious experience serving as a corrective mechanism occurred to Shehu, as it does widely in Muslim Africa. In the telling Shaker metaphor, religious experience might be compared to a tunnel: the deeper one gets into it the narrower it becomes, until finally one is out of range of recognizable landmarks and within range of the devil and wicked spirits. In that condition one is extremely vulnerable to the insinuations of the evil one and to straying. For Muslim religious masters the answer might be in other forms of experience that would contain corrective instruction.

One of the most typical forms of such corrective experience is the lucid or perspicacious dream/vision (*ru'ya al-salihah*), instructing the subject on what course of action to follow. In that regard, shortly after his mystical installation, the Shehu decided to depart from Gobir on what would be his hijrah from infidel rule. However, before he carried out his plans 'Abd al-Qadir al-Jilani appeared to him in a vision to forbid the action. Eventually in 1803 or 1804 he was instructed, again in a vision, to leave Gobir for

Gudu, a move that opened the formal stage of the Islamic revolution that left a permanent mark on all Muslim West Africa.

If dreams and visions are able to restrain impulsive conduct, they can also boost flagging resolve. The Shehu was once assured in a vision that the prophet would come to greet him, about which he remained doubtful. He agreed, nevertheless, to submit the message to the test to prove its truthfulness, so he prayed for guidance. As a result, he claimed, the prophet appeared to him 'in circumstances that dispelled his doubts'.

Many people enter the tunnel experience of dreams and visions by cultivating special religious exercises and devotions. As discussed, khalwah (religious retreat) is a standard practise that is employed to induce dreams and visions for a special purpose. Another highly popular practise, the salat al-istikharah, became the classic dream incubation method of Muslim reformers in Africa, the midnight calm before the day's storm. J. Spencer Trimingham, a pioneer scholar of Muslim Africa, claims that virtually all Muslim reformers in Africa employed al-istikharah. It occurs widely in Muslim literature. For example, Ibn Khaldun (1332–1406) wrote extensively about it and said he tried it to effect. Ibn Battuta mentioned the practises and said that he used it with benefit. What is crucial about khalwah, al-istikharah and other forms of religious retreat is that the experience acquired thereby should not become permanently peripheral but instead should leave things different from what and how they were. The tunnel should bring what passes through it to the surface.

The special importance of dreams and visions for the fomenting and culmination of Muslim religious experience strikes a somewhat discordant note in our own austere, sceptical age. Freud's decisive legacy about dreams as pathological symptoms has sundered them from their roots in religion and society, though dreams and visions occur in the Qur'an, and for that matter in the Bible, with great frequency. Even in Salman Rushdie's *Satanic Verses* dreams are treated as a distortion of reality, a position Rushdie vehemently defends. For example, in an open letter to Rajiv Gandhi, then prime minister of India, Rushdie complains that Muslim critics failed to recognize how the offending parts of the novel hang on the dreams of sick persons and how, therefore, the book is far removed from reality. Given that dreams are considered sacred in Islamic theology, being rated a forty-sixth part of prophecy, Rushdie's protestation amounts to self-incrimination. It is instructive to reflect on how dreams may function for us as a veneer of fantasy or stress, whereas in both Islam and the Bible dreams are the polished horn of the spirit's utterance. It would be instructive to look at the Christian African example at this point.

The African Christian Reinstated

The central question Harris compels us to face is how, in spite of its personal nature, religious experience need not condemn us to marginal isolation but may provide the motive for change and renewal. That Harris deployed his religious vocation without military or economic instruments is a further validation of religion's power. Accordingly, religious experience need not make us retreat into a subjective mood and lose all connection with reality. Some forms of religious experience may, indeed, be what Shakespeare describes as the elegiac bourn from which no traveller returns,[9] leaving the world to darkness and to us; but that is a long way from where Harris stood. Mystical experience, for example, can induce 'such transport of delight' as to leave the subject delirious, if not unhinged. We saw some evidence of that with Mamadou Juhe and his millenarian community of Boketo. Appropriately, that experience led to a dead end.

In contrast, Harris—and Dan Fodio in his own right—is an object lesson in why scholars are unjustified to treat religion simply as a composite residue of power. Harris and Dan Fodio sought visions and received dreams as a mandate to dispel the darkness induced by crisis and moral decline, not as an opiate of oppression and suffering. For them religion was no false consciousness, and so they left us with the attendant challenge to reinstate experience by chronicling the depth and scope of their achievement.

---

9. *Hamlet* Act III, Scene 1.

Religious Experience and Transformation of the Self

Let me take up the third and final theme of our subject, the transformation of self, by drawing on Muslim examples that evoke—and invoke—Christian parallels. Reference may be made to the militant Black Nationalist Malcolm X, who was from a Black Baptist background, converted to Islam through the Black Muslims, and was assassinated in February 1965, before he was forty. In his autobiography, Malcolm X describes his conversion in language that reflects the social dimensions of religious experience. He speaks of it as a dramatic change from guilt and moral twistedness to truth as personal responsibility. In terms of the theoretical formulations just considered, Malcolm X traversed the stages of liminality to emerge at the point where he was invested with a chastened, purified view of the world. The politics of race gave way to the politics of a common humanity; race is subordinate and subject to truth. Of that experience Malcolm X writes as follows:

> Many a time, he confessed, 'I have looked back, trying to assess, just for myself, my first reaction to all this. Every instinct of the ghetto jungle streets, every hustling fox and criminal wolf instinct in me, which would have scoffed at and rejected anything else, was struck dumb. It was as though all of that life was back there without any remaining effect, or influence. I remember how, sometime later, reading the Bible in the Norfolk Prison Colony Library, I came upon, then I read, over and over, how Paul on the road to Damascus, upon hearing the voice of Christ, was so smitten that he was knocked off his horse, in a daze. I do not now, and I did not then, liken myself to Paul. But I do understand his experience . . . I have since learned—helping me to understand what then began to happen within me—that the truth can be quickly received, or received at all, only by the sinner who knows and admits that he is guilty of having sinned much. Stated another way: only guilt admitted accepts truth . . . The very enormity of my previous life's guilt prepared me to accept the truth. Not for weeks yet would I deal with the direct,

> personal application to myself, as a Black man, of the truth. It still was like a blinding light' (Malcolm X 1968: 257ff).

Elaborating on his experience, Malcolm X said he was compelled to re-examine some well-set ideas about the cultural and racial representation of truth and virtue. It resulted in an ethical transformation that he likens to a religious experience, which identifies the sort of religious anthropology that shapes language and thought. For Malcolm X, Islam's inclusive anthropology stood in incriminating contrast to his experience of the racial profiling of Western Christianity. What he learned about God from Christian racism crippled him and undermined his capacity for any act of spontaneous gracious response. He said up to that point he scrutinized everything he or anyone did with suspicion and distrust. On a visit to Mecca on pilgrimage, and out of range of Western racial stereotypes, Malcolm X was shaken in his long-held attitudes. Commenting on the generous hospitality of his Arab host in Jeddah, Malcolm came to this unsettling reckoning:

> I was speechless at the man's attitude, and at my own physical feeling of no difference between us as human beings. I had heard for years of Muslim hospitality, but no one couldn't quite imagine such warmth ... There had before been in my emotions such an impulse to pray—and I did, prostrating myself on the living-room rug. Nothing in either of my two careers as a Black man in America had served to give me any idealistic tendencies. My instincts automatically examined the reasons, the motives, of anyone who did anything they didn't have to do for me. Always in my life, if it was any White person, I could see a selfish motive. But there in that hotel that morning ... was one of the few times I had been so awed that I was totally without resistance (Malcolm X 1968: 445–446).

Malcolm testified that for him Islam reconciled the *One* and the *Many*, bringing together *One* God and the *Many* nations and races of the world who find in God a common source of truth and solidarity. This is what

Pope John Paul II called 'the unity of humankind with regard to the eternal and ultimate destiny of man' (Sherwin & Kasimov 1999: 27–29). Malcolm spoke of Islam having 'proved the power of the One God' as it relates to the unity of human experience and the obligation to acknowledge mutual responsibility for one another. At Mecca itself, after he had completed the pilgrimage obligation and kissed the black stone of the Ka'ba, Malcolm declared:

> I understood it better now that I had before. In the Holy World, away from America's race problem, was the first time I ever had been able to think clearly about the basic divisions of White people in America, and how their attitudes and their motives related to, and affected Negroes. In my thirty-nine years on this earth, the Holy City of Mecca had been the first time I had ever stood before the Creator of All and felt like a complete human being (Malcolm X 1968: 482).

It says something both for the personal and general character of religious experience that, in spite of bitter lessons gained from experience of injustice and discrimination, all of that tending to make individuals feel hemmed in an impenetrable tunnel, Malcolm X should go on to discover a specific underlying connectedness in his quest for truth and meaning. He found that sharing helps to deepen religious experience, rather than to drain it, and that spirituality plumbs the depths of the *imago dei* that makes for a visible community of mutual affirmation. On a strictly sociological level, racial injustice breeds in victims nihilist attitudes of rejection, suspicion, and defiance, whereas in the crucible of spirituality, experience of injustice may lead to a person seeking and finding a community of forgiveness and mutual support. Accordingly, spirituality offers a rich potential for affirming the dignity of persons by inspiring the pursuit of peace and justice.

The imperative of our shared humanity need not and should not conceal our divergence on the roots of our identity grounded in faith, practise, and nurture. However, it should not minimize our unity on the theocentric character of faith and worship. John Paul II expresses it as a spirituality of faith and justice, saying:

> I believe that we, Christians and Muslims, must recognize with joy the religious values that we have in common, and give thanks to God for them. Both of us believe in one God, who is all justice and all mercy; we believe in the importance of prayer, of fasting, of almsgiving, of repentance and of pardon; we believe that God will be a merciful judge [of] us at the end of time, and we hope that after the resurrection he will be satisfied with us and . . . that we will be satisfied with him (Sherwin & Kasimov 1999: 63).[10]

This theme of shared religious values, including the Pope's insistent appeal to the dignity of the human person, is recapitulated in a remarkable passage in a thirteenth-century Sufi text. The text offers a spiritual commentary (*ta'wil*) on the words of Jesus about being born again in order to enter the realm of truth. In other words, for this Islamic writer, the teaching of Jesus is the root of an original moral reality from which rises the purpose of human existence. Given its Islamic origin, the document takes no cognizance of the incarnation or the atonement. For all that, it points in a direction of the ultimate divine vindication that Christians can recognize. The text says:

> Jesus said, 'None will enter the dominion of the heavens unless he is born twice' [John 3:3]. It continues by claiming that the most marvellous, wonderful, mighty, and perfect divine act is the human being, who is compounded of all the worlds. Everything that is scattered throughout the two engendered worlds [of the higher and lower dominions] is brought together within him. He is the vicegerent of God, the shadow of the divinity, and the epitome and quintessence of the engendered

---

10. Address to the young Muslims of Morocco, Casablanca, August 19, 1985. The phrase, being satisfied with God, is echoed in the Arabic verse, 'The Lord shall give thee, and thou shalt be satisfied' (Qur'an 93: 5]. The reference is to Muhammad's straitened circumstances as an orphan (*yatim*).

things. Everything was created to perfect his level. When he attains completion and returns to his own world, the heavens will be rolled up. On that day the bodies will be lost within the spirits, just as today the spirits are lost within the bodies. *On the day We shall roll up heaven as a scroll is rolled up for the writings. As we originated the first creation, so We shall bring it back again—a promise binding on Us; so We shall do* [Qur'an 21: 104] (Chittick 1992: 44ff).

Conclusion: Foresight in Hindsight

When the pope affirms with pastoral solicitude that Muslims and Christians 'believe in the importance of prayer, of fasting, of almsgiving, of repentance and of pardon,' he intends us to understand the peculiar and universal character of religious obligation without respect to persons. It is that ethical commandment that is most evident in the career of Prophet Harris, whereas for the Shehu, the commandment was structured in the form of chains of transmission whose links serve as tokens of commitment and as a voice for change. In this respect, I am perplexed to know what value to place on the contrasting experiences of Dan Fodio and Harris, separated not only by the span of a century but also by the methods, goals, and consequences of reform expressed in radically different ways. The ideas, structures, and institutions that Dan Fodio created in north Nigeria have remained virtually intact, if only in reinforced forms. The heartlands of Muslim north Nigeria remain what the Shehu and his successors created. If this writer may be permitted a personal word here, it was a unique privilege once to be invited personally by the Wazirin Junaidu of Sokoto to visit the Hubbaru, the final resting place of the Shehu in the grounds of the palace and long a pilgrimage centre. The mausoleum is wrapped in fine black and green velvet adorned with Qur'anic verses in gold calligraphy, with low dome echoing with the hum of pilgrims' prayers and their receding footsteps. It was a powerful reminder that the Shehu's spirit continues to brood over centuries of devoted Muslims whose lives have been shaped by the reforms he put in place.

In contrast, I grope now in vain for evidence of a corresponding monument to the legacy of Prophet Harris except to note the equally significant truth that his community has survived, as have the churches he helped to found or to revitalize. The tangible institutions and structures of the Sokoto Empire, along with the prayers of travelling pilgrims, however, have no equivalents in the careers of African Christian leaders who laboured for a kingdom that is not of this world and whose ministers answer to no earthly power. Yet as pioneers of faith, these leaders demonstrated the unbounded potential of Africans when they are stirred by the wind of change, and their ideas and example have continued to exert a powerful influence on the contemporary African Christian resurgence.

If today in the midst of prevailing economic and political crisis, we can contemplate with equanimity rather than with incredulity the future of the church in Africa, that is because African pioneers dreamed and received visions while fear fell upon the people and their land. It is fitting that we should conclude with an appeal to sacred history by recalling how at a pivotal point of the genesis of the Christian movement Peter, the prince of apostles, turned to Scripture to shed light on the novel and puzzling events of conversion for which no one seemed prepared, not even the most attentive in all Judaism. Claiming fidelity to the prophets and the seers of Israel rather than to any blueprint of a worldly kingdom, Peter cited the prophet Joel as pointing to the reality that was now unfolding before their own eyes. We should step in Peter's shoes for a corresponding perspective on the events of Christian Africa today:

> And in the last days it shall be, God declares,
> That I will pour out my Spirit upon all flesh,
> And your sons and your daughters shall prophesy,
> And your young men shall see visions,
> And your old men shall dream dreams;
> Yea, and on my menservants and my maidservants in those days
> I will pour out my Spirit; and they shall prophesy . . .
> And it shall be that whoever calls on the name of the Lord shall
> be saved (Acts 2:17–18, 21, citing Joel 2:28).

References

Akyeampong, E.K. and Gates, H.J. Jr. *Dictionary of African Biography*. Oxford: Oxford University Press. http://www.dacb.org/stories/liberia/legacy_harris.html.

Arendt, H. 1964. *The Origins of Totalitarianism*. New York: Meridian Books.

Armstrong, C.W. 1920. *The Winning of West Africa*. London: Wesleyan Methodist Missionary Society.

Baëta, C.G. 1962. *Prophetism in Ghana: A Study of Some 'Spiritual' Churches*. London: SCM.

Battuta, Ibn. 1957. *Travels in Asia and Africa 1325–1354*, Reproduced and translated by H.A.R. Gibb, 1929. London: Routledge & Kegan Paul.

Blyden, E.W. 1967. *Islam, Christianity and the Negro Race*. Edinburgh: Edinburgh University Press, originally published 1887.

Bolaji-Idowu, E. 1962. *Olodumare: God in Yoruba Belief*. London: Longmans.

Boubacar, Barry. n.d. L'Expansion du Fouta Jallon vers la Cote et les Crises Politiques et Sociales dans la Sénégambie Meridionale au Cours de la Premiere Moitié du XIX éme Siècle. (Unpublished manuscript).

Burton, R. 1863. *Wanderings in West Africa*, 2 vols. London: Tinsley Brothers.

Chittick, William C. (ed.) 1992. *Faith and Practise of Islam: Three Thirteenth Century Sufi Texts*. Albany: State University of New York Press.

dan Fodio, U. 1978. *Bayan wujub al-hijra 'ala 'l 'ibad*, translated and edited by F.H. El-Masri. Khartoum: Khartoum University Press.

Gennep, van A. 1960 *The Rites of Passage*, Translated by Monika B. Vizedom and Gabrielle L. Caffee. Chicago: University of Chicago Press.

Gibbs, N. 16 May 1994. The Killing Fields of Rwanda. *Time*, Monday.

Al-Hajj, M.A. 1967. The Thirteenth Century in Muslim Eschatology: Mahdist Expectations in the Sokoto Caliphate. *Research Bulletin, Centre of Arabic Documentation* 3(2), July: 100–115.

Hargreaves, J.D. 1969. *France and West Africa: An Anthology of Historical Documents*. London: Macmillan.

Hiskett, M. 1973. *The Sword of Truth: The Life and Times of the Shehu Usuman dan Fodio*. New York: Oxford University Press.

Hunwick, John. 1985. (Tr.) *Sharia in Songhay*. Oxford: OUP.

Macdonald, D.B. 1985. *The Religious attitude and Life in Islam*. London: Darf Publishers Ltd., originally published 1909.

Malcolm X. 1968. *The Autobiography*. (with the assistance of Alex Haley) London: Penguin Books.

Murray-Brown, J. 1972. *Kenyatta*. London: Allen & Unwin.

O'Brien, C.C. 1962. *To Katanga and Back: A UN Case History*. London: Hutchinson

Onyinah, O. 1994. *Ancestral Curses*. Accra: International Missions Office.

Onyinah, O. 1995. *Overcoming Demons*. Accra: Pentecostal Press International Missions Office.

Platt, W.J. 1935. *From Fetish to Faith: The Growth of the Church in West Africa*. London: Cargate Press.

Premièr Livret. 1956. *Premièr Livret de l'Education Religieuse a l'usage des Missions Harristes*. Petit-Bassam, Ivory Coast.

Sanneh, L.O. 2008, *Disciples of All Nations: Pillars of World Christianity*. Oxford: Oxford University Press.

Shank, D.A. 1997. The Taming of the Prophet Harris. *Journal of Religion in Africa* 27(1): 59–95.

Sherwin, B.L. and Kasimow, H. (eds.) 1999. *John Paul II and Interreligious Dialogue*. Maryknoll: Orbis Books.

Spong, J.S. 13 August 1998. Anglicans Get Literal. *New York Times* Op-Ed essay.

Turner, V.W. 1969. *The Ritual Process: Structure and Anti-structure*. Chicago: Aldine Publishing Company.

Walker, S.S. 1983. *The Religious Revolution in the Ivory Coast: The Prophet Harris and the Harrist Church*. Chapel Hill: University of North Carolina Press.

Walls, A.F. 1989. The Significance of Christianity in Africa. Edinburgh: The Church of Scotland, St. Colm's Education Centre and College, The St. Colm Lecture.

CHAPTER 2

Patterns of Christian-Muslim Encounters in Africa

John Azumah

In the present world context of inter-religious tensions and conflicts, it is crucial for Christians in Africa to find the right balance in our response to Islam. Some have tended to be virulently anti-Islam and anti-Muslim while others tend to be naïvely romantic about Islam. It is within the wider context of Christian engagement with Islam and Muslims that African Christian responses and engagement will be examined in this chapter. The main thrust of my argument is that African Christian views on Islam and attitudes towards Muslims have been, and continue to be, informed by fluctuating existential situations. In such situations, the line between naïvety and hostility is very thin. We will seek to demonstrate how this line has been crossed in different historical contexts and regions of Africa by looking at different models of Christian-Muslim encounters in Africa. We will then argue for a consciously biblical and theological engagement with Islam and Muslims within the African context.

Christians and Muslims encountered each other in various ways in Africa, which resulted in different dynamics in the relationships between them in different parts and periods on the continent. In some cases, the encounters took the form of immigrant/host community relations; in others, they took the form of invader/ruler and ruled relations. In still others, the encounters took the form of competition for commercial, missionary and political interest.

Christianity's First Contact with Africa

In an interesting parallel, both Christianity and Islam first made contact with Africa out of persecution. According to Matthew 2:13–23, in the face of imminent danger from Herod, Joseph was advised in a dream to escape with his wife and the infant Jesus to Egypt where they remained until the death of Herod. So not only was God in Africa long before the arrival of Western missionaries in the nineteenth and twentieth centuries, Africa also provided sanctuary for Jesus long before the arrival of Christian missions. Similarly, Christianity was on African soil nearly seven centuries before Islam even though the Islamic presence in much of sub-Saharan Africa precedes Christianity by centuries.

Encountering Muslims as Immigrants

According to Muslim tradition, in the year 615 the prophet of Islam, in the face of severe persecution, advised over eighty male converts and their families to seek asylum in Abyssinia (Ethiopia) because 'it is a friendly country'.

During this first encounter between Christians and Muslims on African soil, one of the female refugees who later became a wife of Muhammad is reported to have said, 'When we reached Abyssinia, the Negus [the Christian king] gave us a kind reception. We safely practised our religion, and we worshipped God, and suffered no wrong in word or deed' (Guillaume 1955: 146–150).

Muslim traditions would have us believe that this meeting was more than just one of warm African hospitality accorded to refugees but was a meeting of minds. Islamic traditions recount that at the king's request, Ja'far, the leader of the delegation, recited a passage from Qur'an chapter nineteen, the chapter of Mary. Upon hearing it: 'The Negus wept until his beard was wet and the bishops wept until their scrolls were wet, . . . then the Negus said, 'of a truth, this and what Jesus brought have come from the same niche'.' (Guillaume 1955: 152).

Some Islamic sources have claimed (without empirical evidence) that the Negus later converted to Islam.[1] The mention of tears of joy and the claim of the King's endorsement of Islamic teaching should be viewed within the context of the nascent religion's quest for validation and affirmation from key Christian figures and sources. This is evidenced in the story of Bahira, the monk who is alleged to have first prophesied Muhammad's prophetic role, and of Waraqa, a Christian monk who allegedly confirmed it when Muhammad had his first prophetic experience.

What is interesting, however, is that apparently the Negus of Abyssinia did not bother to ask about the content of the belief system of the refugees until a delegation arrived from Mecca seeking the repatriation of the refugees. And when he did, none of the verses recited to him constituted a political, legal or military threat from the new religion. Hence, the Negus sent the Meccan emissaries back empty-handed. It is reasonable to surmise that if, for instance, Qur'an sura 9:5 known as the sword verse, or sura 9:29 known as the poll tax or *jizya* verse had been recited to the Negus, he would have seen the new religion as a threat and sent the Muslim refugees back to Mecca. As it turned out, the face of Islam presented to the Negus, and which was, in all probability, the only one the refugees knew, was that of a religion which even recognized the virgin birth of Jesus, albeit with some colourful extra-biblical additions.

Be that as it may, the result of this positive experience is that Abyssinia was granted a special status in classical Muslim jurisprudence. Rather than being designated in the 'realm of Islam' (*dar al-islam*) nor the 'realm of war' (*dar al-harb*), Abyssinia was assigned its own category, the 'realm of neutrality' (*dar al-hiyad*). Indeed, William Muir has speculated with justification that 'if an Arab asylum had not at last offered itself at Medina, the prophet might happily himself have emigrated to Abyssinia' (Trimingham 1965: 45). The Abyssinian model of the first encounter between African Christians and Muslims provides us with some insights. It was the first encounter between Muslims living as minorities within an

---

[1]. Evidence in traditional Muslim accounts point to the fact that some of the refugees converted to Christianity and poked fun at their former co-religionists that 'We now see clearly, but you are still blinking' (Trimingham 1965, p.46).

African (Christian) political system. This model of Muslim encounter with African political institutions was to be replicated in successive centuries throughout the rest of sub-Saharan Africa, especially in the west and the central Sudan region. As Muslims spread out from the Sahel into sub-Saharan Africa as merchants and clerics, their first point of call was always the centre of traditional authority, the chiefs' court. Traditional rulers provided patronage and protection to vulnerable 'stranger' Muslim groups, welcoming and accommodating them as respected and even revered guests. This crucial role played by political patronage in the Islamization of Africa as evidenced by Islam having made more gains amongst ethnic groups with chieftaincy institutions than amongst with those without them (Azumah 2001: 24ff).

From about the eighth to the fifteenth century, immigrant Muslim groups were given land to settle across western and central Sudan as privileged minorities. Muslim clerics, by virtue of their literacy in the Arabic script, attained privileged status as scribes and advisors in traditional courts; they were exempted from war and granted right of free and safe passage during times of conflict. In some traditional societies, Muslims were metaphorically referred to as 'wives' of the chief, who provided for their needs. In all of this, immigrant Muslim groups posed no threat to the traditional political institutions that provided them with patronage (Azumah 2001: 55–60). On the contrary, in West Africa, the most influential clerical tradition during this period, the Jakhanke, was known for its pacifism and aversion to militancy as a means of religious and political change. The Jakhanke, who were responsible for the spread of Islam amongst the Mande, were well known and respected for pursuing religious study, producing charms and amulets, and travelling and farming. They made an enduring impact upon the character of Islam in the Western Sudan (Sanneh 1979: 13ff).

That Muslims lived and flourished as minorities under non-Islamic African political systems is noteworthy. This is not to gloss over instances of difficult relationships but to point out that African Islam has a non-ideological, a-political and pacifist tradition, and that Muslims in Africa have lived and even flourished under non-Islamic political systems. Certainly, this was to change in large parts of the region between the sixteenth and nineteenth centuries with the rise of ideological and militant Islam. Even then, a significant proportion of the Muslim leadership opposed the jihadists' campaigns because 'they were too firmly established, on too good terms with their [indigenous] neighbours and made too good a living from trade to wish to upset the system' (Azumah 2001: 80).

Muslims as Invaders and Rulers

The second encounter between Muslims and Christians on the African soil occurred during the first wave of Muslim conquest of Egypt in 640. Coptic Christians in Egypt, like their Nestorian and Jacobite counterparts in Palestine and Syria, welcomed the invading Arab Muslim armies as liberators. At the time, Christian Byzantium had declared these Christian groups to be heretics and discriminated against and persecuted them. A thirteenth-century Coptic historian offers the following interpretation for the Muslim conquest of Egypt:

> This was the period during which the [Byzantine] Emperor oppressed the orthodox people, and required them to conform to his creed, which was contrary to the truth. From these two men [i.e. Emperors Heraclius and Muqauqas] the Christians suffered great persecution . . . But in their time the Hanifite [i.e., Arab] nation appeared, and humbled the Romans, and slew many of them, and took possession of the whole of the land of Egypt. Thus the Jacobite Christians were freed from the tyranny [of the Romans] (Browne 1933: 40).

The first Muslims came to Africa seeking refuge, the second group came as invaders, yet both were welcomed with open hands. Copts, like their Nestorian and Jacobite counterparts elsewhere in the region, allied themselves with the new rulers who granted them freedom of worship in exchange for the payment of *jizya*. Many educated Christians rose to positions of influence, serving as doctors, scribes and scholars. The relationship periodically came under pressure because of persecution against Christians, which rose from anti-Christian sentiments aroused by Muslim preachers or the harsh government policies and struggles with Christian Byzantium. Indeed, things did not always work out as set out in treaties. John of Nikiu, who lived towards the end of the seventh century, records the following mixed feelings of the Copts towards the Muslim conquest:

> 'Amr [the Muslim general who led the conquest] had no mercy on the Egyptians, and did not observe the covenant they had made with him, for he was of a barbaric race. And 'Amr became stronger every day in every field of his activity . . . And when he seized the city of Alexandria, he had the canal drained in accordance with the instructions given by the apostate Theodore. And he increased the taxes to the extent of twenty-two *batr* of gold till all the people hid themselves owing to the greatness of the tribulation, and could not find the wherewithal to pay (Browne 1933: 43).

From the mid-thirteenth century onwards, Christians in Egypt, like their counterparts in the rest of the Middle East, came under severe persecution provoked partly by the crusaders from the West and partly by the Mongol invasion from the East. During those difficult times, Christians were viewed as collaborating with the foreign invaders, accused of causing calamities, and treated as terrorists. At the beginning of the fourteenth century, systematic persecution of Christians became an official policy in Egypt.

Muslim rulers in Egypt extended the standard Islamic treatment of Christians to the old Christian kingdom of Nubia. In a treaty known as the *baqt*, Nubia was allowed to retain its sovereignty in return for allowing free passage and settlement for Muslim traders and payment of an annual tribute in the form of 360 slaves to their Muslim overlords. This arrangement lasted until Nubia was attacked in 1275 and the might of Mamluk Egypt overran a weak Christian kingdom. Nubian Christianity, the state religion and a cult intimately associated with foreigners and Greek culture, was also weak because it had lost contact with the Coptic Church in Egypt, which was its source of leadership and inspiration. Sudanese Christianity eventually disappeared with the fall of the political structure it had depended upon (Trimingham 1965: 76–80).

Islam continued its march as an ideological, political and military force. After Abyssinia's special status had outlived its usefulness, sporadic attempts were made to take it militarily. In the early sixteenth century, emissaries were sent from Mecca to preach jihad against the Christian kingdom. This led to the launch of a full-scale jihad in 1529 by Ahmad bin Ibrahim, called by his Abyssinian adversaries as Ahmad Granj (the 'left-handed'). In the process he destroyed a great number of churches and monasteries and Abyssinia needed help from the Portuguese to defeat him in 1543.

In western and central Sudan, some chiefs had converted to Islam, taken Islamic names, wore Muslim garb and observed the pillars of Islam haphazardly, while they continued to observe traditional religious practises as part of their official duties. The ideological, political and militant face of Islam surfaced in 1493 when Askiya Muhammad overthrew Sonni Ali, the founder of the Songhay Empire. In the eighteenth and nineteenth centuries, this was followed by sustained jihads in present-day West Africa, the most celebrated of which is that of Uthman Dan Fodio, which covered present day Northern Nigeria. The ideological refrain of the jihadists, in the words of Dan Fodio, was 'The government of a country is the government of its king without question. If the king is a Muslim, his land is Muslim, if he is an unbeliever, his land is a land of unbelievers' (Azumah 2001: 63ff).

When Uthman Dan Fodio unleashed his jihad on Gobir, the ruler of Gobir, or *Sarkin Gobir*, sent messages to other Hausa chiefs telling them that he had neglected 'a small fire in his country until it had spread beyond his power to control. Having failed to extinguish it, it had now burnt him'. The chief's letter, cited by Muhammad Bello of the jihadist tradition, ended with a dire warning: 'Let each beware lest a like calamity befall his town too' (Trimingham 1962: 199). This warning came too late for most of the traditional rulers who had flirted with Islam. In the Sarkin Gobir's letter, we have the chief confessing his own naïvety, and, it could be said, that of the many other traditional rulers who fell victim to jihadist Islam, in failing to recognize the inherent challenges in the new religion.

The naïvety was, however, not just on the part of the traditional rulers, but also of the wider Muslim community, who were, in most cases, the first victims of the jihadists' swords. Many leading Muslim clerics opposed the militant face of Islam and paid with their lives. Clerics in Yandoto in Northern Nigeria who had opposed Dan Fodio's jihad had their town overrun and most were put to the sword. As a result, ordinary Muslims across Western Sudan were as relieved as their traditional counterparts with the emergence of European colonial powers, mainly the French and British, who put an end to most of the jihadist mayhem. An old Hausa Muslim woman recounting the British intervention in Northern Nigeria had this to say:

> We Habe wanted them to come; it was the Fulani who did not like it. When the Europeans came the Habe saw that if you worked for them they paid you for it, they didn't say, like the Fulani, 'Commoner, give me this! Commoner, bring me that!' Yes, the Habe wanted them; they saw no harm in them (Smith 1954: 64).

Muslims in the Francophone areas also appreciated the stability and security that resulted after the French defeated Samori Toure, a nineteenth-century jihadist. An address from 'Muslims of Korhogo to the people of Mecca' written during the 1914 to 1918 war, expresses their relief; it reads in part:

> Whoever does not wish to see the French in our colony [Côte d'Ivoire] is also held in contempt by us Muslims, since our prosperity depends entirely on the arrival of these latter in our colonies. It is moreover thanks to the French that we are spared the ravages and pillages of Samori, slavery, and wars between one village and another. At present, we are free, we can live, work in peace, and perform our prayers in tranquillity (Launay 1992: 59–60).

The persecution of and violent attacks against non-Muslims by Muslim invaders in North Africa and jihadists in the western Sudan region left a legacy of suspicion, fear and outright hatred and hostility towards

Islam amongst Christians in affected countries and regions. In Ethiopia, for instance, by the late seventeenth century, a royal decree of religious discrimination forced Muslims to live in segregated ghettoes to contain what was perceived as 'the Muslim threat'. Subsequent emperors more or less continued with this policy up to the modern period and in 1878 an even harsher edict was issued requiring all Muslim subjects to convert to Christianity or be killed. It was not until 1994 that the constitution of Ethiopia granted equal status to all citizens, including Muslims, and to all forms of religious expression.

It is clear from the foregoing that the militant and ideological faces of Islam present serious challenges and even threats to Christians as well as to traditionalists, Muslims, and others. It is also worth pointing out that, during the medieval and modern eras, the Christianity that Islam encountered in Egypt, Nubia and Ethiopia was imperialistic and just as militaristic. Christians regarded success on the military and political fronts as signs of divine favour and viewed setbacks as divine retribution. In other words, Christianity was not necessarily a peaceful tradition and Islam a militant one. Both traditions were locked in ideological and military struggles, in which Christendom won in Ethiopia while Islam won in Egypt and the Sudan.

Africa as a Theatre for Islamic and Western Christian Missions

In the fifteenth century, the Portuguese were the first Europeans to venture south of the Sahara in significant numbers. These were sailors and soldiers accompanied by missionaries. During this period, the Portuguese mainly encountered Islam in Africa on the East Coast where they established a stronghold, Fort Jesus, in Mombasa. They engaged in armed struggles with the Ottoman Empire for control of the sea routes and subsequently allied themselves with Abyssinia in defeating Ahmad Granj in 1543. The Portuguese later fell out of favour with the Abyssinians because the Society of Jesus had an aggressive policy of converting and re-baptizing Orthodox Christians into Catholicism and trying to Latinize the Orthodox Church.

An unholy alliance between Muslims and Ethiopian Christians led to the defeat of the Portuguese. Fort Jesus fell to Muslims in 1698 and the Portuguese were forced to abandon their mission work on the East Coast (Trimingham 1965: 98–100).

On the West Coast, Diogo Gomes, who visited the Senegambian region in 1456 and 1458, gives the following account of his discussion with a Muslim cleric in the court of a chief:

> A certain bishop of their church was there, a native of Mali, who asked me about the God of the Christians, and I answered him according to the intelligence God had given me. I finally questioned him respecting Muhammad, in whom they believe. What I said, pleased his lordship the king so much that he ordered the bishop within three days to leave his kingdom (Gamble & Hair 1999: 263).

European Christian involvement in Africa was stunted following the Portuguese debacle on the East Coast.[2] This coincided with a period of great internal turmoil within Christendom as a result of the Protestant Reformation Movement, which had begun in 1517. Bloody Catholic-Protestant wars raged in Europe and they continued in Northern Ireland until the last century, which meant that for nearly three centuries European Christians were too preoccupied with their own internal strife to undertake foreign adventures. This changed in the nineteenth century with the Protestant missionary movement and European colonial expansionism, which also meant that from the fifteenth to the late nineteenth century, Muslim-Christian encounters in Africa were basically the encounters between European Christians and African Muslims. In this encounter, the two traditions were pitted against one another as rival competitors vying mainly for commercial and political dominance and converts.

As can be seen in the quotation from Gomes, European missionaries resorted to a dogmatic presentation of Christianity in their encounters with Muslims, with the goal of eliciting intellectual assent. They made it their

---

2. The main enduring legacy of Portuguese missions was in Mozambique and the Congo.

duty to undermine the Islamic religious system and sought to prove to the Muslim by argument and controversy that Christianity was superior to Islam. During the nineteenth century, Western thought had become embroiled in a debate *with* Islam in the Indian sub-Continent, and an academic debate *about* Islam back in Europe. On one side of the debate were those like Reginald Bosworth Smith, who argued that even though Islam was not as sophisticated a religion and was irrelevant to Western society, it could meet and improve social and national aspirations and living standards whenever it encountered a people such as Africans at a lower stage of development than itself. Consequently, Colonial policy makers in Africa considered Islam best suited to the less sophisticated and 'untutored' mind of the African and also as a religion in its own right, not one that had to be replaced by Christianity. As rightly observed by Lamin Sanneh:

> Prejudice against Islam in Victorian as in later times was being covertly perpetuated in the guise of tolerance, even paternalistic indulgence, for Islamized Africa. This apparently tolerant attitude also concealed a corresponding prejudice against Black Africans (1996: 75).

On the other side of the debate, Christian missionaries took strong exception to what they considered to be ill-informed liberal academic views on Islam. Missionaries working in Africa pointed to the atrocities of jihadist Islam and the evils of Muslim slavery and slave raiding as evidence of the bankruptcy of Islam. Responding to views that Islam suited native Africans, the Edinburgh 1910 mission conference in its report asked:

> Can Islam [affect] the redemption of Africa? What has Islam made of the Africa it has dominated for centuries? What can it make of the future of Africa? It is a religion without the knowledge of the Divine Fatherhood, a religion without compassion for those outside its pale, and to the whole of womanhood of Africa it is a religion of despair and doom (World Missionary Conference 1910: 243).

The report is littered with examples of missionary competitive zeal couched in combative language. The Commission I Report states: 'the threatening advance of Islam in Equatorial Africa presents to the Church of Christ the decisive question whether the Dark Continent shall become Mohammedan or Christian'. It goes on to declare:

> If we do not counteract the advance of Islam with all our energy and along the whole line, we shall lose not only the large parts of the now Pagan Africa but even the territories already Christianised. The main battle against Mohammedanism in the immediate future will be fought on East African soil. Here the enemy is already before our doors (World Missionary Conference 1910: 435).

The mission to 'stay the advance of Islam' in Africa will not be successful 'until the foundations of Islam in the north are shaken and removed'. And in any case, 'the north needs Christ as much as Pagan Africa farther south, and into this long-neglected field the church ought to send her specially trained missionaries, not in units as hitherto, but in tens and hundreds' (World Missionary Conference 1910: 244).

Leading African clergymen were caught up in the debate. One was E.W. Blyden (1832–1912), a celebrated nineteenth century African-American Presbyterian missionary, who worked in present day Sierra Leone. In response to the Western demonization of Islam, he romanticised Islam in the African context, arguing that it had made enormous contributions towards inter-tribal harmony, inspired 'new spiritual feelings' and hastened tendencies to independence and self-reliance, all of which Christianity had failed to do.

> Islam has done for vast tribes of Africa what Christianity in the hands of Europeans has not yet done. It has cast out the demons of fetishism, general ignorance of God, drunkenness, and gambling, and has introduced customs which subserve the highest purposes of growth and preservation (Walls 2002: 149).

Blyden surely erred in his romanticism of Islam. However, the core of his argument was that Islam had become an integral part of the African experience and contributed to its heritage for which it must be respected and not demonized. Even more importantly, Blyden argued that 'if the desire is to convert Mohammedans, Christians should give up their bitter hostility and study Islam—not at second hand, but as far as possible in its original records—with greater sympathy and liberality' (Blyden 1888: vi). The debate about the suitability or otherwise of Islam to the African continued unabated and Sanneh writes of a parliamentary-style debate held in Freetown, Sierra Leone, in 1888, with the motion: 'Is Christianity or Islam best suited to promote the true interests of the Negro race?' (1996: 67). This was a wholly Christian debate about Islam; the speakers to the motion on both sides were Christians and so was the audience.

In this context, Samuel Adjai Crowther (1806–1891), a Yoruba Church Mission Society (CMS) missionary, emerged to chart a different path. Crowther's encounter with Islam started at a village school in Sierra Leone where, as a fervent young teacher and evangelist, he found a Muslim boy wearing an amulet. He cut it off and warned the boy not to bring such superstitious things to school. Following protest from the boy's father, Crowther offered to debate and prove his point before Muslim elders in the village. He turned up for the debate armed with his Bible and Qur'an, and at the end was disappointed because his well-marshalled arguments were rendered useless. The Muslims simply stuck to the position that God could not have a son. The outcome, in Crowther's own words, 'sobered me down a great deal in my zeal' (1892: 8). This led to a turning point in Crowther's approach to Islam and engagement with Muslims. He realised that confrontational polemics, which was the standard European missionary approach to Islam in both India and Africa, didn't work.

Crowther then developed a more apologetic and respectful approach, relying solely on the Bible to answer Muslim objections, an approach that Andrew Walls calls:

> an African Christian approach to Islam in an African setting. It parted company from the assumptions about Islam that had been current in missionary writing in Crowther's formative

years; there was no denunciation, no allegation of imposture or false prophecy . . . For the future he looked to an African Christian community with an effective knowledge of the Bible (2002: 146).

Crowther recounted a dialogue with the Muslim ruler of Ilorin in 1872, where this time he was armed with copies of an English Bible and Prayer Book and their Yoruba translations. The dialogue was identical in style to the dialogue between the Nestorian patriarch Timothy I and the Caliph al-Mahdi in 781. Crowther then reported how his use of the Yoruba Bible and prayer from the vernacular version of the Prayer Book impressed the Muslim ruler the most (1892: 16–21). Crowther was perceptive in using the mother tongue as a potential bridge with his Muslim kinsmen.

Africa as the 'Spiritual Lung' of the World: Problems and Prospects

In a homily to the second special Assembly for Africa of the Synod of Bishops, Pope Benedict XVI observed, 'Africa constitutes an immense spiritual "lung" for a humanity that appears to be in a crisis of faith and hope.' The pontiff went on to point out that 'this "lung" can also become ill. And at this moment at least two dangerous pathologies are infecting it'. These include materialism and 'religious fundamentalism, combined with political and economic interests'. The Holy Father goes on to talk of the spread of various religious groups in Africa who do so in the name of God 'but according to a logic opposed to divine logic, in other words, not by teaching and practicing love and respect for freedom but rather by intolerance and violence' (Benedict XVI 2009: 2).

Like the lung, Africa's life-giving role is evidenced in a number of ways. In a recent survey on religious tolerance and tension in Africa, the *Pew Forum on Religion and Public Life* noted the religious nature of Africa, something that every African takes for granted: 'Africa is clearly among the most religious places in the world. In many countries across the continent, roughly nine-in-ten people or more say religion is *very important* in their lives'. By this key measure, even the least religiously inclined nation in Africa, Botswana, scores higher (69 per cent) than the United States (57 per cent), which is the most religious of the advanced industrial countries. The vast majority of Africans, more than 95 per cent, claim adherence to the Islamic and Christian faiths. sub-Saharan Africa now is home to about one-in-five of the worlds' Christians (21 per cent) and more than one-in-seven (15 per cent) of the world's Muslims (*Pew Forum* 2010: 1–3). Purely from the point of view of religiosity, Africa qualifies to be characterised as the spiritual lung of the world.

Breathing is the primary functions of the lungs. As indicated, from the beginning Africa provided protection and life to both Christianity and Islam, by offering sanctuary to the infant Jesus and his family and to early converts to Islam. Indeed, Africans like Tertullian, Origen, Cyprian and Augustine led the way in shaping Latin Christian thought (Oden 2007). Early Anglo-Saxon Christians learned literacy and scholarship from an African mentor, 'an abbot called Hadrian, by nation an African, well versed in Holy Scripture, trained in monastic and ecclesiastical teaching, and excellently skilled both in the Greek and Latin tongues.' Hadrian founded the tradition of learning at what would become the great ecclesiastical centre of Canterbury (Isichei 1995: 56). So, like the human lung, Africa played a vital role in providing early Christianity with its spiritual and theological oxygen.

The lungs also play an important role in defending the body against infection and other harmful environmental elements. Africa has acted as a filter of both the Christian and Islamic traditions. Africa moved from being a host to taking ownership for Christianity and Islam by Africanizing them. In its survey, the *Pew Forum* notes that, 'Despite the dominance of Christianity and Islam, traditional African religious beliefs and practises have not disappeared. Rather, they coexist with Islam and Christianity. Whether or not this entails some theological tension, it is a reality in people's lives' (2010: 9). Islam and Christianity are missionary religions, dogmatic and ideologically exclusivist with little tolerance for foreign elements and outsiders. Traditional African religions, on the other hand, are adaptable, open to accommodation and appropriation, and are non-missionary with no membership roll books. This African worldview has over the years served as the wineskin into which both Islam and Christianity have been poured.

The appropriation of Christianity (and Islam) into the traditional African religion meant that in Africa both traditions have different configurations from what pertains in Western and Arabic heartlands. The dogmatic and exclusivist instincts in these two missionary religions are some of the harmful elements that Africa has had to exhale. The end result, to use the words of Lamin Sanneh, is that:

> African Christianity has not been a bitterly fought religion: there have been no ecclesiastical courts condemning unbelievers, heretics, and witches to death; no bloody battles of doctrine and polity; no territorial aggrandizement by churches; no jihads against infidels; no fatwas against women; no amputations, lynchings, ostracism, penalties, or public condemnations of doctrinal difference or dissent. The lines of Christian profession have not been etched in the blood of enemies. To that extent, at least African Christianity has diverged strikingly from sixteenth- and seventeenth-century Christendom (2003: 39).

African Christians may be intolerant and divisive on grounds such as ethnicity, power, money and personalities. Indeed, many churches have sprung up for some of these reasons. However, doctrinal and missiological issues rarely take centre stage or generate heated discussions at many African church synods and general assemblies.

On the Christian-Muslim front, religious and theological differences apparently do not form the primary basis for intolerance and violence. One of the revealing findings of the *Pew Forum* survey is the level of tolerance and respect that exists between African Muslims and Christians:

> The survey finds that on several measures, many Muslims and Christians hold favorable views of each other . . . In roughly half the countries surveyed, majorities also say they trust people who have different religious values than their own.

Sizable majorities in every country surveyed say that people of different faiths are very free to practise their religion, and most add that this is a good thing rather than a bad thing. In most countries, majorities say it is all right if their political leaders are of a different religion than their own. And in most countries, significant minorities (20 per cent or more) of people who attend religious services say that their mosque or church works across religious lines to address community problems (2010: 7).

It can be said, therefore, that in African hands both Islam and Christianity have been divested of their inherently dogmatic basis of exclusivism, intolerance and violence. Having said that, in some parts of the continent, the African spirit of tolerance and peaceful co-existence is under severe strain if not serious threat.

Africa as a Fault Line in Christian-Muslim Relations

Even though there are generally positive inter-religious relations across Africa, serious challenges and even threats do exist. As observed by the Holy Father, Africa is at risk of dangerous pathologies, including religious fundamentalism. For example, al Qaeda's first major terrorist strike took place in Africa; they were the bombings of the American embassies in Kenya and Tanzania in 1998. More recently, Nigeria has experienced ethnic and sectarian bloodshed and hundreds of Muslims and Christians have been killed. After painting the picture of what he calls 'The Next Christendom', Philip Jenkins examines population growth of key Christian and Muslim majority countries in light of prevailing socio-political, ethnic, and religious tensions, economic and political challenges, and ominously talks of the 'Next Crusade'. He singles out Nigeria as a ticking time bomb (2007: 201–204). The *Pew Forum* also noted the tensions:

> On the other hand, the survey also reveals clear signs of tension and division. Overall, Christians are less positive in their views of Muslims than Muslims are of Christians; substantial numbers of Christians (ranging from 20 per cent in Guinea Bissau to 70 per cent in Chad) say they think of Muslims as violent. In a handful of countries, a third or more of Christians say many or most Muslims are hostile toward Christians, and in a few countries a third or more of Muslims say many or most Christians are hostile toward Muslims (*Pew Forum* 2010: 8).

Africa, in many ways, still serves as a theatre for proxy wars and a laboratory for theological and ideological experimentations. When a Danish cartoonist drew an offensive depiction of Muhammad, Christians in Nigeria and Pakistan who may never have heard of Denmark let alone the cartoonist, had to pay with their lives. In other words, African Christians and Muslims still view each other as extensions of the West and the Middle East.

The irony is that over the last century, the centre of gravity of Christianity has shifted inexorably southward to Africa, Asia and Latin America. In 1900, Europe was home to two-thirds of the world's Christian population; today the figure is less than a quarter of the 2.2 billion Christians and is declining. Today there are as many Christians in Latin America as there are in Europe. In 1900 there were about 10 million Christians in Africa. In 2010 there were about 450 million. A typical Christian today is no longer a Western European but most probably a young Nigerian, Korean or Brazilian. On the Islamic front, more than 60 per cent of the global Muslim population is in Asia and about 20 per cent in the Middle East and North Africa. In other words 80 per cent of the world's Muslim populations live outside the Middle East. There are almost as many Muslims in Nigeria as in Egypt (*Pew Forum* 2009: 2).

While in terms of demographics, Christianity and Islam are no longer Western or Middle Eastern religions, many Christians and Muslims still look to the West and Middle East for leadership. Pews and prayer mats are now found in considerable numbers outside the traditional heartlands of Christianity and Islam. The pulpits and *minibars* (pulpits), however, remain firmly rooted in the traditional heartlands, which remain the centres of religious orientation for African Muslims and Christians. Today, several African churches of various denominational traditions still look to the West for religious and theological orientation. They draw from the catechetical, liturgical, and theological menu cards of the Church in the West. While many mainline Protestant churches are still singing hymns and using liturgies developed centuries ago in Western Europe, the Pentecostal and charismatic churches in Africa crave and adopt any new dogma and preaching style from American churches and theological seminaries.

In the wake of September 11th, the debate with and about Islam is raging in the West. Some circles are rehashing in not so thinly veiled academic sophistry the language used by nineteenth- and twentieth-century missionaries and colonial rulers used of Islam. Deeply committed to the age long Western tradition of debating Islam, Jay Smith declares the purpose of one of his debates in the following words: 'I believe this historical material will eventually destroy the entire edifice of Islam academically, bringing into question the very foundations of this growing religion; something I hope happens within my lifetime. Debates like this, up on the Internet, should begin to bring about the demise of Islam's historical credibility within academia; which will, I trust, then filter down into the mosques, and there begin to create a disillusionment amongst Islam's adherents, starting with the young and bright Muslim students, the future "makers and shakers" of Islam' (2013: 1). They brim with self-righteous indignation and are filled with hatred for everything Islamic. Some of these organisations and individuals are scouring Africa, organizing seminars on confrontational polemics, distributing inflammatory literature and literally sowing seeds of fear and suspicion in African Christians towards Muslims.

It is not the case that African Christians have nothing to learn from the West nor that all religious tensions in Africa are caused by outsiders. The point is that learning from the West has to be two-way. If there is one area in which the West needs to hear from Africa in the post-9/11 world, it has to be in the area of religious tolerance and harmonious Christian-Muslim relations. African Christians cannot, however, share with the rest of the world until we have sufficiently learnt the single most important lesson from the disappearance of the early African church in North Africa and Nubia under Islam. Without deep roots in the African culture and heritage, Christianity's future in Africa is at best fragile and nominal. While contemporary African Christians cannot afford to make Blyden's error in romanticizing Islam, we cannot afford to uncritically imbibe images of Islam and hostile attitudes from other parts of the world. As Sanneh points out, Blyden contributed immensely to 'moving [Western] Christians from their medieval fear and distortion of Islam to the terms and realities of shared experience in society' and helped 'to shift energy from abstract academic debate to living issues' (1996: 80). This should be the calling of the African Christian today.

Towards an African Christian Approach to Islam

Christian Africans need to learn from our great ancestor Samuel Crowther who based his engagement with Islam and Muslims on three axes: the Bible, the Holy Spirit and vernacular translation. Crowther looked forward to an 'African Christian community with an effective knowledge of the Bible' as the key in engaging with Muslims. He used the Bible in answering Muslim questions and objections about Christian belief and practise. The Bible should therefore be our main tool in apologetics. This means that engagement with Islam and Muslims must also be based on and driven by biblical values. While the Bible does not have scriptural texts about dealing specifically with Muslims or Islam, it does not mean Jesus left us without a witness as to how to relate to Muslims. He says in Matthew 7:12 that 'in everything, do to others what you would have them do to you, for this sums up the Law and the Prophets'.

In his engagement with Muslims, Crowther used the vernacular, which in his case was their mother tongue language Yoruba, to powerful effect. Bridges and ties exist between African Muslims and Christians on the basis of marriage, lineage, language, ethnicity, kinship and other forms of affiliations such as membership of educational institutions, political parties, trade unions, professional associations, voluntary organisations and so on which form the basis of social and cultural life. These ties and bonds have acted as unifying forces between the two communities in various parts of Africa and contributed to softening the hard doctrinal edges and divisions of Islam and Christianity. These are resources for building bridges for the promotion of inter-religious harmony and peaceful co-existence between African Christians and Muslims.

But more important, the African church needs to develop its own hermeneutical and theological framework in its encounter with Islam and engagement with Muslims. From Christendom, we inherited a Christ who is on the side of the ruler, the powerful, the victorious. He is the Christ of empire, of exclusivity, triumphalism and intolerance. A God who is 'with us, against others', so to speak. A message such as this has nothing new or radical to offer in an Islamic context. The theological import is that God is aligned with the majority worldview. Majority Christology in general, and African images of Christ in particular, has been the proclamation of a God who is 'with us'—not against—but 'for the sake of others'; a Christ who is on the side of the weak and the marginal irrespective of religious affiliation, and who is most powerful in self-giving death.

Christology itself as a theological edifice is constructed on the title of Jesus, *Christus* or Messiah. In an African context, the true identity of people lies in their proper names rather than titles earned or bestowed upon them. Terms such as Messiah, Christ, one nature, three persons, transsubstantiation, hypostasis, etc, are all wedded to Jewish, Greek, Roman and Western cultures. African Christians need to construct our Christ-talk on the basis of the proper name of Jesus, Immanuel, God with us. Indeed, it can be argued that African views of Christ are properly categorized as an *Immanuelogy*, (a theology of Immanuel), a theology *of* relationship and being *in* relationship. Without denying the divinity of Christ, African images of Jesus identify more with his humanity. It is about Jesus as a healer, a mediator, an ancestor, a loved one and a leader or ruler (Stinton 2004). In the encounter with Muslims, Africans need an incarnational theology, a theology that takes on flesh, a face and a name of a relative, a neighbour etc. We need a theology that takes seriously and wrestles with the African reality of religious pluralism, a refocus from the present inherited henotheism (the 'our God' versus 'their God' mentality) to true monotheism, a belief in the one true God who knows no partiality.

References

Azumah, J.A. 2001. *The Legacy of Arab-Islam in Africa: A Quest for Inter-religious Dialogue*. Oxford: Oneworld.

Benedict XVI. 2009. *Homily*. Vatican Basilica, Sunday, 4 October 2009.

Blyden, E.W. 1967. *Christianity, Islam and the Negro Race*. 2nd Edition. Baltimore: Black Classic Press.

Browne, L.E. 1933. *The Eclipse of Christianity in Asia: From the Time of Muhammad till the Fourteenth Century*. London: Cambridge University Press.

Crowther, S.A. 1892. *Experiences with Heathens and Mohammedans in West Africa*. London: Society for Promoting Christian Knowledge.

Cumming, J. 2008. Toward Respectful Witness, in *From Seed to Fruit: Global Trends, Fruitful Practises, and Emerging Issues among Muslims*, edited by Dudley Woodberry. Pasadena: William Carey Library.

Gamble, D.P., and Hair, P.E.H. (eds.). 1999. *The Discovery of the River Gambra (1623) by Richard Jobson*. London: Hakluyt Society.

Guillaume, A. 1955. *The Life of Muhammad: A Translation of Ibn Ishaq's Sirat Rasul Allah*. London: OUP.

Isichei, E. 1995. *A History of Christianity in Africa*. Grand Rapids: Eerdmans.

Jenkins, P. 2008. *The Lost History of Christianity: A Thousand-year Golden Age of the Church in the Middle East, Africa, and Asia—and How it Died*. New York: HarperCollins.

Launay, R. 1992. *Beyond the Stream: Islam and Society in a West African Town*. Berkeley: Univ. of California Press.

McAuliffe, J.D. 1991. *Qur'anic Christians: An Analysis of Classical and Modern Exegesis*. New York: Cambridge University Press.

Moosa, E. 2003. The debts and Burdens of Critical Islam, in *Progressive Muslims on Justice, Gender, and Pluralism*, edited by Omid Safi. Oxford: Oneworld Publications.

Oden, T.C. 2007. *How Africa Shaped the Christian Mind: Rediscovering the African Seedbed of Western Christianity*. Downers Grove, Ill: IVP Books.

Pew Forum on Religion and Public Life. 2009. Mapping the Global Muslim Population. http://pewforum.org/docs/?DocID=450.

Pew Forum on Religion and Public Life. 2010. Islam and Christianity in Sub-Saharan Africa. http://pewforum.org/newassets/images/reports/sub-saharan-africa/sub-saharan-africa-full-report.pdf.

Rahman, F. 1979. *Islam*. 2nd edition. Chicago: University of Chicago Press.

Sanneh, L. 1979. *The Jakhanke: The History of an Islamic Clerical People of the Senegambia*. London: International African Institute.

Sanneh L. 1996. *Piety & Power: Muslims and Christians in West Africa*. New York: Orbis Books.

Sanneh, L. 1997. *The Crown and the Turban: Muslims and West African Pluralism*. Oxford: Westview Press.

Sanneh, L. 2003. *Whose Religion is Christianity: The Gospel Beyond the West*. Grand Rapids: Eerdmans Publishing.

Smith, Jay. 2013. March 12, 2013 News Letter.

Smith, M.F. 1954. *Baba of Karo: A Woman of the Muslim Hausa*. London: Faber and Faber.

Stinton, Diane B. 2004, *Jesus of Africa: Voices of Contemporary African Christology*: New York: Orbis Books.

Trimingham, J.S. 1962. *A History of Islam in West Africa*. London: OUP.

Trimingham, J.S. 1965. *Islam in Ethiopia*. London: Frank Cass & Co. Ltd.

Walls, A.F. 2002. *The Cross-cultural Process in Christian History: Studies in the Transmission and Appropriation of Faith*. New York: Orbis Books.

World Missionary Conference. 1910. *Report of Commission I: Carrying the Gospel to All the Non-Christian World*. http://www.archive.org/stream/reportofcommissi01worluoft#page/243/mode/1up.

Zebiri, K. 1997. *Muslims and Christians Face to Face*. Oxford: Oneworld.

CHAPTER 3

Hermeneutical and Theological Resources in African Traditional Religions for Christian-Muslim Relations in Africa

Abraham A. Akrong & John Azumah

After surveying the prevalent and pervasive role African Traditional Religions (ATR) play on the socio-economic, political and religious lives of African societies, Noel King remarked that,

> When the question is asked, 'Will ATR survive into the third millennium?' it is reasonable to reply, straight-faced: 'How can you destroy it? Shall we shoot every African?' For ATR is not a close rational and logical chain of belief and practise like Islam, nor an arch with a keystone like Christianity, nor a social banyan tree like Hinduism. It is features of African minds and lives. It is most hospitable (King 1971: 101).

In a 2010 survey, the *Pew Forum on Religion and Public Life* reports that about 95 per cent of Africans are either Muslim or Christian, but goes on to make the observation that traditional religious beliefs and practises are still 'a reality in people's lives'. During times of personal or communal crisis and need, Africans have a tendency to draw from their traditional religious heritage. On the personal level these range from politicians seeking advantage over their opponents, to couples looking for children. At the communal level it ranges from times of conflict and war when fighters look for additional 'powers' from traditional religious practitioners to neutralize the enemy's weapons, and the use of traditional mechanisms of justice and reconciliation in such war torn countries as Liberia, Sierra Leone, South Sudan, Rwanda, etc.

The argument in this chapter is that today Christian-Muslim relations are at the crossroads—the meeting point of opposites and the hotbed of diversity—in many parts of Africa. As the celebrated Nigerian novelist, Chinua Achebe put it; 'When we are thinking of crossroads in our culture, that is where the spirits cross and the people cross, so you can meet the spirits there. It can be dangerous but also very rewarding if you wrestle there and succeed. But if you run away from the crossroads because it is perilous, well, you'll survive but you'll never know' (Achebe 1989: 18). The argument of this chapter is that for African Muslims and Christians to succeed at the crossroads, they may have to knock on the doors of ATRs for additional resources.

African Traditional Religion can and indeed has made profound contributions to the understanding of Christian and Islamic mission, a possibility that has only come to be appreciated in recent years. It is a well-established fact in Africa that where one or both the Christian and Islamic traditions have been inculturated, there are peaceful relations between adherents of the two faiths. This is the case in several parts of West Africa such as Senegal and Yorubaland where Islam and Christianity have been divested of their Arab and Greco-Roman/Western cultural scaffoldings. Conversely in areas such as the middle-belt of Nigeria where major sections of both traditions retain their foreign cultural expressions as in radical Islam and Pentecostal/charismatic Christianity, there are tensions and conflicts. A proper understanding of this can reduce the power and force of prejudices in evangelism that is a crucial issue for Christian-Muslim relations. The African religions and philosophy can give us new insights and strength to be bold to proclaim the benefits of the God we worship and live together in peace and mutual celebration.

Religion as a subject of academic study is of recent development, which began in the nineteenth century. The rationalistic spirit of the nineteenth century created an intellectual climate that insisted on understanding everything in a rational format and contributed to a misunderstanding of African Traditional Religion.

Understanding African Traditional Religion

The nineteenth-century academic study of religion was based on the assumption that there was a rational, as opposed to a revelatory explanation, for the genesis and evolution of religion. This rationalistic project about the nature and origin of religion and other cultural institutions was done under the rubrics of a subject called natural history (Fabian 1983: 2).

Natural history, as a subject, operated on the assumption that the development of cultural institutions like religion has followed an evolutionary path of development from the most primitive forms to their present advanced stages. One can study the evolutionary trajectory of the religious phenomenon from its primary and simple beginnings to its more complete forms. For this reason much of the pre-occupation of nineteenth-century religious study was directed by a quest to find the historical evolutionary process of the development of religious beliefs. This quest was a rational enterprise that gave a rationalistic, as opposed to revelatory, account of the development of various religious systems.

Impact of Evolutionary Theory

Until quite recently much of the study of African Traditional Religion was studied under the umbrella of the evolutionary theory of religion. Charles Darwin's theory of evolution, as applied to religious beliefs, assumes that the earliest forms of religious beliefs were simple and less complex because they emanated from very simple primary cultures. The belief is that one could know the past of human religion from the study of primitive beliefs systems. This created a great fascination about the study of the so-called primary or primitive belief system, because it was believed that the primary religions could give scholars knowledge about the pristine forms of the human beliefs of the past.

The scholars of evolutionism like E.B. Tylor, S. Freud and E. Durkheim sought to accomplish two important tasks. First they sought to explain the origins of human belief systems within a system they refer to as natural history. Second, they sought to give a natural account of the different beliefs. The evolutionary theorists postulated that the most primary or primitive form of religion was animism. Out of animism emerged animatism, then polytheism, which later produced monotheism.

The argument was that in the primitive societies like Africa, the type of belief system that one could expect would be mainly animism, because it was the appropriate belief for the level of development of the African society. The celebrated statement, attributed to Emil Ludwig, illustrates this evolutionary mind set. He is reported to have questioned a missionary about the wisdom of going to Africa to evangelize and to have said that deity is a philosophical concept which savages are incapable of conceiving.

The problem with evolutionism was that its classificatory regimes were so rigid that it did not allow for beliefs to stray from one stage of cultural development to another. Later, when other researchers discovered the idea of the supreme God in African societies, the theory of evolution had to be turned on its head. This led to a rival theory of religion known as devolutionary theory. It argues that there was an original revelation of the Supreme in every culture but that this original revelation has been distorted to the different forms of belief systems that we have—animism, animation and polytheism.

The evolutionary vocabulary concepts and descriptive terms of African Traditional Religion developed a whole sets of terminologies derived from accounts of European explorers and adventurers. The term *juju* comes from the French word *jou-jou*, a doll or a plaything. This was how the French explorers saw the images and idols of African Traditional Religion (Evans-Pritchard 1965: 18). *Fetish* comes from the vocabulary of Portuguese explorers and is derived from the Portuguese word (*fatico*), which means a thing made with the hand. For the Portuguese explorers, the symbols of African Traditional Religion were like objects made for worship.

The cumulative effect of these descriptive terms was a tendency to denigrate traditional religion, which became stereotyped as either primitive, negative, false or simply superstitious. These concepts denigrated traditional religion and put it into a negative light as a religion that should be rejected, abandoned or ignored. The negative stereotypes have unfortunately been bequeathed to the academic study of traditional religion, so the academic study of traditional religion has in-built negative stereotypes. The negative stereotypes also fed into the way European missionaries studied traditional religions, not to uphold its integrity or share its core principles and values with other societies and cultures.

Christian/Islamic Missions and Traditional Religions

In the nineteenth and twentieth centuries, Christian mission enterprise was largely founded on the fulfilment theory, which taught that all other religions were preparations for the gospel, which in turn was the ultimate fulfilment to non-Christian religions. Missionaries therefore went out in search for 'points of contacts', i.e. highest ideals in other religions that coincided with aspects of Christian teaching, which will serve as steppingstones for proclaiming the gospel. In their quest for 'points of contacts', the 1910 Edinburgh Mission conference was faced with serious challenges when it came to African Traditional Religions. Collectively, African Traditional Religions were considered as a 'backward and childlike sort of religion' with little or nothing that could be considered as high ideals. Not only were ATRs considered worthless, they were inimical to Christian teaching and values. In extreme cases, overzealous missionaries embarked on physical destruction of traditional shrines and artefacts to prove that these were not worthy of worship.

The general missionary attitude, however, can be summed up in the *salem* concept; Christian villages created by missionaries for the purpose of quarantining African converts away from their traditional kinsfolk. In other words, missionaries fished out Africans from the sea of paganism into Christian ponds to nurture them in the tenants of the new faith which included raising the converts up culturally as proto-Europeans. Indeed, in southern Ghana, the salems were known as *oburoni-kurom* or 'the White man's village'. The salems were therefore geographical seclusion as well as cultural, spiritual and intellectual alienation of converts from the indigenous heritage. The ghetto mentality resulted in an attitudinal and intellectual distancing of African converts from anything indigenous including traditional costumes, indigenous names, local songs and musical instruments etc. At the institutional level, the negative attitudes persisted in the mission churches where African lyrics, drumming, clapping and dancing were prohibited in worship. Instead Africans were theologically educated with the tools of European rationalism and spiritually fed from catechisms, liturgies and hymnals developed in Europe.

Writing on mission work in East Africa, V.J. Donovan notes that religion had become a subject taught in the school, similar to mathematics or Swahili. The few African clergy trained by missionaries 'had become, through their training, almost completely un-African, and extremely conservative and suspicious of any change'. The end product of the missionary effort was 'an inward-turned, individual-salvation-oriented, unadapted Christianity' (Donovan 1978: 7–8). The ponds created by European missionaries, like rivers cut from their sources, dried up with time. The philosophical and evolutionary approach to religion was found to be inadequate in meeting the deepest spiritual needs of African converts. Many attended church on Sundays but during times of existential crisis would visit traditional priests or shrines for help. A Ghanaian traditional ruler once insinuated that his subjects were members of the various Christian denominations on Sundays but adherents of traditional African religions from Monday to Saturday!

The AICs, variously known in academia as African Independent Churches, African Initiated Churches, or African Indigenous Churches (i.e. the Zionists, Roho and Aladura movements from southern eastern and western Africa respectively), arose mainly as part of the quest to fill the spiritual desert created by missionary Christianity. They did this by 'more self-consciously seeking to be African than the churches of missionary origin' (Bediako, 1995: 63). The AICs employed local lyrics, incorporated indigenous forms of rituals in their worship, the leadership used traditional religious designations and costumes, and in contrast to missionary

Christianity's emphasis on argumentation and rationalism, placed emphasis on prayer, healing, exorcism, prophecy, interpretation of dreams, etc. Their appeal and success, in the words of one observer, was

> due in no small measure to their adoption of less formal, more lively, forms of worship with the use of native music and instruments—their approach was nearer the African ethos whereas the churches of European origin are often so distressingly European and dull (E. W. Smith, cited in Parrinder, 1961: 43).

Churches of the charismatic and Pentecostal orientation which are also largely a post-colonial phenomenon, while maintaining a suspicious, negative and in some cases hostile attitude towards traditional religious forms, also placed premium on such phenomena as prayer, healing, prophecy, interpretation of dreams and less formal liturgical style of worship including African choruses, drumming, singing and clapping (Asamoah-Gyadu 2005: 164–200). The gifts and manifestations of the Holy Spirit are given more prominence in contradistinction to dialectical, rationalistic and systematic theologizing of the mission churches. In his 1995 post-synodal exhortation, *Ecclesia in Africa*, Pope John Paul II addressing the issue of dialogue with ATRs said:

> With regards to African Traditional Religions, a serene and prudent dialogue will be able, on the one hand, to protect Catholics from negative influences which condition the way of life of many of them and, on the other hand, to foster the assimilation of positive values such as belief in a Supreme Being who is Eternal, Creator, Provident and Just Judge, values which are readily harmonized with the content of the faith. They can even be seen as a *preparation for the Gospel*, because they contain precious *semina Verbi* [seeds of the Word] which can lead, as already happened in the past, a great number of people 'to be open to the fullness of Revelation in Jesus Christ through the proclamation of the Gospel' (1995: 67).

While the ambivalence is clear in the Pope's position, there is no doubt of his admission that engagement with ATRs is now inevitable if not imperative. Indeed in the same exhortation, the Holy Father intimated thus: 'The Synod considers inculturation an urgent priority in the life of the particular Churches, for a firm rooting of the Gospel in Africa' (1995: 59). The vast majority of African theologians, in their post-colonial self-theologizing, insist on the inculturation of Christianity into indigenous African cultures. Contextualization, indigenization, Africanization, translation, etc. have become the hallmarks of post-colonial African Christian thought, all aimed at making Christianity authentically African without compromising the integrity of the Gospel. In all of these developments, African Traditional Religions are taken as normative in any construction of an African Christian identity and spirituality. ATRs therefore remain the unmistakable substructure for Christian spirituality and the hermeneutical key for African self-theologizing.

It has to be said that these developments did not come about in spite of European missionary activity, but rather because of it, albeit inadvertently. Lamin Sanneh has consistently and persuasively argued that the vernacular translation enterprise undertaken by the missionaries in Africa inspired and empowered indigenous agency. Sanneh notes:

> Often the outcome of vernacular translation was that the missionary lost the position of being the expert. But the significance of translation went beyond that. Armed with a written vernacular Scripture, converts to Christianity invariably called into question the legitimacy of all schemes of foreign domination—cultural, political and religious. Here was an acute paradox: the vernacular Scriptures and the wider cultural and linguistic enterprise on which translation rested provided the means and occasion for arousing a sense of national pride (1987: 333).

In other words, the negative and suspicious attitudes towards indigenous African values in general and ATRs in particular and the ghetto mentality created by the *salems*, were all undone by the missionary acts of translating the Bible into the various vernacular African languages. With the vernacular translations, African converts now had unmediated access to the Bible, but more importantly, the translations served as a de-stigmatizing factor to indigenous cultures.

Islam and Indigenous African Traditions

On the Islamic front, Ali Mazrui is right that 'on the wider spectrum of comparison, it remains true that Islam has been more accommodating to indigenous African custom and traditions than European Christianity has been' (1986: 146). The folk and mystical dimensions of Islam have had the tendency to appropriate and be appropriated into other cultures. The Folk Islamic arts of fortune telling, divination, interpretation of dreams, and production of amulets all fit very comfortably into traditional African religious worldview. The same is true of social practises like polygyny, which is a deep-rooted part of the institution of marriage in traditional Africa. Commenting on what he regards as the 'syncretizing reality' of Islam in Africa, C.F. Molla observes, 'sacrifices are made in the name of Allah, but one is surprised to note that the former gestures have undergone no change whatsoever. Circumcisions are performed but other rites lead up to them and follow them. The new taboos join ranks with old ones' (1965: 467).

In terms of process and attitudes, the Islamic missions encounter with African Traditional Religions share very interesting similarities and dissimilarities with the Christian experience. Islamic missions, unlike its Christian counterpart, encountered African Traditional Religions from a position of marginality and vulnerability. Itinerant Muslim traders and clerics who formed the core bearers of Islam into sub-Saharan Africa did so as immigrant minorities. Wherever they went, they sought patronage from traditional centres of authority, especially from the courts of traditional rulers. The ruling class were therefore always the first to come into contact with Islam and, in many parts of Africa, to adopt certain rituals and forms of the new religion. The Muslim immigrant groups, however, also tended to live apart from the wider indigenous society. Like the Christian *salems*, immigrant Muslim communities tended to live in separate quarters known in Hausa as *zongos* or 'strangers quarters' in West Africa. The marginality and vulnerability of the Muslim communities referred to above doesn't mean that Muslim groups didn't harbour or express similar ethnocentrism and a sense of religious superiority. Unlike their European missionary counterpart who sought to make Europeans out of Africans, the Muslim clerics and trading classes simply kept Islam to themselves and in some places didn't welcome conversion of indigenous people to Islam (Azumah, 2001: 45–55).

Intermingling between the Islamic and indigenous African traditions however did take place. In the encounter of the two traditions, the appropriation of elements was almost always by the dominant indigenous traditions (whose agents were the ruling classes) from the Islamic tradition. In the words of J.S. Trimingham, 'when assimilation took place between African and Islamic institutions, the basic institution into which the other was assimilated might be either, but was generally the African' (1968: 44). This process was to provoke the righteous indignation from orthodox minded Muslims, mainly the jihadist of the eighteenth and nineteenth centuries who resorted to militant jihad to purify Islam from what was perceived as pagan contamination (Azumah, 2001: 65ff). To quote a leading Gambian Muslim scholar, S.S. Nyang, the jihadist embarked upon a twin programme of 'de-traditionalization and Islamization', i.e. the destruction of traditional African structures and values and an aggressive Arabization (1990: 40).

If orthodox Christianity in European hands in Africa operated from the assumptions of evolution of religions, their Muslim counterparts operated on the assumptions of devolution of religion. Islamic orthodoxy is founded on the belief that God's revelation underwent corruption and devolution in the hands of past generations until the rise of Islam. Pre-Islamic Arabia was branded as *jahiliyya* or a period of ignorance, the dawn of Islam ushered in an era of enlightenment. Muslim militants who took up arms ostensibly against the blending of traditional African elements with Islamic ones, branded the former as belonging to the realm of ignorance. But not even the jihadists' swords could vanquish traditional African customs and religious practises. In fact, many of these crept back into Islam in various forms and guises and continue to play significant part in the spiritual and devotional orientation of African Muslims, including regions where the jihadists tried to exterminate all traces of ATR and its rituals. The findings of *Pew Forum* survey of 2010 bear this fact out. The survey found out that while 95 per cent of Africans claim to be Muslim or Christian,

> many of those who indicate they are deeply committed to the practise of Christianity or Islam also incorporate elements of African Traditional Religions into their daily lives. For example, in four countries (Tanzania, Mali, Senegal and South Africa) more than half the people surveyed believe that sacrifices to ancestors or spirits can protect them from harm (2010: 3).

African Traditional Religions may therefore have no roll books or card bearing members, but they do hold sway and in many ways predominate in the lives of African Muslims and Christians. In other words, they are the substructure for both Islam and Christianity in Africa. To use an analogy, it can be said that ATRs, as the host or receiving traditions, act as the software or operating system within the hardware of the Islamic and Christian traditions in Africa. The case we are making in this chapter is that ATRs act not only as a substructure for Islam and Christianity in Africa, but in many ways act as the bridge for peaceful Christian-Muslim relations in most parts of sub-Saharan Africa. We shall now proceed to demonstrate this by looking at the main features of the African worldview, or the African ontology, and how these act as bridges for Christian-Muslim understanding and relationships on the ground.

Hermeneutical and Theological Resources in ATRs for Christian-Muslim Relations

Reality comes to us interpreted on the basis of perspectives derived from our worldviews. The worldview is like spectacles that help us to see and interpret the world from a definite point of view. The first point of call when it comes to resources for Christian-Muslim relations anywhere, adherents of both traditions will have to turn to the Christian and Islamic source books and historical models. But as we have pointed out above, the African Traditional Religions form the substructure of the worldviews of both Muslim and Christian Africans. In talking about the features of the African worldview, we are by no means suggesting uniformity or a single definable something called 'The African Worldview'. Rather, we are seeking to demonstrate how key features of 'African worldviews' act as a bridge to be relied upon to promote Christian-Muslim conversations and relationship in Africa.

The African world postulates a necessary relationship between the natural order and the supernatural or spiritual world. Thus an African perspective on the nature of reality has led some students of African religion and culture to describe African ontology as a theory of being which is vitalistic and dynamic. Kwame Bediako calls it the 'single-tiered ontology' and Benezet Bujo observes that 'in African religion and ethics, everything in the world is intimately connected. All the elements in the universe are related to each other in an interlocking way. One cannot touch one of them without causing the whole to vibrate' (Bujo 2010: 81–82). This aspect of African ontology leads to a principle of causality that can be described as causal activism (Tempels 1959: 19), which means that relationships at all levels, amongst the material and the empirical world on the one hand and spiritual world are vital for cohesion, well-being and progress.

Crucial therefore for the conceptualization of God in ATRs is a relational being who is understood in terms of the different levels of relationship that he has with the world. God is related to the individual through the destiny which human beings receive before they come to the world. This part of divinity in human beings makes them the custodian of the moral life on earth, a belief one finds in the cult of the earth in the northern parts of Ghana, Togo and Burkina Faso. Therefore at the end of the day we can describe the African God as a community of relationship, that is a being whose nature includes his relationship with the world. God is also known as the creator and sustainer of the world and is usually described in parenthood terms as the father or mother of the world. God is therefore a being to be related to and not a philosophical concept or doctrinal treatise to be argued and proven logically as it is the case in contemporary Western and Islamic missions. African Christians and Muslims are therefore comfortable at letting God be God, whose ways and thoughts are beyond human comprehension. God does not need us to fight on his behalf or in his path either literally in holy wars or in theological argumentation through polemics. Even idols are expected to fight their own battles in ATRs.

In traditional African thought, it is in God that humanity becomes truly one. The African traditional view of the Supreme Being is one who takes only the side of justice and truth, not the side of any particular group of people against another. Of course, everyone always thinks their side is the right and just side. However, the age-long debate between Muslims and Christians as to whether the two faith communities worship the same God does not even arise in traditional African religious thought. It is precisely because God as creator owns everybody that no one single group can claim ownership of God. There is no debate as to whether the Supreme Being who is identified by various names in the different languages is the same being. In traditional thought, God transcends all boundaries. Different ethnic groups and clans have their own deities and idols, but they all look up to only one Supreme Being. If Muslims and Christians truly worship the one Supreme Being, then this should serve as a uniting factor, a bridge, and not a dividing factor let alone grounds for war against one another.

In traditional African thought there are no absolutes, no either/or solutions in religious matters. Unlike the literate traditions of Islam and Christianity where one is either a believer or unbeliever, right or wrong, orthodox or heretical, etc, African Traditional Religions tend to be elastic and gradualist by nature. This is mainly due to the fact that traditional practitioners don't see their beliefs in the abstract terms Muslims and Christians tend to see theirs. On the contrary, traditional religions are free of the dead-weight of a theological bureaucracy which is dealing with the present in terms of the past existing in documents rather than assessing the present in the light of what practitioners need now (Goody 1986: 67). For traditional practitioners 'religion does things rather than thinks things' (Tanner 1993: 382). This takes away the sting of religious controversies and polemics that have not only torn Christianity and Islam from within, but have poisoned Christian-Muslim relations over the centuries.

The guiding principle in ATRs can be summed up in an Akan proverb, *'ade pa na tong no ho'*, literally meaning 'the marketability of a product is in its value'. That is to say, the truism of a thing or claim is its own agent. In other words, the truism of a claim is in the results or services rendered (Sarbah 2010: 155). Traditional religious functionaries therefore tend to be 'known by their reputations rather than by their buildings, books or costumes' (Tanner 1993: 374). Unlike Islam and Christianity which are obtrusive and visually aggressive especially with the places of worship which compete for the skylines, along with the use of bells, muezzins, loud speakers and billboards; traditional shrines and priests have to be looked for. They tend to be tucked away.

The reason for this attitude on the part of traditional religious practitioners, as J. Goody rightly points out, is that traditional religions are responsive rather than supervisory, regulatory let alone dictatorial, as is the case with Islam and Christianity. Religion has no borders, which means there is no need to 'convert' let alone put in measures for retaining members. Indeed traditional religions have no roll books and can only talk of clients rather than 'members'. The universalist, missionary and controlling tendencies of Islam and Christianity which are at the root of the competitive and territorial claims and their attendant conflicts, are alien to African religious thought. S.G. Williamson makes the following observation of traditional priests:

> The Methodist Church may have a good attendance on Sundays, but the priests of Bonweri, Barnig and Brakune lose no sleep over it; they regard it as giving unto Caesar the things that are his due, and know where their flock goes when it is, in real trouble, or when traditional ritual is to be observed (Williamson 1965: 82).

Kinship and Hospitality

A key feature of traditional worldview is the social construct of family, lineage, kinship and the strong sense of community. V. Donovan writes about the two 'idols' of individualism and organisation, which 'mesmerize the Western church'. Westerners, he writes, consistently tend to interpret Christianity either from the individual or organisational viewpoint. The love of organisation and power structures has led to our ideas of lord bishops and pontiff popes and national associations of the right and of the left and a plethora of meetings and chapters and synods and councils and committees. Individualism has its obsessions also: individual responsibility, individual morality, individual vocation to the priesthood, self-fulfilment, individual holiness and salvation. Individualism on one side, and organisation on the other, with little room for community in between (Donovan: 68).

By contrast the sense of kinship and lineage has been rightly described by Tanner 'as the most potent binding force' in African societies. Kinship is reckoned through blood and betrothal, i.e. engagement and marriage. In the words of J.S. Mbiti, kinship 'controls social relationships between people in a given community: it governs marital customs and regulations, it determines the behaviour of one individual towards another . . . [it] is like a vast network stretching laterally (horizontally) in every direction, to embrace everybody in any given local group . . . [and] extends vertically to include the departed and those yet to be born' (Mbiti 1970: 102). This bonded nature of African societies is eloquently expressed by Arch-bishop Desmond Tutu of South Africa. He writes:

In our African idiom . . . a person is a person through other persons. We are made for fellowship, for *koinonia*, for friendship, for togetherness because we can be human only together. We are made for inter-dependence and an absolute self-sufficient human being is that less a human being. When we flout this basic law of our being, then all kinds of things go very wrong' (Tutu 1994: 13).

For John Mbiti the African view of the individual can be summed up as follows: 'I am because we are, and since we are, therefore I am' with the kinship system acting like 'an insurance policy covering both the physical and metaphysical dimensions of human life' (Mbiti 1970: 141). Kinship ties which embrace the whole 'tribe' remain deeply rooted in African societies. One can say without fear of contradiction that across African societies kinship ties take precedence over religious bonds and common citizenship. Hence in Kenya one is first a Kikuyu or Luo before a Christian or Kenyan; in Ghana, one is first and foremost an Asante, Ewe or Dagomba before Christian, Muslim or Ghanaian, etc. In other words, important as the Christian teaching of fellowship and communion of believers (*ekklesia*) and the Muslim sense of the *umma* are to African Christians and Muslims, these identity markers play second fiddle to the primary identity rooted in kinship ties. The Yoruba Christian in Nigeria has closer affinity to his Yoruba Muslim relative or neighbour with whom he shares the same mother tongue and lineage than with a fellow Christian Ibo. Similarly, the bond a Yoruba Muslim shares with his Yoruba Christian counterpart is much stronger than that shared with a Hausa Muslim from the north of Nigeria.

The kinship bonds of African societies are the same social construct that the celebrated Ibn Khaldun refers to as *asabiya* in Arabic. As a corporate body, the 'tribe', clan or *ebusua* in Akan or *ebi* in Yoruba has a founder and head who serves as the temporal and spiritual leader of the group. Members share in a common totem, which is usually an animal members are forbidden to eat, and festivals. A person is a lineage member by birth and for life. As one Ghanaian writer notes, the ebusua is like a forest made up of a variety of individual trees. From a distance the trees seem clustered together. When one gets closer to the family or one enters the forest, one finds individual trees or individual persons (Nukunya, 1992: 16). The ebusua or what the Yoruba historian Akinjogbin identifies as 'The *Ebi* Commonwealth Social Theory', acts as glue for adherents of different religious traditions. Thus, in the words of A.E. Akinade, in Yorubaland,

> Christians and Muslims live next to each other, mingle freely together in all aspects of human endeavour. . . . Both Christians and Muslims are awakened every morning by the voice of the muezzin from the minaret of the mosque . . . , Christians receive Christmas and Easter cards from their Muslim friends, neighbours and relatives. Muslims are present in the church for

baptism, wedding or burial of relatives and friends. Christians also look forward to the great festivity that accompanies the *id ul adha*, or Greater Beiram at the end of the Muslim pilgrimage festival (*hajj*). In this practical dialogue, Christians and Muslims are enriched by each other's experience and spirituality, and strengthened by certain features of the faith of the other (Akinade 1997: 148).

As noted by K. Dickson, members of a given community 'are expected to live and act in such a way as to promote society's well-being; to do otherwise is to court disaster, not for only the actor but also for society as a whole. Any act that detracts from the soundness of a society is looked upon with disfavour, and society takes remedial measures to reverse the evil consequences set in motion' (Dickson 1984: 62). Important as the cohesion of kinship group is, 'unity is not marked by uniformity—rather it is founded on commitment to the founder and hence to [his]/her ideals and the well-being of the community' (Oduyoye 1991: 467). It seems therefore that African philosophy and social organisation steers towards the attainment of a community of people that is based on an intrinsic view of the eternal well-being of the total human being. This has made the goal of community the trust of every African communion. The logic is that in community no one is lost and everybody gets what he/she deserves. Community is the goal of life or of any gathering because in community we constitute ourselves as a corporate whole where key aspects of life are celebrated and shared in common.

The strong sense of kinship and its tenacious bonds in African societies may make us wonder whether the concept of kinship is not just as exclusivist and unwelcoming to the outsider or stranger. In answering such concerns it has to be said that in African societies the sense of kinship is accompanied by an ingrained sense of hospitality to the stranger. Lamin Sanneh refers to this inbuilt traditional African mechanism as 'the African principle of 'enclavement', which accords protection and guarantees to stranger and non-kin groups' (Sanneh 1980: 6). Through the principle of enclavement, traditional societies extended hospitality to non-kin immigrant Muslim communities throughout sub-Saharan Africa for centuries until it was disrupted and overthrown by the jihad/reform movements of nineteenth century (Azumah 2001: 38–61). J.S. Trimingham makes a lucid observation of this principle with regard to the status of different groups within the body politic of traditional African societies:

> In the same way, as each individual had his status in the family defined according to age, sex, and filiation, so in the state each lineage had its hereditary status and role according to occupation (Trimingham 1953: 34–35).

In other words, non-kin Muslim groups who were invariably regarded as of a different lineage from the wider indigenous communities, had their status and heritage safeguarded under the body politic of traditional Africa. Like the non-kin Muslim communities, Christian missionaries owe their welcome, status and survival in many parts of Africa to the inbuilt principle of hospitality in African societies rather than the might of colonial authorities. The principle of enclavement is an extension of the kinship and family system, which are 'an ever-expanding, outward-looking community structures as concentric circles in which relationships are moderated by conventions' (Oduyoye 1984: 466). African societies do not therefore only have inbuilt multi-culturalism within its body polity, but is intensely inter-cultural by nature.

The strong sense of kinship bonds and the inbuilt mechanism of hospitality to the stranger in African societies can and should be examined by Christians and Muslims as a hermeneutical key for African ecclesiology and '*ummatology*', i.e. the theology of the *umma*. This will be an important step towards developing a theology of interfaith relationship between Muslims and Christians. A theology that affirms and expands on the sense of mutual commitment to the common good and individual duties in maintaining the well-being and cohesion of society at large. A theology that seeks to foster relationships developed on the principles of conventions and common sense than ones governed by legislations and abstract dogmatic formulations.

Such a theology is crucial because Africans have something unique (such as shared historical and geographical experiences, cultural values, or languages) that collectively distinguish us from our Muslim or Christian co-religionists in the Middle East or Europe; and a collective and intertwined heritage, i.e., the resulting socio-religious, political, ethnic and linguistic plurality of the African context, which is a permanent and distinguishing marker and a shared African experience (Azumah 2001: 180–3). This means that Africans do not only have to learn to live with but find ways of celebrating this diversity in our theological formulations. Any theology or hermeneutic that fails to take cognisance of the inherent diversity of the African context is bound to be a recipe for conflict. We share in Sanneh's optimism that: 'A recognition of the inclusive, tenacious nature of Africa's ancient heritage should enable us to recover a vast and significant field while helping us to relinquish relics of antiquated feuds. By stripping down this historical and cultural scaffolding the supreme prize of genuine encounter will be within our grasp' (Sanneh 1980: 12).

References

Akinade, A.E. 1997, 'The Enduring Legacy: Christian-Muslim Encounter in Yorubaland', in Studies *in World Christianity*, Vol. 3. No. 2.

Akrong, A.A. 1991. 'Akan Christian View of Salvation from the Perspective John Calvin's Soteriology' (Th. D. Diss., Chicago).

Azumah, John, *The Legacy of Arab-Islam in Africa: The Quest for Inter-Religious Dialogue*, Oxford: Oneworld Publication, 2001.

Asamoah-Gyadu, J. Kwabena, African Charismatics: *Current Developments within Independent Indigenous Pentecostalism in Ghana*, Leiden: African Christian Press, 2005.

Ayandele, E.A. 1966. *The Mission Impact on Modern Nigeria*. London Longmans

Baeta, C.C. 1962 *Prophetism in Ghana*. London: Students Christian Movement Press.

Barrett, David B. et al Ed 2001 *World Christian Encyclopaedia: A Comparative Survey of Churches and Religion in the Modern World* 1, New York: Oxford University Press.

Bediako, Kwame 1998. 'Facing the Challenges: Africa in World Christianity in the 21st Century: A Vision of the African Christian Future' *Journal of African Christian Thought* 1, 8 (1).

Bosch, David J. 1991 *Transforming Mission: Paradigm Shift in Theology of Mission*. Maryknoll: Orbis Books.

Dickson, K.A. 1984, *Theology in Africa*, London: Darton, Longman and Todd.

Donovan, V.J. 1978. *Christianity Reconsidered*, New York: Orbis Books.

Eboussi-Boulaga, F.E. 1984.*Christianity without Fetishes*. Maryknoll: Orbis Books.

Evans, Pritchard, E.E. 1965. *Theories of Primitive Religion*. Oxford: Oxford University Press.

Fabian, Johannes. 1984. *Time and the Other*. New York: Columbia University Press.

John Paul II,'Post-Synodal Apostolic Exhortation: *Ecclesia* in Africa'. http://www.vatican.va/holy_father/john_paul_ii/apost_exhortations/documents/hf_jp-ii_exh_14091995_ecclesia-in-africa_en.html.

King, N.Q. 1971. *Christian and Muslim in Africa*, New York: Harper & Row Publishers.

Idowu, E.B. 1974. *African Traditional Religion: A Definition*. London: SCM Press.

Mbiti, John, 1970, *African Religions and Philosophies*. New York: Doubleday and Company.

Oduyoye M.A. 1984, 'The African Family as a Symbol of Ecumenism', in *The Ecumenical Review*, 43/4.

Sanneh L. 1980, The Domestication of Islam and Christianity in African Societies: A Methodological Exploration', in *Journal of Religion in Africa*, 11/1.

Sarbah, C.J.E. 2010. *A Critical Study of Christian-Muslim Relations in the Central Region of Ghana with Special Reference to Traditional Akan Values*, Birmingham: University of Birmingham, unpublished PhD Thesis.

Tanner, R.E.S. 1993, 'African Traditional Religions and their Reactions to other Faiths', in *Studia Missionalia*, Vol. 42.

Tutu, D. 1994, 'The Religious Understanding of Peace', in Gerrie Lubbe (ed.) *A Decade of Interfaith Dialogue, Desmond Tutu Peace Lectures*, Johannesburg: The South African Chapter of the World Conference on Religion and Peace.

Tempels, Placide 1959. *Bantu Philosophy*. Paris: *Présence Africaine*.

Williamson, S.G. 1965. *Akan Religion and the Christian faith*, Accra: University Press.

CHAPTER 4

The African Christian and Islam: Insights from the Colonial Period

Elom Dovlo

This chapter seeks to contribute to the theme for the conference, The African Christian and Islam, by drawing insights from the period of colonial rule. It briefly describes the context of colonial rule within which Christianity spread and how this rule must have shaped African Christian attitudes to Islam and Muslims. Then it examines the attitudes of two key West African Christian leaders towards Islam and the approaches they used to develop relationships with Muslims; the two are Bishop Samuel Ajayi Crowther and Edward Wilmot Blyden. In conclusion, this chapter draws lessons from this period for contemporary African Christian approaches to Islam and Muslims.

The Colonial Context

From the onset of European presence in West Africa in the fifteenth century, Islam was on the agenda of the Portuguese, though not as highly placed as were exploration and trade. Ghanaian church historian Agbeti (1986) and Frederiks (2003), among others, note that Prince Henry the Navigator charged the Portuguese exploring West Africa with discovering the strength of Muslims who were considered the enemies of Portugal. He also ordered them to repulse Muslims from the continent. As noted by Frederiks,

> Prince Henry had an additional reason for wanting to explore Africa. In the aftermath of the Reconquista Prince Henry a young man had fought the Muslim armies in Ceuta, Morocco in 1415 and had become convinced that Islam formed a threat to Europe both politically and religiously. While in Morocco he had heard rumours of a Christian King behind the Muslim lines of defence. It was said that the voyages to West Africa were co-motivated by the search for this Christian King Prester John, who could serve as an ally for Portugal in defeating the Muslim Armies (2003: 82).

Clearly initial European intentions towards Muslims on the African continent were hostile. However, since trade was the European's principal motive for being in West Africa, African Muslims, who were the earliest trans-continental traders, became the Portuguese's natural business partners. During the slave-trade era, European slave traders benefitted directly and indirectly from Muslim raiders who supplied slaves to them, especially in the Senegambia.

The earliest Christian presence (from the fifteenth to eighteenth century) did not produce an abundant harvest of African converts. As a result, during this period Africa did not have a large and strong community of African Christians whose presence would have allowed for encounters with the established African Muslims presence. Fisher (1973: 32), Sanneh (1983) and Ryan (1986) have labelled this era the 'quarantine' phase, when Christianity was restricted mainly to the Europeans who had brought it to the coastline. As Lamin Sanneh has noted:

> When Christianity was transported to West Africa, mostly as a sterilised European institution, safely quarantined in hygienic enclaves along the coast whence it occasionally timidly emerged to make local contact. Often it returned from such ventures still effectively insulated against cross-cultural influences and with more pronounced symptoms of its European condition (1983: 20).

In the nineteenth century, the African Christian presence grew because European Christians made efforts to reach indigenous people. The establishment of colonies in Africa coincided with the establishment of Protestant missions such as the Church Missionary Society (CMS), the Basel Mission, the Wesleyan, the North German Missionary Society, among others, to Africa. These missions were focused on reaching out to Africans and bringing them into Christianity unlike the chaplaincy efforts of the earlier periods of European contact.

During the colonial period, the European scramble for land in Africa resulted in a redefining of traditional borders as Europeans claimed territories. This action brought a complex plurality of African peoples, who had had their own ancestral territories, into the same colonial dominions. As the Christian missions established African Christian communities, these communities became part of this complexity. Plurality thus moved beyond ethnic pluralism to religious pluralism, and African Christians encountered Islam and African Muslims. Christian communities, which developed initially in places like Sierra Leone, Liberia and the Niger Delta, mainly along the coastline of West Africa, gradually spread inland and had African Muslim communities as their close neighbours.

Hanciles citing Andrew Walls has noted the encounters Christian missions had in Africa differed considerably from those between Christianity and Islam in the European experience in Asia. These encounters were based on the fact that 'European Christianity was long defined as 'Christendom': the experience of Christianity as a territorial faith, binding on the whole of society' (2008: 7). This notion of Christendom, however, was not quite the experience of the Christian mission in West Africa, and colonial expansion took place without the original agenda of pushing out Muslims. Colonial authorities, both in French and British West Africa, were very reluctant to create a geographical African Christendom. This reluctance was manifested in a variety of ambivalent colonial attitudes and practises. In some areas such as Nigeria and Ghana the authorities opposed the territorial expansion of Christianity into areas of Muslim dominion; this made missions view colonial authorities as Islam- and Muslim-friendly. Nevertheless, colonial authorities were also often suspicious of Muslim power and intentions and alert against any Mahdist pretensions.

It has to be noted though, that the colonial authorities had anything near to a consistent approach toward Islam or Muslims. The French, who occupied the largest and most Islamized areas of West Africa, did not have a consistent approach to Muslims in French colonies. Peter B. Clarke posits that:

> If what is meant as colonial policy towards Islam is a well thought out, clearly defined strategy or approach applied with a measure of consistency by the colonial regimes to Muslims throughout West Africa, then there was very little of this in the French approach to Islam (1982: 189).

In spite of the inconsistent French approach to Islam, Clarke citing O'Brien indicates that some of the French tended to favour Muslims and that these attitudes were dictated by pragmatism. Clarke for instance offers a general impression based on the opinion of Governor Faidherbe who '. . . believed that Islam could be used both as a vehicle for the diffusion of higher degree of civilization among Africans and as an instrument for the unification of French occupied West Africa' (1982: 190). Further, the French gradually saw even the radical Islamic Brotherhoods, such as the Muridiyya, as allies in promoting their political and economic agenda (1982: 206). Thus, as noted by Stewart, '. . . By the 1920s most colonial administrations had established a network of Muslim holy men, many recruited from the ranks of the Sufi Shaykhs, who could be counted to dispense mediation and moderate counsel to their communities' (1990: 204).

In the British territories,[1] which were smaller but more populous, the colonial policy towards Islam was similar, though it was more defined through the policy of indirect rule. In the British territories, except for Gambia and Northern Nigeria, Islam was not seen as a dominant religion. Missionaries in British territories therefore ventured beyond the coastlines towards the Islamized (at times only partially) interior. Often the British

---

1. Mainly the areas now occupied by modern day Ghana, Nigeria, Gambia and Sierra Leone.

colonial administrators did not permit them to do so, so as to avoid religious conflicts.

Walls notes that colonial authorities had sought to prevent Christian-Muslim conflict during the earliest attempt at a mission to Muslims. This was crafted by the English Methodist Agricultural Mission and sponsored by Thomas Cook in 1794. Walls writes:

> The event has a comic opera outcome, for the party never got beyond Freetown. One of its members immediately created an incident by accosting a Muslim to denounce Muhammad as a false prophet and the rest were dismayed to realise the implications of the life to which they had committed themselves. The Governor of Sierra Leone, fearful for the colony's credit with its neighbours, easily persuaded them to go home. The first modern mission to a Muslim state collapsed before it started (2002: 45).

Another factor that influenced colonial support of Islam was the stability of the well-organized Muslim states of West Africa, which colonial authorities did not want disrupted by Christianity. Several examples abound in Nigeria and Ghana. Sanneh has recounted the views and actions of colonial officers such as Fitzpatrick, Sir Hugh Clifford, and Barnes, who discouraged the spread of Christianity to Muslim domains in Nigeria (1997: 224ff).

In the Gold Coast (now Ghana), A.E.G. Watherston, chief commissioner of the Northern Territories, and his successor, C.H. Armitage, held positive attitudes toward Islam in the British territories. They tried to implement Lord Lugard's indirect rule, which was born out of the latter's encounter with the Sokoto Caliphate in Northern Nigeria. Between 1906 and 1908 they identified Wa, Walewale, Gambaga and the Mamprusi ethnic group as centres of Islam in which the Muslim leadership could be co-opted into administering colonial rule. Watherston, who also perceived Islam as a 'religion eminently suited to the native' and thus more suitable than Christianity for Africans, prevented Christian missionaries from carrying out missions in the North for fear of upsetting this political arrangement.

Colonial authorities also opposed the spread of Christianity in Muslim areas because they associated Christianity with insubordination and African Christians with not respecting colonial rule, traditional customs or Islamic rule. In 1906 Watherston prevented the White Fathers from starting a mission in Wa on the grounds that the town was an important Muslim settlement. In 1912, his successor, Armitage, banned the Wesleyan Mission for the same reason (see Weiss 2008).

Additionally, with time a Muslim police force enforced and policed British colonial policy throughout West Africa. The West African constabulary, made up of mainly Hausas, pitched by default Muslim communities as military police in key towns along the coast of West Africa. On the Gold Coast towns such as Keta, Accra, Cape Coast, and Elmina had garrisons of Hausa-Muslim military police units. This inadvertently created a Muslim community allied with government and with authority among the communities of Christians that were developing in these trading towns and centres of European Influence.

Could colonial policy have contributed to the stance and civil approach taken to Islam by two of most important African Christian converts of the time: Crowther and Blyden? This question is relevant because unlike the colonial authorities fears of insubordination and disrespect of African Christians towards the status quo, i.e., colonial rule and Islam, we find a contrasting attitude in the leading African Christians in the earliest African Christian encounter with Muslims, Bishop Samuel Ajayi Crowther and Wilmot Blyden.

Bishop Samuel Ajayi Crowther

Bishop Crowther (1807–1891) is credited by Walls with 'the first sustained missionary engagement with African Islam in modern times' (1992: 19). As Walls argues, the middle of nineteenth century saw the renewal of Christian and Muslim interest in converting each other, renewal marked by the Niger expeditions in 1841 and 1854 (1992: 48). The key African figure in these attempts to take the Christian gospel to Muslims was Samuel

Ajayi Crowther who, in 1857, became head of the Niger Mission. In 1864, he was consecrated the first African Anglican bishop.

Crowther's methods can be identified as threefold and intertwined. These are:
- avoidance of confrontation,
- dependence on scriptures in dialogue, and
- mother tongue translations of Scripture.

Crowther is reputed to have avoided confrontation and hostility in reaching out to Muslims because of earlier experiences in Sierra Leone where Crowther, who had been born in Yorubaland, had been taken after being rescued from a slave ship. There he was educated in a Church Missionary Society (CMS) school. On one occasion while serving as a young teacher in Wellington, he had seized a charm from a boy, which led to confrontation with the boy's father (McKenzie 1976: 15; Walls 2002: 49). He learnt from this, among other incidents that he had, to court the friendship of Muslims rather than destroy it. He therefore refrained from disputes about truth and falsehood that would generate rancour and bitterness. Rather he aimed at engendering tolerance and cooperation.

As the Nigerian historian Ade Ajayi points out, 'He learnt that the duty of the evangelist was first and foremost to gain a hearing, which came from mutual respect' (2004). In approaching Muslims, Crowther said, Muslims 'can only be argued with upon the ground of what the Koran admits.' These included the status of the angel Gabriel and the miraculous conception of Jesus among others. In this approach, Crowther was using the pedagogical principle of starting from what the hearers already know and leading them into the new faith and knowledge he propagated.

Another aspect of how he engaged Muslims is evident in his earlier encounter over the Islamic charm. Rather than argue with the father of the child, he opted for a dialogue with the elders of the Muslim community (Walls 2002: 49). This was strategic, and his engagement of leaders rather than of individuals may be conceived as part of his civility.

The civility of Crowther's discourse was possible because he did not stress his personal views. Rather, in his second approach in his evangelistic drives, he used scripture-based dialogue. He invited the Muslims he encountered into a dialogue in which they interrogated each other's scriptures using the

Bible and Qur'an. This allowed for creating scenarios and providing answers within the two faiths based on what would be conceived as authority higher than that of the human being. The resultant engagement with Muslims is summed up by Walls thus:

> 'There was no argument,' says Crowther, 'no dispute, no objection made, but the questions were answered direct from the Word of God.' This insistence on answering from the Scripture, even when another answer might be readily to hand, was essential to Crowther's approach: 'After many years of experience, I have found that the Bible, the sword of the Spirit, must fight its own battle, by the guidance of the Holy Spirit' (2002: 52).

Hanciles notes that Crowther's approach 'also represented a very African understanding of Scripture that is even more evident today: one that emphasizes in the spiritual efficacy of the Word and considers effective knowledge of the Bible as the hallmark of spirituality' (2008: 8).

The reason offered for Crowther's use of the Bible in conversations with Muslims is that he believed that the average Christian knew his Bible better than the average African Muslim knew the Qur'an and that he found a great demand among Muslims for Arabic Bibles. Crowther's use of the Bible was enhanced by his moving beyond English and Arabic into using mother tongue translations. This was Crowther's third method of engagement with other faiths.

Crowther translated the Bible into Yoruba, the main language of his people and indeed of the Niger expeditions. The additional advantage Crowther had over his Muslim interlocutors was that he was working within a cultural context increasingly influenced by Islam which insisted on the use of Arabic over against the vernacular. According to Hancile, 'He emphasized the need to collect words and sentences in the local dialects [s]o as to be able in the course of time to make a primer and vocabulary of the language' (2008: 8). This mother-tongue element in Crowther's approach to Christianity contributed to his attitude of tolerance and cooperation.

J.F. Ade Ajayi notes that:

Ajayi Crowther who, as a growing child must have come to associate with Muslims and babalawo and other elders as religious experts, did not hesitate to consult them to syncronise religious terminologies in Islam and traditional religion with those of Christianity. Hence Christianity borrowed names such as Olorun Olodumare (God), Oga, Ogo (Lord of Glory) and similar appellations of God in the Scriptures of Yoruba traditional religion. From Islam the Malam, Alfa became Alufa, the pastor in Christian terminology' (2004).

'Translating the Message', to borrow a title of our keynote speaker and my distinguished teacher, Lamin Sanneh, 'destigmatises' culture (1989). In formulating local language terms for an emergent African Christianity and in using his mother tongue, Crowther softened the grounds for a dialogical approach in mission. His study of Islamic terms shows the openness of Crowther to other worldviews, which places translation and inculturation beyond individual indigenous cultures to take care of the complex societies that colonialism had created. Ade Ajayi thus rightly acknowledges that, 'Crowther's methods, which grew out of the culture of tolerance and co-operation of traditional Yoruba religion, became the dominant approach of the Yoruba Mission' (Ajayi 2004). This supports the view of Sanneh (1980) on the 'domestication' of Christianity and Islam in Africa, in which the inclusiveness of traditional religion and culture minimized the exclusiveness of Christianity and Islam in Africa.

The confrontational attitudes that made the English Methodist Agricultural Mission a fiasco did not subside throughout the period of colonial rule. As a result, European missionaries viewed Crowther's approach, which other African agents adopted, as a soft and ineffective option; the Europeans demanded a more confrontational approach to Islam. Ayandele notes that the young missionaries who arrived from the University of Cambridge between 1887 and 1890 'were tainted by the quixotic idealism of the Student Volunteer Movement, seeking to evangelise the whole world in one generation' (1966: 213). Relating this attitude to Islam and Muslims in particular, Ayandele further notes that:

> Even before they did any work in Nigeria, they condemned the methods of all Christian Missions in Africa. Professedly dedicated to evangelise the Muslim of the Sudan, they announced that they would adopt Muslim dress, food and lodging (1966: 213).

They condemned the approach of the African agents not only to the Home Committee of the CMS but also to their converts.[2]

In 1890, one outstanding defender of the African pastorate did emerge on the side of Crowther. He was Edward Wilmot Blyden, who, according to Ayandele, 'in his writings . . . had regarded the Niger Mission as the only permanent hope of Christianity in West Africa, because it was in the hands of Africans exclusively' (1966: 217).

Edward Wilmot Blyden

The U.S. Virgin Islands-born, Pan-African scholar, diplomat and journalist Edward Wilmot Blyden (1832–1912) first came to Liberia in 1850. From 1871 to 1873 Blyden lived in Freetown, Sierra Leone, then between 1874 and 1885 returned to Liberia, where he held high academic and public service positions. He also led two important expeditions to Fouta Djallon in the interior, where he came into contact with the Muslim inhabitants. Blyden, in encountering Islam, felt that it was more suited to Africans than Christianity was. He admired its state formation, which unified the different tribes. He was convinced that Islam provided opportunities for economic and cultural progress, without the materialism of Christianity. Blyden expressed his ideas on Islam in his book, *Christianity, Islam and the Negro Race* (1887).[3] Powers says, however, that Blyden had different

---

2. Both Ayandele (1966: 215) and McKenzie (1976: 90) note how this new attitude to Islam was reflected in the dismissal of Reverend Paul from Kipo Hill in spite of the protests of both the Emir of Bida and Crowther.
3. The 1967 reprint is quoted in this article.

reasons than colonial administrators for making a positive appraisal of Islam (2000).

Powers links Blyden's attitude to the racism displayed in a debate by Rev. Isaac Taylor, canon of York, in 1897. Taylor argued that whereas Christianity had had negative effects on African Christians, Islam had had a unifying and elevating influence, because of African racial inferiority. Powers, drawing on Blyden's book, posits that Blyden saw racism like Taylor's as the reason for Christianity's failure in Africa. Citing Blyden, Powers notes that he wrote that such racial attitudes in Christianity are what require Black Christian converts to deny their racial heritage (Blyden 1887: xiii), whereas Islam, lacked racial prejudice and espoused universal brotherhood (1887: xiv). Blyden further argued that it was an insult to the Black race to suggest that Islam was more appropriate for Africans because it appealed to their physical or sensual nature. Instead, he blamed racism for Christianity's failure to spread (1887: viii).

Blyden did not, therefore, seek to have Christianity replaced by Islam. Rather, as Ayandele, points out, Blyden was an advocate for an African church.

> He advocated an African Church principally because he believed that it was only an African Church that could stem the tide of Islam and completely destroy it. For said Blyden, Mohammed himself had prophesied that 'in the last times the Ethiopians shall come and utterly demolish the temple of Mecca after which it will not be rebuilt ever again' (1966: 219).

Both Blyden and Crowther, therefore, had a pragmatic attitude toward encounters with Islam and were careful not to arouse unnecessary hostility and rancour. Both had appreciated aspects of Islam, yet remained firm in their Christian convictions. Both studied and wrote about their experiences and insights into the racial context of Christian-Muslim relations in Africa. In placing their experiences within an intellectual framework through such writings, they revealed the strong rational basis of their pragmatic attitudes.

Why the African Attitude to Islam Differed from the European Attitude

A number of reasons can be offered for the tolerant attitude of these early doyens of African Christianity. To explain them, I will dwell more on Crowther who, as a more active missioner, put his convictions into practise. Sanneh has noted that '. . . Crowther's thinking was modelled on his African experience' (2000: 188). Indeed this experience is complex and may have involved family relationships in a pluralistic society. One reason could be that Crowther had married the daughter of a Yoruba Muslim in 1829 (See McKenzie 1976: 15).

In Africa it has been aptly argued that religious encounters were already pluralistic in what is now called African Traditional Religion and which is noted for its marked inclusivity. As noted, this inclusivity 'domesticated' Islam and Christianity in Africa by providing an environment that diluted their exclusivity. However, the Christian-Muslims encounter was more complex than a meeting of two religious traditions. Many ordinary African Christians regarded the boundaries between them and African Muslims as being flexible on non-religious grounds. For example, they could have connections along family lines through intermarriages. Indeed as Muslim traders settled in communities across West Africa they took indigenous wives. Trade also brought Africans into regular contact with Muslims. As colonialism opened new routes for Muslim traders, they moved towards the coastline where European presence had generated new avenues of trade, and inter-religious contact became unavoidable and increased. This called for pragmatic responses as exhibited by Crowther and Blyden.

Moreover, Crowther, in spite of being caught and sold into slavery as a child by Muslims, seem to have had a different experience of Muslims in mission. He encountered a Muslim population which was not personally hostile to him. When he was ordained, he received a delegation from the Yoruba Muslim community who congratulated him. McKenzie states that, 'He was taken aback when the imam and his companions gloried in having their countryman to be the first clergyman of the Church of England among the liberated Africans in the Colony of Sierra Leone' (1976: 17). As McKenzie rightly comments 'Clearly the solidarity of the Yoruba people survived the effects of their transportation to Sierra Leone and was able to support a high measure of toleration of the strongly theological representatives of another faith'.

When Crowther headed towards the Niger interior, Muslims hosted him. On several occasions, as noted by McKenzie (1976: 24), he was not only well received by Muslims, but also provided with food by some, for example at Bida (1976: 57). Further, Muslims attended his services and listened to his sermons (1976: 50). It may be observed that the hospitality the Muslims offered required a non-confrontational style in response. Within the African environment where hospitality is a virtue, a well-received guest must reciprocate and show respect and decorum towards their hosts. Some Muslim leaders actually took care of some agents of the CMS (1976: 58).

Such positive encounters naturally allowed Crowther to develop an appreciation for Muslims without compromising his faith. He, for instance, acknowledged that Allah is not a false God. As McKenzie writes, 'For Crowther, the Muslim worships the same God as he does, though for him, the Muslim's worship has not the status of authenticity' (1976: 16, 25). In addition, McKenzie notes that, 'In the rhythm of the powerful preaching, Crowther voices the belief that 'the people feel there must be a change in religious system'. Islam according to Crowther had refined that system. He wanted to go much further'. Indeed some Muslims who approached Crowther revealed to him that they saw Christianity as enhancing their efforts at ridding traditional society of some unsavoury practises.

Learning about Islam and, indeed, traditional religion was one of the strong foundations of Crowther's approach. This is manifested not only in his translation of Scriptures but in the attempts he made to record the practises and ritual of the faiths. Even in his last years he is reputed to have tried to analyze the factors leading to the progress of Islam in West Africa (McKenzie 1976: 44, 85).

In her analysis of William Maude's document *Memorandum of Muhammadanism*, which was published in 1910, Frederiks states, 'The document shows that Maude was aware that the Christian witness to Muslims needed a special sensitivity and a contextualization of both the gospel and its messenger' (2003: 272). Clearly, Crowther preceded Maude in this understanding and applied this to his mission. Walls is right to say, '. . . the African leader of an African Mission had developed an African Christian approach to Islam in an African setting' (2002: 52ff). Further, as noted by Peter Clarke, this may not have been the elite African Christian attitude but one applied at the grassroots as well. Clarke writes:

> The relations between Muslims and Christians at the official level in certain areas are characterized by mutual suspicion and competition. At the grassroots, in the towns and the villages, these religions were generally speaking characterized by mutual tolerance and respect, although at this level also there was debate and competition, and occasional attitudes of superiority were adopted by both sides (1982: 229).

Lessons for the Contemporary African Christian

The African inter-religious encounter eventually, and for some time, set up a situation of mutual coexistence. Muslim *wanzams* (circumcisers) circumcised Christians, and Muslims guarded Christian premises as watchmen. Post-Independence Africa further enhanced contact between Muslims and Christians in new political settings of a shared common state and of having to work together toward nation building and patriotism.

Moreover, both Islamic and Christian communities have transformed with time. Transnational contacts make Muslims more aware of the bigger Islamic *umma* (community) and of the issues that affect the global Islamic community. The religious consciousness of Muslims, therefore, at times transcends the national consciousness of the states in which they live. This consciousness has been enhanced by post-independence bilateral relations between African and Muslim countries. This has led to the introduction of a level of sectarianism amongst African Muslims, which means Christians now encounter different shades of Islam and Muslims. This complexity is captured by John Azumah's assertion that '. . . Muslims differ as individual, communities, nationalities and in their spiritual quest and level of knowledge and commitment to Islam' (2006: 12). As he further opines, this means that Christians cannot have one broad strategy towards all Muslims.

The contemporary media was instrumental in this post-independence encounter. Many television and radio stations carry Christian and Muslim programmes; some programmes are polemical and clearly addressed to people of other faiths. Radio, in particular, can and does at times become an arena of faceless polemics and confrontation. That is to say, while preachers who use the media reach a larger audience, they themselves are secluded from the audience in whom they may be generating rancour and bitterness through intemperate polemics. More so, what takes place is not dialogue as in the case of Crowther and the Muslims clerics he met. Rather there may be accusations at one time and responses at another, which leads to tension over a long period of time.

Translation and the use of the mother tongue are still arenas of inter-religious encounter in Africa. After independence, in many states there was a growing emergence of a secular-educated Muslim leadership that called for dialogue. They are conversant with the Bible and secular education. At times, there is a deep linguistic resonance as they now conduct *tafsir* (interpretation) in local languages through the media. Indeed, in Ghana the Ahamadiyya Muslim Mission offers translation of parts of the Qur'an in local languages including Akan, Ewe and Ga. Using the Bible and the Qur'an is also a feature of Muslim evangelism of Christians in Ghana. Zaid Collison-Cofie (2005) has narrated how the indigenous Ga Muslims, who were mostly converted from Christianity, used the Bible in preaching, starting around 1935 to win converts. This practise has continued among Ghanaian Muslims, another reason for Christians to renew the use of Crowther's method and become stronger in using the Bible and the Qur'an in engaging Muslims.

Crowther's experience teaches that one must be thoroughly conversant with the Bible and Qur'an to succeed in his style of dialogue using Scriptures. He had lamented that many Christians, although knowledgeable about the Bible, did not know the Qur'an in Arabic (see McKenzie 1976: 41). This remains the same today. Though the contemporary training offered to Christians in mission to Muslims stresses knowing the Qur'an, at times they carry the Qur'an during outreach to Muslims for confrontational purposes.

In Ghana in 1995 for instance, when a Christian evangelist carried the Qur'an into a Muslim community in Takoradi, he allegedly threw it on the floor and trampled on it. The reaction was physical violence (Dovlo 2004: 48–50).

Conclusion

In spite of the changes in contemporary African context and experiences, contemporary African Christians can still learn much from the experience of the colonial era and from early Christian stalwarts like Bishop Ajayi Crowther. The principles they used were those of tolerance based on their African experience rather than intolerance based on the European experience of Islam. They took pride in the unity of African peoples and their humanity rather than in divisions. They studied and examined their inter-faith context so they could to make responses that gave the right answers. They studied the Scriptures in order to know what to say and brought around those they encountered in dialogue by setting the premises of discourse within Biblical traditions. They were careful to '. . . show that the things that Muslims fear as blasphemous are not part of Christian doctrine' (Walls 1992: 19). They gave Islam its due, acknowledging its strength and advantages on the continent without ever compromising their faith and witness.

The attitudes, approaches and principles of Crowther and Blyden are not out-dated. They are still relevant if critically distilled and applied. This is important for a post-independence Africa where state formation must cater for religious pluralism by encouraging sound inter-faith relationships. Indeed, within this context, John Azumah's suggestion that Christians 'be a witness, and not an advocate and a judge' (2006: 15), which was the attitude of Crowther and Blyden, remains appropriate.

References

Ade Ajayi, J.F. 2004. Promoting Religious Tolerance and Co-operation in the West African Region: The Example of Religious Pluralisms and Tolerance among the Yoruba. *The Guardian*, 25 April, 2004.

Agbeti, J.K. 1986. *West African Church History: Christian Missions and Church Foundations 1482–1919*. Leiden: Brill.

Ayandele, E.A. 1966. *The Missionary Impact on Modern Nigeria 1842–1912*. London: Longman.

Azumah, John. 2006. Christian Witness to Muslims: Rationale and Strategies. *Missionalia* 34(1), April 2006:5–21.

Blyden, Edward Wilmot. 1967. *Christianity, Islam and the Negro Race*. (reprint of 1887 text) Edinburgh University Press.

Clarke, B. Peter. 1982. *West Africa and Islam*. London: Edward Arnold.

Collison-Cofie, Zaid. 2005. Islam among the Ga of Ghana. (BA Long Essay), Islamic University College, Ghana.

Dovlo, Elom & Ofosu Asante. 2003. Reinterpreting the Straight Path. Ghanaian Muslim Converts in Mission to Muslims. *Exchange* 32(3): 214–238.

Dovlo, Elom. 2004. The Engagement of Muslims and Christians in Post-independence Ghana. *Journal of African Christian Thought* 7(2), December 2004: 48–56.

Fisher, Humphrey J. 1973. Conversion Reconsidered: Some Historical Aspects of Religious Conversion in Black Africa. *Africa* 43(1), (1973): 27–40.

Frederiks, Martha T. 2003. *We Have Toiled the Whole Night. Christianity in the Gambia 1456–2000*. Netherlands: Boekencentrum.

Hanciles, Jehu J. (2008). In the Shadow of the Elephant: Bishop Crowther and the African Missionary Movement. Inaugural Lecture, Opening of the Crowther Centre for Mission Education, CMS Oxford.

McKenzie, P.R. 1976. *Inter-religious Encounters in West Africa: Samuel Ajayi Crowther's Attitude to African Traditional Religion and Islam*. Leicester: University of Leicester.

Powers, Jessica. 2000. *Christianity vs. Islam in Africa. A 19th Century Debate*. http://www.suite101.com/article.cfm/african_history/46847.

Ryan, Patrick, SJ. 1986. Is it Possible to Conduct a unified History of Religion in West Africa? *Universitas* 8, 1986: 98–112.

Sanneh, Lamin. 1980. The Domestication of Islam and Christianity in African Societies: A Methodological Exploration. *Journal of Religion in Africa* XI(1), (1980):1–12.

Sanneh, Lamin. 1983. *West African Christianity: The Religious Impact*. London: Allen & Unwin.

Sanneh, Lamin. 1989. *Translating the Message*. Maryknoll, New York: Orbis Books.

Sanneh, Lamin. 1990. New and Old in Africa's Religious Heritage: Islam, Christianity and the African encounter, in *Exploring New Religious Movements, Essays in Honour of Harold W. Turner*, edited by A.F. Walls and Wilbert R. Shenk. Elkhart: Mission Focus Publications: 63–82.

Sanneh, Lamin. 1997. *The Crown and the Turban: Muslims and West African Pluralism*. U.S.A.: Westview Press.

Sanneh, Lamin. 2000. The CMS and the African transformation: Samuel Ajayi Crowther and the Opening of Nigeria, in *The Church Missionary Society and World Christianity, 1799–1999*, edited by Kevin Ward and Brian Stanley. Richmond: Curzon Press: 173–197.

Stewart, C.C. 1990. *Islam*, in *The Colonial Moment in Africa*, edited by A.D. Roberts. Cambridge: Cambridge University Press: 191–222.

Walls, A.F. 1992. The Legacy of Samuel Ajayi Crowther. *International Bulletin of Missionary Research*. January 1992: 15–21.

Walls, A.F. 2002. Africa as the Theatre of Christian Engagement with Islam in the Nineteenth Century, in *Christianity and the African Imagination*, edited by David Maxwell with Ingrid Lawrie. Leiden: Brill: 41–62.

Weiss, Holger. 2008. *Between Accommodation and Revivalism: Muslims, the State and Society in Ghana*. Helsinki: Finnish Oriental Society.

CHAPTER 5

The African Christian and Islam: The Roman Catholic Perspective

John Onaiyekan

In our world we are witnessing an ever-greater awareness of the importance of religion in the life of people. The two greatest religions in the world are Christianity and Islam, commanding between themselves a major portion of humanity. A recent statistic puts Christians at 33 per cent of the world population and Muslims at 18 per cent, for a total of 51 per cent (Arinze 1997). Both religions are fiercely propagandist, each believing in its exclusive truth and universal calling. The result is the occasional clashes that we have been witnessing in many parts of the world.

However, I believe that it is becoming ever clearer to most people that we have to face the reality that both will continue to exist for the foreseeable future. We cannot all be Christians no matter how vigorously we preach nor will the world be all Muslim no matter how enthusiastic the followers of Islam spread their faith. We now know it is possible to seek ways of not only tolerating one another but also of trying to understand each other and, hopefully, to also respect one another so that we can jointly work for the good of humanity. It is in this general context that the theme of this conference is of major importance because it focuses on the approaches of Christianity to Islam in Africa. Because, even within Africa, there is great variety within the Christian and the Islamic communities; the approaches of one to the other are a matter of great complexity. It is hoped that with many competent people contributing to this discussion, the picture will be comprehensively covered and analysed so a clear and realistic view may emerge.

I have been requested to give a Catholic perspective on our topic. The danger with this approach would be to concentrate on those areas we consider specifically Catholic, namely where the Catholic Church differs from others. However the Catholic Church is first and foremost a Christian church and it is my belief that what Christians hold in common is far more important than those things that divide them. Therefore, it is to be expected that the treatment of the Catholic perspective would include a good part of what we have in common with others. I will try to explain in simple terms how our church deals with Islam on our continent, leaving others to assess what they do.

A Bit of History

Before addressing the question of the Catholic perspective on this topic, I believe it is important to make a few remarks about the development of both Christianity and Islam on our continent. It seems to me clear that we cannot talk about our attitude to the Islamic faith without recognizing how history has shaped our relationships.

Christianity: An African Religion

It is often forgotten that Christianity is very much an African religion. Our continent was at the origin of the movement which blossomed into the Christian religion. Africa was present early in the gospel story when the family of Joseph, Mary and Jesus took refuge in Egypt to escape the murderous designs of King Herod to kill the infant 'King of Israel' (Matthew 2:13–18). As Jesus carried his cross to Calvary, an African, Simon of Cyrene, a Libyan, was conscripted to help him carry the cross for the last part of the 'Sorrowful Way' (Luke 23:26). The Acts of the Apostles (2:10) mentioned African people from 'Egypt and the parts of

Libya round Cyrene' as being among the first coverts to Christianity. Even though these may well have been Jews who lived in those nations, they certainly considered themselves indigenes of their African nations. Philip the Deacon baptized the eunuch of the Queen of Ethiopia, who took home his newfound faith (Acts 8:26–40).

No wonder the earliest history of the Christian faith has a strong African component. The Church of Alexandria in Egypt and the Christian communities in what was called *Africa Proconsularis* in the modern day Maghreb countries of Tunisia and Algeria produced great theologians like Athanasius and Cyril of Alexandria, Cyprian of Carthage and Augustine of Hippo. They made a determinant contribution to the foundation of Christian theology. The same early African Church produced 'the great saints of the (Egyptian) desert, Paul, Anthony and Pachomius, the first founders of the monastic life, which later spread through their example in both the East and West' (*Ecclesia in Africa* 1995: no. 31). We should also mention women martyrs like Perpetua and Felicitas and the saintly women Monica and Thecla.

Despite many challenges, this early African Church survives in the Coptic communities of Ethiopia and Egypt. The situation in the Maghreb was different and the church did not survive the onslaught of Islam in the seventh century. But this does not reduce the importance of the point that long before Islam, Christianity was quite at home in some parts of Africa.

Christianity did not spread to other parts of Africa until the Europeans brought it along with their sailors and traders across the seas almost 1500 years later. Even that late effort left no lasting impact except in a few places with Portuguese influence in Angola and Mozambique. Sub-Sahara Africa had to wait until the nineteenth century when Christianity came mainly on the back of, but very rarely in collusion with, European colonialism. The relationship between the spread of Christianity and the colonial enterprise in Africa is a complex matter for a more careful historical assessment than it generally receives. What is clear is that within two centuries, the Christian faith has made giant strides all over Africa. We should also note that it was brought in by a divided Christianity, leaving the heritage of a divided Christian Church, a phenomenon with which we still have to grapple.

Islam in Africa

Islam spread largely by conquest across the North African region soon after its birth in the seventh century. That many of the present Muslim lands used to be Christian is not without grave consequence for the perception of relationship between the two faiths. While the early Christian churches of North Africa did not make any appreciable inroads southwards, Islam moved quickly across the Sahara desert into West Africa. Later it spread across the Indian Ocean to the eastern African coast. Much of this later expansion was by the peaceful infiltration of traders and preachers. Thus for much of sub-Saharan Africa, Islam predates Christianity by many centuries. Despite the appearance of Islam being a monolithic unified religion, Muslims practise Islam in a wide variety of ways, which has an impact on how both faiths relate to one another.

The Scramble for Africa

The situation in Africa today can well be described in terms of a 'scramble for Africa', a concept we use for describing the competition of European nations for control over different parts of Africa beginning at the end of the nineteenth century. For a long time, both Christianity and Islam have been making inroads into African communities, often peacefully competing to grab and convert the peoples of Africa. The African peoples, in their turn, have made themselves generally open to being converted to either Christianity or Islam. This openness must not be misunderstood to mean that Africans had no religion of their own or did not consider their religion seriously enough to resist the appeal of the two global faiths. Rather, it is my conviction that if the African peoples easily admit Islam and Christianity, it is because the major elements of their traditional religion find resonance with much of what Christianity and Islam proposes to them.

The most important religious concepts such as the existence of God, the need for reliance on him, faith in the power of prayer, the sense of and need for sacrifice, the belief in a God who judges the actions and the hearts of men and women and who will call everyone to account on the day of judgment, are all present in the African Traditional Religions. These concepts thus find easy acceptance as they are presented in both Christianity and Islam. This, in my view, explains why our continent has moved within almost just a century from cultures of totally native indigenous religions to people who have widely embraced Islam or Christianity.

We have now reached a stage where only dwindling pockets of so-called 'pagans' are left to be converted. The result is that the competition for claiming them has become keener and sharper. Furthermore, Christianity and Islam now find themselves facing one another in many of the African countries. Sometimes problems arise because each is now directing its efforts of conversion to the other. The situation has become rather interesting and the need to devise a peaceful way for this keen competition is increasing every day.

Christian Approaches to Islam

As Christians in Africa, we need to seriously consider how we approach Islam not just as a religious structure but also in terms of its people, Muslims, with whom we live day by day, with whom we share common joys and sorrows, aspirations and frustrations. It is not a straightforward matter of 'how does Christianity approach Islam', but more a matter of how do Christians in their wide diversities approach Muslims who have their wide diversities. How do the many Christian groups in Africa approach the many Muslim groups in our continent?

There are, of course, many ways of going about this, depending on the ideas one has about one's own faith and that of the other. It also depends on the experience of relationship that different people and groups have had.

Confrontation is the primordial approach with each side thinking, 'my religion is the true faith, every other religion is error. The only approach I have towards the other faith is to convert and eliminate.' This attitude is strong in both faiths, because each is theoretically and theologically intransigent, claiming to be not the only true faith but also the best way to reach God. The zeal to convert the other is not only a matter of seeking the pleasure of victory. It can also often be perceived as the greatest form of love and charity. Because we love the other whom we believe is in error, we feel it our obligation to rescue him or her from the error in which they live, hoping also to save the person from the tragic consequences of remaining in error. Much of human history has operated on this basis with horrible consequences.

In our days we live in a world of tolerance where it is considered the right thing to live and let live—to allow everybody to have his or her say, to tolerate even things we know to be wrong. Many Christians approach Muslims on the basis of sheer tolerance: 'You are wrong but I allow you the right to be wrong. You are going to hell but I cannot stop you and I should not disturb your journey to wherever you want to go.' While this may be politically correct, it is often quite problematic. Indeed, as Christians, we are not supposed to tolerate evil, which error is. The same seems to be true of Islam too. How then do we move forward?

The third route is openness to dialogue with others. The bottom line is to recognize that no one has all the truth and no has all the error and that there are common elements of truth that God has given to all. This attitude is promoted through dialogue and becomes the basis for positive co-operation between religions and religious communities. They may be different in many ways but still see one another as having a common basis for living together in harmony and peace.

The three approaches can be found within Christianity and Islam. Even within Christianity are Christians who cannot stand fellow Christians whom they consider as totally in error. Sometimes they merely tolerate one another. But we hope that there are also times when they allow common elements to bring them together to work for the glory of God and the good of humanity. I believe the same can be said within the Islamic community.

Catholic Perspectives of Islam

I wish to stress from the outset that while today the Catholic Church can be said to have a well-articulated policy that is supposed to form a Catholic perspective on Christian approach to Islam, things have not always been so. Even today, Catholics may have a variety of attitudes depending on where they are, the experiences they are living through, and their own theological feelings.

Era of Confrontation

Let us look back into history to examine the roots of confrontation between Christianity and Islam. Christianity started as a religion of the poor people living in a Roman Empire that was dominated by an official pagan religion. Within three centuries, it became the official religion of the Roman Empire and spread quickly over the empire. By the year 600, when Islam came on the scene, Christianity was well established in most of the lands of the Middle East and Southern Europe. During the first encounters, Christians viewed Islam as an attack on the gospel of Jesus Christ. Even though the Islamic faith in many ways expresses some affinity both with the Jewish faith and the Christian faith, the *de facto* relationship between Islam and Christianity from the beginning until recently has been one of confrontation.

The approach was to convert the other if you could. The history of religious wars, which was exacerbated by the theory that the religion of the people was dictated by the religion of the ruler, has filled the pages of history with rivers of blood. Battles have been fought between kingdoms seeking domination and power in the name of religion. Perhaps the high point of this confrontation was the crusades in which European kingdoms mobilized military forces to invade the Middle East with the intention of liberating the Holy Land from the control of Muslim rulers. The adventure was in many cases heroic but it can be said to be a tragic adventure. The Holy Lands remained under Muslim control and seeds of hostility and mutual hatred were sown and continued to grow and fester for centuries afterwards. This happened when most of the West was a Catholic community, well before the sixteenth-century Protestant Reformation.

In addition, we should not forget that the crusades of Western European nations did nothing to help relationship between the Western Catholic Church and Eastern Orthodoxy. Again, the bitter fruits of those events still dog efforts for better relationship today between the Orthodox churches and the Catholic Church.

For many centuries, the main theology or philosophy that guided church life was contained in the famous adage *Extra ecclesia nulla salus* (Outside of the Church, no salvation). And the 'church' was understood in the strict sense of the only true Church, the Catholic Church. Everyone else was in error. Those who were not Christians were considered pagans and heathens who needed conversion. Christians who did not agree with the Catholic position were considered as either schismatics who refused the discipline of Rome while maintaining the unity of dogmatic communion or outright heretics who had embraced dogmatic errors. This covered all those whom we now call 'Protestants'. The desire was to bring everybody 'back to the Mother Church'. The history of the inquisition within the Church and of the crusades outside the Church is in line with this logic. This idea contributed to the religious wars, even between Christians, that devastated most of Europe. This long history of intolerance later carried over to the missions, as has been mentioned.

In the last century or two, people have been moving beyond their traditional narrow attitudes. The link between state and religion has been considerably slackened. The presence of people of different faiths in the same nation has become more and more a normal phenomenon. By the middle of the last century, a new world order had begun to emerge, and it became not only necessary but also possible to devise different and better patterns of relationships and approaches.

Era of Respect Begins—The Second Vatican Council

At this point, when people were becoming more tolerant, the Catholic Church went through the providential revolution of an Ecumenical Council, the Second Vatican Council (1962–1965). This council can be considered a watershed in almost every aspect of Church life. In theology, biblical reflection, church organisation and pastoral practises, Vatican II was a moment of great decisions. We see this in particular with regard to the relationship of the church towards others.

Vatican II came with a new spirit. Pope John XXIII led the church to open itself to others whether non-Catholics or non-Christians. The dogmatic framework was issued in the great document on the Church called *Dogmatic Constitution on the Church* (*Lumen Gentium*). In order of theological proximity to the Catholic faithful, there are the Christians who are not Catholics, but 'who are honoured by the name of Christians, but who do not however profess the Catholic faith in its entirety or have not preserved unity or communion under the successor of Peter' (*Lumen Gentium* 1964: para. 15). Towards them was directed a vigorous programme of ecumenism. Then there are the Jews whose Old Testament we acknowledge as being the inspired Word of God. On the roots of Israel grew the new people of God, the Christian community. St Paul reminds us that it was among them that Jesus, as well as his Mother Mary and all the apostles, came in the flesh (Romans 9:4–5). Indeed, the first Christian church was a church of the Jews. This was enough reason therefore to vigorously pursue improvement of relationship with the Jews.

Next are the Muslims, which brings us to our topic. But first let us note that the same spirit of openness was extended to 'other religions which are found throughout the world' (*Nostra Aetate* 1965: para. 2). This includes the African Traditional Religions.

For its relationship with Muslims, the Church designed an attitude of respect and collaboration. While the Catholic Church has never given up its position that it is the true faith, it also states that the truth about God is present elsewhere and must be appreciated. The Vatican Council II spells out some of these truths as it concerns Islam. Two passages are worth quoting in full:

On Muslims, *Lumen Gentium* paragraph 16 says:

> But the plan of salvation also includes those who acknowledge the Creator, in the first place amongst whom are the Moslems: these profess to hold the faith of Abraham, and together with us, they adore the one merciful God, mankind's judge on the last day (*Lumen Gentium* 1965: para. 16).

In a dogmatic document, this is a very significant passage. The expression, 'in the first place' among other believers in God must be given its full value.

The *Declaration on the Relation of the Church to Non-Christian Religions* (*Nostra Aetate*) is even more detailed, devoting a whole paragraph to Muslims as follows:

> The Church has also high regard for the Muslims. They worship God, who is one, living and subsistent, merciful and almighty, the Creator of heaven and earth, who has also spoken to men. They strive to submit themselves without reserve to the hidden decrees of God, just as Abraham submitted himself to God's plan, to whose faith Muslims eagerly link their own. Although not acknowledging him as God, they venerate Jesus as a prophet, his virgin Mother they also honour, and even at times devoutly invoke. Further, they await the day of judgment and the reward of God, following the resurrection of the dead. For this reason they highly esteem an upright life and worship God, especially by way of prayer, alms-deeds and fasting.
>
> Over the centuries many quarrels and dissensions have arisen between Christians and Muslims. The Sacred Council now pleads with all to forget the past, and urges that a sincere effort be made to achieve mutual understanding; for the benefit of all men, let them together preserve and promote peace, liberty, social justice and moral values (*Nostra Aetate* 1964: para. 3).

Since the mid-sixties, this text has guided the perspectives of Catholics in their approach to Islam.

On a more general note, the Council enjoined Catholics to welcome the truth that we find among others and to see them as what God himself has put in them to promote his kingdom well beyond our own efforts. Sometimes, too, such spiritual values are to be considered as 'seeds of the gospel'.

There is also the clear policy of respecting our differences on the basis of the inalienable right of all to freedom of religion. Today we are all familiar with the idea of freedom of religion. But it was not easy in days of the Ecumenical Council to develop a policy that everyone is free to practise his or her religion. Many believed that error has no right and therefore we could not be speaking of the right to hold different faiths. Thanks be to God, the Holy Spirit broke through and so the Council came out with a whole document on religious freedom: *The Declaration on Religious Liberty* (*Dignitatis Humanae* 1965).

The Era of Dialogue

Once the theological and policy foundation had been laid, it became possible to work out programmes for dialogue, leading to efforts at cooperation at various levels. On the theoretical and theological level, a new theology of the church gradually emerged. This was specifically articulated in *Dogmatic Constitution on the Church*. In respect of our topic, what is important is that in this document the church was understood as the 'sign and instrument', that is a 'sacrament' of God's work in the world to promote his kingdom. The church is a community of the people of God. But at the same time, the concept of the 'people of God' was opened up to welcome anybody, whatever religion they may say they are following, who believe in and live according to the demands of the kingdom of God. This concept of the church made it possible for the Catholic to see others as brothers and sisters on a common journey heading towards a common destiny and objective.

With regard to Islam, serious studies were undertaken about the basic elements of the teachings of Islam and how Christians can understand them. Accurate information about Islam became an important element in the formation and training of the clergy. Many great Catholic universities opened up departments of Interreligious Dialogue, some specifically for Islam. For example, in Rome there is a prestigious Pontifical Institute for Islamic and Arabic Studies. This institute has been running masters and doctoral programmes in Arabic and Islamic studies. Its graduates are spread all over the world, making a valuable contribution to the formation of Catholic priests and other church agents in the area of, and dialogue with, Muslims. They publish in journals and monographs of the highest academic level. The institute is also famous for the occasional *Journées Romaines*, a forum for experts and practitioners in Christian-Muslim relations to interact and compare notes.

Similar institutes emerged in other parts of the Catholic world and their work has been also brought down to grass roots Church members. Thus a lot of effort has gone into enlightening Catholics about what Islam is, at least theoretically.

Post-Vatican II Directives

Soon after the Vatican II, which ended in December 1965, the Catholic Church issued more directives to guide Catholics involved in dialogue with Muslims.

The Guidelines

The first of the directives was published in 1969 by the newly established secretariat for non-Christians under the title *Guidelines for a Dialogue between Muslims and Christians.* It was a well-written document meant to spell out in greater detail the brief but powerful statements of the council documents. The contents are as valid today as they were over forty years ago.

First African Synod, 1994

Of particular relevance to Africa are the directives which emanated from the proceedings of the African Synod of 1994, which were summarized in the Post-Synodal Apostolic Exhortation *Ecclesia in Africa* of Pope John Paul II, issued in September 1995. While encouraging positive relations with Muslims, the document did not gloss over the difficulties on ground. Referring to the fact that both Christians and Muslims believe in the one 'living God, Creator of heaven and earth and the Lord of history', the document continues in paragraph 66 as follows:

> Far from wishing to be the one in whose name a person would kill other people, he (God) requires believers to join together in the service of life in justice and peace. Particular care will therefore be taken so that Islamic-Christian dialogue respects on both sides the principle of religious freedom with all that this involves, also including external and public manifestations of faith. Christians and Muslims are called to commit themselves to promoting a dialogue free from the risks of false irenicism or militant fundamentalism, and to raising their voices against unfair policies and practises, as well as against the lack of reciprocity in matters of religious freedom (*Ecclesia in Africa* 1995).

In the light of the events of 9/11 and its aftermath, these words are prophetic indeed.

Second African Synod, 2008

A second African Synod took place in Rome in October 2008, with the theme, 'The Church in Africa in the Service of Reconciliation, Justice and Peace'. The papal document on this synod is yet to be promulgated. But before the close of the synod sessions, the more than 250 bishops of Africa gathered at the synod approved *Message* which gave a good expression of the general mood of the sessions. The issue of Christian-Muslim relations was addressed in clear terms in a chapter titled 'Joining our Spiritual Forces'. It placed emphasis on the need for Christians and Muslims in Africa to work and walk together with our combined spiritual energies to deal with the many problems plaguing our continent. The document stressed good relations and mutual respect as necessary conditions for such collaboration. The relevant text, from paragraphs 39–41, is worth quoting at length:

39. . . . From our traditional religious culture, Africans have imbibed a deep sense of God, the Creator. They have brought this into their conversion to Christianity and Islam. When this religious fervour is misdirected by fanatics or manipulated by politicians, conflicts are provoked that tend to engulf everyone. But under proper direction and leadership, religions are a strong power for good, especially for peace and reconciliation.
40. The synod heard the testimony of many Synod Fathers who have successfully walked the road of dialogue with Muslims. They have given witness to the fact that dialogue works and collaboration is possible and often effective. The issues of reconciliation, justice and peace generally are concerns for entire communities, irrespective of creed. Working on the many shared values between the two faiths, Christians and Muslims can contribute greatly towards restoring peace and reconciliation in our nations. This has already happened in many cases. The synod commends these efforts and recommends them for others.

41. Dialogue and collaboration will thrive when there is mutual respect. We Catholic Bishops have clear guidelines for dialogue, holding firm to our faith but leaving others to freely choose. The synod received good news of Islamic communities which allow the Church freedom of worship. They also gladly welcome and benefit from the social works of the Church. While we commend this, we insist that this is not enough. Freedom of religion includes also freedom to share one's faith, to propose, not impose it, to accept and welcome converts. Those nations which by law forbid their citizens embracing the Christian faith are depriving their own citizens of their fundamental human right to freely decide on the creed to embrace. Although this has been going on for a long time, it is time to revisit the situation in the light of respect for fundamental human rights. This synod warns that such restriction of freedom subverts sincere dialogue and frustrates genuine collaboration. Since Christians who decide to change their religion are welcomed into the Muslim fold, there ought to be reciprocity in this matter. Mutual respect is the way forward. In the emerging world, we need to make room for every faith to contribute fully to the good of humanity (*Message* 2009, paras. 39–41).

This powerful text will need to be followed up by vigorous and sustained action at all relevant levels.

Action on Ground

On the practical level, structures began to emerge after Vatican II to promote relationship between the Catholic Church and the Muslim community. At the highest level of the Holy See, a special office was established in 1964 by Pope Paul VI for the promotion of relations with all non-Christian believers. Originally called *Secretariat for Non-Christians,* its name was changed in 1974 to *Pontifical Council for Interreligious Dialogue* (PCID), to better highlight the positive thrust of its mandate. Within that council, a Commission for Religious Relations with Muslims was created by Pope Paul VI in 1974. In the Vatican Directory, the *Annuario Pontificio* for 2008, Prof. Lamin Sanneh features as a worthy member of the group of consultants to this commission. See PCID (1994) for an account of their work.

At local levels, the Catholic Church, especially National Bishops' Conferences, have followed this example setting up official structures for engaging other religions especially Islam.

Because of these studies and initiatives from the highest level of the Vatican to the lower levels of National Episcopal Conferences and even dioceses, the Catholic Church has been able to reach out to Muslims in a variety of ways. Efforts are made to break down prejudices so the road is cleared for mutual respect and collaboration in doing good things, especially where serious social and political challenges negatively affect everyone. The average Catholic in Africa is constantly being assisted and enlightened to understand in a positive way the spiritual values of the Islamic faith.

We must, however, admit that the reality on the ground is often not so smooth. Even within the Catholic Church not everybody has imbibed the new spirit of accommodation and mutual respect. Many still live in the old era of confrontation and rejection of anything not Catholic. It seems there is not much one can do about this, provided such people are not in positions of authority where they can impose their views on others.

Unfortunately, not every Christian group accepts or endorses the position of the Catholic Church. I have often been challenged by people who wonder how any Christian can say that we worship the same God with Muslims. When you have such Christians in positions of leadership in their churches, this creates a problem of co-ordinating our activities with regard to our approach to the other party. That is why in Africa and especially at the national level, the challenge of an ecumenical dimension to interreligious matters cannot be ignored. If we do not have a common mind in regards to whom we think the Muslim is, it becomes extremely difficult to have any attitude or approach to him or her in concrete and daily living circumstances. This challenge continues and calls for urgent attention.

There is also the impact of the other party in the relationship. Whatever may be the good intentions and broad-minded approach of the Catholic

Church, what will happen in our relationship with Muslims will also depend on what the Muslims think or say. Because the Catholic Church is part of a wider Christian community the Muslim community tends to look at Christians as one body. The experience of Nigeria is clear on this matter. When the church finds itself in an environment where the prevailing attitude of Muslims is one of hostility and even persecution, the church is left with no room to manoeuvre. This is the situation in those countries which have described themselves as Islamic by nature and refuse to accommodate other faiths. It means that the church is simply tolerated and often allowed to engage in pastoral activities only for foreigners and visitors but not for the citizens of the country. This is the situation in many of the Maghreb lands today. The plight of Christians in Algeria is sensitively reported by Henri Teissier (1967, 2002). This is the situation referred to in the text quoted from the *Message* of the Second African Synod. Despite all difficulties, we still believe that progress can be made with good intentions and firm purpose while keeping our eyes open to the realities around us.

The Nigerian Case

By way of an example, I wish to conclude with a few remarks about the position of the Catholic Church in my country, Nigeria, towards Muslims. As Catholics, we endorse and promote the general policy of the Catholic Church in this matter. Our church has issued many guidelines. Every year, the Holy See sends out letters to Muslim communities all over the world on the occasion of the two major Islamic feasts of *Id-el-Kabir* and *Id Fitr*. The Pontifical Council for Interreligious Dialogue also sends many documents. All these form the basis for our efforts at reaching out to Muslims in our country. We may not have recorded any clamorous success, but some effort is going on.

The Bishops' Conference has a special committee, which is headed by a bishop, for working with Muslims. That committee has been holding regular consultations, assisted by a think tank of Nigerians from all walks of life, which have special competence in how to work and walk with Muslims. We should not underestimate the importance of some well-publicized individual efforts by some bishops who have struck good relations with Muslim leaders within their communities. A good example is the Archbishop of Jos, Ignatius Kaigama; at the height of the Jos crisis in 2008–2009, he and the Emir of Wase doggedly tried to give leadership for peace and reconciliation in an atmosphere of general distrust and confrontation.

The Catholic Church as an integral part of the Christian Association of Nigeria (CAN) is also an important element in the Nigeria Interreligious Council (NIREC), which brings Christian and Muslim leaders together. In that forum, Catholic members make known their positions, especially their positive attitude towards the Muslims. This has had a positive impact on the work of the Council as well as on the perceptions of many members, both Christian and Muslim. Nevertheless, at the end of the day, relationship boils down to person to person. It depends therefore on the attitude of each individual how he or she will relate with a Muslim brother or sister. Our experience is that it is always possible to forge good relations with others even when there are instances of betrayal of trust.

Conclusion

We live in a constantly changing world. Some changes are bad. But some are good. I believe one of the good things in our world is the readiness for and the emphasis on co-operation among peoples. This has spread into the area of religion, and religious people are more and more trying to come closer together. The two greatest religions in the world today, Christianity and Islam, have generally understood the necessity to come closer together so that the world may be better served. The power of religion is obvious, sometimes shown in tragically negative ways. We see this when religion is being used and misused to promote violence and hatred in our society. But the good news is that the same force can be harnessed and used for greater good for our people and to the greater glory of God. This is the challenge that is before all of us. The Catholic Church has its own approach towards this. We expect that others will look into their own spiritual resources to find ways of linking up to achieve this objective. The urgency is great, not only for our countries and for our continent of Africa, but for humanity today in general.

References

Arinze, F. 1997. 'Christian-Muslim Relations in the 21st Century' (talk given at the Centre for Muslim-Christian Understanding in Georgetown University, Washington DC, 5th June 1997). http://www.sedos.org/english/arinze.htm

Dignitatis Humanae, 1965. Declaration on Religious freedom Dignitatis Humanae on the Right of the Person and of Communities to Social and Civil freedom in Matters Religious Promulgated by His Holiness Pope Paul VI on 7th December 1965. http://www.vatican.va/archive/hist_councils/ii_vatican_council/documents/vat-ii_decl_19651207_dignitatis-humanae_en.html

Ecclesia in Africa, 1995. *The Church in Africa: Ecclesia in Africa: And Its Evangelizing Mission Toward the Year 2000*. United States Catholic Conference. http://www.vatican.va/holy_father/john_paul_ii/apost_exhortations/documents/hf_jp-ii_exh_14091995_ecclesia_in_africa_en.html

Kenny, Joseph, 2004. *West Africa and Islam: What every Catholic Should Know*. Lagos: AECAWA Publication

Lumen Gentium, 1964. Dogmatic Constitution on the Church Lumen Gentium Solemnly Promulgated by His Holiness Pope Paul VI on 21st November 1964. http://www.vatican.va/archive/hist_councils/ii_vatican_council/documents/vat-ii_const_19641121_lumengentium_en.html

Message, 2009. Message of the Second Special Assembly for Africa of the Synod of Bishops 23rd October 2009. http://www.asianews.it/index.php?l=en&art=16681&theme=2&size=A

Nostra Aetate, 1965. Declaration on the Relation of the Church to Non-Christian Religions Nostra Aetate Proclaimed by his Holiness Pope Paul VI on 28th October 1965. Encounter PISAI November 1997, no.239. http://www.vatican.va/archive/hist_councils/ii_vatican_council/documents/vat-ii_decl_19651028_nostra-aetate_en.html

Pontifical Council for Interreligious Dialogue (PCID), 1994. *Recognize the Spiritual Bonds Which Unite Us: Sixteen Years of Christian-Muslim Relations*. Vatican City.

Secretariat for Non-Christians, 1969. *Guidelines for a Dialogue between Muslims and Christians*. Vatican City.

Teissier, H. 1967. *Eglise en Islam: Meditation Sur l'existence Chrétienne en Algérie*. Paris: Centurion.

Teissier, H. 2002. *Chrétiens en Algérie: Un Partage d'espérance*. Paris: Desclée de Brouwer.

Part Two: A Thematic Assessment

CHAPTER 6

Fault Lines in African Christian Responses to Islam

John Azumah

One of the crucial issues facing Christians today is finding the right balance in our response to Islam and engagement with Muslims. The quest for an appropriate Christian response to Islam has sadly polarized Christians along 'evangelical' versus 'ecumenical', 'truth' versus 'grace', 'tough' versus 'soft', or 'confrontational' versus 'conciliatory' or 'dialogue' lines. Christians accuse each other of spreading fear about Islam and engendering hostility towards Muslims (Islamophobia) on the one hand, and naïvely going soft on and becoming apologists for Islam (Islamophilia) on the other. In the wake of the 1998 bombings of Dar es Salaam and Nairobi, the 9/11 attacks, the Iraq war, violence in Nigeria, etc., the division amongst Christians has deepened. But this division is as old as Islam itself. Kate Zebiri chronicles the different approaches down the centuries and makes the point that;

> In contrast to the Muslim view of Christianity, in the absence of any clear scriptural mandate there has never been, and there in the nature of things never could be, a unified or official Christian attitude towards Islam . . . Paradoxically, the lack of specific scriptural restraints accounts in part for both the greater virulence of Christian anti-Islamic polemic in the medieval period, and the greater flexibility and openness in the contemporary period (Zebiri 1997: 6–7).

Reflecting on the post 9/11 Christian responses to Islam, Joseph Cumming talks of a titanic struggle; a struggle not between Muslims and Christians, a struggle not between Islam and the West, but 'a struggle within Christianity itself, a struggle for the soul of the Christian faith' (Cumming 2008: 319). Cumming's point is that Islam per se is not necessarily the greatest challenge facing Christians today but rather how Christians choose to respond to Islam. One of the biggest sources of the misunderstanding and mudslinging amongst Christians regarding an approach to Islam and engagement with Muslims is that Islam is often spoken about and presented as a monolithic entity, as a *homo Islamicus*. It is common to read or hear statements like, 'Islam says or teaches X, Y, Z'; 'Islam does not permit or teach X, Y, Z'. Such statements are rather misleading as they assume that there is one unified system of belief called 'Islam'.

As we may be aware, right after the death of the prophet of Islam in 632 AD, Muslims have differed on many issues. The first civil war broke out as a result of the differences barely three decades after the death of Muhammad. Islamic scripture and traditions lend themselves to different interpretations. Islam is also domesticated in many different cultures around the globe and is one of the highly contextualized religions. Islam in Yorubaland is very different from Islam in Hausaland. Islam is therefore far from being a monolithic entity. Ebrahim Moosa, a leading South African Muslim scholar makes the following instructive observation:

> No one has seen 'Islam' in its transparent glory to really judge it. But what we have seen are Muslims: good Muslims and bad Muslims; ugly Muslims and pretty Muslims; just Muslims and unjust Muslims; Muslims who are oppressors, racists, bigots, misogynists, and criminals as well as Muslims who are compassionate, liberators, seekers of an end to racism and sexism and those who aspire for global justice and equity (Moosa 2003: 115).

In light of the above factors, it is important to state from the outset that, it is more appropriate to speak of Christian 'approaches' or 'responses' rather than give the impression there can only be one Christian approach or response to Islam. One way of exploring the different approaches is to identify the different faces of Islam Christians engage with in different contexts. I want to suggest five faces of Islam in need of considered Christian responses. These are: 1. The militant and violent face of Islam including Islamic terrorism; 2. the ideological face of Islam in the form of Islamist conceptions of an Islamic state; 3. Islamic/Muslim criticism, rejection and polemics against Christian beliefs; 4. Islamic missionary activity—da'wah; 5. the progressive face of Islam. These faces of Islam impact Christians in different ways in different contexts and will therefore elicit different responses.

Responding to Militant Islam

Islamic militancy seems to have become the main determining factor for Christian responses to Islam. The daily headlines of violence involving Muslims in different parts of the world have had as far reaching psychological and even theological impact on Christians as it has on the general non-Muslim world. This situation has provoked an age-old Christian anti-Islamic polemical discourse, i.e. debating the question as to whether Islam as a religious belief system is intrinsically violent. Some Christian experts on Islam argue that violent acts committed by Muslims are deeply grounded in the Qur'an, the traditions, Muhammad's example (*sunna*), Islamic history and jurisprudence. 'The primary motivation of terrorists and suicide bombers', writes Patrick Sookhdeo, 'is theological, compounded mainly of duty and reward . . . Without a theology to fuel it, Islamic terrorism would eventually shrivel and die' (Sookhdeo 2004: 143). Riddell and Cotterell on their part have no doubt that 'the roots of the problem' are embedded 'in Islam's own history, both distant and present' (Riddell & Cotterell 2003: 7–8).

Others on their part are of the view that the root-causes of Muslim anger and violence are primarily geo-political; the Arab-Israeli conflict and unjust American foreign policies in particular. Ben White in his critical review of Patrick Sookhdeo's *Global Jihad*, criticizes Sookhdeo for downplaying and ignoring geo-political causes and motivations for violence carried out by Muslims. White then quotes from a Chicago-based political scientist, Robert Pape, that what 'nearly all suicide terrorist attacks have in common is a specific secular and strategic goal' and that 'religion is rarely the root cause, although it is often used as a tool by terrorist organisations in recruiting' (White 2010). These are very legitimate discussions. We need to know the causes in order to know how to respond. But we also have to bear in mind that when it comes to Muslim discourse on the relationship between religion and politics, the point has always been made that the two are inextricably linked.

The question however remains as to whether Islam as a religion is intrinsically violent. There are lots of ambiguities in the Qur'an as well as Muslim tradition and history on the issue of violence. For example, one key Qur'anic verse often quoted to back the thesis that Islam is a peaceful religion is 2:256, '. . . there is no compulsion in religion'. Yet there are also verses like 47:4, 'So when you meet those who disbelieve smite at their necks till you have killed and wounded many of them'. But religious traditions themselves neither speak nor act. It is adherents who speak and act in the name of their traditions. And talking about adherents, there are Muslims who assert and genuinely believe that Islam is a religion of peace, while there are others whose discourse and activities proclaim the opposite. All of these groups are using Muslim scripture and traditions, and all claim their version of Islam is the 'true' Islam. As Colin Chapman rightly observes, 'There is a convincing logic that lies behind both these ways of interpreting the Qur'an, because both are based on accepted principles of interpretation' (Chapman 2007: 6). So, Muslims may be singing from the same hymn-sheet, but they are singing very different tunes.

Western experts have tended to take sides in this intra-Muslim discourse. In my own research on the history of Islam in Africa, Western scholars overwhelmingly sided with eighteenth and nineteenth centuries jihadists as standard bearers of Islamic orthodoxy and branded as venal and corrupt those Muslims who opposed the jihadists' interpretation of Islamic sources (Azumah 2001: 80). It is amazing how mainstream Western academia today has shifted camps, now siding with the moderate Muslim interpretation and branding the radical as extremists, fanatical and deviants. I personally don't think it is appropriate for non-Muslims to get involved in pontificating as to what constitutes orthodox or heretical Islam.

My own thinking on the issue of violence is that seeds of violence can be found in Islamic source books and history. But one cannot always and simplistically draw a straight line between a historic text and a particular action or behaviour. Individual human choice of hermeneutics intervenes, as do particular circumstances. Millions of Muslims around the world recite the same Qur'anic texts daily but do not go out to commit acts of violence. If it is okay to brand Islam as violent on the basis of the acts of the radical groups, it is even more appropriate to argue that Islam is peaceful because the peaceful nature of the vast majority of Muslims. One has to consider the way particular circumstances, as well as historical and contemporary socio-political factors, provide fertile soil for the seeds of violence in Islamic source books.

In order to think of a Christian response to Islamic militancy, it is vital that certain facts are stated. For as Jesus said in John 8:32, there is freedom in knowing the truth. First, apart from instances of communal violence in places like Indonesia and Northern Nigeria, Christians are not the primary targets of jihadists Muslims. The recent attacks on Christians in Iraq and Egypt by elements of al-Qaeda horrified the general Muslim public as it did non-Muslims. The targets of the militants are specific governments and states, including Islamic states. Western democracies have tended to be prime targets. Second, whilst Christians and several other non-Muslims have been victims of Muslim militancy, the actual number of Christians killed in Muslim violence pales into insignificance when compared with the number of Muslim victims. In other words, Muslims are the main victims of militant Islam. Third, research shows that Islamic militancy creates disaffection in Muslims about Islam, resulting in some converting to Christianity (where there is a friendly Christian presence) while many others simply become atheists (Bongoyok 2008: 297–310).

All the facts point to the conclusion that Islamic militancy is more of a threat to Muslims and Islam than it is to Christians and Christianity. For Christian citizens, whose nations are targets of Islamic terrorist groups, Paul makes clear in Romans 13 that dealing with such threats is the responsibility of governments and state security forces. In times like these, Christians should remain as patriotic citizens without compromising their prophetic calling or sacrificing their pastoral care for the weak and vulnerable. As part of their civic responsibilities, one of the contributions Christians are uniquely placed to make is to resource the secular authorities (politicians, security forces, and public policy makers and opinion shapers) to understand, appreciate and engage intelligently with the role of religions in public policy matters.

With weak and corrupt security agencies in many African countries, in places like Nigeria where Christians suffer violence from the hands of Muslims (and vice versa), the long term goal for Christians should be aimed at strengthening these institutions whose duty it is to handle law-and-order issues. In a country like Nigeria with such a delicately poised religious make-up, it is not in the strategic interest of Christians to over-play the religious card. For instance reports such as, 'The Muslims have come to attack and burn down our churches' or 'Muslims are attacking and killing Christians', make it difficult for the authorities to go after the perpetrators. No government will want to be seen fighting 'Muslims' or for that matter any particular religious group. However, if the perpetrators are portrayed as criminals and terrorists and their actions as criminal, it makes it easier for security agencies to go after them. As the saying goes, there are many ways of killing a cat.

The following wise counsel from Martin Luther King, Jr. on violence is very powerful:

> The ultimate weakness of violence is that it is a descending spiral, begetting the very thing it seeks to destroy. Instead of diminishing evil, it multiplies it . . .
>
> Through violence you may murder the hater, but you do not murder hate. In fact, violence merely increases hate . . .
>
> Returning violence for violence multiplies violence, adding deeper darkness to a night already devoid of stars. Darkness cannot drive out darkness; only light can do that. Hate cannot drive out hate; only love can do that.

Our Christian calling is to love our enemies and pray for those who persecute us (Matt. 5:44–45). This may sound tough and unrealistic, but it is what Jesus requires of his followers.

Responding to Islam as an Ideology

Related to, but different from, Islamic militancy is the Islamist concept of an Islamic State where Sharia is enforced as the legal code in civil and criminal matters. The history of early Islamic conquests of Palestine, Syria and North Africa, teaches us that Muslim militancy per se has never been the main factor for demographic changes in favour of Islam. As Muslim conquests and rule gained roots over Christian populations, 'circumstances [became] such that it took considerable tenacity, often a kind of hopeless doggedness, to remain Christian' (Cragg 1956: 307), let alone to propagate Christianity. Quoting extensively from the Covenant of Umar and elaborating on the discriminatory prescriptions of the Sharia against Christians, a leading eighteenth-century Egyptian Muslim Jurist by the name of al-Damanhuri had no doubt as to the desired effects of the Sharia. He wrote:

> The Companions [of the prophet] agreed upon these points in order to demonstrate the abasement of the infidel and to protect the weak believer's faith. For if he sees them humbled, he will not be inclined toward their belief, which is not true if he sees them in power, pride, or luxury garb, as all this urges him to esteem them and incline toward them, in view of his own distress and poverty. Yet esteem for the unbeliever is unbelief (Damanhuri 1975: 55–57).

In the words of Hans Kung, therefore, 'Islam did not prevail by missionary activity in our sense; as a system, it is simply not designed for that sort of thing. But, perhaps without always realizing it, Islam exerted social pressure on the unbelievers, and that, in the long run, is stronger than religious conviction' (Kung 1993: 106–7).

The socio-political and religious pressures imposed by an Islamic state on minority groups pose a serious challenge to Christians in Muslim majority countries. There are varied reasons for the clamour for the implementation of the Sharia within some African Muslim circles. For some, Sharia is God's law that cannot be compromised and must be observed in its totality at all cost. For others, secular democracy is the anti-thesis of Islam and a Western Christian system aimed at undermining Islam. Yet for others Sharia is an integral part of their Islam and to deny Muslims from implementing it is an infringement on their freedom of religious expression (Azumah 2008: 69–72). For Muslim politicians, Sharia can be a vote winner as was proven to be in the northern parts of Nigeria in the early 2000s.

Yet Christians have legitimate concerns that implementing a legal system like the Sharia in a religiously pluralistic society like Africa poses many challenges and relegates non-Muslims to second-class citizenship status. For instance, in a Sharia run state, Christians are barred from high political offices; they are allowed to profess but not proclaim their faith, certainly not to Muslims; their testimony is inadmissible in a Sharia court, etc. Well-meaning Christian leaders and scholars have spoken and written in favour of the Sharia as a personal status code for Muslims. The Archbishop of Canterbury, Dr Rowan Williams' suggestion of 'a constructive accommodation with some aspects of Muslim law' in the British context is well known.

Such calls for the Sharia as a legal code in Muslim personal and family matters fail to take into full account its implication for religious freedom. As perceptively pointed out by Kenneth Cragg;

> As long as religious communities have an exclusive prerogative over matters of marriage, divorce, and inheritance, relating to their members, there will remain a serious infraction of genuine religious liberty. Change of status will not be freely possible if marriage rights, inheritance and the rest are not brought into line (Cragg 1956: 310).

For instance, in many African countries converts from Islam may not be subjected to capital punishment but they will still be subjected to disinheritance and forceful divorce from their Muslim spouses. Sharia, even as a code for Muslim personal and family matters, is therefore still problematic in a religiously pluralistic context. Hence, in light of 1 Corinthians 12:25–26, Christians everywhere have a duty to stand in solidarity with and speak on behalf of Christian minorities who are subjected to the socio-religious and political pressures in Islamic countries. These pressures are very powerful especially in developing countries where poverty and corruption are rife. This does not mean, for example, that British Muslims should be demonized for the treatment of Christian minorities in Pakistan. Indeed, such advocacy can and should be done in partnership with Muslim scholars and activists who feel equally strongly about human rights and religious liberties issues.

As part of a Christian response, there is also a need to resource churches in Muslim majority contexts to theologically and biblically reflect on their engagement with Islam. In many of these places, Christians are preoccupied with bread and butter issues, and in some cases, even life and death matters, with the result that theological and biblical reflection either takes a back seat or is skewed. A sound theology of the cross, for instance, is crucial if churches in Muslim majority countries are to avoid the two extremes of cultivating a *dhimmitude* mentality preoccupied with self-preservation as is the case in some parts of the Middle East and other Muslim majority countries, or the so called '*third cheek theology*' in the name of self-defence, as is happening within some Nigerian and Sudanese Christian circles where Christian seek to respond in kind to Muslim pressures. Above all, Christians and Muslims need to have a proper conversation as to what extent it is appropriate for the state to be involved in enforcing matters of faith.

Responding to Islamic Anti-Christian Polemic

In its scripture and traditions, Islam is generally critical and polemical of Christianity. Anti-Christian polemic is deeply rooted in Islamic source books and individual Muslims and groups have taken it up as their vocation. I have had occasions to challenge my Muslim friends to substitute the term 'Muslim' into every place the word 'Christian' appears in the Qur'an and to read the passages and tell me how they would feel if they were reading that about Muslims from the Bible. Of course, I also tell Christians that in order to appreciate the Qur'anic anti-Christian material, they should read what the New Testament, especially the Gospel of John, says about Jews in general and Jewish religious leaders in particular. Many prominent Muslim scholars, activists and preachers have employed anti-Christian polemic in their works down the centuries; the most notorious Muslim polemicist Africa has produced is Ahmed Deedat (d. 2005) of South Africa.

The question therefore is not whether Christians should respond to Islamic anti-Christian polemic but *how* they should respond. In past and contemporary times, Christians have sought to respond in kind to Muslim polemics. Christian anti-Muslim polemics reached its peak in the nineteenth century in India as Christian missionaries engaged Muslim and Hindu preachers in open debates. The debates produced some of the most outstanding literature in the field of polemics, with Gottlieb Pfander's *Mizan ul-Haqq* standing tall amongst the lot. The problem with the polemical approach, in the words of J.S. Trimingham, was that the missionaries gave a

> dogmatic presentation of Christianity. They thought that it was their work to attack and break down the Islamic religious system, and their method was developed accordingly . . . They sought to prove to the Muslim by argument and controversy that Christianity was better, and to force an intellectual assent. They failed, for they were fighting on the Muslim's own ground (Trimingham 1948: 45–6).

The missionaries might have convinced themselves that they won many of the debates, but what is evident is that they made few converts. On the contrary, the controversies fomented hostile anti-Christian feelings and directly contributed to the birth of the most virulent anti-Christian Islamic movement, the Ahmadiyya Movement, which has specialized and championed anti-Christian polemics in the last century in many parts of Africa. Ahmed Deedat was set on his path of anti-Christian polemics by the constant attacks mounted by a Christian missionary in South Africa.

Together, the Ahmadiyya and Ahmed Deedat have subverted the cause of the gospel amongst Muslims and converted more Christians in Africa to Islam than anyone could ever have imagined. Chawkat Moucarry is therefore right that polemics 'is counter-productive as it usually inspires Muslims to become more radical in their beliefs, and often provokes an offensive reaction too—Muslims attacking Christianity even more vehemently' (Moucarry 2010).

I have heard some Christians say the best form of defence is attack. I personally don't like the word *defence*, let alone *attack*. That sounds to me like seeking revenge, which, I think, is unbiblical (Rom. 12:19). The Bible is clear in defining the role expected of Christians, which is to be that of *witnesses* (Acts 1:8) not *defenders* of the faith. Now let us imagine a courtroom scenario as a metaphor to clarify what we are driving at here. In a courtroom, some of the principal characters include the judge, advocate/lawyers, witnesses, and, of course, the accused and accuser. The duty of the advocates or lawyers is to argue the cases in order to seek conviction or acquittal; the witnesses are simply called upon to testify to what they have seen, heard or experienced; the judge has the task of passing judgment as well as the sentence. If we apply this to biblical teaching, God (and Jesus in his second coming) is the one and only Righteous Judge with the power to pass judgement and sentence. The role of the advocate or lawyer is that of the Holy Spirit. Christians are the witnesses. Throughout the book of Acts and the Epistles, the apostles reminded their audience that they were merely testifying to what they had witnessed in the life and works of Jesus, as well as his death, resurrection and ascension.

The defence of the Gospel is the sole duty of the Holy Spirit. The Greek word used for the Holy Spirit in John 14:16, 26; 15:26 and 16:7 and translated as Counsellor or Comforter, is *parakletos* which means 'one who pleads another's cause before a judge, a pleader, counsel for defence, legal assistant, or an advocate'. The scoring of points in order to seek conviction is the duty of the Holy Spirit. Of course the Holy Spirit works through witnesses, and that is precisely why witnesses are duty bound to exhibit the fruit of the Spirit described in Galatians 5:22–23. The point here therefore is that we should guard against confusing and assuming the role of God or that of the Holy Spirit.

Others say we can't avoid confrontation because the truth has to be told and falsehood has to be exposed. While exposing falsehood and upholding the truth are essential components of Christian witness, it is the message that confronts and exposes, not the messenger. Furthermore, Christian witness is about calling people into a *relationship* with God and others, and we do not argue people into relationships! Witness can be compared to courtship. The use of polemics as a form of witness to Muslims is like trying hard to point out to a young lady in courtship how terrible and bad her family situation is, and why that is a good reason for her to leave her parents and come marry you! How many young ladies can be won into marriage by such an approach?

The Bible warns us very clearly not to judge: 'Do not judge, or you too will be judged' (Matt. 7:1–2). Paul warns against passing judgements in 1 Corinthians 4:5, and goes on to make it even more explicit in 5:12: 'What business is it of mine to judge those outside the church? Are you not to judge those inside?' Does this make the task of the witness any easier or less crucial? Definitely not! When faced with strong evidence in a law court, attorneys normally try to question the credibility of the witness in order to undermine the evidence. In the same way, the cause of the gospel can and has been undermined by Christian witness. That is why Paul warned the believers in Rome that, 'the name of God is blasphemed among the Gentiles because of you'.

Furthermore, some of the images used by Jesus to describe his followers in the world include *leaven, light, salt* and a *city on hill*. It is not by accident that Jesus uses the images of light or lamp and salt. Salt and lamp or light are the most silent yet most effective agents of change. Christians are familiar with expressions such as, 'I am on fire for the Lord!' The mentality of 'being on fire' has with it ideas of burning, destroying, getting rid off, which in turn harbours notions of judgement. A student once asked me whether higher studies have 'quenched my fire'. My reply was, *Yes!* I added that I have ceased burning and only started shining! I don't believe Christians are called to 'burn'. We are called to shine or glow.

But my biggest reservation about polemics as an African has to do with the dogmatic presentation of Christianity for the purpose of intellectual assent. For Africans, religious phenomena are much more than propositional statements or creeds that have to be logically explained and intellectually subscribed to. Religious phenomena include mysteries that are deeply rooted in the metaphysical world. These defy logic and argumentation. What they call for is faith, which as defined in Hebrews 11:1, is 'being sure of what we hope for and certain of what we do not see'. The writer of Hebrews goes on to add that it was 'by faith that the ancients were commended for', not by logical reasoning. Africans therefore have a duty to be critical of the evangelistic methods developed in other contexts.

Finally, a lesson we can learn from the early Christians. This is found in the story of the Christians from Najran and their meeting with Muhammad in Medina in 630 AD. After discussing and disagreeing with Muhammad on the divinity of Jesus, Muhammad challenged the Christians to a mutual invocation of cursing (Guillaume 1955: 277). The Christians resisted the temptation to take the bait. A biblical example can be found in the story of the temptation of Jesus when Satan challenged and provoked Jesus to prove himself. Jesus refused to give in to the provocation. Likewise, it is my considered opinion that rather than pander to the provocation of Muslim anti-Christian polemics in a tit-for-tat game, the aim of our response should be to correct and remove the misunderstanding as far as we are able. My own view therefore is that robust apologetics, not polemics, should be the Christian response to Islamic anti-Christian polemic.

Responding to Islamic Da'wah

Islam and Christianity are the two main missionary religions. While both religions have always taken their missionary calling seriously, it could be said that from the late eighteenth up to the mid twentieth century, Christian missionary activity far outstripped their Islamic rival. However, since the post-colonial era (late 1950s onwards), Christian mission in Western hands has come under a lot of suspicion, accusations and attacks. It has since been on the retreat into university departments and theological seminaries. The few who venture into missions in Muslim countries do so clandestinely. During this same period, Muslim governments and organisations embarked upon very aggressive da'wah in Africa, Asia and the West. The dissemination of Islam is an integral part of Saudi Foreign Policy. Islamic da'wah itself however is not the real challenge to Christianity.

The challenge lies in the criminalization of Christian missions resulting in Christian missionaries resorting to strategies that raise serious questions about the credibility of the gospel and the integrity of missionaries. Another challenge is governments (mainly Islamic) and fundamentalist groups who put legal impediments in the way of people who want to change their religion, especially conversion to Christianity.

Under such circumstances, Christian mission in an Islamic context should go beyond the making of converts. As the only two missionary religions, it is in the interest of adherents of both traditions to have an open discussion on missions itself. In such conversations, the point has to be made that there can be no missions unless there is freedom of religion and that there is an inherent contradiction between mission or da'wah and apostasy laws. As Kenneth Cragg puts it, 'A true understanding of freedom, as freedom of movement of mind, demands that the option should exist' and 'freedom of belief must include freedom of disbelief'. This is so important, Cragg believes, because 'Freedom of conscience has an absolute value that transcends all special pleading. We are not seeking such changes primarily for the benefit of potential converts. Nor should thoughtful Muslims resist them for the sake of deterring such converts' (Cragg 1956: 306–11).

A belief system that denies freedom of disbelief is a prison and no self-respecting faith wants to be a prison. Also, Muslims have to recognize the changing face of Christian missions in contemporary Africa, which is now borne by Africans. This means that instead of continuing to beat the dead donkey in western missions, Muslims have to engage with African Christians and their understanding of missions. For the majority of African Christians, missions is to the church what water is to a fish. Worship and witness, profession and proclamation, are like breathing-in and breathing-out to the church in Africa. The question Christians need to raise with Muslim scholars, activists, governments and organisations in particular, is how Islam can criminalize an activity it is itself actively engaged in across the world.

Christian mission in an Islamic context should therefore involve open and consistent conversations on religious freedom instead of the present situation where missionaries are forced to behave like drug traffickers or terrorist operatives constantly devising ways to evade law enforcement agencies. Timothy Tennent is right in observing that the clandestine behaviour that has characterized Christian missions in Muslim countries in the last couple of decades is unethical and damaging to the credibility of Christians, breeding further distrust towards missions. I share Tennent's counsel that: 'A more open witness in a straightforward, but contextually sensitive way seems to hold the greatest promise for effective and ethical Christian penetration into the Muslim world' (Tennent 2006: 113).

Christian Response to Progressive Islam

The phenomena characterized here as 'progressive' constitutes what many will see as voices from the margins of Islamic discourse which tends to take a more critical reading of the sources in favour of new interpretations in light of contemporary realities. This face of Islam is as old as Islam itself. The Mu'tazilite, an Islamic school of speculative theology that flourished during the eighth to tenth century Basra and Baghdad, is one of the earliest. This school of thought has always sought to be the voice of reason and tolerance against a tide of uncritical adherence and compliance to Islamic source books. As a result they have always been subjected to all forms pressures from the traditional clerical and juridical classes.

In Africa we recall the Muslim scholars who stood up and spoke against the jihadists of eighteenth and nineteenth century West Africa and had to pay with their lives. These scholars, properly identified as pragmatists rather than progressives, took exception of the jihads, arguing among other things that war was not desirable and indeed has the potential for evil, within the pluralistic African context. They challenged the rigid and puritanical interpretations of the jihadists preferring a gradualist and more pragmatic approach to the realities (Azumah 2001: 74–80). This tradition of critical re-reading of Islamic sources was taken up by Mahmud Taha (d. 1985) of Sudan who called for a reversal of the traditional Muslim abrogation theory for the more peaceful verses of the Qur'an to take precedence over the more militant ones. The Nimeiry government executed Taha for blasphemy.

Taha's reformist views persist today in the works of disciples like Abdullahi Ahmed An-Na'im.

The specific use of the term 'progressive' is a post-9/11 coinage by a group of Muslim scholars who pursue a more critical reading of Islamic source books and reject what they call 'the arrogant authoritarian discourse of Muslim literalist-exclusivists'. Their main aim is to reflect 'critically on the heritage of Islamic thought and to adapt it to the modern world' (Safi 2003: 5). Direct engagement with Islamic source books is imperative in the view of progressives because, even though

> it is not difficult to find progressives from a Muslim background who tackle issues of social justice, disparate distribution of wealth, oppression of Muslim women, etc. However, it has been our experience that too often such activism lacks the necessary engagement with the specifics of Islamic traditions (Safi 2003: 7).

In other words, progressive Muslims are keen not only to demonstrate that Islam has resources within its source books for social justice, but more importantly, that Islamic traditions need to be redeemed from the clutches of traditionalist, literalist conservatism. They see what they call 'progressive *ijtihad*' or 'committed critical thinking based on disciplined but independent reasoning, to come up with solutions to new problems', as a form of jihad they are waging (Safi 2003: 8). The primary areas of concern for progressive Muslims are: 1) Critically engaging with Islamic traditions such as the Qur'an, Haddith and accumulated legal opinions through the prism of a new hermeneutical key, a new ijtihad. 2) Standing for social justice for all and against injustices perpetuated by fellow Muslims in the name of Islam. Safi writes:

> The time has come to stand up and be counted. As Muslims and as human beings, we stand up to those who perpetuate hate in the name of Islam. We stand up to those whose God is a vengeful monster in the sky issuing death decrees against the Muslim and the non-Muslim alike. We stand up to those who

apologetically claim that the beautiful notions of universal brotherhood and sisterhood in the Qur'an have somehow made Muslim societies immune to the ravages of classism, sexism, and racism. To all of these, we say: not in my name, not in the name of my God will you commit this hatred, this violence. We stand by the Qur'anic teaching (5:32) that to save the life of one human being is to have saved the life of all humanity, and to take the life of one human being is to have taken the life of all humanity. That which you do to my fellow human beings, you do to me (Safi 2003: 9–10).

3) Attending to issues of gender justice within Muslim society. And in talking about gender justice, 'we are not just talking about women. Far too often Muslims forget that gender injustice is not just something that oppresses women; it also debases and dehumanizes the Muslim males who participate in the system. . . . The human and religious right of Muslim women cannot be 'granted', 'given back', or 'restored' because they were never ours to give—or take—in the first place. Muslim women *own* their God-given rights by the simple virtue of being human' (Safi 2003: 10–11). 4) Wrestling with the challenges of pluralism and seeking inclusivity and eschewing exclusivity and intolerance,

> pluralism is the great challenge of the day not just for Muslims, but for all of humanity: can we find a way to celebrate our common humanity not in spite of our differences but *because* of them, through them, and beyond them? Can we learn to grow to the point where ultimately 'we' refers not to an exclusivist grouping, but to what the Qur'an calls the *Bani Adam*, the totality of humanity? (Safi 2003: 12).

Leading African Muslim scholars who fall within the broad categorization of progressive Muslims include Abdullahi Ahmed An-Na'im of Sudan, Farid Esack, Ibrahim Moosa, Sa'diyya Shaikh all of South Africa and several others who may not refer to themselves as 'progressive Muslims' but share in the above approaches and sentiments. The following titles of some of the works of some of these scholar/activists speak for themselves: *The Second Message of Islam* (1996), by Mahmoud Taha; *Toward an Islamic Reformation: Civil Liberties, Human Rights and International Law* (1990), by Abdullahi Ahmed An-Na'im; *Qur'an, Liberation & Pluralism: An Islamic Perspective of Interreligious Solidarity against Oppression* (1997), by Farid Esack.

Christian writers who revel in conspiracy theories dismiss these attempts as part of *taqiya*, dissimulation or pretence on the part of these Muslim scholars, and that the true nature and real agenda of Islam is to conquer and rule. Some declare that there is no such thing as 'moderate Islam' or 'moderate Muslims', which is rather uncharitable looking at the fact that some of these scholars have paid with their lives and most have to live in exile. Other critics will not go as far as to cast aspersions on the personal integrity of these scholars but will rather question the integrity of their approaches and works. This school of thought still goes with the dictum that 'Islam reformed is no longer Islam'. The argument goes that a faithful reading of the Qur'an can only lead to the intolerant, misogynist and militant expressions of Islam. If this is true, then it means Muslims are trapped in their traditions.

But some of us are of the opinion that the Qur'an is made for Muslims and not Muslims for the Qur'an. Indeed, as the title of one of Farid Esack's forthcoming book puts it, 'Whose Qur'an?' Muslims everywhere don't need authorization from anyone as to how to interpret their sacred texts. If African Muslims truly desire it and wish to be part of an interdependent pluralistic Africa, they can interpret the Qur'an in terms that addresses their realities. This is what progressive Muslims are seeking to do. It is certainly not the duty of Christians to set themselves the tasks of pontificating which Islamic interpretation is right and which is wrong. We need to be informed about this type of discourse and reach out to progressive Muslims as partners in dialogue against all forms of discrimination and oppression.

Christian Response as a Witness to Islam

It is essential that any Christian response to Islam is not seen to be driven by fear and self-preservation. Jesus is very clear; 'If anyone would come after me, he must deny himself and take up his cross and follow me. For whoever wants to save his life will lose it, but whoever loses his life for me and for the gospel will save it.' The crusades are a very good example of a Christian response to Islam undertaken out of fear and self-preservation. The legacy of the crusades and the witness they left in the Muslim psyche about Christianity speaks for itself. To quote Joseph Cumming once more:

> It used to be commonly said that Islam was Satan's greatest masterpiece. I believe that is not true. I believe that Satan's greatest masterpiece was the Crusades. Why? Is it because the Crusades were the worst atrocity that ever happened in history? I think Hitler was worse. Stalin was worse. Pol Pot was worse. What is so horrible about the Crusades is that it was done under the symbol of the cross, that Satan succeeded in distorting the very heart of the Christian faith.
>
> The cross is at the heart of the entire Christian faith, and for the Muslims and the Jews of the world, what does the symbol of the cross now signify? The cross now signifies, 'Christians hate you enough to kill you.' What is the cross suppose to signify? It is suppose to signify, 'God loved you enough to lay down his life for you, and I love you enough that I would lay down my life for you.' Satan succeeded in taking the very heart of the Christian faith, and turning it around to mean not just something different, but to mean the exact opposite of what it was supposed to mean (Cumming 2008: 322–3).

It is true that African Christians had nothing to do with the crusades and therefore have nothing to be guilty about or to apologise for. In fact, Egyptian Christians were victims of the crusades along with their Muslim counterparts! However it is not enough for us to dismiss the crusades as belonging solely to the domain of erstwhile Christian Europe. The crusades have done a lot of damage to Christian witness and left a stain on the gospel of Jesus Christ. Sanneh describes the crusades as 'a coup d'etat against the teaching of Jesus' (Sanneh 2003: 32). Moreover, engaging with Muslims is a form of Christian witness and we cannot afford to dismiss their historical hurts (real or perceived) caused by Christians just as we wouldn't like Muslims to dismiss the historical hurts caused us by past generations of Muslims. History is a mistress when it comes to contemporary Muslim-Christian relations and needs to be taken seriously.

Conclusion

In conclusion, I would like to reiterate the following: Do Islamic militancy, terrorism, ideology, anti-Christian polemic and da'wah pose challenges and, even in some cases, threats to Christianity, Christian values and rights of Christian minorities? *Yes!* The danger however is to let radical Islam succeed in radicalizing the gospel and ourselves. Some evangelicals are very close to allowing radical Islam to not only define and drive their missions, but also their attitude towards Muslims and even other Christians who think differently. Archbishop Desmond Tutu is reported to have said to Black South Africans: 'Be kind to the Whites. They need you to rediscover their own humanity'! Radical Muslims need Christians to rediscover their own humanity.

The main casualty in the collateral damage of radical Islam is the fruit of the Spirit described in Galatians 5:22–23, expressed in qualities such as love, peace, compassion, gentleness, kindness, etc. These biblical characterisations of Christ-likeness have, unfortunately, become virtually dirty words in some Christian circles as far as engaging with Islam and Muslims is concerned. Some Christians enthusiastically use the fruit of the Holy Spirit in anti-Muslim polemic to show the superiority of Christianity to Islam, while at the same time dismissively brand their fellow Christians as going 'soft' on Islam and thus betraying the Christian cause when they call for a greater demonstration of Christ-like graces towards Muslims. Such sentiments only betray what's on the inside, for Jesus says in Matthew 7:16–20 (NIV),

> By their fruit you will recognise them. Do people pick grapes from thorn bushes, or figs from thistles? Likewise every good tree bears good fruit, but a bad tree bears bad fruit. A good tree

cannot bear bad fruit, and a bad tree cannot bear good fruit. Every tree that does not bear good fruit is cut down and thrown into the fire. Thus, by their fruit you will recognise them.

There may be no scriptural texts dealing with Muslims or Islam in the Bible, but that doesn't mean Jesus did not leave us without a witness on how to relate to Muslims. For he says in Matthew 7:12 that 'in everything, do to others what you would have them do to you, for this sums up the Law and the Prophets'. Some of us believe Jesus is the way, the truth and the life, and there is no other way in engaging with Muslims than the Jesus Way! And Jesus' way is not a broad way, but a narrow one; it is not wide gate but a small one. Jesus' way is not a 'soft' option. On the contrary, it is a tough one!

References

Azumah J. 2001, *The Legacy of Arab-Islam: A Quest for Inter-Religious Dialogue*, Oxford: Oneworld Publications.

Azumah J. 2008. *My Neighbour's Faith: Islam Explained for African Christians*, Nairobi: Hippo Books.

Bongoyok M. 2008, 'Islamism and Receptivity to Jesus,' in Woodberry, (ed.), *From Seed to Fruit*.

Chapman C. 2007, 'Christian Responses to Islam, Islamism and 'Islamic Terrorism' ' in *Cambridge Papers*, 16/2.

Cragg K. 1956, *The Call of the Minaret 3rd Edition*, Oxford: Oneword Publications.

Cumming, J. 2008, 'Toward Respectful Witness', in Dudley Woodberry, (ed.), *From Seed to Fruit: Global Trends, Fruitful Practises, and Emerging Issues among Muslims*, Pasadena: William Carey Library.

Guillaume A. 1955, *The Life of Muhammad: A Translation of Ibn Ishaq's Sirat Rasul Allah*, Oxford: Oxford University Press.

Kung H. et al. 1993, *Christianity and the World Religions: Paths of Dialogue with Islam, Hinduism, and Buddhism*, 2nd ed., London: SCM Press.

Moosa E. 2003, 'The Debts and Burdens of Critical Islam,' in Omid Safi (ed.), *Progressive Muslims on Justice, Gender and Pluralism*. Oxford: Oneword Publications.

Moucarry C. 2010, 'A Plea for Dialogue between Christians and Muslims,' http://conversation.lausanne.org/resources/detail/10023 [accessed 30 May 2010].

Perlmann M. (trans.) 1975, *Shaykh Damanhuri on the Churches of Cairo (1737)*, Berkeley: University of California Press.

Riddell P.G. & Cotterell P. (eds.) 2003, *Islam in Conflict: Past, Present and Future*, Leicester: InterVarsity Press.

Ridgeon L. 2001, *Islamic Interpretations of Christianity*, Surrey: Curzon Press.

Safi O. 2003, *Progressive Muslims on Justice, Gender and Pluralism*, Oxford: Oneworld Publications.

Sanneh L. 2003, *Whose Religion is Christianity? The Gospel Beyond the West*, Grand Rapids: Eerdmans Publishing.

Sookhdeo P. 2004, *Understanding Islamic Terrorism*, Pewsey: Isaac Publishing.

Tennent T. 2006, 'Followers of Jesus (Isa) in Islamic Mosques: A Closer Examination of C-5 'High Spectrum' Contextualization,' in *International Journal of Frontier Missions*, 23/3

Trimingham J.S. 1948, *The Christian Approach to Islam in the Sudan*, London: Oxford University Press.

White B. 2010, Review of Patrick Sookhdeo's *Global Jihad*. http://www.fulcrum-anglican.org.uk/page.cfm?ID=380 [accessed 30 May 2010].

Zebiri, K. 1997, *Muslims and Christians Face to Face,* Oxford: Oneworld Publications.

CHAPTER 7

Competition and Conflict: Pentecostals' and Charismatics' Engagement with Islam in Nigeria

Matthews A. Ojo

Since the 1980s in Nigeria, Pentecostals' and charismatics' attitudes to Islam have largely been determined by the nature of Christian-Muslim relations in the country, particularly after the Sharia debate of the late 1970s. This relationship has been characterized by suspicion, bitterness, competition and mistrust. It has also been affected by the legacies of British colonialism, the predatory nature of national politics, the prevalence of confrontational relations in governance, Pentecostals' self-identity as a revivalist movement, and by the attempt to expand the scope of Sharia.

Relationship between Christianity and Islam

Since 1976, four significant issues have dominated the relationship between Christianity and Islam in Nigeria. In that year, a Constitutional Drafting Committee was appointed to provide a new constitution for the country after eleven years of military rule during which the country had been governed without recourse to constitutional provisions. The first issue is the attempt to expand the scope of Sharia beyond its jurisdiction in personal law and beyond its restriction to certain geographical areas to become national in scope with constitutional guarantees. To Muslims, this quest was seen as providing for and respecting their religious rights to determine their lives based on the precepts of the faith. On the other hand, the response of Christians was to affirm the secular nature of the state by arguing that any affirmation of religious laws in a pluralistic society would eventually discriminate against the adherents of other religions.

The second issue centres on religious violence, which has surfaced frequently since December 1980. Between December 1980 and February 2006, fifty-eight major instances of religious cum ethnic violence were reported in the media; most of them occurred in Northern Nigeria. In fact, in Jos and its environs, twelve major ethnic and religious incidents of violence were recorded between April 1994 and March 2010, in an area previously prized for its peace and multiculturalism. The perpetrators of these religious riots have mostly been Muslims and Islamic groups, and the violence has been directed against Christians and Christian institutions with dire consequences. In about three cases, Christians have instigated violence against their Muslim neighbours. During incidences of violence, Christians and Muslims often traded accusations. Lives have been lost on both sides, properties destroyed, and communities estranged as hostility and suspicion have come to characterize the Christian-Muslim relationship.

The third issue is the rise of religious revivalism within Christianity and Islam. These revival movements have been fundamentalist in nature and by the 1990s had become globalized. The consequence for Christian-Muslim relations is that religious events elsewhere now have symbolic meanings in Nigeria, thus stimulating disruptive local responses. As a result of the revivalism, there has been a heightened consciousness that both religions exist in a competitive relationship, hence distrust and suspicion have characterized the relationship. Indeed, a number of youth organisations in both religions have continued to champion their cause in militant ways.

Fourth, the precarious situation of striving to maintain equality in religious matters has affected Christians and Muslims, particularly in the area of gaining access to the public space, including access to government-controlled media. Generally, government support for religious activities and institutions has been vested with meaning and the allocation of economic and social resources has often attracted complaints of discrimination from both sides. The educational institutions, the public sphere, land resources, and the media have been the context for the playing out of these issues in the lives of Nigerians. Since Christianity and Islam account for over 80 per cent of Nigeria's population of 140 million, the contestation between the two religions continues to reflect in other aspects of the national life.

Therefore, one may argue that the rise of Pentecostal and charismatic movements in the 1970s coincided with the rise of Islamic fundamentalism, which was fuelled by global events. Although Islamic fundamentalism and Christian revivalism were not restricted to Nigeria in the 1970s, their impact in Nigeria was intensified by the failing state and economic recession of the 1980s and 1990s. This situation alienated many Nigerians, who had to resort to their religious constituencies for the security and social services which the state failed to provide. The deep-rooted hostility between Christians and Muslims erupted when governance became ineffective and rule of law and security were abandoned. With some diligence, it may be possible to isolate the response of Pentecostals and charismatics towards Islamic affirmation in the country. In this regard, it is better to treat each of the two religions as monolithic and gloss over the varieties within each. I begin by providing an overview of the Pentecostal and charismatic movements in Nigeria.

Overview of the Pentecostal and Charismatic Movements

Pentecostalism, both in its old form as a sectarian religion and in its contemporary form as a global religion, has continued to attract attention among scholars of religion as well as the general public. Pentecostal and charismatic movements constitute major areas of growth for Christianity and have moved into positions of power in many countries.

Pentecostal spirituality centres on the experience of the baptism of the Holy Spirit and the practise of the charismatic gifts (Anderson 2004: 24). This inward experience of baptism of the Holy Spirit, as they claim, is often identified by the initial and outward sign of speaking in tongues and the exercise of the gifts of the Holy Spirit—principally the gift of healing and demonstration of power—mostly in miracles and in personal social transformation (Hamilton 1975). Both Pentecostals and charismatics believe in the Pentecostal doctrines of baptism of the Holy Spirit and speaking in tongues.

However, charismatics are trans-denominational and more ecumenical in their religious expression than the Pentecostals, who often come from the classical Pentecostal denominations such as Apostolic Faith Mission, Assemblies of God, Foursquare Gospel Church, The Apostolic Church, Elim Gospel Church, etc. The demarcation between Pentecostals and charismatics in Africa is a thin one. The charismatic renewal of the 1960s and early 1970s carried with it no desire to form any independent existence as the Pentecostal assemblies did in the early decades of the twentieth century. However, since the 1980s, some charismatic groups in Africa have adopted independent existence, and some have indeed become new denominations. Generally, independent charismatic churches in Africa are still led by solitary figures who are founders and general overseers, have built up mega churches, and exercise authority over their organisations as personal empires without a constitutional framework.

Growth of the Movements

Pentecostal and charismatic movements are proliferating in Africa, and in a wide range of types and sizes in many countries (Ojo 2001: 2–6). In fact, since the late 1970s new forms of Pentecostalism have been making a significant advance in many African countries. This explosion of Christianity was at first identified with young men and women who labelled themselves as pastors and evangelists despite lack of pastoral or theological training. Their proselytizing activities, which largely occurred within existing Christian churches and in public places, were remarkable and daring as these young people called on other Christians to repent from all kinds of evil associations. 'Are you born again?' or 'You must be born again' was a common way they approached their listeners. Although their activities were based on the old evangelical tradition of conversion, they had a newness because they proselytized even in public places. The young puritan preachers also offered prayers for deliverance from every kind of malevolent spiritual force. This new evangelism was also promoted by and through literature, crusades, camp meetings, 'Fire or Holy Ghost or Power' conferences, 'Holy Ghost Nights', healing and deliverance services, etc. In addition, the new evangelists erected their sign boards in conspicuous places in the cities and used the media and the emerging media technologies to advertise themselves. By the mid-1980s, the new phenomenon had been institutionalized in new independent churches most of which go by descriptions of 'ministries' or 'fellowships' or evangelistic associations or churches.

Pentecostal and charismatic movements are the fastest growing religious endeavour in Africa. The number has grown from about thirty independent charismatic organisations in the mid-1970s located mainly in Nigeria, Ghana and Malawi to more than ten thousand groups across the continent by 2000. The membership has become substantial with about 8 million of the estimated 52 million Christians in Nigeria, about 2 million of the Christian population in Ghana, about half a million in Cameroon and Cote d'Ivoire, and about 300,000 each in Benin and Burkina Faso, about 150,000 in Togo, and about 2,000 in Niger Republic. In southern Africa, these new Pentecostal and charismatic groups have added greatly to the demographic and social importance of the Pentecostal churches, which have existed as part of the Zionist churches or as new religious entities. It is remarkable that within three decades the charismatic movements have moved into a position of power in many countries.

As a result of this religious change on the continent, Nigerian Pentecostal churches are playing significant roles. For example, by the mid-1980s, the growth of the charismatic renewal across West Africa had been greatly facilitated by Nigerians as they interacted with other Africans at regional and international meetings, through trade and business activities on personal and official levels, and through direct missionary activities, which Ojo (1997, 2005) has documented. By the mid-1970s, the Nigerian movements had become transnational as they forged linkages across the continent and with similar organisations in North America and Europe. From the mid-1980s on, increased migration facilitated constant networking with charismatic groups of the African Diaspora in the West.

Pentecostalism in the Literature

The literature has some useful information on Pentecostal movements, but is in dire need of deeper research. From its historical and anthropological slant on the early *Aladura* movement in the 1930s to 1960s (Peel 1968; Barrett 1968; Omoyajowo 1982), research has moved to focus on the social and demographic changes in Nigeria since the 1970s that gave a fillip to the growth and expansion of particular Pentecostal groups and churches as new religious expressions (Ojo 1988a, 1988b; Marshall 1992, 2009). In turn, Ojo (2001) advances a typology of Pentecostal groups. Gifford (1992) examines nuanced experiences across Africa, while Ojo (1997, 2006) examines their dispersal from Nigeria to neighbouring countries. Hackett (1998) analyses the use of media technology by Pentecostal movements in Nigeria and Ghana, while Ukah (2008) details how the Redeemed Christian Church of God in Nigeria has deployed biblical as well as secular doctrines to create new transnational identities and, hence, make huge social and financial capital for itself. Ihejirika (2006) discusses how independent charismatic groups fare in mainline churches.

In general, religion or highly expressive forms of religion such as Pentecostalism have come across in the literature in two main ways. One argument made by social scientists tends to regard religion as a means of keeping popular anger below the radar of social discontent or as a tool in the hands of ruling elites to legitimize the social order. On the other hand, some scholars of religion have tended to see Pentecostals as acute social transformers.

Other scholars like Ogbu Kalu (2008: 4) have argued that Africans have always been attracted to the charismatic and pneumatic elements of the gospel because these resonate with the goals and practises of traditional religion. Thus, people come to the charismatic churches to seek answers to questions raised within the interiors of the primal worldviews. The implication is that Pentecostalism is growing because of its cultural policy and attitude to indigenous worldview and culture. This buttresses the argument that African Christianity is an extension of African Traditional Religion.

Impact of Pentecostalism

The explosion of Pentecostalism in Africa led to new power relations in social and political activities. Without doubt, Pentecostals now draw huge numbers of people and diverse interest groups to their rituals and their non-religious activities.

Pentecostal spirituality is intriguing for several reasons. Among these is the enthusiasm in its services, the relative novelty of its message, and the proliferation of a large number of new churches advertising themselves widely in the print and electronic media in a competitive religious landscape. Other reasons include how the pietism of the early years gave way to constructs of 'earthly paradise' and to a triumphal and entrepreneurial outlook on the part of clergy, leaders, and members.

Pentecostalism also affects millions of non-believers in various ways. It can be passed off as the cultural product for these times, designed as it were to address individual, group, and societal needs in disruptive socio-economic and political contexts such as obtained in Nigeria from the late 1970s through the 1990s (Ojo 2006; Marshall 1991, 1992, 2009). Pentecostalism is uniquely modern, imbued with a 'can-do' spirit, market-oriented, success-directed, and charismatic in style, with ever-growing multi-ethnic congregations largely using English as a medium of communication. These are but the main characteristics that have enabled the Pentecostal movements to propagate their doctrines of power and change in nearly every nook and cranny of Nigeria.

Although the membership of charismatic churches is still small in comparison to that of the existing mainline churches, the movements are marked by vigorous activity, committed membership, and rapid growth. The Pentecostal and charismatic movements have changed the pace and direction and have enlarged the scale of communicating the gospel in Africa. They continue to utilize media communication technologies for the re-packaging of a new spirituality. Consequently, they reconstruct religious life and landscape through specific missionary strategies and ethics.

Largely an urban phenomenon, Pentecostalism has been a purveyor of modern culture. Starting with the use of modern musical instruments, Pentecostals and charismatics have appropriated sophisticated media technologies such as videos, satellite broadcasting, and the Internet. Hence, their sermons, healing and miracle services, breakthrough programmes, and advertising of conventions and special programmes often dominate the airwaves, providing huge and easy revenue to many cash-strapped radio and television stations. Moreover, the use of literature, including their own printed magazines, tracts and booklets, has aided in the wider dissemination of Pentecostal spirituality across Africa. Unlike the African Independent Churches, charismatic organisations often lay claim to their movement as being international in scope. Indeed, some of them maintain linkages with similar charismatic organisations in North America and Europe.

The movements, which had begun as an indigenous religious phenomenon in the early 1970s, became more institutionalised within a decade or so. In Nigeria, the movements took their roots from a revival among young Christian students in the colleges and universities. The revival, which was based on the Pentecostal experience of baptism, spread rapidly in the tertiary educational institutions and into the mainline Protestant churches. The revivalists encountered strong opposition from these churches, and some of these young religious enthusiasts were expelled from the churches as rebels. Certainly, this expulsion provided part of the early stimuli that created independent existence for the movements.

Hence, the rise of denominationalism was a major development within charismatic movements from the mid-1980s on. The revival became routinized into stable religious organisations with bureaucratic structures. Thereafter, Pentecostal and charismatic organisations adopted many strategies to maintain their denominational structure. The major features of this development include holding Sunday services instead of meetings during the week as in their early years. They erected their own church buildings instead of using rented spaces and created a structure of paid and full-time clergy instead of the earlier democratic leadership.

The doctrinal emphasis and messages shifted from ones of personal evangelism and baptism of the Holy Spirit, to ones of healing, miracles and prosperity, all as paradigms for personal empowerment. To a large extent, these changes were conditioned by the socio-economic changes in the society. Denominationalism also brought internal changes that affected Pentecostals' and charismatics' orientation to worldly values. Instead of rejecting secular values, some began to be involved in social and political issues to gain relevance. The emphasis on healing and personal empowerment for success and upward social mobility has continued to attract a large class of socially impoverished Nigerians. Indeed, the rapid expansion of Pentecostalism in Nigeria and perhaps across Africa could be linked first to a pragmatic approach to the social and religious issues affecting the lives of millions. Second, it could be linked to an emphasis on supernatural empowerment, which Pentecostals believed could address the needs of its members within disruptive socio-economic and political contexts (Ojo, 1995; Marshall, 1991, 1992, 2009). For example, the emphasis on healing was constructed to take care of physical illness, deliverance from all past ancestral curses and demonic attacks. Similarly, the emphasis on success and prosperity was constructed as means of addressing contemporary socio-economic difficulties, social dislocation, the failure of the centralised state, and the general frustration among Nigerians. Consequently, in their messages, the pastors emphasize the name of Jesus and the power of Jesus to address daily existential needs.

Although the Bible has broadened the outlook of Pentecostals and charismatics, their basic traditional African cosmology was little affected; hence, they continue to grapple with power in its various manifestations. The emphasis on healing, success, prosperity, and deliverance are all rooted in the appropriation of power in its traditional and modern forms. The increasing popularity of the charismatic and Pentecostal movements, as noted by Birgit Meyer (1999), stems from the fact that it ties into historically generated local understandings of Christianity despite a dislike of African Traditional Religion.

Historical Legacy of British Colonialism

The mistrust and bitterness that exist between Christians and Muslims in Nigeria have been largely conditioned by the historical legacy of British colonialism and its impact in formulating the sphere of influence of the two religions and their relationship to the state.

Islamic expansion and Christian evangelisation occurred within existing geographical and ethnic boundaries, which have contributed to problems between the two religions. Nigeria is largely divided into three major geographical areas, each with a regional government. Islam is dominant in Northern Nigeria where over two-thirds of the population is Muslim. Eastern Nigeria has an overwhelming Christian presence. And the two religions co-exist in Western Nigeria, though with a slight Christian majority. The creation of these three regional governments was a British colonial framework partly reflecting when and how colonialism was entrenched in the different regions.

Islam was largely confined to a restricted space in Northern Nigeria until the first decade of the nineteenth century when a jihad instigated by Uthman dan Fodio, a Fulani cleric, succeeded in expanding the influence of Islam and creating an almost theocratic state where Islamic culture began to replace much of the indigenous culture of the people. John Paden (1973) has noted that Islam eventually succeeded in providing regional integration as both the rulers and the people had subscribed to the same religion before the advent of colonialism. Obaro Ikime opined that 'the success of the jihad meant that from that time on the Sokoto Caliphate adopted more intensively a foreign culture and a foreign religion' (Ikime 1979: 12), though the British tended to treat this Arab religion and culture as if it were indigenous to Northern Nigeria.

Because the British colonial administration lacked the personnel and finances to create a new administrative structure, it preserved this monolithic culture and regional integration for political expediency. It went to great efforts to increase and expand the power of the emirs, Islamic rulers, over areas not previously subjugated by the jihad. From the first decade of the twentieth century, the colonial administration restricted the penetration of Christian missions into this region. The frustration of the Christian missionaries was soon shared by Christian converts who saw Christian missions as a means of ethnic self-determination and as a bulwark against Islamic oppression. The reason for such a policy is tied to the British notion of ethnicity.

Ethnic identities have existed in Africa before colonialism because most of the pre-colonial empires were built around ethnic configurations.

However, the British constructed the framework of state formation based on nineteenth-century anthropological thinking of superiority of certain ethnic groups, hence giving different groups different level of access to political power. Once the colonial administration began to play an important and often determining role in ethnic relationship, ethnicity took up new social and political force.

Again, for political expediency, British colonial administration preferred to deal with big ethnic blocs rather than with thousands of small ethnic groups. Thus, Nigeria's political structure from the colonial era was moulded on ethnic considerations. From 1939 onwards, three regional administrations (East, West—both making up the South—and North) emerged, and this dominated the political structure until the eve of the civil war in 1967 (Vickers 2000). Because these administrative units were quite large and were dominated by large ethnic groups, by the 1950s 'smaller' ethnic groups began to demand political and cultural autonomy. Even after the creation of states from the regions in 1967, which happened in response to the ethnic agitation and in an effort to forestall ethnic militancy, the North-South or East-West dichotomies still linger politically.

The contest between ethnicity and religion was played out in Northern Nigeria. In the 1950s, most of the ethnic associations of minorities in this region championed self-determination and social justice against what was seen as the oppression of the Hausa-Fulani aristocracy, which enjoyed support from the British colonial administration. For example, when the Northern People's Congress was formed in October 1951 as the biggest political party in Northern Nigeria, it was closely aligned with the Hausa-Fulani aristocracy. Hence, it was seen by ethnic groups with a large Christian population as an Islamic party seeking the continuation of the dominance of the Hausa-Fulani. The United Middle Belt Congress, for example, was formed by smaller ethnic groups in the region, and therefore, had a large Christian support particularly in the Adamawa part of the region (Kastfelt 1994: 70–73). The mistrust and suspicion among the regions and among the ethnic groups continued leading to large-scale ethnic hostilities and eventually the Nigerian Civil War (1967–1970).

The presence of Christian missionary work symbolized resistance to Islamic domination for some minority ethnic groups in the Middle Belt.

Sustained Christian missionary work in Nigeria began in the Western region from 1838 and was well established by the end of the century. The material culture of Christianity, particularly its Western education, became a veritable tool of socio-political transformation in Southern Nigeria. In 1900, Christian missions' attempt to establish a presence in Kano, Northern Nigeria, was resisted by both the emirs and the British, who were seeking the favour of the Islamic aristocracy to introduce British rule. As noted, indirect rule—ruling through local and traditional rulers—enabled the Hausa-Fulani to extend their influence over other ethnic groups not conquered by the jihad of Uthman dan Fodio. More important, as noted, the indirect rule system increased agitation by ethnic groups over whom the British had imposed Hausa-Fulani rule. Turaki wrote an insightful study on the role of British colonialism in the institutionalization of the status and socio-political role of Muslim and non-Muslim ethnic groups and the consequences of such a policy, which created a superior status and hence dominance for the Hausa-Fulani group and socially inferior status and subordination for the non-Muslim ethnic groups. This resulted in subordination for the non-Muslim ethnic groups (1993: 63). By the 1940s and 1950s, Christian missions among the non-Islamised ethnic groups had had much success in the Middle Belt of the region among ethnic groups seeking to resist the Hausa-Fulani rule.

Although Christian missionary work was never intended as means for resisting Islam, this view went a long way to reinforcing existing cleavages. As noted by Kastfelt (1994: 72–76), the meaning of religion and ethnicity was different for Western missionaries and Nigerian Christians. To the missionaries, religion was most important, but for Nigerian Christians, religion and their ethnic interest went hand-in-hand in the various organisations, churches, ethnic associations, and political parties. The common enemy was the Hausa-Fulani, whose Islamization programme was evident even under the British colonisation. Overall, those who felt oppressed sought succour in a new religion, Christianity, and looked down on their oppressors and their religion.

Relationship to the State

The mistrust and competition that have heightened between Christianity and Islam since the mid-1980s could be attributed to certain ideological and structural orientations of the two groups. Specifically, while Islamic fundamentalist groups have sought for a centralization of the religious and social order by trying to use the power of the state to its advantage, Pentecostal groups have favoured a decentralization of the political and social order. Such decentralization has in the past favoured religious creativity that has stimulated more Christian growth. Decentralization is more suited to Pentecostalism, which, with its emphasis on the personal empowerment of the Holy Spirit, has created alternative centres of power to solving human needs against the background of the failure of the centralized state.

More important, it is within this framework of decentralization that the ability of the Pentecostal movements to simplify the complexities of modern life in more pragmatic ways has been realised. Ideologically, while Islamic groups seek to solve the problems of the ambiguities of the modern state, Pentecostal groups are concerned with solving problems confronting the individual. This contradictory orientation continues to create gaps between Pentecostal churches and Islam.

Pentecostals' and Charismatics' Attitude towards Islam Since 1980

Since 1980 two major approaches have determined the attitude and response of Pentecostals and charismatics to Islam and Islamic affirmation. First are those issues and activities that are internal to Pentecostal movements and which have been nurtured by certain doctrinal emphases and practises. Second are those external issues which attracted responses from Pentecostals and charismatics and other Christians.

Internal Factors

Five issues internal to the Pentecostal movements have shaped Pentecostals' and charismatics' attitudes to Muslims. They are their interpretation of the story of Abraham, Haggai, and her son, Ishmael; the emphasis in evangelistic training programmes; the targeting of Muslims for evangelism; overzealousness by some Pentecostals; and the minority ethnic background of many Pentecostal leaders in Northern Nigeria.

Interpretation of Dismissal of Hagar and Ishmael

The interpretation that Pentecostals and charismatics give to the story of Abraham and his concubine Hagar, and her son, Ishmael, in Genesis 16 and 21 and Galatians 4:22–31, has largely informed Pentecostals' attitude to Islam. The often-quoted passage is Paul's epistles to the Galatians.

> For it is written that Abraham had two sons: the one by a bondwoman, the other by a freewoman. But he who was of the bondwoman was born according to the flesh, and he of the freewoman through promise, which things are symbolic. For these are the two covenants: the one from Mount Sinai which gives birth to bondage, which is Hagar—for this Hagar is Mount Sinai in Arabia, and corresponds to Jerusalem which now is, and is in bondage with her children—but the Jerusalem above is free, which is the mother of us all. For it is written:
> 'Rejoice, O barren,
> You who do not bear!
> Break forth and shout,
> You who are not in labour!
> For the desolate has many more children
> Than she who has a husband'.
> Now we, brethren, as Isaac was, are children of promise. But, as he who was born according to the flesh then persecuted him who was born according to the Spirit, even so it is now. Nevertheless what does the Scripture say? 'Cast out the bondwoman and her son, for the son of the bondwoman

shall not be heir with the son of the freewoman'. So then, brethren, we are not children of the bondwoman but of the free (Galatians 4:22–31 NKJV).

Based on this story some Pentecostals and charismatics allude to Islam as the 'usurper'. In sermons, Bible studies, and talks, etc., speakers have mentioned the 'religion of the bondwoman', 'the religion of the slave', 'the religion of force and violence', 'the slaves', 'the spirit of anti-Christ', and similar expressions. This biblical story has become used as a potent metaphor that depicts Islam as the 'unwanted' and 'violent' religion and has had a major bearing on relations between Christians and Muslims. This perception has also been sustained by a few Northern indigenes who are converts from Islam and who had become Christian evangelists.[1] They often refer to their previously violent backgrounds and the persecution they suffered from their family on becoming Christians to justify their hatred of Islam or to heighten Christians' fear of Islam.

Some of these evangelists regularly publish magazines to portray the violent activities of Muslims against Christians, thus continuing to fuel anti-Islamic sentiments. The headlines and captions to photographs are usually provocative, often depicting Islam as the enemy. Samples of such headlines include 'The Violent Truth About Islam', 'Why Muslims Attack Christians and What Jihad is All About', 'Plateau Genocide: Is Islam the Religion of Peace or Zenith of Wickedness', and 'How Hundreds of Kids, Women Were Butchered by Muslim Fanatics'. In mid-2010, Pentecostals and charismatics circulated a video of the March 2010 killings and destruction of Christian villages in religious cum ethnic violence in Jos, Northern Nigeria. Overall, these materials have reinforced the perception of Pentecostals and charismatics about Islam as the 'enemy'.

Evangelistic Training Materials and Targeting of Muslims

The second and third internal issues relate to the evangelistic training activities of Pentecostal and charismatic groups and churches, particularly

---

1. Because of confidentiality, the names and locations of these evangelists cannot be mentioned here.

in geographical areas where there is a sizeable population of Muslims. Behind Christian evangelistic programmes are the training programmes which often consist of the rudiments of 'how to witness to Muslims' or 'the challenge of other religions' or a general course on Islam. Although the courses present historical facts to illustrate the growth pattern of Islam in Africa, the essence of the programmes is the presentation of Islam as a challenge to evangelism and church growth in Africa.

A number of Pentecostal and charismatic organisations and churches target Muslims in their evangelistic and missions programmes. One major group is the Calvary Ministries, which was established in Zaria in April 1975 with the aim of evangelizing Muslims and other ethnic groups in the Sahel region. The first outing of the Calvary Ministries in Zaria on 25 December 1974 was met with violent reaction from Muslims who had gathered at the open air evangelistic meeting, initially oblivious of the religious purpose of the programme. The success of such evangelistic programmes in Northern Nigeria has often provoked the anger of Muslims because Christianity is seen as an encroachment and as a harbinger of Western values, which Islam has been resisting. These anti-Western and anti-Christian sentiments have ignited iconoclastic actions during religious riots.

Minority Ethnicity

Another issue that has bearing on Pentecostals' attitudes to Islam is the ethnic background of their leaders. Most Pentecostal evangelists and church founders in Northern Nigeria come from the minority ethnic groups that are predominantly Christian and have always opposed the feudalistic powers of the emirs.

The Northern indigenes, who were pioneers of the charismatic renewal, include Dr. Samuel Kujiyat, a veterinary doctor, who with others founded the Rhema Living Word Church based in the city of Kaduna in 1984. Another prominent leader is Simon Kwasau, who graduated with a Higher National Diploma from the Ramat Polytechnic, Maiduguri, and who in 1987 founded the Love Divine Ministry in the same city. Peter Ohidah, another college graduate established the Healing the Nations Bible Church about 1987 in the same city. In Zaria, Professor Ishaya Audu, Nigeria's former foreign minister (1979–1983), established the Faith and Charity

Ministries. In Jos, Dr. Steve Onoja, a medical doctor, and Mai waizi Dandaura, a health technologist, founded Faith Deliverance Ministries in 1986, and the Prevailing Faith Ministries in 1980 respectively. Their churches have a substantial number of Northern indigenes. Therefore, the active participation of these Northern indigenes in the charismatic renewal became a practical way of channelling their political aspirations for self-determination by creating alternative moral communities where they could exercise their religious freedom.

The emergence of Northern indigenes as evangelists and leaders of charismatic organisations from the mid-1980s on brought political initiatives into the charismatic movement because some of its leaders had to address events unfolding around them. The 1980s was an era of political and religious turmoil in Northern Nigeria, and these events affected the response of charismatics to the socio-political situations. Among these events were the rising tide of Islamic fundamentalism and violence against Christians.

Overzealousness

Pentecostal and charismatic churches have also demonstrated an overzealousness which has fuelled anti-Christian sentiments. In one regional meeting of the Christian Association of Nigeria I attended in the late 1980s, there were complaints from ministers of mainline Protestant churches in Northern Nigeria that certain Pentecostal churches were becoming provocative by siting their churches close to existing mosques or mounting their speakers in the direction of mosques. The report added that such actions have attracted the ire of Muslims during religious riots.

The fanaticism of Pentecostals and charismatics has created conflicts in the past. An incident at the University of Ibadan shows the extent to which some Pentecostals and charismatics could act on their doctrinal perception that Islam is a 'false religion'. On Friday, 14 August 2010, Oluwaseun Adegunsoye, a fourth-year female law student and a member of the Mountain of Fire and Miracles Ministries, a prominent independent charismatic church, disguised herself and joined other Muslims in the *jumat* prayer on the campus. (The central mosque is just about 100 yards from the Protestant chapel). While the imam was leading prayers, Adegunsoye stood up, interrupted the prayers and preached against Islam. She was reported to have said, 'Except you accept Christ in your life, you are not saved. All of you here no matter the number of the congregation, accept Jesus Christ. Allah is not God; Jesus is God' (*Nigerian Tribune*, 15 August 2010). She was rescued by the imam and the security personnel from being lynched. The aggrieved Muslim students organized a violent protest on Monday, 16 August, disrupted academic activities on the campus, and called for the expulsion of the student and the banning of her religious organisation from the campus, although there was no evidence of support from her group (*Vanguard*, 18 August 2010). The matter was considered so serious that Muslim leaders outside the campus were still commenting on it a week later.

Since the 1980s, Christians have developed institutional forums for articulating their response to Islamic affirmation and for creating and solidifying Christian attitude to Islam. *Today's Challenge,* a bi-monthly magazine published by the Evangelical Church of West Africa Productions in Jos, has served as a Christian media organ to counteract Islamic fundamentalism and champion the rights of Christians in the North. It carried news and commentaries on perceived injustices and discrimination against Christians, and in various write-ups has led the media crusade against Islam.

The magazine has devoted space to the Christian perspectives of the major religious conflicts in the North; by the late 1990s, it was focusing on the activities of the fundamentalist Islamic groups. For example, it gave good coverage to the kidnapping of a Christian preacher in Kafachan in the late 1990s by El Zakzaky's Shiite group, among many others. In addition, it promotes fear of an Islamization project in Nigeria. Hence the closure of three Christian schools by the Kwara State Ministry of Education in December 1995 was described as nothing but an 'extension of the implementation of an Islamic agenda aimed at the Islamization of Nigeria' (1996: 6–12). The magazine regularly carries the press releases and responses of CAN and other Christian bodies to the pronouncements of *Jama'atu Nasril Islam* and the Muslim Students Society, two organisations regularly championing 'Islam Only' and 'Islamic Revolution Now' agendas.

By the mid-1990s, the magazine had become an important actor in creating solidarity among evangelicals and Pentecostals in the on-going competition with Islam.

External Factors

The external factors that have an important influence on Christian-Muslim relations in Northern Nigeria include the larger issues affecting religious pluralism and having political implications beyond the Pentecostal constituency. They include perceptions about Islamization and the issue of extending Sharia law, the admission of Nigeria into the Organisation of the Islamic Conference, Pentecostal political activism, and increases in ethnic violence.

Perceptions of Islamization

The perception of certain Pentecostals, charismatics and other evangelicals is that Muslims have a grand agenda for the Islamization of the country using political machinery. This perception began to take root in 1977 when the country was embroiled in a controversy over the quest to enlarge the scope of Sharia and incorporate it into the national constitution. For the first time in the country's judiciary history, provisions were made in the 1976 draft constitution for the establishment of a Federal Sharia Court of Appeal, which would have equal powers to those of the existing High Courts and Federal Courts of Appeal (Report of the Constitution Drafting Committee 1976: 73–78).

During the sittings of the Constituent Assembly to examine the draft constitution and approve it, the Sharia issue divided the assembly into two opposing camps. Most Muslims from Northern Nigeria favoured the proposed role for the Sharia, arguing that it would help protect the rights of Muslims who have been disenfranchised over the years. In the opposing camp were the Christians from Southern Nigeria who opposed the expansion of the scope of Sharia, arguing that it would undermine the secular nature of the nation and encourage discrimination based on religious grounds (Ofonagoro 1977: 368–371). During the course of the debate and the stalemate, Christian awareness rose and some churches organized prayer meetings to seek God's intervention to stop what they considered the Islamization of the country. Eventually, the federal government forced a compromise such that the status quo ante would remain. That saved the situation. However, the compromise offered the possibility for each state that wants to create a Sharia high court.

Between October 1988 and March 1989, there was a repetition of the 1977–1978 Sharia debate in the new Constituent Assembly, which was given the task of fashioning a suitable constitution for the country. Once again, an imposed compromise saved the situation. The Sharia controversy marked a fundamental change for the worse in Christian-Muslim relations. For the first time, religious differences were deliberately fanned for political purposes. Pentecostals and charismatics were also influenced in their perception of Islam as a result of the controversy.

The Sharia issue surfaced in a new dimension when the Zamfara State House of Assembly promulgated the new Sharia law in October 1999 and expanded its scope to include criminal matters. The subsequent adoption of Sharia by other northern states increased the fear of Pentecostals and charismatics. Eventually, the climax came with the religious riots in Kaduna city in February 2000 over the Sharia issue. As a result of the crisis, Kaduna city was divided along religious lines with the northern part of the city becoming an Islamic enclave and the southern part becoming a Christian community. Pentecostals played prominent roles in the crisis because many of their churches, which were on the fringes of the two communities, were destroyed by irate Muslims.

The recent propositions for the expansion of the scope of Sharia can be seen as attempts by certain Muslim politicians to redefine the status of Islam in a pluralistic Nigeria. This re-definition aims at self-assertion and internal regeneration. This internal regeneration undoubtedly has the support of the grassroots who see religion as a cultural defence against the secularism of the West (Clarke 1987: 128–129), as a strategy to counter Christian advance in the North, and as a bulwark against the rampaging capitalist economy and the failure of the centralized state. Moreover, it was also an attempt to reverse the decline of Islam in a community that had looked upon the jihad of Uthman Dan Fodio of 1804 as a landmark in

African history. This Islamic renewal, which was marked by an internal self-assertion and popularized by the Sharia slogan, sought to capture the public space and consequently transform the social milieu. Thus Sharia has become a symbol offering religious solidarity and group togetherness for renewal.

The main protagonists of Sharia are a new class of Muslim youth, Sharia implementation committees, and intellectuals who want to invest the civil religion in Nigeria with Islamic symbols. Among the grassroots organisations, the *iztibah*, (semi-official Sharia police) have attempted to enforce public morality based on Islamic precepts. These Muslim groups are in direct competition with Christianity, which they view as having benefitted from colonial legacies to the detriment of Islam.

The admission of Nigeria into the Organisation of the Islamic Conference (OIC) in January 1986, after it had maintained an observer status for seventeen years, caused a deterioration in Christian-Muslim relations. After a Nigerian newspaper leaked the news to the public, there were arguments for and against the membership, and generally, Christians called for the immediate withdrawal of Nigeria from the OIC. Eventually, the matter accentuated the suspicion among Pentecostal and Christian groups against Islam and Muslim political leaders. The notion that there was a secret agenda to Islamize the country became more credible when the second in command in the military government, Ebitu Ukiwe, who is a Christian, claimed that he was not consulted about Nigeria membership in the OIC and the matter had not been discussed in the Federal Military Council (Ojo & Akinrinade 1992). A committee of equal numbers of Christians and Muslims constituted to look into the issue could not function because it could not agree on a chairman.

Religious and Ethnic Violence

Since the 1980s Nigeria has witnessed religious and ethnic violence on large scale, leading to killing, destruction of religious buildings and properties, and large-scale social displacement. The religious riots and the attendant destruction of places of worship and loss of lives have had a greater influence on Christian-Muslim relations and on Pentecostals' attitude towards Islam than any other issue. Religious riots first began in December

1980 when Maitatsine, a radical Islamic sect, first attacked other Islamic groups and then the police in Kano in its attempt to introduce a purer form of Islam. Although the sect's enclave was destroyed by the Army and its leader killed, the remnants of the sect carried out similar religious riots in October 1982 in Maiduguri and in February 1984 in Yola. These riots set the pace for subsequent religious violence between Christians and Muslims in Northern Nigeria.

In 1983, Christians were directly targeted and attacked by radical Muslims in Kaduna and churches destroyed. In March 1987, violence erupted on the campus of a college of education in Kafachan within Kaduna State when a disagreement over a sermon preached by a Christian evangelist, who had converted from Islam, drew the anger of members of the Muslim Students' Society. The ensuing fracas spilled into the town where Christians and Muslims retaliated against one another by burning churches, mosques and properties. By the next day, news of the fighting has filtered into Kaduna city where Muslims mobilized for reprisals against Christians. Mayhem spread to other towns in the state (Ibrahim 1991). The 1987 Kafachan riots proved that Christians in general were at great risk in Northern Nigeria as they lost more in the religious riots.

Media Influence

The manipulative role of the mass media in heightening religious and ethnic conflicts was clear in this religious riot. Radio Kaduna, a federal government radio and TV station, aired sentimental statements to mobilize Muslims in the state to rise up against Christians. This went beyond news broadcasting because the inflammatory broadcast was made every hour for two days. This was replayed in the Kano crisis in October 1991 when the government radio station promoted anti-Christian feeling against the Reinhard Bonnke's Christian evangelistic programme in the city. By the 1990s, the news media were reflecting religious sentiments. *New Nigerian*, which was published by the Northern states, spoke for Muslims, while *Today's Challenge* did the same for Christians.

Pentecostals and Charismatics become More Active in Opposition toward Islam

In the late 1980s, Pentecostals and charismatics started to be more politically active to protect their rights against Islamic onslaught. A significant involvement of Pentecostals in politics followed the pronouncement of the late Sheikh Abubakar Gumi, the Grand Khadi of Northern Nigeria, in late 1987 that Muslims would never allow non-Muslims to rule the country as head of state or president. He also said that in the event of this happening, Muslims would seek to divide the country (*Quality* 1987: 35–39). Consequently, in Kaduna in 1988, charismatics joined with other Christians to field candidates, eventually won majority of seats in the city elections, and eventually installed a Baptist minister as the chairman of the local government in a city that had been considered a Muslim stronghold. This mass political mobilization of Christians made charismatics aware of the influence they could wield if they took socio-economic issues seriously. In addition, two prominent charismatics, S.S. Salifu and Jerry Gana, were candidates in the party-level primaries for the presidential elections in 1991 and 1993.

After the Kafachan riots, Christian attitude to Islamic aggression changed. Before 1987, Pentecostals, in particular, had intensified their prayer activities and eventually sustained a strong spirit of hope for supernatural intervention as they frequently faced the challenge of Islamic onslaughts. After the Kafachan riots, Christians abandoned non-retaliation as an option and began to retaliate forcefully whenever attacked by Muslims. This eventually changed the nature of Muslim attack, and made Muslims more cautious.

Following the 1987 riots, the Christian Association of Nigeria (CAN), an ecumenical body of Christian churches, became the main spokesperson for Christian denominations, championing the political and religious rights of Christians in Northern Nigeria through press conferences, press releases and other publications.

During this time, while the clergy dominated CAN leadership, the Youth Wing of CAN was sustained by evangelicals and Pentecostals who organised prayer sessions and embarked on pamphleteering. At the local level, it was vibrant as it consolidated opposition to Islamic and other anti-Christian forces. By 1988, most of the militant CAN publications that challenged the pro-Islamic policy of General Babangida's administration had had input from the Youth Wing. One such publication is *Leadership in Nigeria*, which seriously criticized the religious imbalance in the leadership of the Federal Military Government. Statistics were published to reflect the religious imbalance of those appointed to positions of authority in the country. Eventually, the perception of Islam as a common enemy helped CAN to bridge the gap between the evangelicals and the Pentecostals in the North, and brought them together to form one solid bloc to counter Muslim fundamentalism.

The involvement of Pentecostals in CAN activities indirectly influenced Pentecostals to moderate their negative perception of Islam because of CAN's insistence on using dialogue to resolve disagreements with Muslims. In addition, CAN gave a series of talks to its members' churches on how to act without provoking the anger of Muslims. Consequently, by the mid-1990s Pentecostals were participating in the inter-faith dialogues held under the auspices of CAN.

In October 1991, Pentecostals teamed up with evangelicals to host the German evangelist Reinhard Bonnke for an open air evangelistic programme in Kano. This was the first time such a meeting was to be held in a city with an overwhelming Muslim population, but the organizers were confident of its success. As expected, there were muted Muslim protests, and then Muslims resorted to violence, looting, destruction of property including businesses owned by Christians, and killing to prevent the programme from being held. In this riot, Christians, for the first time, mounted a response. Igbo Christians, mostly from south-eastern Nigeria, counterattacked the rioters and other Muslims in an attempt to defend their businesses. The Christian Association denied planning this retaliation and insisted that it was a spontaneous response by a threatened people (Boer 2003). Thereafter, it was not uncommon for Christians to fight back when attacked by Muslims.

Christians have not always been on the receiving end of religious riots. One exception was the Zagon-Kataf riot in which indigenous Kataf Christians overwhelmed their Muslim neighbours in a dispute over the relocation of the town's market from a site closer to Muslims to one closer to Christians. In many of these riots, churches and religious buildings belonging to Pentecostals and charismatics were destroyed, often because they were located in suburbs or far away from areas populated by Christians.

Similar religious riots have occurred in Northern Nigeria with dire consequences. In the first three months of 2010, indigenous people in Jos, who were mostly Christians, and their Muslim neighbours battled over rights to land and access to political power. Overall, these religious riots have significantly diminished prospects for national integration because they contributed to Christian-Muslim polarization while mobilizing Southern sympathies for Northern Christians.

Pentecostals and Inter-faith Mediation and Bridge Building Efforts

Usually, the federal and state governments have shown concern after each religious riot and sometimes have taken steps in promoting inter-faith mediation efforts. Individuals and non-governmental organisations are also making efforts at bridge-building. One successful effort was initiated by a Pentecostal, Rev. James Wuye. As a young man he had participated in one of the Zagon Kataf riots and lost an arm to Muslim mobs. While on a revenge mission in the mid-1990s, he met Imam Mohammed Ashafa, an Islamic priest who also was on a revenge mission. Coming together in 1995, both renounced vengeance and opted for religious dialogue and reconciliation. A public forum in 1996 focused on verses from the Qur'an and Bible that affirm forgiveness and love of neighbours. Eventually their efforts were institutionalized through two programmes: Interfaith Mediation Centre and Muslim-Christian Dialogue Forum, both of which have their offices in Kaduna. These institutions have experienced notable success through workshops on reconciliation and non-violence organized within and outside Kaduna State. The organisations use preventive and curative approaches that open channels of communication between Christian and Muslim leaders, reorient militant youths toward dialogue and forgiveness, facilitate peace agreements between warring groups, and use radio and television as platforms for advocating dialogue and reconciliation. In August 2002, Wuye and Ashafa were instrumental in persuading religious leaders of each faith in Kaduna to sign a peace agreement in the aftermath of the religious violence that occurred in the city in February 2000 (*The Imam and the Pastor*).

Conclusion

This chapter has attempted a discussion of Pentecostals' and charismatics' attitude to Islam from a historical perspective. Overall, Christian-Muslim relations have changed in response to events unfolding in the country. The competition between Islam and Christianity seems to have been heightened by the existing power competition that is endemic in national politics. In poorly integrated nations like Nigeria, religious and ethnic-geographical identities tend to be coterminous. Although every identity is constructed, religious identity can be difficult to alter because it is also based on religious experience, either group-generated or personalized. Where religion and ethnic identities overlap, there is a tendency for ethnic and religious issues to be politicized as experience in Nigeria shows. Christian-Muslim relations have deteriorated largely because the country has not achieved the minimum levels of trust required for political stability. Hence, Nigerians continue to use memories of the past as their point of reference, with dire consequences.

The rise of Pentecostal political interests also coincides with the rise of radical Islamic reformism, which also claims interests in the political sphere. During the presidency of Ibrahim Babangida (1985–1993), Pentecostals began to link the overt support of his government for Islam with an Islamisation agenda. Consequently, the demonisation of Islamic groups became a feature of Pentecostal discourse. That moderated somewhat as a result of political sensitization and mobilization under the umbrella of the Christian Association of Nigeria, which united evangelicals and Pentecostals against Islamic fundamentalism. In fact, from 1999 on, the Sharia debate came to be seen by charismatics as Muslims' attempt to control national politics. Interestingly, both charismatics and radical Muslims conjured the devil in the name of the other—a reflection of the distrust and competition between the two religions, whose adherents make up more than 80 per cent of Nigeria's 140 million population.

Overall, many Pentecostals and charismatics have tended to spiritualize the danger which Islamic fundamentalism poses to Christian mission. Nevertheless, the charismatic movements are politically relevant because they have provided a mechanism for wider linkage of opposition to Islamic fundamentalism.

References

Anderson, Allan. 2004. *An Introduction to Pentecostalism.* Cambridge: Cambridge University Press.

Barrett, D. 1968. *Schism and Renewal in Africa: An Analysis of Six Thousand Contemporary Religious Movements.* Nairobi: Oxford University Press.

Boer, Jan H. 2003. *Nigeria's Decades of Blood: Studies in Christian and Muslim Relations.* Jos: Stream Christian Publishers.

Clarke, Peter. 1987. The Maitatsine Movement in Northern Nigeria in Historical and Current Perspectives, in *New Religious Movements in Nigeria*, edited by Rosalind Hackett. Lewiston, N.Y.: The Edwin Mellen Press: 93–115.

Gifford, Paul. (ed.) 1992. *New Dimensions in African Christianity.* Nairobi: All African Conference of Churches.

Hackett, Rosalind J. 1998. Charismatic/Pentecostal Appropriation of Media Technologies in Nigeria and Ghana. *Journal of Religion in Africa* 28(3): 258–277.

Ibrahim, Jibrin. 1989. The Politics of Religion in Nigeria: The Parameters of the 1987 Crisis in Kaduna State. *Review of African Political Economy* 45(46): 65–82.

Ihejirika, Walter C. 2006. *From Catholicism to Pentecostalism: Role of Nigerian Televangelists in Religious Conversion.* Port Harcourt: University of Port Harcourt Press.

Ikime, Obaro. 1979. *Through Changing Scenes: Nigerian History Yesterday, Today and Tomorrow.* Ibadan: Ibadan University Press.

The Imam and the Pastor. [DVD]. 2008. London: FLTfilms.

Kalu, Ogbu. 2008. *African Pentecostalism: An Introduction.* Oxford: Oxford University Press.

Kano Disturbances Tribunal of Inquiry. 1981. *Report of Tribunal on Inquiry on Kano Disturbances (Maitatsine).* Kano.

Kastsfelt, Niels. 1994. *Religion and Politics in Nigeria: A Study in Middle Belt Christianity.* London: British Academic Press.

Marshall, Ruth. 1991. Power in the Name of Jesus. *Review of African Political Economy* 52: 21–38.

Marshall, Ruth. 1992. Pentecostalism in Southern Nigeria: An Overview, in *New Dimensions in African Christianity*, edited by Paul Gifford. Nairobi: All African Conference of Churches: 8–39.

Marshall, Ruth. 2009 *Political Spiritualities: The Pentecostal Revolution in Nigeria.* Chicago: University of Chicago Press.

Meyer, Birgit. 1999. *Translating the Devil: Religion and Modernity among the Ewe in Ghana.* Trenton, NJ: Africa World Press.

Ojo, M.A. and Akinrinade, Olusola. 1992. Religion and Politics in Contemporary Nigeria: A Study of the 1986 OIC Crisis. *Journal of Asian and African Affairs* 4(1): 44–59.

Ojo, Matthews A. 1994. Religious Pluralism and National Integration in Nigeria. *Journal of Religious Pluralism* 4: 31–58.

Ojo, Matthews A. 1995. The Charismatic Movements in Nigeria Today. *International Bulletin of Missionary Research* 3(19): 114–118.

Ojo, Matthews A. 2001a. African Charismatics, in *Encyclopedia of Africa and Africa-American Religion*, edited by Stephen Glazier. New York: Routledge: 2–6.

Ojo, Matthews A. 2001b. Media Evangelism, in *Encyclopaedia of African & African-American Religion*, edited by Stephen Glazier, New York: Routledge: 180–184.

Ojo, Matthews A. 2005a. Religion, Public Space, and the Press in Contemporary Nigeria, in *Christianity and Social Change in Africa*, edited by Toyin Falola. Durham, NC: Carolina Academic Press: 233–250.

Ojo, Matthews A. 2005b. Nigerian Pentecostalism and Transnational Religious Networks in West African Coastal Region, in *Entreprises Religieuses Transationales En Afrique d l'Ouest*, edited by Laurent Fourchard, André Mary, and Rene Otayek. Paris: Editions Karthala & Ibadan: IFRA: 395–415.

Ojo, Matthews A. 2006a. *The End-Time Army: Charismatic Movements in Modern Nigeria.* Trenton, NJ: Africa World Press.

Ojo, Matthews A. 2006b. American Pentecostalism and the Growth of Pentecostal-Charismatic Movements in Nigeria, in *Freedom's Distant Shores:*

American Protestants and Post Colonial Alliances with Africa, edited by R. Drew Smith. Waco, TX: Baylor University Press: 155–168.

Ojo, Matthews A., and Lateju, Folaranmi. 2010. Christian-Muslim Conflicts and Interfaith Bridge-building Efforts in Nigeria. *The Review of Faith and International Affairs* 8(1): 31–38.

Omoyajowo, J. Akinyele. 1982. *Cherubim and Seraphim: The History of an African Independent Church*. New York & Lagos: Nok Publishers.

Paden, J.N. 1973. *Religion and Political Culture in Kano*. Los Angeles: University of California Press.

Peel, J.D.Y. 1968. *Aladura: A Religious Movement among the Yoruba*. London: International African Institute by the Oxford University Press.

Quality newsmagazine. 1897. Lagos, Nigeria: 35–39.

Turaki, Yusufu. 1993. *The British Colonial Legacy in Northern Nigeria: A Social Ethical Analysis of the Colonial and Post-colonial Society and Politics in Nigeria*. Jos: Challenge Press: 143–184.

Ukah, Asonzeh F.K. 2008. *A New Paradigm of Pentecostal Power: A Study of the Redeemed Christian Church of God in Nigeria*. Trenton, NJ: Africa World Press.

Vickers, Michael. 2000. *Ethnicity and Sub-nationalism in Nigeria: Movement and Mid-West State*. Oxford: Worldview Publishing.

CHAPTER 8

The African Christian and Ideological Islam

Josiah Idowu-Fearon

Dr. Azumah, in his letter of invitation, wrote: 'I want to suggest five faces of Islam needing *missiological* and *theological* Christian engagements. These are
1. the militant face of Islam;
2. The ideological face of Islam in the form of Islamicists' conceptions of an Islamic State and the implementation of Sharia;
3. Islamic/Muslim criticism, rejection and polemics against Christian beliefs;
4. Islamic Missionary activity—da'wah; and
5. Islamic Mysticism, tassawuf.

He then concludes:

> . . . these faces of Islam impact Christians in varying degrees in different contexts and will therefore elicit different responses from Christians in Africa.

Because of how these 'faces' are inter-connected, I propose we begin with some definitions so as to have shared meanings as we use these concepts. In my topic are two basic concepts: 'Ideology' and 'Islamism'. In other words, what do Islamists mean by 'ideological Islam'?

Origin of the Word 'Islamism'

According to Mozaffari (2007: 17), it is almost certain that the etiquette of 'Islamism' was used for the first time by French writers at the end of seventeenth century. *Le Petit Robert* gives 1697 as the first reference to the word. The Enlightenment philosopher Voltaire is one of the first writers to use the term: 'this religion is called *Islamism*'. These scholars used the term 'Islamism' only in the sense of 'Islam' without any specific political or ideological connotation. By Islamism they meant Islam and Islamism were interchangeable terms. Prior to the Islamist revolution of Iran in 1978–1979, the terms Islamism and Islamists were virtually absent from the vocabulary of newspaper reporters.

The change in the vocabulary occurred with the outbreak of the Islamic revolution under the leadership of Ayatollah Khomeini, who preached a political Islam and established the first 'Islamist government' in the twentieth century. This religious revolution made it imperative to find a new vocabulary to outline the specificity of this new phenomenon. This event gave rise to new frequently used terms: 'Islamic fundamentalism', 'radical Islam', 'Islamic revival' and 'political Islam'. These terms, which became titles of numerous books and multiple articles, were clear and ambivalent at the same time. They indicated that this kind of Islam is quite different from other versions of Islam. What precisely does this new form of Islam contain? The ambiguity remains almost complete. Surely, it has become evident that this particular form of Islam was (more) political, often violent and severely critical towards the West, and last but not least, determined in its hostility towards established regimes in the Muslim world.

The clear conceptualization of this new phenomenon came after the tragic events of 9/11, which increased the use of the word 'Islamism' among politicians and journalists worldwide. Scholars have also progressively focused their attention on the ideological contests of Islamism. Islamism is no longer the simple Islam but rather a new and independent concept. This change is observable in scholars' works, and particularly so in books and articles published after 9/11. For example, two eminent French Islamologists, Olivier Roy and Giles Kepel, previously used both 'political

Islam' and 'fundamentalist Islam' extensively, whereas they now tend to use Islamism more and more often. For Roy, Islamism denominated the new form of activist Islam (Roy 2002).

What Muslim Authors Think of Islamism

The Muslim equivalent to Islamists is *Islamiyun,* used only in this form and with a significantly limited and restricted sense. It is worth noting that the Qur'an uses the terms *Muslimun* along with *Mu'minun* (believers), but never Islamiyun. Theologians from the leading schools (Hanafi, Maliki, Shafi'i and Hanbali) use Muslimun and Muslim, not Islamiyun. The same can be noticed in the works of great medieval historians, jurists and thinkers such as Ibn Ishaq (d. 768), Ibn Hisham (d. 833), Bukhari (810–870) Farabi (870–950), Mas'udi (d. 958), Mawardi (972–1058), Avicenna [Ibn Sina] (980–1037), al-Ghazali (1058–1111), Averoes [Ibn Rushd] (1126–1198) and Ibn Khaldun (1332–1406). The same tradition is observed in modern times among Muslim authors such as Muhammad Ibn Abd al-Wahhabi (1703–1792) (the founder of Wahhabi sect), Sayyid Jamal al-Afghani (1838–1897), Muhammad Abduh (1849–1905) and Rashid Rida (1865–1935). Muslim leaders who played a crucial role in the twentieth century did not use Islamism in their abundant work either. Hassan al-Banna (1906–1948) used 'Muslims' and 'Muslim Brothers' especially when addressing his own disciples. The zealous ideologue of the Muslim Brotherhood Sayyid Qutb (1906–1966), and finally, Ayatollah Khomeini (1902–1989) who brought political Islam from theory into reality did not also use the term Islamism.

Some Muslim thinkers and scholars, however, such as Mawdudi (1903–1979) from Southwest Asia together with a number of other later Muslim authors, are known to have used 'Islamism' (Islamiyun). These include the Sudanese Hassan al-Turabi (b. 1932). In his book *Al-Islam Wal Hakm* (Islam and Government) he uses Islamiyun to designate 'political Muslims' for whom Islam is the solution, Islam is religion and government, and Islam is the constitution and the law (Hasan al-Turabi 2003: 49).

Islamism: A Conceptual Framework

Fuller notes that Islamism is an effort by Muslims to draw meaning out of Islam that is applicable to some problems of contemporary governance, society, and politics (1999). This understanding captures some aspects of related concepts such as political Islam, fundamentalism, revivalism and renewal. These concepts have been explained in the works of the following scholars: Esposito (1994, 1995), Marty and Appleby (1993, 1994), Eickelman and Piscatori (1996), and Hussein (2008). In another document, Islamism is further understood as synonymous with 'Islamic activism' and defined as the active assertion and promotion of beliefs, prescriptions, laws, or policies that are held to be in Islamic character (*Africa Report* No. 37–2).

Totalism

Having studied the way Muslim and non-Muslim scholars used this term Islamism, Shepherd (1987: 307–335) adopts the term 'Islamic totalism' to describe:

> . . . the tendency to view Islam not merely as a 'religion' in the narrow sense of theological belief, private prayer and ritual worship, but also a total way of life with guidance for political, economic, and social behaviour . . . commonly, this takes the form of the claim that Muslims should have an 'Islamic State', that is, a state in which all law is based on the Sharia.

According to Mozaffari, Shepherd brought in a new concept: 'Islamic totalism' which, in his view is the tendency to view Islam as an ideology. He commends Shepherd for defining the concept he wants to use in his work and especially his efforts to point out that labels such as 'fundamentalist', 'modernist' and 'secularist' have undoubtedly often functioned as obstacles to understanding the actual people and tendencies involved, in part, because they are frequently used without explicit definition. However, he questions Shepherd's failure to elaborate on the difference between 'Islamic totalism' and 'Islamism'. It is also of interest to non-Muslims to note that the Muslim authorities who are against Islamists often call them *Irhabiyyun* (terrorists) or *Mutatarriffun* (extremists).

Taking into consideration the two definitions above and in the light of Shepherd's definition and its commendation, our working definition of Islamism for this paper would be:

> . . . a religious ideology with a holistic interpretation of Islam whose final aim is the conquest of the world by all means (Mozaffari 2007: 21).

Ideology

Ideology, the second key concept in our topic, may be defined as 'sets of ideas by which men explain and justify the ends and means of organized social action, with the aim of preserving or reconstructing a given reality' (Sternhill 1982: 329). In totalitarian systems, ideologies are a powerful instrument for the mobilization of the masses as well as sources of legitimacy and sources of the sense of mission of a leader or a ruling group (Linz 2000: 77).

In this sense, Islamism is more than merely a religion in the narrow sense of theological belief, private prayer and ritual worship, but also serves as a total way of life with guidance for political, economic and social behaviour (Shepherd 1987: 308). Islamists selectively pick up some elements in Islam and turn them into an ideological precept. Islamism indeed fulfils all requirements of an ideology, but it goes beyond the purely ideological dimension and sacralises the essence of ideology. A car bumper sticker from *Jamat-e-Islami* with the following quote from Hasan al-Banna sums up the ideology of Islamists:

> Allah is Our Lord.
> Mohammed is Our Leader,
> The Koran is Our Constitution,

> Jihad is our way,
> Martyrdom is our Desire (Husain 2007: 52).

Islamism therefore differs on this point from other totalitarian ideologies as it takes its legitimacy from a *double* source: *ideology* and *religion*. Owing to Islam's double character, Islamists regard the actions they undertake as religious duties. Where a Nazi felt responsible to the Führer, an Islamist is responsible to his leader and before Allah. Islamism is also a regressive ideology because it is oriented towards the past. Its ideal is the Madinan model under Prophet Muhammad as well as the Caliphate of the first four caliphs (*Khulafa al-Rashidun*). In this respect, Sayyid Qutb is explicit when he declares: 'If Islam is again to play the role of the leader of mankind, then it is necessary that the Muslim Community be restored to its original form' (Qutb 1991).

How Islamists Interpret Islam

Islamists argue, first, that their set of selected elements is, in reality, the true Islam and, second, they are convinced that this true Islam is holistic and embraces all aspects of Muslims' life in eternity. The holism is based on the absolute indivisibility of the trinity: *din* (religion), *dunya* (way of life), and *daula* (government). This indivisibility is supposed to be permanent and eternal. Its ultimate goal boils down to the fulfilment of this mentioned triad on a global scale.

The Ideology of Islamists

To Islamists, the existing world order is both wrong and repressive. It is wrong because the existing world does not correspond to Islamic principles. Islam, as a political power, is no longer as predominant as it used to be in the past. The world is also considered repressive because non-Muslims occupy what the Islamists consider to be Muslim territory (e.g., Palestine,

Kashmir, Chechnya) or because Muslims live under severe repression from their own (anti-Islamic) governments.

To get rid of the repression and wrong-doing, Islamists mainly propose two other 'ideal reference points'. The first is the 'Madina Model', which is society as it was shaped by Muhammad himself. The second is the classical era of the Caliphate, one of the longest political institutions in history. It spanned the period from 632, right after the death of Muhammad the prophet, to 1924, when Mustafa Kemal [Ataturk] abolished it. During this long period, the experiences of the Caliphate were of course not all the same, and not all the experiences were glorious. However, according to the general position of Shia, the Imamate and not the Caliphate, is the rightful and legitimate institution. In spite of this position, Shia Islamists like Ayatollah Khomeini, without hiding their preference for the Imamate, have moved slowly but consistently towards a more consensual attitude. Together with the Sunni Islamists, they share pride in and a nostalgia for the disappeared past. Therefore, it is fair to say that the restoration of the Caliphate represents a general aspiration of all Islamists, independent of their sectarian membership (Mozaffari 2007: 23). To the Islamists the restoration of the Caliphate is the first step towards the Islamization of the world.

How They Plan to Achieve Their Goal

The Islamists' spectrum of means to achieve Islamization is quite wide, ranging from propagation, peaceful indoctrination and political struggle to violent methods such as assassination, hostage taking, terrorist and suicide actions, and even massacre of civil populations. Regarding violence, it seems right to say that some Islamists in some parts of the world use violence while other Islamists in other parts of the world use non-violent methods. This variation is determined by different factors, though I would not hesitate to say that the quietist attitude of some Islamists is an exception. In general, the use of violence is integral to the strategy of the Islamists for achieving their ends. Among the various violent methods, terror has proven to be the preferred one and is frequently used by their groups (Mozaffari 2007: 24).

Confirming this observation, in a recent poll in the U.K., 58 per cent of people associated Islam with extremism, 50 per cent of people associated Islam with terrorism and nearly 70 per cent believe that Islam encourages repression of women (Patterson 2010: 3). In concluding her studies of totalitarianism, Hanna Arendt confirms the above observations:

> Total terrorism (is) the essence of totalitarian government ... guiding principles and criteria of action are, according to Montesquieu, *honour* in monarchy, *virtue* in a republic and *fear* in a tyranny (1996: 446–467).

As Mozaffari concludes, terrorism and diffusion of fear in the civil population is the instrument of choice in the hands of Islamist groups (Mozaffari 2007: 24).

Some political analysts have identified three streams within Islamism.

1. Political: There is the Islamic political movement (*al-harakat al-islamiyya al-siyassiyya*), exemplified by the society of the Muslim Brothers in Egypt with its offshoots in Algeria, Kuwait, Jordan, Palestine, Sudan and Syria. There are also locally rooted movements as the Justice and Development Party in Turkey and the Party for Justice and Development in Morocco—whose purpose is to attain political power at the national level. All these political movements now accept the nation-state, operate within its constitutional framework and eschew violence (except under conditions of foreign occupation). The characteristic actor in this stream is the party-political militant who makes an issue of Muslim misgovernment and social injustice and gives priority to political reform to be achieved by political action (advocating new policies, contesting elections, etc.)
2. Missionary: The Islamic mission of conversion (*al-da'wa*) which exists in two main variants is exemplified by the highly structured *Tablighi* movement on the one hand and the highly diffuse *salafiya* on the other. In both cases political power is not an objective; the over-riding purpose is the preservation of the Muslim identity, the Islamic faith and moral order against the

forces of unbelief, and the characteristic actors are missionaries (*du'a*) and the *Ulama*. To achieve their main goal, they make an issue of the corruption of Islamic values (*al-qiyam al-Islammiya*) and the weakening of faith (*al-Iman*) and give priority to a form of moral and spiritual rearmament that champions individual virtue as the condition of good government as well as of collective salvation.

3. Jihadi: The Islamic armed struggle (*al-jihad*), internal (combating nominally Muslim regimes considered impious); irredentist (fighting to redeem land ruled by non-Muslims or under occupation); and global (combating the West). The characteristic actor is, of course, the fighter (*al-mujahid*). Jihadi Islamists make an issue of the oppressive weight of non-Muslim political and military power in the Islamic world and give priority to armed resistance (Crisis Group 2005: 3).

Though there are numerous currents of Islamism, as demonstrated previously, one common objective holds them together and that is their founding of their activism on the traditions and teachings of Islam as contained in the Qur'an and authoritative commentaries.

In the African Christian response to ideological Islam, it is essential to note some key differences between Islam and Christianity. Apart from the theological conflict between Christian belief in the divinity of Jesus and in the Trinity and Islam's rigorous monotheism, Islam is a religion that contains and transmits a framework of law held to be of divine origin and binding on all believers, in a way that—the Ten Commandments and the like notwithstanding—has no counterpart in Christianity (Crisis Group 2005, note 2). As Christians, it is necessary to remember that Islam is not so much a religion of peace as a religion of law. Unlike Christianity, it has is no universal agreed definition of Islam. For practical purposes, what matters is what Muslims believe their religion to be, and this varies with circumstances and has changed over time. The view of Nazih Ayubi that denies the significance of the legal prescriptions contained in scripture, is very much a minority view (Nazih 1991: 210–213). Furthermore, unlike in the Christian faith, Islam postulates and transmits a corpus of legal prescriptions as well as moral injunctions and is, therefore, 'The blueprint of a social order' (Gellner 1981: 1).

The African Christian Responses to Islam

In their search for responses, African Christians need to avoid the mistake of the West in equating ideological Islam with Islamic fundamentalism, radicalism and extremism. They need to do an honest and objective analysis of the three streams and work with groups that are willing to construct alliances and win over public opinion. Christianity is obliged to adapt to contemporary realities and innovate within the medium of the Islamic tradition. African Christians, in working out a response or responses must, of a necessity, read between the lines and see whether it is not more accurate to suggest that it is the religious or missionary, rather than political activists, who are the real fundamentalists. The missionary stream is uninterested in political action and dependent for their authority on the literalist reading of scripture of which they claim a virtual monopoly. These are they who push for a universal reinstatement of Caliphate.

The *Salafiya*, which these days is Wahhabi-dominated, is expanding rapidly in sub-Saharan Africa, South and South-East Asia and Europe today. This expansion of *Salafiya* around the periphery of the Islamic world and in the Muslim Diaspora is increasingly difficult to dissociate from the galvanizing impact of the *Salafiya Jihadiya* on the younger and increasingly mobile elements of the Muslim population.

Do Political Islamists Still Call for 'The Islamic State' Today?

According to *Middle East/North Africa Report* (2005: 6), Islamic movements no longer operate with a definite and demanding conception of the Islamic state to be counterposed to existing states in the Muslim world. Islamist political movements have come around to acknowledging that scripture (the Qur'an, the Sunna and the hadith) contains no clear definition of the

'Islamic state' and that it can, accordingly, take different forms. At the same time, recognition of the limitations of scripture in this respect had led these movements to drop the simplistic slogans such as *Islam huwa al hall* (Islam is the solution) and *al-Qur'an dusturna* (the Qur'an is our Constitution) which they previously favoured and to dissociate themselves from the backward-looking conceptions of fundamentalist Islamic movements inclined to invoke the original Islamic community of seventh-century Arabia as the political model to emulate.

Today these movements, having abandoned the (*dawla Islamiya*), emphasize other themes, most notably the demand for justice (*al-adala*) and freedom (*al-hurriya*). These movements believe that the key to their realisation is the consecration by the State of Islamic law, the Sharia. This call has been qualified by two key elements:

1. Political Islamists now recognize the need for Muslims to 'live in harmony with their time rather than try to recreate the original Islamic community of seventh century Madina'. This has led to the need for ijtihad, the intellectual effort of interpretation, in order to establish precisely how the principles embodied in the Sharia may best be translated into actual legislation in contemporary Muslim countries.
2. In addition to ijtihad, they recognize the need for deliberation and deliberative instances representative of the community and parliaments, in the process of law-making.

The outcome of these developments is that Islamist political streams are moving away from theocratic conceptions of the Muslim polity, in which sovereignty (*al-hakimiya*) is conceived as belonging to God alone (*al-hakimiya li-llah*), to more or less democratic conceptions which recognize that sovereignty belongs to the people (*Crisis Group report* July 2004: 30).

What to Do about Ideological Islam

Based on the analysis above, it would not be out of place to say that Islamism, or ideological Islam, runs against the interests of our corporate existence as a continent and of the democratic world. Christian communities, wherever they are found on the continent, need to get engaged with Muslim communities as Africans. In whatever ideological responses we adopt, it is necessary to bear in mind, first and foremost, that we are Africans; we own this continent together, and we have a joint responsibility to keep it safe for our generation and the next. Second, Africans must come to terms with the reality that neither of these two communities can drive the other out of the continent; Africa will always be a continent of both Christians and Muslims for as long as it takes the Lord to return. For these reasons, we need to have clear ideological standards in the formulation of the Christian response to Islamic ideology on the African continent. Here are some proposals for our studies and consideration.

1. The Christian community needs to understand what ideological Islam teaches and encourage non-Islamist Muslims to reject the 'jihadist' and 'political' streams in all their ramifications. 'Muslims have a responsibility to stand up and reclaim our faith. It is Muslims who are able to recognize Islamist extremists most easily' (Husain 2007: 278). An example of this type of standard was the coming together of the Jamat Nasil Islam (JNI) in the early 1980s and the formation of the Council of Ulama in 1986 in Nigeria to counter the disunity caused by the Maitatsine followers who accused the traditional Islamic leaders of materialism and un-Islamic practises (Falola 1998; Loimeier 1992; Kastfelt 1989). On a positive note, it would be in the interest of the Christian community to study the methods of the da'wah stream and intensify its own methods as a counter to the missionary method of the da'wah Islamists.

2. The desire of Islamists is to put in place an 'Islamic state' where theologians and Imams will run government on their interpretation and implementation of Sharia. One Islamist group is the Nigerian-based Izala group, which Birai calls 'revivalist' (1993) and some have call 'reformist' (Kane 1994). Its leader once campaigned for Sharia at the highest level of the Nigerian judicial system and had publicly spoken in favour of electing a Muslim president for Nigeria. Christians need to collaborate with non-Islamist Muslims, especially where Muslims constitute a majority

and work together against Islamists. Rather than fight the Muslim Umma, Nigerian Christians would do better by joining hands with the *tariqas* who disagree with the Izala and several similar groups in the other countries on the continent.

3. Christians in Africa must not make the mistake of equating Islam with 'terrorism'. Terrorism is an act and the jihadists use this method for a political change. Christians are therefore to collaborate with their fellow African non-Islamist Muslims who represent the progressive voice and jointly condemn terrorism as a tactic for political change. Some progressive Muslim scholars are critical of the refusal of the elites to accept the right of the Muslim to ijtihad (rational analysis and interpretation of law) (Esposito 1998). I suggest that Christian theologians and scholars from other disciplines must work in tandem with such progressive non-Islamist Muslim elites.

4. In responding to Ideological Islam, African Christians must advocate for individual freedom and liberty. In the same vein, they need to work with African Muslims against Islamist laws concerning blasphemy and apostasy within and outside the Islamic community. Furthermore, African Christians, as a matter of urgency, need to work with Muslim scholars and human rights activists to challenge their countries on the need to avoid ambiguity in legal matters. In Nigeria for example, the federal government from the Colonial period on, has been ambiguous in its treatment of religious matters, and the ambiguity makes it easy to challenge the constitution. The Nigerian constitution for example, lays emphasis on the *federal* structure, which provides opportunity for Islamism to challenge the constitution's position on Sharia.

5. Other issues central to the concerns of Islamism and therefore open to an appeal for religious solutions include rising violent crimes and corruption in private and public spheres, need to be taken up and acted upon by the Christians. The existing Sharia courts mete out justice more efficiently than the civil courts do on these matters (*The Economist* 2002: 4). This also makes Islamic

ideology attractive to the youths who feel powerless in the face of the political and legal arms of their governments.
6. The Sharia situation is not a good model for a pluralist continent like Africa. The different regimes have always avoided debates about religion for fear that such debates would tear the country apart. Unfortunately, the present situation in such countries as Nigeria, Sudan and Kenya is not any better. In the light of da'wah activism, Christian and non-Islamist Muslim leaders should cooperate and initiate civil debates among the citizens of their countries, most of which call for compromise and tolerance.
7. It is in the interest of Christians and the non-Islamist Muslims in Africa to work together to ensure that peoples' religious practise does not clash with the law of each country, provide a secular education of a high standard for all, conduct foreign policies that do not fuel the fantasies of angry young men and women looking for a cause, and generally do everything within its power to foster the view that religion is about prayer, not politics.

Conclusion

An analysis of Islamism and how it affects the African continent could be a positive step towards bringing about a general peace and peaceful co-existence between the Christian and Muslim communities on the continent. Without wanting to be perceived as naïve, I want to suggest that the contextualized studies of Islamism, as has been attempted in this chapter, could bring about a new understanding between Christians and Muslims on the continent.

Having said that, I am fully aware that Africa is not an island; Africans have international connections and are bound to be influenced by non-African Christians and Muslims. However, I strongly believe that an objective and contextualized analysis of Islamism could be a harbinger of a new face of co-operation on the continent, which could lead to the stabilization and a new irenic relationship that could give birth to an even form of development.

References

Birai, Umar. 1993. Islamic *Tajdid* and the Political Process in Nigeria. *Fundamentalism and the State, Vol. 3: The Fundamentalism Project*, edited by Martin E. Marty and R. Scott Appleby. Chicago. The University of Chicago Press: 184–203.

Esposito, J.L. 1984. Political Islam: Beyond the Green Menace. *Current History*. January.

Esposito, J.L. 1995. *The Islamic Threat: Myth or Reality*. New York; Oxford University Press.

Etienne, B. 1987, *L'Islamisme Radical*. Paris: Hachette.

Falola, Toyin. 1998. *Violence in Nigeria: The Crisis of Religion, Politics and Secular Ideologies*. Rochester N.Y; University of Rochester Press.

Gellner, E. 1981. *Muslim Society*. Cambridge University Press.

Graham, F. 1999. Is Islamism a Threat? A Debate. *Middle East Quarterly*, 6 (4).

Hassan al-Turabi. 2003. *Al-Islam wal Hakam*. London, Al-Saqi.

Husain, E. 2007. *The Islamist*. Penguin books, London.

Kastfelt, Neils. 1989. Rumours of the Maitatsine: A Note on Political Culture in Northern Nigeria. *Africa Affairs*. 88:83–90.

Kane, Ousmane. 1994. Izala: The Rise of Muslim Reformism in Northern Nigeria. *Accounting for Fundamentalisms, Vol.4: The Fundamentalism Project*, edited by Martin E. Marty and R. Scott Appleby. Chicago: University of Chicago Press: 490–512.

International Crisis Group Working to Prevent Conflict Worldwide. 2005. *Understanding Islam*. 2 March 2005.

International Crisis Group Working to Prevent Conflict Worldwide. 2004. *Islamism, Violence and Reform in Algeria: Turning the Page*. July 2004.

Linz, J. 2000. *Totalitarian and Authoritarian Regimes*. Boulder: Lyn Rienner.

Loimeier, Roman. 1992. The Dynamics of Religious Unrest in Northern Nigeria. *Afrika Spectrum* 1: 59–80.

Marty, Martins E. and R. Scott Appleby (eds.) *Fundamentalisms and the State: Remaking Politics, Economics and Militancy, Vol. 3: The Fundamentalism Project*. Chicago: University of Chicago, Press.

Middle East/North Africa Report 2005. No 37, 2 March 2005.

Mozaffari, M. 2007. What is Islamism? History and Definition of a Concept. *Totalitarian Movements and Political Religions* 8(1), March: 17–33.

Nazih Ayubi, 1991. *Political Islam: Religion and Politics in the Arab World*. London and New York.

Patterson C. 24 June 2010. Moderate Islam Must Find its Voice. *The Independent*, Thursday: Viewspaper 3.

Qutb, S. 1991. *Milestones*. Delhi: Markazi Maktaba Islami.

Roy, O. 2002. *Globalised Islam: The Search for a New Ummah*. London, Hurst and Company.

Sternhill, 1982. Fascist Ideology. *Fascism: A Reader's Guide,* edited by Laquer, W. London. Penguin Books.

CHAPTER 9

The African Christian and Muslim Militancy

Moussa Bongoyok

Islamism is a global preoccupation. Our world is still shaking from terrorist attacks in the U.S.A. and many other countries. One need not be a prophet to foretell a future with more attacks perpetrated by militant Muslims, even in places where people least likely expect them. Muslims and non-Muslims are equally concerned and asking serious questions about the rise in Islamist terrorism: What went wrong? What do we need to do in order to re-establish security, peaceful cohabitation between various religious communities and ensure the survival of our global village?

More than any continent, Africa, whose population is about 40 per cent Muslim, cannot afford to ignore these questions. In many African countries, Christians and Muslims have co-existed peacefully for centuries. Some people have long forgotten the challenging periods of jihad and its disastrous consequences on local populations. In sub-Saharan Africa, it is not rare to find Christians, Muslims and followers of African religions in the same family. The Bamoun of Cameroon, for example, did not allow religion to disturb their society. Christians and Muslims generally have good relationships and are involved in joint social events. The spread of Sufi brotherhoods like the Tijaniyyah, Qadiriyyah and Muridiyya, to name only a few, have helped shape an image of tolerant Islam in Africa.

The course of events in recent years has shown that peaceful relations between Muslims and Christians can deteriorate rapidly. Signs that Africa is seriously affected by Muslim militancy include the on-going situation in Sudan where Osama bin Laden lived before establishing himself in Afghanistan, the 1998 bombings in Kenya and Tanzania, the 2010 bombings in Uganda, the armed conflict in Somalia, and the numerous violent confrontations between Christians and Muslims in Northern Nigeria. There is a severe risk of large violent confrontations between Christians and Muslims. We already hear Christians in Northern Nigeria say, 'Militant Muslims have already slapped both cheeks; we do not have a third one'. It is imperative that African Christianity takes the rise of Islamism seriously.

I have witnessed a change in the Muslim community in the region where I grew up. The Islam I knew when I was a child was popular Islam, mostly Sufi, and largely peaceful. I was not exposed to Islamism until after I started to work as teacher and pastor in Maroua, the largest Muslim city in Cameroon. In 1998, when I was the leader of the Protestant community in the city, we were confronted with an open verbal Islamist attack against the Bible and Christianity through the public media in Maroua. The Catholic bishop Philippe Albert Joseph Stevens and I went to see the leader of the Muslim Fulbe community to complain. He explained that he was also amazed because such an attack had never happened before. He raised the issue of division inside the Islamic community and pointed to the Islamists, mainly the *Wahhabiya*.[1] He noted that they perpetrate verbal, and sometimes physical, attacks not only against Christians but also against Muslims who do not share their doctrinal views.

That experience, and the alumni reports I heard while on the faculty at Bangui Evangelical School of Theology in Central African Republic, influenced my work on Muslim militancy. While I was at Bangui, Dr. Isaac Zokoue, who was president of our seminary, sent Dr. Jack Robinson, a

---

1. In addition to the pastoral, administrative and teaching ministries, I served as a part time chaplain in two public high schools of Maroua from 1994–1996 (Lycée Bilingue and Lycée de Domayo) where I taught classes about Christian religion. During the first year, I had many Muslim students in my class and they seemed to enjoy the teachings. They were eager to learn more about the Christian faith. The second year, because of the increasing Islamist pressure, Muslim students did not attend Christian religion classes although they told me that they liked it. Some of them attended classes on Islam organized by Islamists instead while others did not take any religious class.

professor, to West African countries to see how our alumni were doing. Former students reported that they were confronted with many new questions raised by Muslims (especially Islamists) and wished the courses on Islam would have deepened their understanding of these questions instead of focusing on folk Islam. This confirmed what I have observed in Cameroon and caused me to pay more attention to the development of Muslim militancy and to think about appropriate responses. That led me to write my Ph.D. dissertation on Islamism. One of my main preoccupations was to identify the root causes of Muslim militancy.

This chapter is an attempt to describe some key aspects of Muslim militancy and its manifestation in Africa, to identify the root causes of Muslim militancy, and to make suggestions as to how the African Christian should respond to the Militant Muslim. Its aspiration is to contribute to the ongoing reflection on contextual Christian responses to militant Islam in Africa and globally.

I define Islamism as 'the ideology held by fundamentalist and conservative Muslims that all life, including the political and social realms, should be regulated by the way of God' (Bongoyok 2008: 298). Sometimes, I use 'Muslim militancy' to refer to Islamism although scholars have different views on this.

Muslim Militancy in Africa

Islam first penetrated Africa in a peaceful manner. In 615 AD, Muslims who were persecuted in Arabia found refuge in the Christian kingdom of Abyssinia (currently Ethiopia), which welcomed and protected them.

A little more than twenty years later, in 639, the Islamic conquest of Africa started in Egypt. Soon after, Islam spread through jihad. In sub-Saharan Africa, Islam mainly spread through peaceful means like trade, relationship with local rulers, marriage, education or Islamic missionary activities. *The History of Islam in Africa* (2000) edited by Nehemia Levtzion and Randall L. Pouwels provides important data on the historical development of Islam in Africa and confirms this. Boer provides an interesting summary of Islam in West Africa (1968: 108), where its development was similar to that in East Africa.

The jihad tradition has an undeniable impact on the current developments of Muslim militancy in Africa. As far as jihad is concerned, Azumah wrote:

> There is certainly no question that the socio-political, judicial and intellectual legacies of the jihadists have left an indelible imprint on Islam and Muslim identity in areas with a long and sustained jihad tradition as Northern Nigeria. Muslim religious and political awareness and self-assertions in most parts of Africa, in addition to contemporary global and local factors, are directly and indirectly inspired by the jihad tradition (2001: 101).

The end of the colonial era and the advent of independence had provided hope for a reduction in Muslim militancy and improved relationships between various religious groups, this in spite of the activities of the Muslim Brotherhood, which was founded in 1928 in Egypt. However, in the 1990s, religious Muslim militancy rose up again. In 1991, the Islamic Salvation Front in Algeria organized a general strike and many violent attacks followed, with some Christians losing their lives. Egypt went through a series of violent confrontations as well. During the same period, sub-Saharan nations were shattered by a series of attacks perpetrated by Islamists.

Today, Islamists are active in all the regions of Africa: North, South, East, West and Centre. The movement is more entrenched in Northern Africa where al-Qaeda and similar movements are well established. The situation in Nigeria could also have a significant impact on other neighbouring West African and Central African countries. The activities of Libyan President Mu'ammar al-Qaddafi and his discourses deserve attention as well. East Africa is under the fire of Islamic militancy. Arab television and radio channels are carrying Islamist teachings in cities and villages where they were not heard or seen just ten years ago. Islamic universities and colleges are multiplying thanks to generous Saudi investment and that carries the Islamist influence further and further. Islamism is making a strong impact on the younger generation of Muslim religious leaders; most of them were or are being trained in Saudi Arabia and other nations where they are exposed to militant Islam. As a result, the religious map of Africa will dramatically change shortly if nothing is done to wisely reverse the situation.

Root Causes of Muslim Militancy in Africa

I want to stress my sincere desire to be as objective as possible while talking about Muslim militancy and even Islamist terrorists. On this, I agree with Tracy L. Scott when she writes:

> People tend to stereotype terrorists in one of two ways. Some see all terrorists as evil thugs given to mindless violence. They are viewed as being either crazy or controlled by fanatical leaders. Other people see terrorists as misguided idealists who have become so frustrated by the oppressive situation under which they live that they resort to violence. There is some truth in both of these views. But what we want to remember is that terrorists are not all alike. Motivations, methods, and goals differ among various terrorist groups and individuals. And our emotional support of or opposition to a group's purposes will colour or image them. For as it has been said: one person's 'terrorist' is another person's 'freedom fighter' (1989: 136).

Militant Muslims are not a band of crazy people. They are fellow humans. They have feelings and dreams. Most of them do not have a history of violence or crime, and some are highly educated and wealthy. They deserve our attention and objectivity in the way we approach their lives and actions. Sometimes, all they crave for is a group of people to listen to them, a group who are willing to understand their challenges, struggles and aspirations. Instead, they encounter people who fight them or try to silence them by any means. There is a real need for more understanding if we are to address the issues that give birth to Muslim militancy.

The methodology of medical practitioners inspires my overall approach to Islamism. Good medical doctors do not treat only the symptoms but also seek above all to address the causes of a disease. They know that symptoms may give them an idea that something is wrong and even indicate the person has a certain type of disease but, ultimately, they do further testing to identify the causes of the symptoms. I think this approach is not only logical but is best suited for exploring responses to Islamism without neglecting the manifestations of Islamism; it is imperative that we further consider the root causes of this global phenomenon. This is what this chapter is trying to achieve.

As Einstein said, 'The formulation of the problem is often more important than the solution'. Identifying the root causes of Muslim militancy is fundamental, but it is not an easy task. People have various views. Dan Radlauer, who deals with the terrorist aspect of Muslim militancy, claims terrorism is an industry (2010). I do not think it is so simple. How can he explain the fact that someone like Osama bin Laden sacrificed his money and his comfort, and risked his own life for the Islamist cause? Bin Laden could have earned more money in his mega construction business and other businesses.

Political figures like former U.S. vice-president Al Gore pointed to poverty, ignorance, disease, environmental disorder, corruption and political oppression as causes of Muslim militancy. Jean Chretien, former prime minister of Canada, said that the root cause of Islamic militancy is poverty. Both of them were right and suffered severe criticism from some journalists and writers. Steven Martinovitch (2010), a freelance author in Sudbury, Canada, responded to Jean Chretien by saying that the root cause is rather 'hatred of the secular and free West and what we represent'. He pursued his argument by adding:

> If there is a root cause of terrorism, it's far more complicated than simply material success. The common denominator that unites terrorists—regardless of their ideology or ultimate goals—is their hatred of rationality, individualism, secularism—whether political or religious, and capitalism. Their common enemy is Western culture itself (2010).

Although Martinovitch went a step further, he did not provide a satisfactory answer either. Akiko Fukushima explores more fundamental causes. He writes:

> Looking at these commonly suggested underlying causes, one can extract a common thread of a sense of injustice and inequality of those who are not on the good side of poverty, governance, globalization, conflicts, etc. They must have reached a level of desperation that compelled them to believe that resorting to violence was the only way to resolution (Fukushima 2003).

He has covered even more causes but still missed many aspects in his analysis. For practical and methodological reasons, I have classified the root causes of Islamism in six main categories: historical, psychological, political, socioeconomic, doctrinal, and ethical and cultural roots[2] (2001: 27–55). Let me briefly revisit some of the root causes.

Historical

Historically, the relationship between Muslims and non-Muslims has not been always peaceful. During early Islamic conquests, jihad prevailed and it re-surged in the eighteenth and nineteenth century. Many Africans were forced to embrace Islam, leaving deep hurts in numerous ethnic groups even today. Unfortunately, some militant Muslims still think that jihad is the most effective way to have greater impact and to get rid of anything that prevent them from fully applying the Sharia. Although colonial powers sometimes favoured Islam, many Muslims think the Christian invaders from the West hindered their progress and hurt Muslim populations. Islamism offers them opportunity to revenge and regain territory. One can then easily understands why, on the streets of many African nations, some Muslims were rejoicing following the September 11 attack.

---

2. The ethical and cultural roots are classified in the same category.

The impact of colonialism and neo-colonialism continues. People may be powerless before the new world superpowers, but they have enough freedom to ask themselves tough questions like these in which Matthew Hassan Kukah expresses openly what many murmur in their hearts:

> The world is divided into the powerful and the weak, saints and sinners, through such images as the Group of 7 Industrialized Nations, the Developed World, the Civilized World, and so on. If there are developed and civilized worlds, then those of us who are outside these worlds must be uncivilized and undeveloped. Yet do these artificial divisions and power paradigms really confer any superiority on anyone by virtue of these contrived aggregations of God's creation and creatures? How can dialogue be constructed when history has been so falsely designed? (Kukah 2007: 161).

This mistake in the design of history fuels the anger of militant Muslims.

Psychologically

Psychologically, there is a mixture of fear, anger, desperation and hatred in the Muslim community, particularly in regard to the Western domination of world affairs. Of course, the West is portrayed as Christian although the spiritual reality is far from truth. In such a context, violence seems to be an easy response. It should be added that similar reactions occur when Islamists view many corrupt Muslim governments or the impact on their religious experience of other teachings and values.

Politically

Politically, militant Islam is claiming more power. The poor leadership of some African political leaders gives militant Muslims reasons to push their political agenda more aggressively, as the on-going situation in Somalia illustrates. Sometimes, militant Muslims make strong cases in favour of the victims of injustices and of political corruption. The blind embrace of Western democracy without proper contextualization does not help either. In North Africa, it led to more problems when militant Muslims won elections and held offices, or when they won and were deprived of their victory, as was the case in Algeria in 1991. By aiming at key leadership positions, they hope to be able to rule the population more justly and, more importantly, to fully implement Sharia even if it means that followers of other religions will suffer and be deprived of many rights. From an Islamic perspective, the move seems logical because there is no divide between politics and religion in Islam.

James Piscatori provides additional insights in regard to the political root causes of Muslim militancy:

> The formation of fundamentalist movements is thus not so much a reaction to the failures of modernization, though that acute sense of disappointment is obviously present; but, rather, a reaction to the failures of religious leaders as well as political—to deal with these failures (1994: 361).

Piscatori supports his argument with examples of Upper Egypt and the crowded suburbs of Cairo, Algeria and Palestine where local and national political leaders have failed to respond to various difficulties and crises.

Graham E. Fuller puts political issues on the top of the list of preconditions for the emergence of Islamist movements in the Muslim world. Like Piscatori, he points to the inefficiency of states and regimes in dealing with economic and social problems as a cause of militancy. Other political weaknesses include illegitimacy, corruption, favouritism, moral weaknesses, political repression, authoritarianism, absence of political opposition or questionable political alliances with foreign powers (1997: 144–145).

Socioeconomic

In the socioeconomic arena, poverty is one of the most important issues. Although some African countries are making progress (for example, South Africa and Equatorial Guinea), the pauperization of the continent is rampant. Africa is still the poorest continent in the world although it has outstanding natural resources. Because of this, it has become a fertile soil for militant Muslims who do not hesitate to use 'petro-dollars' to push their agenda at national, regional and even individual levels. Many people have embraced Islamist views in exchange for financial and material benefits.

Many scholars criticised the former British Prime Minister Tony Blair who stated that poverty could breed terrorism, but I do not think he was completely wrong in his analysis. Although poverty is not the only root cause of Islamist terrorism, it must never be minimized, especially in developing nations. In various African nations, I have observed how many people were involved in Islamism out of a genuine struggle with poverty. Expanding on Islamism in Kano, one of the most influential Muslim cities in Nigeria, Bawuro M. Barkindo writes, 'However, for the majority the recourse to Islamism is the result of their frustration with the failure of "modern" measures to cope with the worsening social and economic problems' (1993: 105).

These examples clearly indicate that poverty weights the balance of the root causes of Islamist terrorism. It is dangerous to think that our world can neglect poverty and succeed in the struggle to trump Islamist terrorism. This is even worse in Africa where the majority of the population live on a dollar a day or even less.

While discussing the socio-economic roots of Islamism, one may not minimize the fact that greed has corrupted our world in such a way that some highly respected companies, organisations and institutions are directly or indirectly encouraging Islamist terrorism. This is particularly true in Africa where corruption has reached a dangerous level. Burleigh's comment illustrates this point:

> Universities are allowed to use free speech arguments to defend sinister Islamist organisations active on campuses, rather than

challenged about their greed for high overseas fees. What are already highly politicized universities are allowed to receive dubious foreign funding for regional-studies or Islamic studies programmes which are biased against Western interests, at a time when they routinely reject Western government funding if it emanates from the military (2009: 483).

This is not good for African institutions of higher education.

Socio-economic dissatisfactions are not only roots of Islamic terrorism but also the leading reason for its rapid growth all over the world. In a *New York Times* article entitled 'Taliban Enlist an Army of Pakistan's Have-Nots', Jane Perlez and Pir Zubair Shah described the strong influence of the Taliban in the Swat Valley, a Pakistani region. The Taliban had taken advantage of a situation where wealthy landlords were exploiting landless tenants and orchestrated a violent class revolt. 'To do so, militants organized peasants into armed gangs that became their shock troops', the residents, government officials and analyst said' (2009, A1). Government officials and investors all over the world need to take this situation seriously because when Islamists convince populations they are coming with Islamist teachings and restrictions and a message of hope, justice and economic redistribution, it will take a long time to convince these populations to move away from Islamist rule and influence.

Doctrinal

Doctrinal arguments also influence Muslims to adopt militant Islam because the teachings of the Islamists seem to be appealing. In most African nations, new Muslim leaders have come on the Islamic religious scenes with more formal education and sometimes more money than their parents who were mainly educated locally or regionally in the Sufi tradition. From a technical standpoint, the most recent chapters of the Qur'an (like *surah at-tawbah*[3]) carry more weight according to the Islamic

---

3. Chapter 9.

rules of interpretation and are more in tune with the teachings of Muslim militancy. Instead, Muslim militancy is presented as a calling to return to the fundamentals of Islam and to reject innovations and corrupted religious teachings in the process. Tibenderana has rightly observed, 'Islamic fundamentalism is partly a response to Christo-Western superiority to and dominance of the Islamic world, and partly a rejection of folk-religious tradition' (2006: 22).

Many Islamist movements clearly indicate their religious dissatisfaction in their goals or names. For example, the Izala's full name is *Jama'at al-Izalat al Bid'a wa Iqamat al-Sunna*, which means 'Society for the Removal of Heresy and Reinstatement of Tradition'. They openly denounced and condemned common practises of the dominant Sufi brotherhoods such as 'curing charms, use of holy water, divination, excessive veneration of the founders of Sufi brotherhoods, and so on' (Kane 1994: 499). They struggle for the purification of Islam. The fact the *Kitab al-Tawhid* of Muhammad Ibn 'Abd al-Wahhāb constitutes the source of their preaching is also a clear indication of the link with the wahhābi doctrine.

Ethics and Culture

In respect to ethics and culture, the alarming moral decadence in the so-called 'Christian West' gave more fuel to the Islamist fire. Radical Islam is presented as the ideal solution to the moral corruption of our globe. Unfortunately, Hollywood, television and the Internet spread many movies or programmes that push Muslims to take radical actions to protect their populations, especially the youth. Issues like paedophilia, sexuality and homosexuality are among topics that anger Muslims. Militant Islam is portrayed as the only solution to the moral decadence of our world.

All these root causes have contributed to the growth in militant Muslim anger and acts of terrorism perpetrated in the name of Islam.

Islamic Terrorism: An invitation to Take Seriously the Root Causes of Muslim Militancy

The words 'terror' and 'terrorism' have been used much more since 9/11. Just mentioning them brings to mind violent images of planes crashing into the twin towers, train and car bombings, suicide bombers, numerous victims and multiple other scenes of violence and hatred that make us ashamed of our humanity.

Terrorism is hard to define (See Benegas 2004: 550–567 and Burns & Peterson 2005: 8–14). Most authors seem to agree that terrorism is the intentional use of violence (or the threat to use violence) against civilians or innocent people thus inspiring fear for political, ideological or religious ends. Terrorism cannot be linked to a specific nation, ethnic group, ideology, political party or religion.

By Islamist terrorism, I mean acts of terror carried out by an Islamist group or an individual Islamist in the name of Islam or in the name of Islamic teachings or convictions. These convictions can be as diverse as historical, economic, psychological, political, religious, ideological, doctrinal, cultural, ethical, etc. It is not rare to find specific militant groups who claim responsibility for a terrorist act and provide a reason for that act.

Islamist terrorists come from various backgrounds. Some of them are highly educated; others are barely literate (if literate at all) even in their own languages. Some of them are civilians; others are skilled and experienced military personnel. Some of them are rich; others are poor. Some are scientists; others are modest peasants. Some of them are young; others are old. Some live in large Western cities; others live in remote villages of Asia or Africa. Yet, all of them identify with the same ideal and objectives. All of them are ready to kill or to lose their lives in the name of their shared convictions. All of them feel that they are right in perpetrating acts of violence against fellow humans even if the victims belong to their own family, religion, ethnic group or country. All of them rejoice when they succeed to carry out a plan or a strategy, even if it means the death of innocent people. After a terrorist act in one corner of the world, it is not rare to find groups of people who shout 'victory' and celebrate in other regions. We witnessed such reactions in African countries after 9/11.

Is terrorism only an Islamic phenomenon? Terrorism is not a new phenomenon. It is as old as human existence. As Alex de Waal wrote in the introduction to a book on Islamism that he edited, 'A focus on Islamism runs the danger of feeding into the 'clash of civilizations' hypothesis, and presenting Islamism as a monolithic phenomenon with an inevitable tendency towards violence' (Waal 2004: 3). I am aware of this risk and for that reason I would like to clearly state that Islam and even Islamism are not synonymous with terrorism. Around the world, a vast majority of peaceful Muslims, and many Islamists, strongly believe that terrorism is not the appropriate way to carry out their intentions.

In addition, let me make it clear that terrorism is a universal phenomenon. It is not peculiar to Islam or Islamism. To a certain degree, it can be found in almost all religious and ideological groups. Thus, Islam or any other religion must not be portrayed extremist, violent or perpetrators of terrorism. In this paper, I am focusing on Islamist terrorism because of its global impact and because of the nature of our subject.

It must also be noted that Islamist terrorism is not limited to the Islamist milieu. An individual or a group, Muslim or not, who willingly agrees with people who carry out Islamist terrorism and acts in the same spirit, even if the result is not the same, can be called agents of Islamist terrorism.

Some Islamic groups have been clearly identified as terrorists. However, one must be prudent about generalizations. Some members of groups identified as terrorists may have joined against their will or under menace. Others may have been forced to accept Islamists' radical views out of fear. While doing research on the ground among the Islamist Fulbe, I realised that the situation is not as simple as many people think. Various social, cultural, religious and ethnic dynamics can only be mastered by informed insiders and so many analysts may not have the full picture. The fact that someone is part of an Islamist terrorist group does not make him or her terrorist. Likewise, an individual or a group that is not clearly identified as an Islamist terrorist could be a disguised terrorist. This is an area where it is important to use wisdom and discernment to avoid a dangerous naïveté than could cost many innocent lives.

Nevertheless, it is important to keep in mind that the impact of Islamic terrorism is far greater than what the public media describe. It is a global phenomenon with a global agenda. It is as diverse as individuals who identify with it today and who will join the movement tomorrow.

It is equally important to understand the clear signals that militant Muslims are sending through terrorism. The 'war on terror' may have won some victories such as preventing other attacks, but the reality of terrorism is as vivid as it was in 2001. Said Ali al-Shihri, who had been held at Guantánamo, is currently the deputy leader of al-Qaeda in Yemen. The Taliban are regaining full strength in Pakistan and Afghanistan. They are fighting Pakistan's military in an attempt to seize control of the nuclear state. Muslim and non-Muslims alike live in fear of Islamist terrorist attacks. The threat is not gone. The message of these events is that we have not found the right response or responses to Islamism yet.

Michael Burleigh sums up what many informed people think when he writes, 'It seems probable, to most informed commentators, that the 'war on terror' is becoming what the generals call the 'long war' which may last for fifteen, thirty or fifty years' (2009: 479). This war could be even worse if we fail to address the cause roots of Islamists' terrorism more efficiently and rapidly.

The African Christian's Responses to Muslim Militancy

How can a Christian respond to Muslim militancy if its global root causes are not clearly identified? It would be as dangerous for a medical doctor trying to cure a disease to guess at its cause when he or she could have determined the cause by investigation. Although I have provided a general description of the root causes of Islamism, a more contextual approach is necessary. Each African country, and sometimes each region in a country, is dealing with issues that are unique to the context and that deserve to be taken into consideration in the effort to appropriately respond to Muslim militancy. Following are some of the important issues to take into account.

Research Partnership

Research needs to be conducted prior to any analysis or action. Because of the diversity of the root causes, it is also important have a holistic approach and involve people with various gifts and expertise. This requires partnerships, which would also re-enforce unity and collaboration among Christians from various denominations. Evangelical Christians, for example, can develop strong and lasting relationships that will help them to grow spiritually and have a greater success in their ministries. To achieve this, a solid but flexible structure must be put into place, if it does not exist. Qualified leaders must be designated. Once the root causes in each country and region are properly identified, they should be analyzed. Proper actions could then be taken.

Prayer

In the process, prayer is important. Muslim militancy is a delicate and complex phenomenon and God's wisdom is needed. There is no easy solution that is universally applicable. Each context, each situation, may require specific actions. Our Christian values of love, peace, humility and respect are always valid but the way to react may vary according to circumstances and locations.

Education

Education of the whole body of believers (from the highest level of church leadership to the Sunday school children) is a must. Ignorance of Islamic teachings and practises is dangerous. False teachings about Islam do not help either. Unfortunately, few Christian seminaries, colleges and universities give solid and balanced teachings on Islam to current and future church leaders and prepare them to love, respect and live peacefully with their Muslim neighbours without diluting their Christian doctrines and values. The need is even bigger in African francophone nations.

Cooperation

One of Antoine de St-Exupery's most famous quotations is, 'To love is not to look at one another: it is to look, together, in the same direction.' This can be applied to African Christianity's response to Muslim militancy. Militant Muslims, even the more violent ones, are people too. Some are willing to talk to Christians, to hear or to be heard; however, they face confrontation. There is a need to take down the walls between Christians and Muslims and to build bridges through friendly encounters and, more important, through involvement in joint activities to meet the felt needs of their communities. In this area, African Christianity can bring a unique contribution to global Christianity and to humanity, especially in sub-Saharan Africa where Christians and Muslims share common parents or grandparents.

In taking concrete steps toward Muslim neighbours, Christians can start with those who are open-minded, peaceful and welcoming; preferably religious leaders, Islamic educators and opinion leaders. By listening to their concerns, exchanging ideas and working together in a non-threatening way on solutions to contextual problems, the two could achieve much, and Christian-Muslim relations would improve. These friendly Muslims can then have a positive impact on their fellow Muslims and even on those who are militant.

Here is a concrete example where input from moderate Muslims can be helpful. Several countries around the world run de-radicalization programmes aiming at deprogramming Islamist terrorists. These programmes involve moderate Muslim scholars or clerics who re-examine the Qur'anic texts generally used to justify terrorism or violence and offer substantial financial and material help to rehabilitate the prisoners when they are released. Although some find that these programmes are generally short and do not offer full guarantees that the former terrorists will not resume acts of violence, I think that they must be encouraged. Burleigh, who reports that according to the Saudis the programme has an 80–90 per cent success rate, describes how it works. Here is an extract of his description:

> The Interior Ministry has established a series of advisory committees, consisting of experts on Islam and psychologists, almost all of them drawn from the universities and mosques. Initially, the experts simply ask why the person is in jail, which leads to a discussion on their beliefs. The clerics concentrate on explaining to prisoners, who invariably have a little or no grasp of the religion, that their understanding of it is false, based on corrupt heretical understandings of Islam (2009: 481).

The Saudi government found the right approach because nothing can frighten somebody who is ready to die and is convinced that he or she is doing the right thing in the light of his or her religious convictions. Changing the mindset is the best approach. However, it is not wise to set general rules for the rehabilitation of Islamist terrorists. Each one has his or her own religious pilgrimage, life experiences, mental health issues, character and sources of influence. The leaders of such programmes must take these factors into consideration and provide appropriate long-term follow-up. But even this is not sufficient. Since most of those who fall into the Islamist terrorism trap have a wrong view of Islam, it is of high important to re-educate the whole population through schools, media, religious centres, families and other public or private means. African Christianity must take this task seriously.

It is also good to draw the attention of political and religious leaders to the danger of Islamist terrorists disguising themselves and using the system to their advantage. The risk is even higher in Europe and North America where some governments have fallen into the trap and let in the Trojan horse because of their national policies. If they were willing to do so, it would not be difficult to carefully monitor and implement well-established regulations to correct the mistake.

Religion plays an important role in the life of a believer. However, it is important to avoid the trap of incoherence. For example, Raphael Israeli observed that:

> Hundreds and thousands did protest in London against the invasion of Iraq, carrying banners which read, 'not in my

name'. But neither the MCB [Muslim Council of Britain] nor any other Muslim groups saw fit to make similar public declarations against the wanton murder of their fellow citizens on 7/7 by their fellow Muslims (2008: 431).

In such circumstances people may easily be attracted by Islamophobia. But I do not believe that Islamophobia is a good reaction to Muslim militancy. However, it will likely grow if Islamists carry out more attacks. The statistics provided by Clive D. Field in his article entitled 'Islamophobia in Contemporary Britain: The Evidence of the Opinions Polls, 1988–2006' (2007: 447–477) gives an idea of how 'the Islamophobic storm clouds' can easily tarnish the image of Islam in such circumstances. In the best interest of their religions, Muslims must proudly join with the rest of the world in search of better ways to address the root causes of Islamism and, hopefully, stop the spiral of violence and bloodshed. That is why African Christianity must include peaceful Muslims in its strategy to trump Muslim militancy. However, Christians must fully take their responsibilities before God even if there is no cooperation from followers of other religions.

Politics

With the rise and growth of Muslim militancy in Africa, Christians need to intentionally permeate all spheres of the society including the media and politics. In regard to Muslim and Christian involvement in politics in Africa, Lamin Sanneh rightly observed, 'We may say that the contemporary Muslim encounter with Christianity is essentially an encounter with the religion as anti-theocratic and pluralistic in tendency. Consequently, in the wake of Christian retreat from theocratic politics we have a rising tide of Muslim demand for religion as a state idea' (1996: 112). Without advocating for the creation of Christian states, I think that Christians must be more involved in the political life of their nations. And once they are elected, they must live a godly life and make a difference in their leadership. Africa needs leaders like Deborah, Joseph, David and Daniel today.

Poverty

In a context where poverty is particularly prevalent, the church needs to be more involved in social and economic development. It should explore all the ways to meet the felt needs of the population. This will require a more holistic approach to theology and particularly missiology. This will also require the creation of more Christian universities where followers of Christ can be properly prepared to meet these multiple needs in the best way possible.

Non-violence

In our efforts to deal with the historical roots of Muslim anger, there is no need to waste energy in pessimism. Although our generation cannot change the past, it has the full ability to re-design the present and the future of humanity, with God's help. This will require more humility, courage, wisdom and genuine love, but African Christianity can do it if it is willing to pay the price.

How should the church react when innocent Christians are killed and church buildings are burned, as is the case in Northern Nigeria? There is no easy response. I am personally in favour of non-violence. The use of violence to end violence is not the smartest way to proceed, because it will only generate more violence. However, I do understand those who think otherwise:

> Sometimes, the command to love means that we must use force to stop an enemy from injuring the innocent. However, any military force used must be aimed at evil doers. With terrorism, we must be sure that we do not harm the 'enemy's' innocent people in order to protect 'ours' (Scott 1989: 142).

During my readings, I was struck with these lines written by a Jewish author:

> If as some claim, only a small percentage of Muslims are 'radical', 'fundamentalist' or simply 'Islamists', while the majority are 'peace-loving', what explains the teeming crowds who erupt violently in Cairo, Gaza, Karachi, Teheran and Kabul at every manufactured 'provocation'? What happens to those supposedly peace-loving majorities if they are not represented by the violent crowds? (Israeli 2008: 4).

Although I do not agree with the conclusion of the author because the reality is far more complex, it is important to stress the importance of Muslim leaders around the world being courageous enough to condemn acts of violence and to preach a message of peace. It is important for the image of Islam itself since the whole world is judging those who kill others in the name of their religion.

Because Muslim militancy also uses terrorism in order to achieve its goals, Scott is right when she writes, 'As a prophetic witness, the Church should continually bring biblical principles to bear on the public debate about terrorism. We need to get beyond slogans and stereotypes and call for public honesty in the discussion of terrorism' (1989: 144).

However, she fails to stress the important role of theologians and church leaders, being deeply rooted in the church, not only in educating the church but also in echoing the prophetic voice in the public arena with honesty and faithfulness to the Holy Scriptures. The teachings of our Lord Jesus Christ on love, humility, prudence, simplicity and other virtues are fundamental.

Before closing this section, I would like to underline that although responding to Muslim militancy in Africa is primarily the task of African Christianity, this does not exclude external contributions. In the conclusion of the book he edited, *Africa and the War on Terrorism*, John Davis makes seven important recommendations (2007: 182–86). He does well to address issues like African prioritization, political violence, marginalization of African institutions, the need of economic assistance, anti-terrorism measures and the preoccupant situation in Sudan and Somalia. Our world needs to pay attention to them because we cannot neglect Africa in our responses to Islamist terrorism. However, Davis fails to address the need to encourage specific anti-terrorism measures at the level of each country that will involve citizens of all religious groups as well as foreign experts. This is a serious task for the Africa Union and the United Nations because it not only about Africa.

Christians from the West, East and other regions of the world can share their expertise with their brothers and sisters in Africa and come alongside as they deal with the significant growth of Islamism on their continent. In the process, they will learn valuable lessons that will help them better meet the Islamist challenges in their own contexts.

Conclusion

An African proverb says, 'If the beard of your neighbour catches fire, wet yours.' The beards of many Africans have been already burned by Islamists and others are on fire. There is no single country or region in Africa where the risk is absent. For this reason, Muslim militancy should be taken seriously.

In that effort, it is necessary to go beyond the symptoms of Islamism and to deal with its root causes, which are historical, psychological, political, socio-economic, doctrinal, ethical and cultural. This requires godly wisdom, serious research, partnership, proper education, peaceful Christian-Muslim relations and concrete actions geared toward meeting the felt needs of the populations, both Muslim and non-Muslim.

African Christianity is uniquely positioned to make a substantial contribution to the global scholarship on Christian-Muslim relations and responses to Muslim militancy. If this is done properly among all the Muslims, it will be a major victory for humanity.

At the end of this paper, one may ask: Is there hope? This is the type of question to which Mahmood Monshipouri wisely responded when he wrote:

> Can Islamists and secularists find a way to coexist in the Muslim world? The answer is yes. As indicated before, contrary to the prevalent assumption, cultural modernity is neither a product of Western secularism nor wholly incompatible with Islamism.

> Continuity and change underlie the broad foundation of Muslim existence, experience and traditions (1998: 234).

Although Monshipouri comments only on a specific aspect, the principle is valid for the overall responses to Muslim militancy. Yes, militant Muslims can renounce violence and co-exist peacefully with their fellow humans if the root causes of their anger are properly addressed. It is not an easy task and requires the active involvement of people from various religious, political, social and intellectual backgrounds, but it can be done. It may not put an end to acts of violence perpetrated by militant Muslims as individuals or as groups, but they will eventually become marginal. For me, the real question is not whether it is possible to respond appropriately to Muslim militancy; the question each government, each society, each movement, each association and each individual must ask is, 'Are we willing to pay the price that such enterprise requires for the survival of our humanity? Are we willing to put into our responses a good dose of genuine love, peaceful relationship with others, sacrifice, compassion, ethics, mercy, justice, perseverance, patience and wisdom?'

In his famous encyclical *Pacem in terres* Pope John XXIII identified four pillars of peace: truth, justice, love and freedom. That is a wise declaration. However, the more I think about Muslim militancy, the more I humbly dare to say that we need a fifth pillar: partnership. Violence has no friend. It turns even against those who think that they have mastered it and can use it to make a case, get attention, fight enemies, or further their agenda. Religious violence is a crime against the very soul of the human condition. Muslims and non-Muslims, Islamists and liberals, men and women of all races need to join in the struggle for peace.

References

Azumah, John A. 2001. *The Legacy of Arab-Islam in Africa: A Quest for Interreligious Dialogue*. Oxford: Oneworld.

Barkindo, Bawuro M. 1993. Islamism in Kano City Since 1970: Causes, Form and Implications. *Muslim Identity and Social Change in Sub-Saharan Africa*, edited by Bloomington Louis Brenner: Indiana University Press: 91–105.

Benegas, José María. 2004. *Diccionario espasa Terrorismo*. Madrid: España.
Burleigh, Michael. 2009. *Blood and Rage: A Cultural History of Terrorism*. New York: Harper Collins Publishers.
Boer, Harry. 1968. *A Brief History of Islam*. Ibadan: Daystar.
Bongoyok, Moussa. 2008. Islamism and Receptivity to Jesus, in *From Seed to Fruit*, edited by J. Dudley Woodberry. Pasadena: William Carey Library.
Bongoyok, Moussa. 2006. *The Rise of Islamism Among the Sedentary Fulbe of Northern Cameroon and Its Implications for Theological Responses*. Pasadena: Fuller Seminary.
Burns,V., and Peterson, K.D. 2005. *Terrorism: A Documentary and Reference Guide*. Westport: Greenwood Press.
Davis, John. 2007. *Africa and the War on Terrorism*. Farnham: Ashgate Publishing Limited.
Field, Clive D. 2007. Islamophobia in Contemporary Britain: The Evidence of the Opinions Polls, 1988–2006. *Islam and Christian-Muslim Relations* 18(4): 155–164.
Fukushima, A. 2003. *Understanding and Addressing the Underlying Causes of International Terrorism*. http://www.yorku.ca/yciss/activities/documents/CanadaJapanUnderstandingandAddressing.pdf.
Fuller, Graham E. 1997. Islamism(s) in the Next Century. *The Islamist Debate*, edited by Martin Kramer. Ramat Aviv: Dayan Centre Papers: 141–160.
Israeli, Raphael. 2008. *The Spread of Islamikaze Terrorism in Europe: The Third Islamic Invasion*. London: Vallentine Mitchell.
Levtzion, Nehemia, and Randall L. Pouwels (eds.) 2000. *The History of Islam*. Athens: Ohio University Press.
Kane, O. 1994. Izala: The Rise of Muslim Reformism in Northern Nigeria. *Accounting for Fundamentalisms: The Dynamic Character of Movements*, edited by M.E. Marty and R.S. Appleby. Chicago: University of Chicago Press: 490–512.
Kukah, Matthew Hassan. 2007. Christian-Muslim Relations in Sub-Saharan Africa: Problems and Prospects. *Islam and Christian-Muslim Relations* 18(2): 155–164.
Martinovitch, S. 2010. The Root Cause of Terrorism? The Arab World. UJA Federation of Greater Toronto. http://www.jewishtoronto.net/page.aspx?id=33090.
Monshipouri, Mahmood. 1998. *Islamism, Secularism and Human Rights in the Middle East*. London: Lynne Rienner Publishers.

Perlez, Jane, and Shah Pir Zubair. 17 April 2009. Taliban Enlist An Army of Pakistan's Have-nots. *The New York Times*, Friday: A1 and A12.

Piscatori, James. 1994. Accounting for Islamic Fundamentalism. *Accounting for Fundamentalisms*, edited by Marty, Martin E., and R. Scott Appleby. Chicago: The University of Chicago Press: 361–373.

Radlauer, D. 2010. The London Bombings and the 'Root Causes of Terrorism'. Institute for Counter-Terrorism. http://212.150.54.123/editorials/editorialdet.cfm?editorialid=1.

Sanneh, Lamin. 1996. *Piety and Power: Muslims and Christians in West Africa*. Maryknoll: Orbis.

Scott, Tracy L. 1989. Terrorism—What is Our Response? *Issues in focus*, edited by Rosenberger, Margaret. Ventura: Regal Books: 135–145.

Tibenderana, Kazenga P. 2006. *Islamic Fundamentalism*. Kampala: Fountain Publishers.

Waal, Alex De 2004. *Islamism and Its Enemies in the Horn of Africa*. Bloomington: Indiana University Press.

Zeidan, David 2002. Typical Elements of Fundamentalist Worldviews. *Islam and Christian-Muslim Relations*, 13(2).

CHAPTER 10

The African Christian and Islamic Da'wah and Polemics

John Chesworth

Islam is a missionary religion, and it is the duty of all Muslims to call others to their faith. This imperative has often been undertaken by ordinary Muslims, rather than by trained missionaries. A number of approaches have developed over the centuries, some of which have caused tensions within society. This paper seeks to demonstrate how Islamic da'wah is being conducted in Africa, focusing on the use of polemics and suggesting responses from African Christians.

Definition of Terms

The terms that are central to the paper can be defined in these ways:

> *da'wah*: is the call, or invitation addressed by God and the prophets to people to believe in the true religion, Islam (Arabic). Maqsood says that 'the term applies more broadly to the duty of Muslims to invite others to find the Sharia the 'straight path' of Islam. The call should be carried out with wisdom, gentleness, tact and good manners' (1996: 25).

polemic(s): controversial discussion and debate, especially in theology. In Christian-Muslim relations, it refers to an approach that is disputatious and deliberately sets out to be provocative. Maqsood says 'Aggressive and arrogant preaching cannot qualify as da'wah, since it drives people *away* from Islam' (1996: 25).

apologetics: A systematic, argumentative discourse in defence of a religion or doctrine. Reasoned defence or vindication, a reasoned defence, especially of Christianity or Islam.

However, the application of these terms needs further clarification. Khurshid Ahmed discusses three aspects of da'wah:

> The *what?* of Islamic *da'wah* means invitation to Islam as a faith and as a way of life, as *al-din*.
>
> The *why?* of Islamic *da'wah* . . . Man is not self-sufficient and needs divine guidance.
>
> [T]he *how? da'wah* is presented primarily through conveying the message, and by practising it and presenting before the world its living example. Islam has ruled out techniques of coercion as instruments of *da'wah*. The methods it has enjoined and actualized in history are methods of communication, discussion and persuasion on the one hand, and the gravitational pull of godliness as exemplified in the lives of the people and realised in the social order. There is no professional class of priests or preachers in Islam. Every Muslim is responsible for the *da'wah* whatever be his vocation in life (in al-Faruqi 1976: 401–402).

Religious polemics has a long history and Hava Lazarus-Yafeh, discussing the medieval period, states that it is:

> [A]n indispensible part of the continuous competition between great civilizations. They may include many different kinds of literature, . . . One may even say that the crystallization of every great civilization is based to a large extent on its contacts, clashes, and competition with rival forces, for no civilization can develop or prosper on its own (Lazarus-Yafeh 1992: 4–5).

Kate Zebiri, commenting on contemporary Muslim polemic, says:

> Contemporary Muslim polemic tends to draw more on sources external to the Qur'an, in particular higher biblical criticism which can be used to demonstrate that the Bible is not 'revealed' in the sense that Muslims generally understand revelation, i.e., the verbatim word of God preserved without any alterations . . . Despite benefiting from higher criticism, however, the modern polemic is not demonstrably superior to the classical works and indeed often shows an inferior knowledge of empirical Christianity (Zebiri 2004: 124).

Apologetics as a defence of one's own faith, should, in its strictest sense, only use the resources provided by that faith. In an ideal situation, the practise of apologetics should be conducted in an irenic (promoting peace) manner. In reality, apologetics is practised as a defence of one's own faith through the refutation of the other's faith. Rather than using reason, polemical argument can be aggressive and negative, which can easily lead to a rise in tensions between two faith communities.

These definitions and qualifying statements serve to set the scene as we examine Islamic da'wah and polemics in Africa.

Islamic Da'wah in Africa From a Historical Perspective

From the first contact between Muslims and Africans, da'wah has been carried out. Islam had arrived in both East and West Africa by the eighth century. Muslim traders arriving in West Africa, having crossed the Sahara, attracted adherents to Islam. In East Africa, traders arriving on the coast also attracted followers to Islam.

The Muslim traders' primary purpose was trade, but they were also conducting da'wah. In some instances, they travelled with imams and *ulama* (scholars) for their own spiritual benefit, and these Muslims also taught those who were interested in Islam. In other cases local people initially imitated the actions of the traders when they prayed and only later came to understand the faith. Some were attracted to Islam because they could see advantages in associating themselves with Muslims and the success of the Muslim traders. Some were drawn to Islam through the Sufi *turuq*, attracted by the mystical aspects and the use of music, which they could relate to. In some regions, the rulers turned to Islam, whilst the people remained as traditionalists; in other areas the rulers were unable to convert because of their cultic roles, but the people became Muslims.[1]

As people became Muslims, they saw education as being important and by the fourteenth century a renowned university had been established in West Africa at Sankore, in Timbuktu. In East Africa, ulama set up schools with students sitting at their feet.

As Islam spread, a Muslim community developed, following a form of Islam, which came to be regarded as orthodox within its own setting.

This chapter cannot examine all the organisations involved with da'wah in Africa, so to illustrate some of the approaches, it is examining two international Muslim organisations that have da'wah as the centre of their programmes.

---

[1]. See Trimingham 1998 on the role of Sufi *turuq*; see Kenny 2000; Levtzion and Pouwels 2000 and Robinson 2004 for examples of da'wah and the spread of Islam in Africa.

Da'wah and the Islam in Africa Organisation[2]

In November 1989, the Islam in Africa conference held in Abuja, Nigeria, led to the founding of the Islam in Africa Organisation (IAO) which was formally constituted in July 1991.

The establishment of the IAO showed that Islam had a new seriousness in establishing its identity in Africa, with an increase in Islamic pride and a commitment to enable both development and da'wah in Africa.

The official communiqué and the resolution to establish IAO, which were published as appendices to the conference proceedings in 1993, included the IAO's purposes in regard to the propagation of Islam. Some were:

> To encourage the teaching of Arabic language which is the language of the Qur'an as well as the lingua franca of the continent and to strive for all restoration of the use of Arabic script in vernacular.

> The conference salutes and highly commends the efforts which the Muslim youth are making in the service of Islam and pledges its full support for them in this worthwhile endeavour.

> To urge Muslims to establish strong economic ties between African Islamic countries and other parts of the Muslim world in order to facilitate mutual assistance and cooperation in commerce, industry and finance with a view to evolving a sound economic system based on Islamic principles (Alkali 1993: 433, appendix 6).

In addition to the purposes stated in the communiqué, the 'Resolution to Establish the Islam in Africa Organisation' specifically refers to da'wah:

---

[2]. This section draws on pages 119–124 of Chesworth 2007. Challenges to the Next Christendom: Islam in Africa. For further views on IAO and the 'Abuja Declaration' see also Hunwick 1997: 41–42 and Wijsen 2007: 64–65.

> To establish Islamic Tertiary and Vocational Centres which are designed to train Da'wah workers who will be trained to acquire trades and skills which will equip them to be self-employed and productive.
>
> To support, enhance and co-ordinate Da'wah work all over Africa on Islamic matters and publicize the research findings; (Alkali 1993: 435–436, appendix 7).

These extracts from the official 1993 communiqué and the resolution show a desire to propagate Islam within Africa particularly through da'wah and Islamic literature in various vernaculars. The statements reveal something of the desires of the Islamic world—that Islam should be spread throughout the world; that Muslims should call others to the faith; that states with a Muslim majority should be ruled in an Islamic way, with Muslims in key government posts; and that other religions are seen as inimical to the progress of an Islamic community.

The IAO website lists the objectives of the organisation and number three is:

> To support, enhance and coordinate Da'wah work in all parts of Africa and propagate the knowledge of Islam throughout the continent (IAO Objectives).

This objective accords with the communiqué; however, present activity seems to be limited and, as at 20 June 2010, the website was not functioning, leading to questions as to the current viability of the IAO. Nevertheless, the sentiments and aims expressed in the Abuja Declaration are still real and guide Muslim groups and individuals in their desire to call all within Africa to Islam.

World Islamic Call Society (WICS)

One group that has managed to move to active involvement in da'wah is the World Islamic Call Society (WICS). It was founded in 1970 as the

Islamic Call Organisation (*al-Da'wa al-Islamia*) by the Libyan head of state, Mu'ammar Al-Qaddafi, subsequently becoming the World Islamic Call Society in 1982. Their website gives the structure of the society and its work, giving regular press releases on its worldwide activities.

The section on Rightly Guided describes the da'wah activities:

> Through various programmes designed and supported by the Society, local Islamic Callers organized cultural courses and forums to better educate recent converts. These programmes focused on the principals [*sic*] of dialogue and consultation in Islam and corrected misconceptions propagated by organisations hostile to Islam. The programmes also provided information on religious jurisprudence 'Fiqh,' Da'wah, techniques of Qur'an recitation (Tajweed), schools of recitation (Qira'at) and the Arabic language (WICS Rightly Guided).

WICS has thirty-four offices outside Libya with eighteen of them being in Africa. From their own reports, it appears that Africa is the focus of much of their work. The website gives details of the numbers of people who have declared *shahada* as a result of their work. For Africa the figures are 62,901 from twenty-eight African states. The website notes that:

> the great increase in the number of new Muslims in Ethiopia and Congo is mainly due to entire villages coming into the fold of Islam. During the historic tour of the Leader, he extended an invitation to those who were present to accept Islam. As a result of his logical and spiritual message, a great number of people responded positively to his invitation (WICS Rightly Guided).

In addition, on Mu'ammar Al-Qaddafi's various tours, notably in 2003 and 2005, 'he met a number of Sultans, and leaders of tribes in Niger, Ghana, Togo, and southern Sudan. Responding to the invitation of the Leader they all declared the Shahada in front of a large gathering' (WICS website).

The use of declaration of the shahada as an identifier is of special note, as this is all that is required for someone to become a Muslim. However, the figures given do not differentiate between those who are already Muslims and those who are newly making a decision to submit to Islam.

It is not easy to differentiate between spiritual and political purposes when Mu'ammar Al-Qaddafi is involved. The declaration of shahada by traditional rulers before the leader appears to be taken as a symbol of support for Mu'ammar Al-Qaddafi. This became apparent in August 2008 when Mu'ammar Al-Qaddafi was reported to have invited many traditional rulers to declare their support for him, and they declared him to be king of kings prior to his being chosen as president of the African Union in January 2009 (BBC 2008, 2009, 2010).

WICS, unlike IAO, is still active and its website regularly gives reports, issuing twenty different press releases during one week in June, half of them concerning work in Africa. These press releases give an indication as to how WICS carries out its da'wah activities. An example is a press release: 'WICS organizes caravan to Kisumu and Kagyado [sic] in Kenya', which reported that:

> The office of the World Islamic call society in Uganda has of recent dispatched a caravan to Kisumu and Kagyado [Kajiado] districts in Kenya. The caravan supervised by WICS's Du'at in Kenya comprised lectures and lessons about Islam, ethics and how to perform various acts of worship, beside visits to Muslim families (WICS News 14 June 2010).[3]

This reveals that the work is comprised of teaching about Islam, although we are not told who was taught, nor how many, and of visits to Muslim families, the purpose of which could be seen as being to support and encourage them.

It has also reported on similar caravans to the Gambia and a da'wah trip to Kano, Nigeria, which describes the reception of new converts:

---

3. Kisumu is on Lake Victoria Nyanza, whilst Kajiado is to the south of Nairobi and populated predominantly by Maasai pastoralists.

Within the framework of catering for new converts and offering orientation programmes, the office of the World Islamic Call Society in Kano made a Da'wah trip to Shanono local government in Kano state to inspect the condition of Muslims there. The trip took place on June 7th and witnessed 59 Nigerians profess Islam . . . During the function, WICS' Secretary briefed the new Muslim brothers and sisters on the tenets of Islam and various acts of worship as well as some of its ethical and social aspects (WICS News 10 June 2010).

This statement is both informative and opaque! The implication is that people declared shahada before the WICS officials and were subsequently briefed on the practise of the faith that they had newly embraced. The press release does not explain whether those who professed Islam had previously declared a wish to do so or whether they had been attending classes on Islam before the WICS' secretary 'briefed them . . . on the tenets of Islam'.

With the changes that occurred in Libya during 2011, future developments of WICS work is far from certain.

Methods of Da'wah in Current Use

As noted, these are the initiatives of international organisations such as IAO and WICS, whose approach to da'wah is through Islamic education and forms of assistance, including health, development and relief. Groups and individuals also use many other, less open, methods of da'wah.

It is not possible to go into detail here as to how Islam is being spread through da'wah in the whole of the continent; however, research in Tanzania and Kenya recorded a number of methods used by Muslims, including:
- *Mihadhara:* (public debates), mainly using the comparative religions approach.
- Tracts and pamphlets: Many are in circulation, written to challenge Christians to question their faith.
- Newspapers and magazines.

- Radio and television, both local and via satellite: Local broadcasters are generally circumspect lest they be closed down, whereas the content of satellite channels is virtually unregulated. Whilst the primary aim of satellite channels *alarabiya* and *aljazeera* is dissemination of news, other channels have da'wah as their aim, such as *Peace TV* which promotes itself as being a '24 hour Islamic Spiritual Edutainment International Satellite TV Channel' broadcasting in English and Urdu, and regularly shows programmes of Ahmed Deedat, Zakir Naik, Bilal Philips (Peace TV).
- Internet, both local and international: Few sites are hosted locally, because of the unreliable infrastructure. Many sites are set up by African Muslim diaspora, but these often fail to be maintained (Chesworth 2007b: 257–259). International sites are also becoming known and receive many 'hits'.
- Cassettes and videos, now DVDs, VCDs: These are readily available in shops and on the streets. They include material from Deedat and recordings of *Mihadhara* (Swahili: public debates), some of which are extremely offensive to Christians.
- Mosque building: This can be understood as not only establishing a 'presence', but also as 'claiming the ground' for Islam.
- Financial support: such as enhanced bride price or assistance in land purchases.
- Employment and trade: work and accommodation are offered to jobless young Christians by Muslim traders.
- Schools: Muslim-run secondary schools are offering places to Christians and in some cases then influencing the students to become Muslims.
- Scholarships: offered to the youth to study abroad in a Muslim university.
- Health services: Hospitals and dispensaries are being run by Muslims. In some cases, service will include active propagation of Islam.

- Relief services: various Islamic agencies are becoming involved in providing relief.

(Chesworth 2007a: 124–126 adapted; See also Wijsen and Mfumbusa 2004: 54, for methods of da'wah in Tanzania.)

Some of the methods appear to be underhanded and could be regarded as either enticing or entrapping people into becoming Muslims. However, it should also be noted that many of these methods are not that different from those used by early Christian missionaries in Africa.

How is Someone Received into Islam?

If someone has decided that they wish to become a Muslim, that is to convert,[4] how do they do this? Declaration of shahada before two reliable Muslim witnesses is all that is required.[5] However many Muslim groups take responsibility to assess the genuineness of the desire to become a Muslim. Muhammad Al-Maawi, the *da'i* (propaganda officer) at Jamia Mosque in Nairobi, explained the process for receiving a new convert at the mosque, saying that a person wishing to convert would be interviewed carefully, ascertain their understanding of Islam and to discern the genuineness of their intent to convert. The new convert is then given literature and asked to return after a period of time, usually within a month, for a further interview, after which if the da'i is satisfied that the desire is genuine and through free-will, the convert then declares the shahada and is given a certificate of conversion (Personal interview 2005).

This could be regarded as being a responsible approach to conversion, ensuring that the person knows what they are joining to and that they

---

4. To convert is the most readily understood term, however Muslims also use the term 'revert', on the premise that all are originally Muslims and when they acknowledge this they are reverting to Islam, rather than converting to it.
5. If the witnesses are male, only two are required, if only one is male, then two women are needed.

are doing so voluntarily with no coercion. However, how widespread this approach is and how carefully it is actually practised is another question.

Muslim Polemics in Africa

Having looked at da'wah, the focus now is on one of its aspects, the use of polemics by Muslims in Africa. The origins of the present approach to polemics go back to debates held in Agra in 1854. Karl Pfander (1803–1865), a German who worked with Church Missionary Society (CMS), went to Persia at the age of twenty-two, and worked there for twelve years. At the age of twenty-six, he wrote *Mizan al-Haqq* (The Balance of Truth). He then worked in India, where he spoke at a number of public debates and wrote apologetic literature (Chapman 1995: 211). In 1854 Pfander engaged in a series of public debates in Agra with Rahmat Allah al-Kairanawi (1818–1891), who 'by most accounts bested Pfander' (Goddard 2000: 131). Some years later, in 1867, Rahmat Allah wrote *Izhar al-Haqq* (The Truth Revealed). Rahmat Allah 'won' because he was aware of biblical criticism which was then current, whereas Pfander knew nothing of this. It is of note that both books are still readily available.[6]

Ahmed Deedat and the Comparative Religions Approach

Ahmed Deedat (1918–2005) discovered a copy of Rahmat Allah's book whilst working in a general store and found in it the answers to the 'crude questioning and jibes' which he received from Bible college students who came to the shop. Deedat went on to develop what has come to be known as the comparative religions approach, which is at the heart of much current polemical discourse.

---

6. A new edition of Rahmat Allah's *Izhar al-Haqq* was published in 2003 and is available on the internet, as is Pfander's *Mizan al-Haqq*.

Deedat used the Bible to refute the claims of Christianity and to challenge Christians. His talks were then used to produce a series of pamphlets, which are widely distributed and translated into several African languages. His lectures and debates with prominent Christians were filmed and have become very popular. Even though he died in 2005, Peace TV broadcasts *Man with a Mission*, starring Ahmed Deedat, three times a week, because 'his ardent passion for da'wah still motivates minds of young Muslims and his legacy continues to inspire people of all ages' (Peace TV). The Peace TV website for *Man with a Mission* says:

> Have you seen a Muslim observing a method of preaching that ironically had been conventionally the very tool of Western Christian missionaries? If not, watch Shaikh Ahmed Deedat . . . the 'Man with a Mission'. Shaikh Ahmed Deedat, popularly known as the Muslim Scholar of the Christian Bible, is considered to be a pioneer in the field of public talks and debates on Islam and comparative religion. He took comparative religion to a new effective dimension, which involved a comparative and critical analysis of the Bible, rather than the traditional method of Da'wah (propagation) that involved expounding on the Qur'an and Hadith to a non-Muslim audience

The comparative religions approach has been imitated by many 'children of Deedat' throughout Africa. His first visit to East Africa in 1981 led Muslims there to develop their own material using a local language, Swahili, rather than English.

Two of the earliest proponents of this method in East Africa were Mussa Fundi Ngariba (d. 1993) and Mohammed Ali Kawemba, from Ujiji, Western Tanzania. Ngariba studied under Shaykh Mussa Hussein in Ujiji (Chande 1998: 153). Ngariba and Kawemba became well-known during the 1980s when they travelled extensively through Tanzania and Kenya with *Jumuiya ya Wahubiri wa Kiislamu Tanzania* (Society of Muslim Preachers of Tanzania) (JUWAKITA) (Chesworth 2006: 170). Their method was to hold *mihadhara* (Swahili: public debates) with titles such as *Mungu Mmoja dini moja* (One God, one religion) and *Biblia inakana Uungu wa Yesu* (The Bible denies the Divinity of Jesus), where the two speakers would use the Bible to present reasons why Christians had been misled. Other groups have copied this method and are still very active in East Africa.[7]

Use of the Bible to Refute Christianity

How does the comparative religions approach work, and how is the Bible turned against Christians? It is often done through taking verses out of context or picking out apparent inconsistencies in the text. When this is done in the context of a public meeting, it can sound very convincing. Muslims are in a quandary, as they find statements in the Qur'an that do not match those found in the Bible. As they believe that the Qur'an is an exact copy of the *umm-l-kitab* in paradise, the inconsistencies cannot be in the Qur'an, therefore the Bible must be inconsistent. This leads to some of the strands of argument used by Muslims; however, other arguments rely on the text of the Bible being reliable to prove their case.

Here are examples of how the Bible is used by Muslim preachers in pamphlets (Chesworth 2008).

Muhammad in the Bible

To find verses in the Bible that point clearly to the coming of Muhammad legitimises Islam as having been foretold by prophets in the Old Testament and implies that Jesus also knew that Muhammad would come. One passage that is often used is Deuteronomy 18:18a: 'I will raise up for them a prophet like you from among their own people'.

Jews initially understood this to mean that God would raise up a succession of true prophets among Israel. With time, it came to be understood as referring to one specific prophet, a second Moses. Early

---

[7]. For a detailed exploration of the methods used by Ngariba and Kawemba, see Chesworth 2006: 168–172; 201. Joseph Mutei analysed video recordings of *mihadhara* conducted by Ngariba and Kawemba as a part of his MA research. See Mutei 2006, for reports of groups working in different parts of Kenya; also Ahmed 2008, for groups in Tanzania and Kenya.

Christians identified this expected prophet as Jesus. Muslims understand the verse to show that Moses was clearly announcing that Muhammad would be the prophet like him, and God would raise him up.

Uislamu Katika Biblia (*Islam in the Bible*) by Ngariba and Kawemba quotes verse 18, and then sets out a series of comparisons between Moses and Muhammad and Jesus.[8]

Having quoted verse 18, the tract makes clear that it is a reference to Muhammad, not to Jesus. This is demonstrated by five statements, which compare aspects of Moses' life with those of Muhammad and Jesus. In each of the following, Muhammad's history is seen to be closer to that of Moses's than is Jesus': in having both a father and mother; in being married; in being accepted by his people whilst alive; in being a leader; in bringing new laws for their people.

Jesus is Not the Son of God

Muslims deny that Jesus is the Son of God, because it is clearly stated in the Qur'an that God has no associates and that 'He begot no one nor was He begotten' (Sura 112:3). Thus attempts are made to show that Jesus cannot be God's son.

Abbas Kanoni Gombo in *Kwa Nini Niliacha Ukristo na Nikawa Muislamu* (*Why I Left Christianity and Became a Muslim*) uses verses from Hebrews and Acts to show that 'to be born without a father is not a sign of divinity'.[9]

He begins by referring to Christians' use of Jesus having been born without a father as a 'sign' of his divinity. The passage starts by comparing Adam with Jesus, to demonstrate that Adam's origins are even more unusual than those of Jesus'. It asks, 'If Adam was born without father or mother, likewise Melchizedek, what is so surprising about Jesus being born with only a mother?' in order to make the reader consider what was so special about Jesus. Acts 2:22 is then quoted in full to show that the miracles and signs that Jesus performed were signs that God did 'by his hand'. This is

---

8. Ngariba and Kawemba 1987: 12–13, see appendix for text. For further examples of Ngariba and Kawemba's use of the Bible see Chesworth 2008a, 2008b and 2011.
9. Kanoni nd: 24, see appendix for text.

used to show that Jesus was a prophet and not the second person of the Trinity, because any action he did was because God permitted it. Kanoni uses these reasons to explain why he began to have doubts about 'the truth of the teaching of the religion of Christianity'.

The Five Pillars of Islam in the Bible

Verses from the Bible are used to demonstrate the Five Pillars of Islam. In an example concerning prayer, Ngariba and Kawemba quote Bible passages about removing shoes (Exodus 3:3–6; Joshua 5:13–15), ablutions (Exodus 30:17–21; Matthew 5:17–20; John 13:5–11), and prostrating (Exodus 34:8–9; 2 Chronicles 7:3; Matthew 26:38–44; Revelation 7:1–4). In each case the passages are explained as being the actions of the followers of Moses and Jesus. 'It is absolutely clear that it was necessary for the followers of Moses and Jesus to follow these actions. . . . These things are done by Muslims and forgotten by Christians' (1987: 25).

The challenge to Christians is then, if Moses and Jesus did these things, who is being more faithful to them? It is the Muslims who do what they did, whereas Christians do not. This argument is then used to attack Paul, who is seen as having perverted the message of Jesus and led his followers astray.

Paul's Misleading of Believers

Ngariba and Kawemba question Paul's right to claim to be an apostle and claim that he 'came to plant bad seeds after Jesus Christ' (1987: 8). They quote a series of Bible references to attack Paul's claim to apostleship: Romans 11:13; 1 Corinthians 2:1–2; Philippians 2:5–7; 1 Timothy 3:14–16; Titus 2:13–14 (1987: 8–10; See appendix for text).

They reject Paul's claim to be an apostle. This is because Paul had 'greatly persecuted Jesus in his time' and his mission to be an 'Apostle to the Nations' came to him from Jesus 'in a dream'. The pamphlet writers use these statements, all of which are contained in the Bible references mentioned, in such a way as to imply something that is not actually correct.

Ngariba and Kawemba see Paul as having falsely claimed to have been given authority by Jesus; they believe that Paul changed the direction of the faith of Jesus' followers and that had this not happened those followers would have recognised Muhammad and become Muslims.

Inconsistencies Found in the Bible

A common accusation made by Muslims, from the earliest times, is that Christians and Jews deliberately changed the text of the Bible. Later, other scholars began to accuse both Christians and Jews of corrupting the text itself that is, deliberately changing the text for their own purposes.

Muslim writers have continued to charge Christians with *tahrif* (corruption of scripture), mainly using the classical arguments set out by the early writers. Some recent writers, particularly in polemical writings, have used the charge of tahrif against the editors of new versions of the Bible in various languages.[10]

Abbas Gombo Kanoni uses different versions of John 1:18 to accuse Christians of tahrif. (See appendix for text.) Kanoni begins by asking what it means to call Jesus 'Son'. He then makes his argument based on different words found in two versions of the Swahili Bible which have different readings of John 1:18 centring on the presence or absence of 'God'.

> John 1:18 No one has ever seen God. It is God the only Son, who is close to the Father's heart, who has made him known. (New Revised Standard Version)
>
> 'WHAT DOES IT MEAN TO CALL JESUS 'SON'?'
>
> In the Bible that was printed in 1945
>   John 1:18 is written: 'The only son that is in the Father's breast.'
>
> But in the Bible that was printed in 1950
>   John 1:18 is written: 'God the only Son that is in the Father's breast.'
>
> (p. 22)

---

10. For further information on tahrif see Hava Lazarus-Haveh, 1992, 1999.

The first version, which Kanoni calls the Bible of 1945, is *Kitabu cha Agano Jipya la Bwana na Mwokozi Wetu Yesu Kristo Kimefasirika katika Maneno ya Kiyunani* (New Testament in Swahili, Zanzibar), which had been reprinted from an edition which had last been corrected in 1923. The second version, which he calls the Bible of 1950, is *Kitabu cha Agano Jipya la Bwana na Mwokozi Wetu Yesu Kristo* (The New Testament in Swahili, Union Version), which was the first edition of the new Union Version.

The Zanzibar Swahili version says *Mwana wa pekee* (the only son) whilst the Union Version says *Mungu Mwana pekee* (God the only son).[11] It is not surprising that Kanoni, finding these two different versions, says: 'This word is inserted on purpose', that is tahrif (deliberate corruption). It is perhaps not surprising that Kanoni was shocked at the difference between the two versions of the passage as it originates in variant readings in the text of the Greek New Testament, something that is unlikely that a layperson would be aware of.

Kanoni gives two reasons as to why the change was made:

> . . . in order that the desire of theirs to raise up Jesus should succeed.

> It was only added so that they could dare to make the lie of their faith that has no foundation, that of the Holy Trinity.

In his arguments, Kanoni does not appear to be referring to the classical attacks on Christians using tahrif; rather his argument seems to be based on the differences between two versions of the Swahili Bible. The resulting attack is not dissimilar to classical attacks and appears to be rooted in Muslims and Christians having different understandings of the text of the Qur'an and the Bible. For Muslims, the Qur'an is the true text only in the original Arabic and anything in a different language can only be an interpretation of the text and not the text itself. Whereas for Christians,

---

11. When these versions were being prepared, those who were translating more often relied on English versions of the New Testament, rather than using the Greek version as a basis. Because the variant reading was known, those working on John's Gospel would have discussed the possibility of using *Mungu Mwana pekee* rather than *Mwana wa pekee*.

the Bible is the Word of God, in whatever language it is read in. The New Testament was written originally in Greek, but has been translated into the languages (vernaculars) of the people using it from the time of the early church, in order that the believers could understand it clearly.

Propagation of Polemics

Historically, polemics involved the use of face-to-face debates and print media; today it is also being promulgated using new media.

Christian Responses

Understanding that Islam, as a missionary religion, is seeking to 'call' others to Islam, how should the African Christian respond? Lamin Sanneh, discussing Christian experiences of Islamic da'wah, makes this helpful contribution:

> Christian experience of Islamic da'wah in Africa can be both stimulating and challenging. It is stimulating because it has shown Christians how seriously the vocation to witness needs to be taken. The devotion and sense of self-sacrifice which Muslims have shown in obedience to the call to spread and establish the faith are a poignant reminder of what lies at the heart of Christian discipleship (Sanneh 1976: 422).

A frequently asked question from Christian students in courses on Islam in Africa is, 'When can we throw "stones" back at the Muslims?' Surely, we are taught to 'turn the other cheek'? Does throwing 'stones' actually help? Does a Christian polemical response do any more than add more heat than light to the situation?

The use of polemics by Christians gives rise to an important question: Who are we trying to reach with it? It is likely to cause offence to the Muslim listener. If the message a Muslim hears from Christians is that

Islam is 'of the devil', are they likely to be willing to stay and listen and be open to being convinced by the speaker?

Polemics is more likely to exacerbate a situation where relations between Christians and Muslims are already poor and to increase tensions so much that violence may occur.

What Methods Can We Use?

In many parts of Africa today, relations between Christians and Muslims are worse than in the past. In some communities where families used to include both Muslims and Christians without any tensions, those tensions are now apparent, for example amongst the Yoruba in Southern Nigeria. How can we as Christians fulfil our missionary imperative and 'go and tell' Muslims?

Two Possible Approaches

Friendship Evangelism

Barbara Cooper, in her study of Christians in Niger, discusses what can be termed as 'friendship evangelism':

> Christian women do participate in the major life events of their Muslim kin and neighbours, offering the same kinds of wedding gifts to the bride or mother that any Muslim woman would (cloth, kola nuts, cash, kitchenware). They go to great lengths to visit ill neighbours, whether Muslim or Christian, and offer help with minding their children or advice on how to treat the ailment . . . And so I imagine that this gentle and loving approach to their Hausa Muslim neighbour has, in the past, contributed to feelings of sympathy and commonality (2006: 377).

Many of us involved in work amongst Muslims are men and so we are precluded from working amongst at least half of the Muslims, who are women. Christian women can 'gossip the gospel' with their Muslim neighbours, through their lives and witness. This approach should be encouraged, and men should seek ways to develop friendship with Muslim men.

Reading the Bible with Muslims

In Britain over the past ten years, groups have grown up where members of the Abrahamic faiths read and discuss their scriptures together. This is called Scriptural Reasoning and allows each faith to present their own scripture and to explain their understanding of a text. This is followed by a discussion where those from each faith can ask questions and draw out similarities and differences from their own faith tradition.[12]

George Joseph, working in Senegal, used the Wolof Bible, translated by Protestants, to discover whether it 'penetrates the double filter of a Senegalese Muslim audience, who read the Bible, not only through the lenses of Senegalese Islam, but also through conceptions that come with a long contact with Senegalese Catholicism' (Joseph 2004: 87–88). He reported on the 'enthusiastic willingness of Senegalese Muslims to discuss the Bible' (Joseph 2004: 98).

> Although they do consider the text to contain the Word of God, they do not grant it the same status as the Koran because of what they consider to be the corruptness of the text. They also consider the Bible from a position of a religion that completes and refines the truths of Christianity. Thus they interpret with confidence and will find ways to circumvent the meaning in favour of one compatible to Islam, much the way in which Christians read Hebrew texts. Yet, when all is said and done, I, a Christian, felt very close to the participants after our discussions (Joseph 2004: 98–99).

---

12. See Ford and Pecknold 2006; Scriptural Reasoning http://www.scripturalreasoning.org/index.php.

Reading the Bible with a small group of Muslims who want to understand what the scriptures say allows the Christian to explain what the gospel message really means.

These examples show two possible responses, but they are not the extent of methods that can be used.

Conclusion

Muslims have a missionary imperative to call others to Islam. This is unlikely to change. In the same way, Christians will continue to 'go and tell' to fulfil their missionary mandate.

Respect and courtesy should be an integral part of attempts to conduct da'wah and evangelism. With these in place, individuals can demonstrate their faith in their witness and life, allowing the other to make their choice of religion from a standpoint of positive interaction.

References

Ahmed, C. 2008. *Les Conversions à l'Islam fondamentaliste: Le Cas de la Tanzanie et du Kenya*. Paris: L'Harmattan.

Alarabiya Satellite Channel. http://www.alarabiya.net/english.html

Aljazeera Satellite Channel. http://english.aljazeera.net/

Alkali, N., Adamu, A., Yadudu, A., Motem, R., and Salihi, H. 1993. *Islam in Africa: Proceedings of the Islam in Africa Conference*. Ibadan: Spectrum Books Ltd.

An-Na'im, A.A. (ed.) 1999. *Proselytization and Communal Self-determination in Africa*. Maryknoll: Orbis.

An-Na'im, A.A. 1999. Competing Claims to Religious Freedom and Communal Self-determination in Africa. *Proselytization and Communal Self-determination in Africa*, edited by A.A. An-Na'im. Maryknoll: Orbis: 1–28.

BBC. 2008. Gaddafi: Africa's 'King of Kings'. http://news.bbc.co.uk/1/hi/world/africa/7588033.stm 29 August 2008.

BBC. 2009. Gaddafi Vows to Push Africa Unity. http://news.bbc.co.uk/1/hi/world/africa/7864604.stm 2 February 2009.

BBC. 2010. African Union Row Over Muammar Gaddafi's Role. http://news.bbc.co.uk/1/hi/world/africa/8485477.stm 28 January 2010.

Brenner, L. (ed.) 1993. *Muslim Identity and Social Change in Sub-Saharan Africa*. London: Hurst.

Chande, A. 1998. *Islam, Ulamaa and Community Development in Tanzania*. Bethesda: Austin and Winfield.

Chapman, C. 1995. *Cross and Crescent: Responding to the Challenge of Islam*. Leicester: IVP.

Chesworth, J.A. 1999. Muslim Affirmation through Refutation: A Tanzanian Example. Birmingham University, MA. (Unpublished dissertation).

Chesworth, J.A. 2003. The Use of the Qur'an in Swahili *Da'wa* and Evangelism Literature. Paper presented at Qur'an: Text, Translation and Interpretation conference, held at SOAS, 16–17 October 2003.

Chesworth, J.A. 2004a. *Dhimmi* Status in Islam from an Historical Perspective with Implications for Present Day Africa. *From the Cross to the Crescent, Procmura Occasional Paper 1.1*, edited by J. Mbillah, and J. Chesworth. Nairobi: Procmura: 64–85.

Chesworth, J.A. 2004b. Muslims and Christians in East Africa Since Independence: Shifting Fortunes and Perceptions. *Journal of African Christian Thought* 7(2): 39–47.

Chesworth, J.A. 2006. Fundamentalism and Outreach Strategies in East Africa: Christian Evangelism and Muslim *Da'wa*. *Muslim-Christian encounters in Africa*, edited by B.J. Soares. Leiden: Brill. 159–186.

Chesworth, J.A. 2007a. Challenges to the Next Christendom: Islam in Africa. *Global Christianity: Contested Claims*, edited by F. Wijsen, and R. Schreiter. Amsterdam: Rodopi B.V.: 117–132.

Chesworth, J.A. 2007b. A Study of Selected Islamic Internet Sites in East Africa. *Masaryk University Journal of Law and Technology*. 1(2): 253–262.

Chesworth, J.A. 2008a. The Cross and 'Outreach' Literature in East Africa. *Jesus and the Cross: Reflections of Christians from Islamic Contexts*, edited by D. Singh. Carlisle: Regnum: 105–111.

Chesworth, J.A. 2008b. The Use of Scripture in Swahili Tracts by Muslims and Christians in East Africa. http://etheses.bham.ac.uk/150/

Chesworth, J.A. 2009. Polemical Revival: Attacking the Other's Texts. *Forum* 21(4), 2009: 72–76.

Cooper, B. 2006. *Evangelical Christians in the Muslim Sahel*. Bloomington: Indiana University Press.

Deedat, A. 1991. *Desert Storm—Has it Ended?* (previously published as *Christ in Islam*). Durban: IPCI.

Deedat, A. 1992a. *Is the Bible God's Word.* Durban: IPCI.

Deedat, A. 1992b. *Combat Kit Against Bible Thumpers.* Durban: IPCI.

Deedat, A. 1995. *Who Moved the Stone?* Durban: IPCI.

Deedat, A. 1997. *Muhummed (p.b.u.h.) The Natural Successor to Christ (p.b.u.h.).* Durban: IPCI.

Deedat, A. 2000a. *Muhummed (p.b.u.h.) The Greatest.* Durban: IPCI.

Deedat, A. 2000b. *The God Who Never Was.* Durban: IPCI.

Deedat, A. 2003. *Crucifixion or Cruci-fiction?* Durban: IPCI.

Deedat, A. 2005. *What the Bible Says about Muhummed (p.b.u.h.)* Durban: IPCI.

Deedat, A. n.d. 'A high quality video Collection of Sheikh Ahmed Deedat's Debates and Lectures'. http://english.truthway.tv/ (also includes pdf copies of Deedat's booklets).

El-Miskin, T. 1993. 'Da'wa and the Challenge of Secularism: A Conceptual Agenda for Islamic Ideologues'. *Islam in Africa: Proceedings of the Islam in Africa Conference.* Eds. N. Akali, A. Adam et al., Ibadan: Spectrum Books, 266–275.

Faruqi, al I. 1976. 'On the Nature of Islamic Da'wah'. *International Review of Mission,* Vol. 65. 391–409.

Ford, D. And Pecknold (eds.), C.C. 2006. *The Promise of Scriptural Reasoning.* Oxford: Wiley-Blackwell.

Goddard, H. 1996. *Muslim Perceptions of Christianity.* London: Grey Seal.

Goddard, H. 2000. *A History of Christian-Muslim Relations,* Edinburgh: Edinburgh University Press.

Hansen, H.B. & Twaddle, M. (eds.) 1995. *Religion and Politics in East Africa.* London: James Currey.

Haynes, J. 1996. *Religion and Politics in Africa.* London: Zed Books.

Islam in Africa Organisation 1993. 'The Communique' [Appendix 6]. In Alkali, N. et al *Islam in Africa: Proceedings of the Islam in Africa Conference,* Ibadan: Spectrum Books Ltd., 432–434.

Islam in Africa Organisation 1993. 'Resolution to Establish the Islam in Africa Organisation' [Appendix Seven]. In Alkali, N. et al *Islam in Africa: Proceedings of the Islam in Africa Conference,* Ibadan: Spectrum Books Ltd., 435–436.

Joseph, G. 2004. 'Reading Wolof Bible with Muslims'. *Biblical Texts and African Audiences*, edited by E.R. Wendland and J-C. Loba-Mkole. Nairobi: Acton Press, 86–99.

Kairanawi, R. 2003. *Izhar-ul-Haqq: The Truth Revealed*. London: Ta-Ha Publishers. http://www.islam4all.com/newpage71.htm

Kanoni, A.G. n.d. *Kwa Nini Niliacha Ukristo na Nikawa Muislamu*. Mombasa: Adam Traders.

Lacunza Balda, J. 1993. 'The Role of Kiswahili in East African Islam'. *Muslim Identity and Social Change in Sub-Saharan Africa*, edited by L. Brenner. London: Hurst & Company, 226–238.

Lazarus-Yafeh, H. 1992. *Intertwined Worlds: Medieval Islam and Bible Criticism*. Princeton: Princeton University Press.

Lazarus-Yafeh, H. 1999. 'Taḥrīf', In *Encyclopedia of Islam CD-Rom Edition V. 1.0*, eds. C.E. Bosworth et al, Leiden: Brill Vol X, 111–112.

Levtzion, N. & Pouwels, R.L. (eds.) 2000. *The History of Islam in Africa*. Oxford: James Currey.

Maqsood, R.W. 1996. *Islam a Dictionary*. Birmingham: Islamic Vision.

Mbillah, J. and Chesworth J. (eds.) 2004. *From the Cross to the Crescent*, Procmura Occasional Paper 1.1, Nairobi: Procmura.

Mutei, J. 2006. *The Effectiveness of Mihadhara as a Method of Islamic Da'wah in Kenya*, MA dissertation, St. Paul's University, Limuru, Kenya (unpublished).

Ngariba, M.F. & Kawemba, M.A. 1987. *Uislamu Katika Biblia*. Zanzibar: Al-Khayria Press.

'Objectives of the IAO', the Website is no longer active, but an archived version of the site from June 2008 is available at: http://web.archive.org/web/20080316174237/www.islaminafrica.org/objective.htm

Peace TV 2010. *Home Page*. http://www.peacetv.in/index.php

Peace TV 2010. *Man with a Mission*. http://www.peacetv.in/eng_manwithmission.php

Pfander, C.G. 1986. *The Mizan-ul-Haqq: Balance of Truth*. Villach: Light of Life. http://answering-islam.org/Books/Pfander/Balance/index.htm

Sajaad, M. 2007. *The Fiqh of Da'wah: A Commentary on 40 Hadiths*. Birmingham: As-Suffa Institute.

Sanneh, L. 1976. 'Christian Experience of Islamic Da'wah, with Particular Reference to Africa'. *International Review of Mission*, Vol. 65, 410–426.

Scriptural Reasoning. 2010. *Scriptural Reasoning*. http://www.scripturalreasoning.org/index.php

Soares, B.F. and Otayek, R. (eds.) 2007. *Islam and Muslim Politics in Africa*. Basingstoke: Palgrave.

Stenger, F., Wandera, J. and Hannon, P. (eds.) 2008. *Christian-Muslim Co-Existence in Eastern Africa*. Nairobi: Paulines Publications.

Trimingham, J.S. 1998. *The Sufi Orders of Islam*. Oxford: Oxford University Press.

Wendland, E.R. & Loba-Mkole, J-C. (eds.) 2004. *Biblical Texts and African Audiences*. Nairobi: Acton.

Westerlund, D. & Rosander, E.E. (eds.) 1997. *African Islam and Islam in Africa*. London: Hurst & Co.

Wijsen, F. & Mfumbusa, B. 2004. *Seeds of Conflict: Religious Tensions in Tanzania*, Nairobi: Paulines Publications of Africa.

Wijsen, F. 2007. *Seeds of Conflict in a Haven of Peace: From Religious Studies to Interreligious Studies in Africa*, Amsterdam: Rodopi B.V.

Wijsen, F. & Schreiter, R. (eds.) 2007. *Global Christianity: Contested Claims*, Amsterdam: Rodopi B.V.

World Islamic Call Society 2010. 'The Rightly Guided'. www.islamic-call.net/english/modules/smartsection/item.php?itemid=49, accessed 11 June 2010

'WICS Organizes Caravan to Kisumu and Kagiado in Kenya'. http://www.islamic-call.net/english/modules/news/article.php?storyid=1839

'WICS Undertakes Da'wa trip in Kano'. http://www.islamic-call.net/english/modules/news/article.php?storyid=1826.

Zahniser, A.H.M. 2002. 'Invitation'. *The Encyclopaedia of the Qur'an*: Volume Two E-I. Ed. J.D. McAuliffe, Leiden: Brill, 557–558.

Zebiri, K. 2004. 'Polemic and Polemical Language'. *The Encyclopaedia of the Qur'an*: Volume Four P-Sh. Ed. J.D. McAuliffe, Leiden: Brill, 114–125.

Appendix
Examples of Muslim Use of the Bible

These are translations, by the author, from the short extracts from Swahili texts by Mussa Fundi Ngariba and Mohamed Ali Kawemba, *Uislamu Katika Biblia* (1993) and Abbas Gombo Kanoni, *Kwa Nini Niliacha Ukristo na Nikawa Muislamu* (no date) used in the section Use of the Bible to Refute Christianity of this chapter.

Muhammad in the Bible

> Deuteronomy 18:18a: 'I will raise up for them a prophet like you from among their own people'.

The Apostle named here without doubt is Prophet Muhammad (s.a.w.) nor is it Jesus as the Christians claim. The kin of the Jews are the Arabs.

The prophet Moses was more of an example for Prophet Muhammad than Jesus. If we look at a number of examples:

(a) Prophet Moses was born with a mother and a father as Prophet Muhammad, but Jesus was born without a father.
(b) Both Prophet Moses and Prophet Muhammad were married and gave birth to children, but Jesus did not marry.
(c) Both Prophet Moses and Prophet Muhammad were accepted by their people when they were alive, Jesus was rejected and until today he is rejected by his people the Jews.
(d) Both Prophet Moses and Prophet Muhammad were Apostles and rulers but Jesus announced that he himself was only an Apostle.
(e) Prophet Moses and Prophet Muhammad brought new laws to lead their people but Jesus came to fulfil the laws that Prophet Moses brought.

(Ngariba & Kawemba 1987: 12–13)

Jesus is not the Son of God

One of the few signs that are brought by Christians concerning the Divinity of Jesus is that he was born without a father. I would like to remind you that Adam was born without father or mother. Adam did not suckle milk by any person at all, nor did Adam experience childhood. So, who is it that was created in a more amazing way? Jesus or Adam? So, should we call Adam to be an essence of God because he was not born with a father and mother as we were born?

When we read the Bible, Hebrews 7:3 we see that there was Melchizedek who had no father, no mother, no parents, no beginning of his days, nor end of his life, but he is likened to the Son of God.

If Adam was born without father or mother, likewise Melchizedek, what is so surprising about Jesus being born with only a mother?

Jesus was not God, nor was he the second person of God because even his disciples confirm this thing by saying:

> 'Children of Israel listen to these words: You yourselves know that Jesus of Nazareth was among you as a person that was witnessed to by God himself, by acts of great power, by miracles and by signs that God did by his hand.' Acts 2:22

Following from this testimony that we have read here, it is difficult to agree that Jesus is not a prophet rather that he is the second person of God.

These are the reasons that made me begin to have very many doubts concerning the truth of the teaching of the religion of Christianity.

(Kanoni nd: 24)

Prayer [From: The Five Pillars of Islam in the Bible]

To Remove Shoes
When Muslims enter any holy place, such as the mosque, they remove their shoes, unlike the Christians when they enter Churches and there they wear shoes.

References given Qur'an Sura 20:11–12; Exodus 3:3–6; Joshua 5:13–15

Musa and Joshua were both told to remove their shoes when they stood on holy ground. This rule is followed by Muslims and is broken by Christians.

Ablutions
Almighty God told Prophet Muhammad in the Qur'an 5:7; Exodus 30:17–21

The followers of Jesus were expected to follow the rules that Moses gave as Jesus himself said: Matthew 5:17–20; John 13:5–11

For Moses and Jesus ablutions were essential. Muslims follow this tradition each time that they say their prayers. Christians make absolutely no effort.

Prostration
To prostrate during prayers is a part of Muslim prayers. But present day Christians have abandoned this completely. Let us see what Moses and Jesus and the other messengers did.

> Moses in Exodus 34:8–9;
>
> Solomon in 2 Chronicles 7:3;
>
> Jesus in Matthew 26:38–44;
>
> Jesus 'fell onto the ground' when he prayed, it has the meaning of to prostrate before Almighty God.
>
> Almighty God said in Qur'an 48:29

Revelation 7:1–4

The mark on the forehead is that *sijida* that is named in the Qur'an.

It is absolutely clear that it was necessary for the followers of Moses and Jesus to follow there actions. Therefore when one prays it is essntial to prostate until one's forehead touches the earth. These things are done by Muslims and forgotten by Christians.

(Ngariba & Kawemba 1987: 20–25)

Paul's misleading of believers

The question still remains, 'Who came to plant bad seeds after Jesus Christ?' There are two people who claimed apostleship after Jesus. These are St. Paul four years after Jesus, and Prophet Muhammad about 600 years later.

Paul

Paul was not one of the Companions of Jesus. He greatly persecuted Jesus in his time. Four years after the departure of Jesus, Paul claimed to have seen Jesus in a dream and that he wanted him to go and preach to those who were not Jews. Here again Paul claimed the Apostleship of the people of the Nations.

[The following passages are then quoted: Romans 11:13; 1 Corinthians 2:1–2; Philippians 2:5–7; 1 Timothy 3:14–16; Titus 2:13–14.]

If Paul calls Jesus 'Great God' what will he call his Father who is in heaven? Well let us see what Jesus says in John 14:28. 'You heard me say to you, 'I am going to my place, and again I am coming to you.' If you loved me, you would rejoice that I am going to the Father, because the Father is greater than I.'

This shows that Jesus was born by the command of Almighty God like any other creature and he will die in order to return to Almighty God like other humans.

(Ngariba & Kawemba 1987: 8–10)

Inconsistencies found in the Bible

'What Does It Mean to Call Jesus 'Son'?'

When I was discussing with a certain leader of the Christian religion concerning the second person of the Godhead, that is Jesus, that leader showed me a certain part in the Bible where it was written 'God-Son'. And resulting from this testimony, all Christians believe that Jesus is God's Son and that he is the second person of the Godhead.

To tell the truth, this word 'God-Son' as it is shown in the Bible is a counterfeit word that is inserted only in the Bible. This word is inserted on purpose in order that that desire of theirs to raise up Jesus should succeed. This word 'God-Son' was not in the old Bible, this word was only added in the Bible of these days.

In the Bible that was printed in 1945

> John 1:18 is written: 'The only son that is in the Father's breast.'

But in the Bible that was printed in 1950

> John 1:18 is written: 'God the only Son that is in the Father's breast.'

I think that you will see that the old Bible does not know this word 'God-Son', rather it only knows the word 'Son'. When in this time of light when many of the people are aware, these writers are able to dare to change the Bible and to write words that are able to mislead their followers, so then, how many changes that are greater than this were able to be changed by these writers in the time of darkness? No doubt today's Bible is filled with many things that are not the truth, which were added according to the inclination of those writers.

That way, this word 'God-Son' is not the word of truth; rather it is a 'counterfeit' word. It was only added so that they could dare to make the lie of their faith that has no foundation, that of the Holy Trinity.

(Kanoni nd: 22–23)

CHAPTER 11

The African Christian and Islamic Mysticism: Folk Islam

David W. Shenk

Brisk trade winds blew onshore the July day in 1963 when my wife, Grace, and I arrived at the Mogadiscio airport in Somalia. Our children, two-year-old Karen and two-month-old Doris, accompanied us. Tangy Indian Ocean breezes played about us as we crossed the tarmac to the tight and crowded immigration counters. One word repeatedly intruded into the bedlam of jostling voices: Allah! During the next hour as we pressed through the meandering immigration maze, I believe I heard the name of God more often than during the whole of my previous twenty-six years.

Then a porter discerned that we were members of the Somalia Mennonite Mission (SMM). Appreciatively he exclaimed above the cacophony of voices, 'Then you must be a *wadaad*! Aren't you a wadaad?' (This is a man of holiness and piety who leads others in the ways of piety.) The porter had revealed to the throngs in the airport immigration area that a Christian wadaad had arrived in Somalia.

God Awareness Everywhere!

Our airport introduction impressed on us that the Somali people were pervasively spiritual. God awareness penetrated every nook of their lives. And they were indeed Muslim. The two million Somalis were proud of their Islamic identity. I learned more about that drinking tea with men. Within days of our arrival one of my first Somali acquaintances introduced me to the evening tea-drinking institution. After the heat of the day was safely past, the streets filled with gossipers who sat at tea tables lining the street sides enjoying the evening ocean breezes as they chatted. In those days phones were uncommon, but the tea table oral grapevine took news across the city of a quarter million with an efficiency that the twenty-first century internet cannot duplicate. I suppose that within hours of our arrival to join the SMM team the tea-table network had spread the word across the city that another Somalia Mennonite Mission teacher had arrived in town.

Most often the tea-drinking conversations tuned into spiritual, religious or political concerns. My companions explained to me that they welcomed the SMM schools. I was delighted. In subsequent conversations I was further informed that no Somali would ever become a Christian because all Somalis were born Muslim and because all trace their genealogy back to the Prophet Muhammad, the blood of the prophet courses through the veins of every Somali.

Sufi Spirituality

Those conversations inaugurated me into Somali spirituality, which was significantly formed by Sufism. The Sufis are the mystics of Islam; their quest is to experience God (Azeemi 2005: 51). The movement, which has roots in early Islamic history, first developed in Baghdad two centuries after Muhammad's *hijra* from Mecca to Medina. It was a syncretistic movement, weaving together mystical inclinations within the Qur'an as well as Hindu, Buddhist, Christian, Gnostic and Neo-Platonic spirituality. Occasionally the Sufi movement has had a bumpy ride in relationship to Islamic orthodoxy. At the beginning of the movement al Hallaj, a Sufi saint, was crucified for claiming the possibility of becoming the incarnation of divine presence. The same tensions infected Somalia when in 1909 at Biyolay a Sufi Saint, Sheikh Uways, was martyred with twenty-six of his disciples. The Sufi tension with orthodoxy is rooted within a paradox within the Qur'an between an insistence that there can be no fellowship between

God and humankind (*tanzih*) (Qur'an: Ikhlas: 112) and the doctrine of friendship with God (*awilya*) (Qur'an: al-Maida: 5:53–54; Jonah: 10:63).

There were several Sufi orders in Somalia, as there are across Africa. The most pervasive order in Somalia was the Qadiriya, which was founded by Abd al Qadir al Jilani in Baghdad in the twelfth century.

Sufism is not a sideshow within Somali Islam. All Somalis were in some way formed by Sufi spirituality. I learned that the repeated references to Allah in conversation are rooted in the Sufi commitment to remembering God as commanded in the Qur'an. 'Ye who believe! Let not your riches divert you from the remembrance of God. If any act thus, the loss is their own' (Qur'an: Munafiqun: 43:9). This means that every area of life should be permeated with the remembrance of God! (Fadiman and Frager 1997: 15–16). No wonder God-talk permeated not only the airport but every area of Somali life! Of course, Sufi piety pervades not only Somali Islam but much of African Islam.

Saints and Pilgrimage

Those tea-table conversations gave me an idea. If Sufism is a response to the yearning of Muslims to experience God, could it be that the gospel is the fulfilment of the Sufi quest? As a young missionary in my twenties, I began to explore Sufism. Early on, I wrote to B.W. Andrzejewski, a Catholic Polish anthropologist who had done ethnographic studies of the Somali people. He was a professor at the School of Oriental and African Studies at the University of London.

I asked the professor, 'What are the bridges for the Gospel within Somali Islam?' Andrzejewski wrote back saying, 'Give attention to Somali Sufism. That is the bridge.' He also sent me a fifty-page pamphlet he had published on Somali Sufism (1974). That pamphlet significantly formed my approach to bearing witness to Christ within Somali Sufi-permeated Islam. Andrzejewski was especially impressed with the role of intercessory saints in Somali Islam.

My primary instructors, however, were the Somali people. From them I learned the significance of the intercessory saints. Each Somali clan had their own local saint, and clan identity was nurtured in an annual pilgrimage to the *zawiya* (tomb of a saint) of the local saint. On two occasions, I accompanied Somali friends on their pilgrimage to the zawiya of their clan. The two pilgrimages were to the tombs of saints within the Qadiriya system.

Each local saint was connected to the Prophet Muhammad and the founding saint of the order through a double chain of spiritual authority. The first link to spiritual authority was the *silsila* (chain), which was the genealogical descent from the eponym of the Sufi order. The second link was the mystical *isnad* (connection) through which hidden mysteries have been transmitted down through the generations and become incarnated within the local saint.

One of those pilgrimages took us to a quite remote village of about five hundred inhabitants, who were subsistence agriculturalists with a number of semi-nomadic camel herders. I suppose a couple of thousand pilgrims were in town, some of whom had travelled hundreds of miles through the Somali acacia scrub lands to participate in this annual homecoming. The pilgrims walked together to the site of the tomb, about a mile outside the village. At the tomb, people repeated *dhikr* (remembrances) of God by repeating Allah or other names for God from the 99 names that all Somalis would know. They repetitively chanted the names of Muhammad and Abdulqadir and other saints. People entering the tomb area took dust from the grave and sprinkled it upon their bodies. Others wrote prayers of petition on scraps of paper and tied them to the trees. Finally, the pilgrims began the trek back to the village where animals were sacrificed. On the walk, I was told that pilgrims often shared accounts of blessings they had received through the intercessory powers of their saint.

At nightfall the people began feasting and dancing to rhythmic tunes and chant around a fire. I understand that the singing and dancing continued well into the night.

Lamin Sanneh describes a similar experience of all night prayer, Qur'anic recitations and singing around a bonfire in his boyhood town in the Gambia. These events were organized by the Sufi leadership in his home community 4,500 miles west of Somalia! (1996: 156–158). Surely, such gatherings happen across the continent wherever Sufi spirituality prevails.

As we began our journey home, I asked, 'Is our pilgrimage to the Sheikh's tomb faithful to Islam?' A friend chose his words carefully as he responded,

> We know this is not faithful to Islam. However, we desperately need the baraka (blessing) of God. But we cannot get into the presence of God with our petitions and pleas for blessing because we have done some sins. We need an intercessor. Our saint was a very holy man. When he lived he demonstrated that he possessed true spiritual strength for he performed some miracles. He also knows us for he lived among us. We believe that he is at the door of Muhammad. Muhammad is at the door of God. So we petition our saint who knows us well beseeching him to bring our prayers to Muhammad who takes our prayers to God. Through our local saint, Muhammad can become our advocate and intercessor.

The Gospel and Intercession

When, I asked whether my companions would like to hear what the gospel message says about intercession, they were eager to hear. I pointed out that in the Qur'an we read that there can be no intercessor unless God has appointed the intercessor. We read, 'None shall have the power of intercession, but such a one as has received permission from God most gracious' (Qur'an: Maryam: 19:87). This means that we need to discern whom God has appointed as intercessor. The gospel (*Injeel*) reveals that God has appointed the Messiah as the one true intercessor.

At a later time, I told my host that the Injeel reveals to us, 'The Lord has sworn and will not change his mind: you (the Messiah) are a priest forever' (Bible: Hebrews 7:21). The reasons God has appointed the Messiah as intercessor are because (1) he understands us fully; (2) he is without sin; (3) he gave his life as the sacrificial offering for our sin; (4) he is indestructible for he has risen from the dead; (5) he lives forever (Bible: Hebrews 7:23–28). Because God has appointed Jesus the Messiah as our priest and intercessor forever, Christians pray to God in the name of Jesus the Messiah. This is how Jesus taught his disciples to pray when he was in his earthly ministries. He promised, 'The Father (God) will give you whatever you ask in my name!' (Bible: John 15:16). So I shared several recent ways in which I had experienced God moving in response to prayer in the name of Jesus the Messiah.

My companions were impressed, and one asked for an opportunity to learn more about the ministry of the Messiah as intercessor. Imagine what book of the Bible I used for that study. Hebrews, of course. This scripture is remarkably relevant to the Sufi worldview and the spiritual realities that Sufis quest.

Intercessory prayer is only one dimension of the priestly work of Christ, yet it is a very significant dimension. For example, at the Somalia Mennonite Mission intermediate school that I was directing we experienced a crisis when the water pump in the school well broke down. For about two weeks, we struggled to repair that pump and finally decided that we would give our efforts one more day. If not successful, we would close the school until we could install a new pump. At about midnight, we were ready to give the starter cord a pull. Students from the dormitories crowded around the pump house eager to know if school would have to close. Just before I pulled the starter cord, a student stepped to the front and interjected, 'We have heard that the Injeel reveals that we have authority to pray in the name of Jesus the Messiah. So we have all consulted and decided that you should not pull that starter rope until you have prayed right now in the name of the Messiah that the pump will work.'

What a quandary! It was against the law to propagate Christianity. We had been praying in our homes. But this was a demand for public prayer with Muslim students crowding around us so we had no alternative. I led in prayer in the name of Jesus who is our intercessor, asking that if this was in harmony with God's good will for us, God would touch that pump so that we might have water. We pulled the starter cord. The pump sprang to life and pumped volumes of water; it served the school for some years with no further problems. The pump incident invited a lot of searching conversations about the intercessory ministry of Jesus.

The Quest for Baraka

The Sufi quest for effective intercession permeates African Muslim spirituality. Central to the quest for intercessors is a yearning for authentic power and *baraka* (blessing). In the broadest sense, baraka is peace and well-being (Sanneh 1996: 169–171). The purpose of life is to acquire baraka. *Peace is Everything*, the title of a provocative book by David Maranz, says it well. Maranz, who explores the worldview of the Muslims and traditionalists in Senegambia, insists that all the religious and Islamic themes converge into one overriding quest—peace (1993).

Baraka is a gift given by those who are empowered. Baraka always flows from the top down, never the other way around. No *murid* (disciple) can give baraka to his mentor; only the mentor can transmit baraka to his disciple (Sanneh 1996: 170–171). Sufis believe that empowerment comes from the inner secret baraka that Muhammad enjoyed and that came to him through the mediation of the angel Gabriel in the process of revealing the Qur'an. These began in the cave at Mount Hira outside Mecca. A further most significant step in Muhammad's empowerment was the *mi'raj*, a mysterious night-time journey he took from Mecca to Jerusalem and then into the seventh heaven into the presence of God. Muhammad's ascent into the seventh heaven is viewed by many Sufis as a demonstration of the goal of the murid to ascend stage by stage through the seven steps necessary for absorption into the divine presence (Trimingham 1971: 208–210). Muhammad in his experiences of divine presence has become the supreme pathfinder, leading his devotees into the experience of the presence God (Yusuf Ali 1968: 691–93).

It is not surprising that the respective chains of blessing are so important. Each one has its origin in Muhammad, and devotees have passed it on from generation to generation. Sufi mystics stress that absorption into the intercessor is essential to acquiring the incarnation of baraka. The murid must lose his identity becuse he is devotedly absorbed into the person of his sheikh. The sheikh is one who has experienced personal annihilation because he has been absorbed into the Prophet Muhammad, who has been absorbed into the presence of God (Mirahmadi & Mirahmadi 2005: 65).

This Sufi quest for absorption leaps over the obstacles to experiencing God that both Islam and traditional African religion place before the devout worshipper. The obstacles are formidable. For example, the philosophers of traditional non-Islamic African religion assert that God the creator has gone away and will never return. There are hundreds of myths across the African continent about this God who has left us with no prospect of a reversal of this loss (Mbiti 1970: 177). Even orthodox Islam cannot address this loss, for in Islam God is the one who transcends us and who never meets us. He sends his instructions down to us, but he never comes down to encounter us. God never comes down to save us. He is never affected by us (Cragg 1984: 102–105). This is the reason Islam denies that Jesus was crucified. A sovereign God would never leave the Messiah to suffer on the cross. So in both Islam and African Traditional Religion God is not engaged with us in our plight. There is no God as the Good Shepherd seeking his lost sheep in either African Traditional Religion or in Islam.

Consequently, other ways to acquire empowerment for baraka must be found. For the Sufis it is the sheikh-intercessor. For traditional religionists it is the shaman. Within many regions of Africa the shaman and the sheikh-intercessor roles have been united. In West Africa that unification of the two is the *marabout*. He is the one who has incarnated the baraka and authority of the Qur'an. He is privy to the inner secrets of the Sufi saint. Furthermore he incarnates the powers of the spirits and divinities of the ancestors. Maranz lists some ninety-six powers and forces that need to be manipulated to effect the peace (Maranz 1993: 183–185). The marabouts are the experts in manipulation, which gives them enormous power for either good or evil. The adherent must obey the wishes of his marabout. Otherwise, the marabout will strike his adherent with disaster.

Recently when my wife and I were hosted by churches in Senegambia and Burkina Faso, we met with members for after-church conversation. We always asked, 'Why have you become Christians?' With no exception members responded, 'Because Jesus has broken the power of the marabout.' It is ironic that the marabout, who claim expertise in manipulating the powers in ways that bring baraka, actually bring bondage and fear into the lives of those who venerate them.

Exploring an entirely different context, that of North America, Sayyid Nurjan Mirahmadi insists that the devotee who is seeking baraka must lose his personal identity as his ego is surrendered into his spiritual adviser, the sheikh. The marabout, likewise, demands complete loyalty. In contrast to these themes of ego and personal negation, Christ is experienced as the one who delivers from all powers offering abundant grace and salvation. Believers in Jesus receive the triumph of Christ over the powers as assurance that the peace of Christ prevails over all powers, including those of the marabout. Furthermore, Jesus Christ does not annihilate the person; on the contrary, Christ offers abundant and everlasting personal life.

Experiencing the Presence of God

As mentioned, the remembrance of God is a companion theme to intercession in the quest for God. Islam proclaims that God is closer to us than the jugular vein. But closeness to God does not mean knowing God. In Islam God reveals his qualities, but he does not reveal his essence, for God does not meet us. In his compassion, God sends his will down, but he does not come down to save us. We cannot meet God or know God personally. This reality enshrined in Islamic understanding of God is a perplexity for the Sufis.

The Sufi quest is to experience God. That is the function of dhikr, the remembrance of God by the recitation of his names. The Sufi quest is bolstered by several themes within the Qur'an.

First, nature is described as the *ayat* (signs) of God. Surely this means that creation is a sign pointing us toward an experience of the Creator.

Second, Abraham is described as a *wali* (friend) of God. One can only be a friend with a person who is known, a person whose presence one can experience. Surely this means that God can be experienced.

Third, Moses is described as a prophet with whom God spoke! Speech is the vehicle for experiencing a person (Qur'an: A'raf: 7:144).

The Sufis have built upon these themes to develop a philosophy that pursues the possibility of experiencing God. A foremost dimension of that quest is dhikr, the remembrance of God. For the pious, this might mean only the repetition of the ninety-nine names of God using the beads of the *tasbih* (Muslim rosary of ninety-nine beads). But the devout Sufi will go beyond this, and the breathing and chanting techniques they use when they perform dhikr induces trance-like experiences.

This type of Sufi Islam was practised in the Qadiriya mosque on the block where we lived in Nairobi, Kenya, after our family had to leave Somalia in 1973 because of a socialist nationalization of all SMM programmes. Every Thursday night our Muslim neighbours went to the mosque for dhikr. The congregation gathered and began the hypnotic chants of remembrance of God, their prophet Muhammad and their respective saint. They swayed as they wafted coloured flags in a room filled with the burning incense. They focused on the sheikh, who was leading this remembrance exercise. Occasionally they stopped chanting to drink tea and chewed *khat*.[1] The worship went until about midnight until the participants were in a state of trance-induced absorption into the universal.

Sayyid Nurjan describes this state of absorption into the universal in this way:

> The Shaykh becomes, in our hearts, the mirror of the Absolute Essence. If we are successful in this, we reach the state of self-effacement—absence from the world of the senses. To the degree that this state increases in us, our attachment to the world of senses will weaken and disappear, and we will come into the Station of Absolute Void—not sensing anything other than God (Mirahmadi & Mirahmadi 2005: 65–66).

Jalal al-Din Rumi writes winsomely of the Sufi quest in ways that have attracted the attention of the New Age movement in the West. True to the essence of the Sufi quest, his spirituality upholds the submersion of the person within the Universal. Here is just one glimpse into the Sufi quest as described by Rumi:

---

1. Also known as *Miraa* (*Catha edulis*), a stimulant and hallucinogen.

> If you could get rid of yourself just once,
> The secret of secrets would open to you.
> The face of the unknown, hidden beyond the universe,
> Would appear on the mirror of your perception.
> (Fadiman & Frager 1997: 224)

The process of spiritual ascension into the state of self-annihilation within the divine presence is demanding indeed. Many Sufi teachers describe seven levels within the self, each of which must be transcended stage by stage in the ascent to pure spirituality. Fadiman and Frager describe these stages as follows: Commanding Self, Regretful Self, Inspired Self, Contented Self, Pleasing Self, Self Pleasing to God, Pure Self. The role of the Sufi 'path finder' is to guide the murid through these stages (Fadiman & Frager 1997: 20–22).

However, in Rumi's writings, as well as in the mainstream of Sufi spirituality, we are hard pressed to discern even hints of the I-Thou encounter of biblical theism. Although God as friend is the expressed quest of the Sufi movement, in reality the quest to experience God has taken the devotee direction similar to that of Brahmanism in India in which the person seeks to become absorbed into the universe rather than in the direction of embracing the God who loves us and offers the gift of forgiveness and reconciliation. Sufis speak of experiencing God, not of knowing God or of relating to God as our loving heavenly Father. The gospel of reconciliation can be astonishingly good news for the Sufi quester, precisely because reconciliation with God is so much more than Sufi philosophers have dared dream as a possibility.

The Sheikh as Pathfinder

As noted, the intercessor intercedes so that his devotees might receive baraka. However, in the dhikr routines the devotee is seeking not only blessing but also absorption into the Universal. Only the sheikh can lead his disciple into this demanding spiritual formation, which means he is the pathfinder. His way is known as the *tariqa* (the way). Each Sufi sheikh promulgates his distinctive tariqa, which he has acquired from his eponym founder. The devotees of a sheikh and his tariqa are not isolated individuals. They are part of a community, which is also called tariqa. This community, which is led by the sheikh, is a discipling community that provides devotees with the inner spiritual insights of their respective tariqa and sheikh. The tariqas are alternative communities of piety within the larger Muslim umma (community).

A central theme in all the tariqas is that Muhammad has been absorbed into the Universal Presence and so have the eponymous saints. The goal of the murid is to become absorbed into his sheikh, thereby experiencing personal annihilation. This movement is akin to Hindu Brahmanism and Gnosticism. As I engaged with this Sufi dimension of the Muslim movement in East Africa, I often grieved, for the movement robbed people of the integrity of their personal identity. The eventual dementia that addiction to khat created within some devotees of East African Sufism was a tragic waste of human potential.

Christ the Way

In the context of Sufism, we sought to bear witness that in Christ we meet God in ways that are genuinely life-giving and respectful of the integrity of the person. The respective tariqas are quite often in competition with each other; devotees seek for the tariqa that allegedly offers the most baraka. The same reality informs responses to the invitation of Christ and the church. People will most often develop interest in the gospel because of a perception that Christ and the church offer a more abundant life than is true of the Muslim umma or the tariqas.

I became increasingly convinced that the triune revelation of God within the New Testament is a revelation that fulfils the Sufi quest for experiencing God. The triune God offers salvation and abundant life, not debilitating spiritual practises. This reality was most persuasively expressed in the life of the church, which demonstrates the presence of the abundant life offered in Christ.

Let me illustrate. When we moved to Nairobi from Somalia we deliberately choose to live on Eighth Street in the Eastleigh section of the city on the same block as the Sufi Qadiriya mosque. We rented a five-apartment complex that facilitated the development of an international and inter-ethnic team of believers in Jesus Christ. We were a Christian alternative community, a discipling community for new believers. We were a missionary community that was in some ways analogous to the mosque tariqa, which was an Islamic discipling and missionary community. We had baptisms as a covenant sign of membership; the Sufi tariqa had their membership covenant ceremonies. We served the community in a variety of ways, but especially with a reading room for students; in time we developed a well-rounded community centre that nowadays touches a thousand Muslims a week. The Holy Spirit brought into being a community of Muslim background believers in Jesus.

We always had a lively engagement with the mosque-based Qadiriya tariqa. Occasionally we ate with the leaders of the Sufi mosque and had dialogical encounters. When the imam became ill, I would visit him, lay hands on him, and pray in the name of Jesus the Messiah for his healing.

Then one day after the Friday sermon a friend came straight from the mosque to our home. He was very agitated and, standing in our doorway, he shouted at me,

> 'This must stop! Teaching polytheism cannot continue on this street.'
>
> I responded, 'I don't know what you are shouting about.'
>
> 'Trinity!' he exploded. 'You must stop teaching that there are three gods.'
>
> 'Oh!' I said. 'Trinity is not about three gods. Rather Trinity means that you and I should love one another.'
>
> 'How can that be?' he interjected with a touch of surprise.
>
> I continued, 'Trinity means that within God there is loving fellowship and communion. But God does not hold his love to himself. Rather he extends his love to us. He has done this supremely in Jesus the Messiah. In his outstretched hands on the cross when he was crucified we see the fullness of God's

redemptive and reconciling love revealed. Outstretched hands are for embrace and reconciliation. Jesus, the Messiah God, in his great love invites us to be forgiven and reconciled to God. Through the Holy Spirit, God empowers us to be transformed so that we might receive and express God's love. So God as Trinity is God who loves. He is our creator, our loving heavenly Father. God is Redeemer who has entered human history in Jesus the Messiah. God is also Holy Spirit who lives within all true believers empowering us to participate in and express God's love.

My friend was amazed. He exclaimed, 'That is wonderful. So Trinity means that we should love as God loves. That is surprising!'

Thereafter this young man always referred to me as dear brother David when he would meet me on the street.

Church Engaged with Tariqa Communities

The Sufi tariqas were recognized as communities of peace and piety who were questing for absorption into divine presence. The Christ-centred tariqa we developed in Nairobi was a community reflecting the triune reconciling love of God.

In due course, a companion Christian centre was formed in Garissa in the vast Somali Muslim North East Province of Kenya. The Somalis who inhabited this region were mostly camel-herding nomads. Canadian and Kenyan leadership of this visionary centre worked with a Saalihiya tariqa in the remote northern border regions of Kenya. They met with the sheikh sharing with him their vision to develop a Christian tariqa in Garissa. He most obligingly gave counsel on how to proceed. The architecture of the Garissa tariqa was analogous to that of the Saalihiya tariqa, and the daily routines emulated that of the Saalihiya. Yet the essence of the two communities was different. The Sufi tariqa sought baraka through absorption into divine presence; the Christian tariqa was formed and sustained through the reconciling love of Christ and the empowerment of the Holy Spirit.

The Sufi tariqas were always alternative communities to the mainstream ethos of the Muslim ummah. They were usually communities of peace within the turbulent ethos of Somali Islam. An exception is the Saalihiya led by Sheikh Mahamad 'Abdille Hassan. At the turn of the twentieth century, he and his Saalihiya associates initiated a jihad against British rule in northern Somalia. For him the demands of justice overpowered the claims of peace, especially because he feared that British rule would open the door for conversions to the Christian faith. The wars continued for two decades, with a third of the Somali inhabitants of the north killed. The war expanded beyond primary conflict with the British to fighting against all Somalis who did not embrace the Saalihiya vision promulgated by the sheikh (Lewis 1961: 226–227).

The violence of the Somali Saalihiya is exceptional. Even in the turbulence of Somalia in the last two decades, the various tariqa communities have generally maintained their pacifist inclinations. We grieve, as do the sheikhs who lead the tariqas, that in recent months a number of the tariqas in southern Somalia have decided to arm for self-defence against the violence of the jihadist al Shabaab who vow to attack all expressions of Islam that they do not deem true to Muhammad's sunna (teachings and conduct).

It is not only in eastern Africa that the tariqas have been communities of peace. Lamin Sanneh describes the Jakhanke clerics of Senegambia as an authentic expression of non-violent pacifist Islam (1989). My judgment is that the Sufi tariqas generally contribute to providing space for emerging church within the ethos of the Muslim *umma* and the Dar al Islam. They do this by modelling ways that alternative communities can thrive within mainstream Islam; they salt the society with pacifist ideals that mitigate the harshness of potentially jihadist Islam.

I have stressed that the piety and prayer patterns for the Sufi movements are intended to eventually annihilate personhood as the devotee becomes absorbed into the divine presence. Facilitating that process is an incarnational theology that views Muhammad as the incarnation light, the true light that enlightens the whole world (Trimingham 1971: 161). The authority of the sheikh is derived from his inculcation of that Muhammadan light. The devotees press in to be enveloped and absorbed by that light.

The Christian tariqas in Nairobi and Garissa were also communities of prayer and peace. These communities were centred in Christ, who is the incarnational presence of God. These Christian prayer movements quested for the infilling of the Holy Spirit. He never obliterates personality, but rather recreates the person in freedom to be all that God intends. The Holy Spirit empowers to serve the community in ways that redeems and recreates people. The Holy Spirit convicts of sin and empowers for righteous living. The Christian community is a fellowship of reconciliation and forgiveness centred in Christ. Both the Eastleigh and Garissa Christian communities were recognized within the wider Islamic milieu as congregations of service, reconciliation, and peacemaking.

Over the nearly four decades, since it was first envisioned, the Garissa Christian tariqa has gone through a number of transformations. In recent years, one of the people engaged in that early vision has joined a small Christian intercessory prayer team who minister in prayer for the healing of the Somali people. The Somali population of the region has been tragically traumatized by the wars that have ravaged their clans for over two decades. This small team of intercessors minister day-by-day in prayer for the healing of persons and healing of a nation. Muslims come to this centre requesting prayer. As they are touched with the healing miracle of the touch of the grace of God, occasionally persons report seeing visions of Jesus the Great Physician. These revelations open hearts to the reality that the power for authentic healing is not 'possessed' by Christian saints who have baraka. Rather it is the gift of God revealed in and effected through the ministry of Jesus the Messiah.

The prayer ministry in the name of Jesus the Messiah is analogous to the ministry of Mahzar Mallouhi among Middle Eastern Muslims. He is a prolific writer who casts Jesus within a Sufi spirituality that sees linkages between the Qur'anic Jesus and the Jesus of the Gospels. His reflections on a Sufi reading of Jesus in the Gospel of John have been noteworthy. Likewise the prayer ministry team in Garissa take the stance that Jesus is not a possession that Christians can capture for themselves, but rather that he belongs also within the Muslim community (Chandler 2007).

Bearing Witness to Christ in Ethiopia

Bedru Hussein Muktar describes the progress of the Gospel as a prayer movement among the Hadiya people of Ethiopia. Like the peoples of Senegambia where the *marabouts* integrated the powers of sheikh and shaman, the Hadiya integrated Sufi and occult powers. As Islam was introduced, they simply added Allah to their traditional divinities. The advance of Islam in many African societies is accompanied with the advance of demon possession. Islam claims the power to free from the demons, yet the affliction of demon possession seems to accompany the cure. The energies of the society went into placating and manipulating occult powers and divinities with the fearsome possibility of demon possession lurking in the shadows. Consequently, the indicators of modern progress such as agricultural development or education languished. Infant mortality was horrendously high.

Then the Lord spoke in a vision to evangelist Tesfaye Makango commanding him to go to Korga within the region inhabited by the Hadiya. The vision revealed that Korga was in the centre of a war zone between clans. The Lord commanded him to take the gospel of peace and reconciliation to these people. Friends who knew the region warned that he would likely be killed. Nevertheless, he set out immediately with only the clothing he was wearing and a light blanket. Days later, he arrived and discovered a small intercessory prayer group meeting in the home of a woman believer. A young girl was present who was possessed of a demon. In the name of Jesus Christ, the demon fled. From that moment, the battle was joined. The proclamation of the gospel throughout the region was accompanied by miraculous healings and demon exorcisms. They also encountered much opposition to the gospel.

Then a leading Sufi sheikh saw a vision in which a river of healing water was pouring from his home. He went immediately to the evangelist to seek for the One who produces this life-giving water and learned that the water was a metaphor of the Holy Spirit. He emerged as a key leader and prophet within the Christian movement. Occasionally entire Muslim mosque congregations have turned to Christ. Consequently, some mosques have been transformed into become church buildings where congregations of believers in Jesus Christ now gather for worship.

As the gospel prospered among Hadiya there was enormous uplift. Healthy rainfall patterns developed. Cattle ceased aborting their young. Schools replaced occult shrines. People turned to Christ rather than occult talismans for healing. The wars stopped. The churches that spread among the people were communities of healing and reconciliation (Muktar 2005: 407–411).

Dreams and Visions

The dream of the Sufi sheikh of the Hadiya people was significant in his conversion to Christ and his becoming an emerging leader within the Christian movement. Dreams and visions are an exceedingly prominent phenomena within the Sufi communities (Trimingham: 1971: 190–192). Probably this goes back to Muhammad himself who claimed that the angel Gabriel would appear to him. The Sufi movements are laced with accounts of dreams inspiring and leading the aspirants of the eponymous sheikh. It is, therefore, not surprising that there are recurrent accounts of the risen Messiah meeting Muslims. Such visions are powerfully persuasive.

On a recent visit to Ethiopia, an evangelist described how Christ is appearing to Muslim sheikhs. His appearance is brilliant, often like the sun. He emanates pure love. And his instructions are uniform: meet a Christian evangelist and invite him or her to explain the gospel more fully to you. This is remarkably similar to what Saul experienced on the Damascus Road. In that case, the Lord arranged for Saul to meet Ananias. So in these regions of Ethiopia the sheikhs are seeking out evangelists to hear from them their witness to Jesus as Lord and Saviour. I was told that occasionally these converted sheikhs share with their congregations what has transpired. Occasionally the entire mosque community decides to convert. Consequently, the gospel is being preached in several mosques. Evangelists are quite occupied indeed in discipling these new congregations of believers in Jesus.

Ahmed Ali Haile: I Have Come Home

At present, I am working with Ahmed Ali Haile in writing his memoirs. For the last four decades he has been an indefatigable ambassador of the gospel of peace within the Somali world. He describes his growing up years in central Somalia and the many ways his Sufi-influenced Muslim community and family planted yearnings in his soul that were fulfilled when he met Christ. For example, every year his father would select a perfect newborn lamb and give it special care for a year. When the Muslim world was on the annual pilgrimage to Mecca, he would kill the lamb as a sacrificial offering. He would take the blood and sprinkle the lentel and doorposts of their home. They would eat the lamb together, beseeching God's protection upon their family. As a child, Ahmed often wondered what this could mean, what sign of truth was in the sacrifice of these lambs.

Then when Ahmed was fifteen and recuperating from a bad attack of malaria, a Christian nurse gave him a portion of the Bible to read. For the next two years he studied that book privately. Then one day he prayed that God would open his heart to the truth and was instantly touched by the Holy Spirit, who implanted within him the seed of saving faith. As he continued exploring the Scriptures, he came to believe that the annual sacrifice of the lamb in his home was a sign preparing him to believe in and receive the sacrifice of Christ, the Lamb of God, who gave his life in the cross for our forgiveness and redemption.

In regard to his journey of faith, Ahmed says, 'I will never speak critically of Islam, for the Islam of my community and family, prepared me to believe the gospel!' He adds:

> When I believed in Jesus and became a member of the church, I knew that I had finally come home. My spiritual quest was fulfilled.
>
> My home in Christ is like a Somali nomadic hut. The centre pole is Christ crucified and risen. The ribbing is each of us who have believed. We need to bond together around the centre pole. The matting over the hut is the grace of Jesus

Christ who covers us and provides salvation and security. I have indeed come home!

References

Andrzejewski, B.W. 1974. The Veneration of Sufi Saints and Its Impact on the Oral Literature of the Somali People and On Their Literature in Arabic. *African Language Studies* XV. London: The School of Oriental and African Studies, University of London.

Azeemi, K.S. 2005. *Muraqaba: The Art and Science of Sufi Meditation.* Houston: Plato Publishing.

Chandler, P.G. 2007. *Pilgrims of Christ on the Muslim Road: Exploring a New Path between Two Faiths.* Lanham: Rowman & Littlefield Publishers, Inc.

Cragg, K. 1984. *Muhammad & the Christian: A Question of Response.* Maryknoll: Orbis.

Fadiman, J. & Frager, R. 1997. *Essential Sufism.* San Francisco: Harper One.

Krabill, J.R., Shenk, D.W., and Stutzman, L., (eds.) 2005. *Anabaptists Meeting Muslims: A Calling for Presence in the Way of Christ.* Scottdale: Herald Press.

Lewis, I.M. 1969. *Islam in Tropical Africa.* London: Oxford University Press.

Maranz, D.E. 1993. *Peace is Everything: The Worldview of Muslims and Traditionalists in the Senegambia.* Dallas: International Museum of Cultures.

Mbiti, J.S. 1970. *Concepts of God in Africa.* London: SPCK.

Mirahmadi, S.N., and Mirahmadi, H. 2005. *The Healing Power of Sufi Meditation.* Fenton, MI.: Naqshbandi Haqqani Sufi Order of America.

Muktar, B.H. 2005. Church Formation in a MuslimCommunity: Meserete Kristos Church (MKC). *Anabaptists Meeting Muslims: A Calling for Presence in the Way of Christ.* Edited by J.R. Krabill, D.W. Shenk, and L. Stutzman. Scottdale: Herald Press.

Sanneh, L. 1996. *Piety and Power Muslims and Christians in West Africa.* Maryknoll: Orbis.

Sanneh, L. 1989. *The Jakhanke Muslim Clerics: A Religious and Historical Study of Islam in Senegambia.* Lanham, MD: University Press of America.

Trimingham, J.S. 1971. *The Sufi Orders of Islam.* Oxford: Clarendon Press.

Yusuf, A.A. 1968. *The Holy Qur'an: Text, translation and Commentary.* Beirut: Dar Al Arabia.

Part Three: Country Studies

CHAPTER 12

Egypt

Tharwat Wahba

It is impossible to define a single African-Christian approach to Islam, for each African country has a unique history and context. However, it is important to understand the relationship between Islam and Christianity in Egypt, since it was the first country on the African continent to receive both Christianity and Islam. Egypt became the intellectual centre for both religions and the gateway for both faiths to move into the heart of Africa (Meinardus 1969: 52). The first missionaries for both Christianity and Islam used Egypt as their base for moving into Africa through Nubia, Sudan and Ethiopia (Nazir-Ali 1991: 21).

Despite these profound links with the history of the African continent, the religious situation in Egypt today is different from that of most African countries. Primarily, this is because Christians are a minority in Egypt, and the minority perspective, or mentality, deeply affects Christians' relationships with those of the dominant faith. Egypt, therefore, can provide a valuable case study of Islamic dealings with minorities and of minority Christians' approach to Islam (Hassan 2003: 8).

This chapter will survey the situation of both Christianity and Islam within Egypt, providing a historical overview of the entry and spread of both faiths and an outline of the current situation. Further, it will explore the interaction between the two faiths. Last, this chapter will examine the problems Christians have to face and the variety of methods they use in approaching Muslims.

Christianity in Egypt: A Historical Background

Christianity came to Egypt in the first century AD. The Coptic Orthodox Church in Egypt considers Saint Mark to be its founder, believing that he first preached the gospel in Alexandria about 61 AD. Little else is known about the history of this Church during its first 150 years in Egypt (Roberts 1979: 49). From the end of the second century, the Theological School of Alexandria played an important role. Pantaenus, Clement, Athanasius and Origen were among the leaders connected with the school who made significant contributions to theological thought throughout Christendom (Salama 1982: 22–23). At the end of the third and the beginning of the fourth century, the church in Egypt suffered under the persecution of Roman emperors, especially Diocletian. Because of the great number of Christians who died in his time (284–305 AD), the Egyptian Church was known as 'the Church of martyrs' (Bowman 1990: 191–192). Beginning with 'the father of monasticism', St Anthony, (c. 251–356), and St. Pachomius, (c. 292–348), the Coptic Church also influenced the Christian world by providing the ethos and model for monasticism (Oden 2007: 52).

The Coptic Church, as an oriental church, also made a historical contribution through mission work. In the fourth century, the Coptic Church established the Church of Ethiopia, and continued to support this work until the middle of the twentieth century (Markos 1994: 23). This and other smaller projects throughout Western Africa and Nubia demonstrate the rich commitment of the Coptic Church to missions (Nazir-Ali 1991: 28).

Because of the Chalcedonian controversy of 451 AD, the Coptic, or Egyptian Church,[1] was divided into two bodies. The majority of Egyptians followed the Miaphysitic doctrine and became what is known as the Coptic Orthodox Church (Kamil 2002: 200). A minority, however, followed the Diophysite doctrine and gave their loyalty to the Byzantine Church. They were known as the 'Melkites' or Greeks (Watterson 1988: 46). Egyptians

---

1. The word Copt is an ancient Greek word meaning 'Egyptian', but after the Arab conquest of Egypt the Arabs called Christians 'Copts,' and this is the name used for Christians in Egypt today including Catholics, Evangelicals and the Orthodox.

at the time, and most scholars today would agree that this conflict was not primarily about doctrine but rather, was concerned with national freedom and independence from Hellenistic political and ideological domination (Etteldorf 1959: 56–57).

The Islamic invasion of Egypt, which began in 640 AD, drastically affected Egypt and the Egyptian church. The country itself gradually changed from being Egyptian and Christian to being one of the most important Arabic and Islamic countries in history. Furthermore, the invasion led to the isolation of the Coptic Church from churches in the West and the East (Kamil 2002: 235).

The Coptic Church remained as the national Church of Egypt, but it suffered greatly though it maintained its witness to Christ. However, by the mid-nineteenth century, the strength of the Coptic Orthodox Church was at a low point, weakened by political, social and economic factors (Wahba 2008: 9). In the middle of that century, Protestant missionaries arrived and contributed greatly to the religious and social life of the country. This led to a revitalization of the Orthodox Church.

The first Protestant church to be established was the Presbyterian Church of Egypt. When the American missionaries from the United Presbyterian Church of North America came in 1854, they focused their work in Upper Egypt[2] and Cairo. While they initially sought to reach Muslims, they quickly switched their major emphasis to the evangelisation of the Copts, establishing schools and medical clinics, distributing the Bible and providing theological education for Egyptian leaders (Wahba 2008: 18–21). By the end of the nineteenth century, missionaries from other Protestant denominations had also begun to establish local churches.

Islam in Egypt

Islam came to Egypt after Amr Ibn El Aas, a Muslim military leader, invaded in 640/641 AD. In the early years, Muslim invaders gave conquered peoples

---

2. Upper Egypt refers to the south of the country, while Lower Egypt refers to the delta areas.

three alternatives: convert to Islam; retain their religion with freedom of worship in return for the payment of a poll tax (*jizya*); or death. As a result, many Christians, most of whom could not afford the poll tax, became Muslims (Kamil 2002: 230).

Egypt became an Islamic province, ruled by a line of governors who were appointed by the caliphs in the east. The country was ruled by many Islamic dynasties including the Umayyad dynasty (661–750), the Abbasid dynasty (750–868), the Tulunid dynasty (868–905), the Ekhshidit dynasty (935–969), the Fatimid Caliph (969–1171), the Ayyubid dynasty (1171–1250), the Mamluk state (1250–1517), and the Ottoman dynasty (1517–1918) (Bibawi 2001: 184). Throughout this time Egypt, and Egyptian Christians, provided abundant grain and tax revenue to the cause of Islam.

Following Islam's initial spread throughout Egypt, the Muslims alternatively tolerated and persecuted the Copts. Heavy taxation of Christians encouraged mass conversions to Islam. By the tenth century, Arabic had replaced Coptic as the primary spoken language, and the Coptic language was relegated to the liturgical sphere. The Arabic language became the language of government, culture and commerce. Over time, these socio-economic pressures together with organized persecution changed the country's demographics. By the end of the twelfth century, Egypt's population was no longer mostly Christian; the Muslims had become the majority (Meinardus 1969: 425–426). The number of Christians was reduced to less than one-tenth of the population during the Mamluk dynasties. The numbers became even less during the Ottoman Empire. By the mid-nineteenth century, it is estimated that the number of Copts was a mere 150,000 to 217,000 out of a total population of five million (Butcher 1897: 393).

Just as Egypt played a leading role in early Christian theology, Egypt also became the intellectual centre for Islam. Al-Azhar University and Mosque have held an important position as a leading institution and reference point for the Muslim world. Established in 971 AD, it is the oldest Islamic university and has a large number of students, not only from Egypt, but also from many other nations (Abd Al-Fattah 1998: 154–155). The teachings and writings of its scholars have been highly regarded by the worldwide community of Muslims. The majority of Egyptian Muslims have always been Sunni. Although the Shiite Fatimid Caliph ruled Egypt from 969 to1171, the country adhered to its Sunni traditions and teachings (Abd Al-Fattah 1995: 27).

Islamic Ideologies

The Egyptian society has accepted a wide spectrum of Islamist ideologies as well as many global values.

In Egypt, unlike some Muslim countries, Sufism and Islam are not always mutually exclusive categories. The hundreds of Sufi organisations and groups have their own structure and hierarchy, which the government both recognizes and interferes with. Islamic secularists have attacked Sufism and saint-veneration for more than a century with the Sufi Orders broadly viewed as appealing only to the uneducated. Even the term 'Sufism' is often misunderstood. Yet Sufism continues its vitality and appeals to many who are educated as well as to the uneducated. While some Sufi-oriented religious leaders are not recognized as such by the public, Sufi-influenced groups and individuals promote new interpretations of Islam which are openly critical of the traditional limitations of women's rights and support varying degrees of theological pluralism (Hoffman 1995).

There are also many official Muslim organisations in Egypt today. Al-Azhar plays the major role in such Muslim affairs as education, publishing, da'wah and representing Islam at conferences and inter-religious dialogues. The Supreme Council of Islamic Affairs, which is headed by the grand sheikh of Al-Azhar, has the final authority for giving permission for book publication, sending Muslim scholars (missionaries) to other countries, and organizing international and local conferences (Abd Al-Fattah 1995: 28–29). The House of *Iftaa* also has a major role in declaring religious and legal guidelines (*fatwas*) for Muslims in Egypt and other countries. Most Egyptian Muslims highly respect the decisions, reports and perspective of these official institutions (Abd Al-Fattah 1995: 74).

Among Muslim scholars there is a wide spectrum of perspectives concerning the application of Sharia law, the establishment of an Islamic state, the interpretation of women's statutes, the meaning of Jihad and the rights of religious minorities in Muslim countries. Liberal scholars are published in Western media but their influence within Egypt is very limited compared with that of the fundamentalist, conservative or moderate scholars (Bishri 1988: 669). Muslims in Egypt tend to retain their traditional ways of thinking and find it hard to accept new ideas that would moderate or alter what they have learned from ancient scholars. Traditional views and practises dominate both the Islamic academic and public speech. Al Azhar actively opposes any new school of Qur'anic interpretation or new theological ideas. Accusing scholars of being infidels is a traditionally used weapon to inhibit any widespread reformation of Islamic thought.

Today, most Muslims believe that a Muslim society must be based on Sharia law. Political entities are compelled to adopt religious language in order to regain moral influence over society and to secure their political legitimacy in the eyes of the public. The Muslim Brotherhood, al-*Ikhwan al-Muslimun*, which was established in 1928 by Hassan Al-Banna, has played an important role in developing the ideology of a Muslim state. Their influence on the public has increased through the years and their ideologies in life, state and society, which came mostly from the teachings of Sayyid Qutb, dominate Muslims' thoughts in Egypt today. Although they oppose the teachings of changing society by force, the Mubarak government accused them of being enemies of the state. Regular arrests for the leaders of this movement have taken place in the recent past (Abd Al-Fattah 1998: 207).

Most Egyptian Muslims disapprove of extremism, and the leaders of Egypt's most prominent Islamist groups have renounced violence and attempt to work within the political system. In addition, a religious revival has expressed itself in many ways: increased attendance at the mosque; broad adoption of Islamic dress by both men and women; proliferation of religious literature and electronic media; and the rise of many Islamic organisations (Hassan 2003: 173).

The Current Situation of Christians in Egypt

According to the census of 2009, Egypt has a population of about 80 million. However, it is hard to find exact numbers for many aspects of social, economic or religious life. The number of Christians in Egypt is particularly difficult to determine, and this causes tension between the government and Christians. According to the 1986 government census, which was the last to provide figures by religion, Christians made up 9.43 per cent of the total population of 50.4 million (i.e., 4.75 million Christians) (Bibawi 2001: 92). This means that the number of Christians today, based on the same percentage, is about 8 million. Egyptian Christians claim much higher percentages. Some Muslim sources continue to claim that there are only 4 to 5 million Christians.

It is thought that the Coptic Orthodox Church represents 90 per cent of the Christian population, with all other Christian denominations making up the remaining 10 per cent. The Evangelical (Presbyterian) Church is the second largest denomination in church membership and number of churches (Abd Al-Fattah 1998: 106–107).

Egypt has about 3,000 church buildings for all denominations. If each church can hold up to one thousand people, the capacity of all churches is no more than 2.5 to 3 million people (Habib 2010: 69). This means that more than 5 million people who have no house of worship. Both the lack of accurate statistics and the lack of buildings and Christian clergy, point to the complexity of the situation and the problems Christians face with the government and wider Muslim society.

Problems Facing Egyptian Christians

Discrimination and Marginalization

Since the Arab conquest, discrimination and marginalization have been matters of contention between Christians and Muslims in Egypt. After Islam became the majority religion, these problems were exacerbated. Today, Egyptian Christians complain that the Egyptian government applies discriminatory religious laws and practises concerning conversion, marriage, parenthood and education. They further contend that the government has effectively restricted Christians from senior government, political, military or educational positions and that there is increasing discrimination in the private sector (Hassan 2003: 116–118).

Church Building Permits

Obtaining building permits for churches remains a major difficulty for most Christian denominations in Egypt (Bailey and Bailey 2003: 145). The decree of 1856 by Saied Pasha, ruler of Egypt, put in place a system governing the relationship between church and state, which included a system governing the granting of church-building permissions. A 1934 Ministry of Interior decree added a further ten conditions to this decree. These included the conditions that a church was not allowed to be built within 100 metres of a mosque; that the permission of a utility official must be given where the church building would be near that utility; and that there must be no objection to such construction by any Muslim neighbour (Bibawi 2001: 46–47). It further decreed that the president of the country must also authorize the building of a church. While this law has recently been changed so that local governors can issue a decree for repairs, obtaining permission for repairs or new construction often takes many years. Many see the changed law as a further hindrance because lower officials are more easily influenced by local extremist elements.

Representation in Government and Parliament

Although Christians were very involved in the liberation and nationalization of Egypt during the first half of the twentieth century, they are marginalized in the political system. Of the 454 members of the People's Assembly, currently only six members are Christian. Of these, only one was elected, while the other five were appointed by the president. Christians are likewise restricted in the upper levels of government (Bibawi 2001: 211). By custom, the following positions are occupied only by Muslims: president, prime minister, assistants for prime minister, minister of defence, and heads of the various branches of the Egyptian armed forces. The list includes chair of the People's Assembly, governors (of twenty-eight governors, only one is a Christian), as well as the heads of all government service offices, chiefs of police, and presidents and deans of universities. Copts are also under-represented in ambassadorships abroad.

Violence against Christians

Egypt has witnessed a series of violent practises by Muslim extremists against Christians (Ibrahim 1996: 22) and in recent years, the situation has worsened. A 1995 report on the religious situation published by the official newspaper *Al-Ahram* described the development of radical Islamic groups and their activities, especially in Upper Egypt (Makari 2007: xvi). More than 182 violent events occurred in 1995 between Muslim groups and Christians, who were the victims (Abd Al-Fattah 1998: 194–207).

One of the worst events happened in Al Kosheh in 1999, where Muslims killed twenty-one Christians. Of the ninety-three men tried by the Court of Cassation, only two were found guilty. One was sentenced to fifteen years in prison and the other to a mere three years (Habib 2010: 30). In many cases, the government pressures official religious leaders to seek to calm their people, without, however, ensuring any kind of justice for the oppressed.

Egyptian Christians Approaches to Muslims

Natural Approaches

Egyptian Christians have adopted different approaches in light of their socio-religious and political conditions as minorities in a Muslim majority Egypt and their interaction with Muslims.

Isolation

Historically, Egyptian Christians have largely withdrawn from public life having developed what is termed a battered minority syndrome. In part, this includes a sense of inferiority and a heightened sensitivity to persecution and discrimination. The necessary outward acquiescence to orders that are enforced by the majority and the lack of participation in the political decision-making process are experienced as keenly humiliating (Hassan 2003: 197–198).

The majority of Egyptian Christians live with as little interaction with their Muslim neighbours as possible. Most find their identity in the church. They are satisfied with what they have inside the walls of the church which is not only a place for worship but also the *locus* of their social life. Churches in general are centred on social activities such as trips, education and employment. The church provides a network resource for business endeavours and employment and finding a marriage spouse. Some companies owned by Christians hire only Christian workers. Such practises, together with the pressures of espousing different values than the majority and experiencing discrimination, have spiralled into increasing isolation and withdrawal of Christians from political, social and public life (Hassan 2003: 197).

Emigration

Another response to the situation is seen in the emigration of Copts to the West in search of new opportunities. Since 1965, hundreds of thousands of Copts have migrated to Canada, Australia, the U.S.A. and Europe. Compared to other Christian communities in the Middle East, Coptic emigration is limited; however, it has added to the massive brain drain from Egypt, and contributed to a Coptic lobbying force in the U.S.A. and Europe (Abd Al-Fattah 1998: 284).

The Egyptian Christians who live abroad play an important role in the political support of their churches and families. They openly accuse the Egyptian government of intolerance towards Christians. They have formed themselves into organisations and exert pressure on the government to give more rights to Christians. Furthermore, they provide vital financial support to both families and churches back home (Abd Al-Fattah 1998: 285–286).

Conversion of Christians

Through the centuries and under the Muslim pressures, a huge number of Christians have converted to Islam. Poverty, the desire for economic gain, the longing to escape discrimination, and even the choice of marriage partner, have all motivated thousands of Christians to convert to Islam (Hassan 2003: 107).

It is much easier for Christians to convert to Islam than for a Muslim to convert to Christianity. The religion of every citizen is on each person's identity (ID) card, which makes a change of religion from Islam close to impossible. The ID cards lead officials to treat Christians as second-class citizens. The government and Muslim society in general supports in every way possible those who want to convert to Islam. Meanwhile, Muslims who convert to Christianity are denied all rights. Although there are no statistics on the number of converts to Islam, it is estimated that in the past there were a few thousand conversions to Islam every year. In recent years, this number has declined, as Christian leaders have more actively intervened, and the Christian community has provided more support to those facing pressures to convert to Islam (Hassan 2003: 222).

Intentional Interactions with Muslims: Holistic Approach

Active Christian churches and mission-oriented individuals have approached their fellow Muslim citizens in different ways. Depending on their theological perspective and opportunities for ministry, they use either direct or indirect approaches. Likewise, the approaches can vary from the tolerance and mutual respect that uses dialogue to the more confrontational tactic of polemics.

Dialogue

In Egypt, Christians have instigated numerous dialogue programmes between Christians and Muslims. That between Al-Azhar and the Anglican Church is one of the strategic dialogues that have run for many years, contributing to more understanding between some Christians and Muslims. The Coptic Evangelical Organisation for Social Services (CEOSS) has, over many years, held many meetings between Christian and Muslim scholars and leaders, resulting in numerous publications (Abd Al-Fattah 1998: 412). The Coptic Orthodox Church has established its own forums for dialogue, where both church and Muslim leaders meet for official occasions as the breakfast (*Iftar*) during Ramadan. Likewise, numerous international NGOs and church groups have sought to study Islam and foster dialogue between the two religions (Abd Al-Fattah 1998: 412).

While dialogue is important, there is also reason for concern. All have been initiated and financed by Christians. Furthermore, the dialogues tend to concentrate on issues where there is a common ground, but fail to discuss contentious theological and socio-political issues. Unfortunately, these dialogues also take place between elite scholars and leaders, with little to no impact among the common people or upon public debate (Brewster 1979: 516–517).

Evangelism

Evangelism of Muslims takes many forms. Egyptian law forbids public evangelism outside the walls of the churches; this includes public evangelistic meetings and the initiation of evangelistic conversations by Christians. The government tolerates Christian evangelism of other Christians or of non-believers whose political identity is Christian. Although any attempt to actively evangelize Muslims is illegal (Wahba 2008: 103), Christian churches, organisations and individuals seek to use any open door for evangelism. The Cairo Book Fair and both Islamic and Christian religious festivals provide excellent opportunities to make Christian literature and contact accessible. Christian satellite channels such as Sat-7, Al-Hayat, Al-Karma and Miracle make a strong impact upon both Christians and Muslims. It is hard to measure the results of this work, but the correspondence received by these channels suggests that they are indeed surprisingly successful (Bibawi 2001: 68).

One-to-one evangelism and the distribution of both the Bible and the *Jesus* film are among the most effective methods of evangelism. Again, it is impossible to measure the results. However, some estimate that the total of Muslim converts numbers in the millions. This is more striking when it is realised that a Muslim who converts to Christianity can face extreme reprisals from family, employers and friends—with no legal recourse. When their conversion becomes known, many are forced to move or even emigrate.

Social Work

Taking a more holistic approach, many Christian organisations started with social ministries as a way to interact with Muslims. This method was first used by Western missions, including Church Missionary Society (CMS) and the American Presbyterian Mission. They established schools, medical clinics, and literacy programmes, began family awareness programmes, and organized micro-credit projects to help support needy Christians and Muslims (Wahba 2008: 21). The Presbyterian Church continues to use this approach, as seen in its numerous schools and the multiplicity of CEOSS projects (Hassan 2003: 91). The Catholics were also pioneers in reaching out to Egyptian society through a wide range of organisations such as Caritas, schools and clinics. Likewise, the Coptic Orthodox Church ministers to the needy, but mostly targets its own people, while Presbyterians and Catholics reach out to both Christians and Muslims (Hassan 2003: 159). These social work projects have played an important role in the country's socio-economic development and in promoting more a peaceful co-existence between the two faiths. Many Muslims appreciate Christians because they receive a high quality service and ministry, regardless of their religious background. This kind of work is building a peaceful and tolerant relationship and provides a starting point for evangelism.

Polemics

In recent years, with the advent of satellite channels and the internet, some Egyptian Christians have begun to use a polemical approach with Muslims. They attack the five pillars of Islam, as well as its prophet, The Qur'an, the hadith and Islamic practises. These attacks range from pointing out contradictions and illogical tenets to ridiculing beliefs. This approach has gained popularity among the vast majority of Egyptian Christians because it allows them to express the pressure they have suffered for fourteen centuries (Johnson 2009: 122). However, some Christian leaders fear that this exacerbates hostilities between Christians and Muslims. They believe that this approach could make Muslims more aggressively defensive when they are evangelized, and point to the many Muslim scholars, writers and groups who have reacted against these tactics and are seeking to mobilize Muslims against them. On the other hand, an unknown number of Muslims have sought answers to questions raised by these programmes and some have indeed converted to Christianity (Hassan 2003: 222, 289).

Conclusion

The majority of Christians in the Middle East now live in Egypt. In their long history with Islam, Egyptian Christians have kept their Christian faith and contributed to global Christianity despite centuries of persecution and oppression.

It is to be hoped that the Egyptian Christians can overcome the pressures that have kept them from proclaiming the Gospel freely. They need to defeat the inner fears which bind them so that they can contribute to the spread of the Gospel among Arabs, Muslims and Africans. With their knowledge of Islam and the Qur'an, and their extraordinary experience in dealing with Muslims, Egyptian Christians could cooperate with both Arabic and non-Arabic speaking African Christians in their interaction with Muslims. Egyptian Christians are specially fitted to the task due to their proximity to the Middle Eastern, Islamic, Arabic and African culture, tradition, languages and economic situation. Africans and western missionaries need to discover the Egyptian Church anew, looking to a common future while learning from the lessons of the past (Oden 2007: 10–11).

References

Abd Al-Fattah N., & Rashdan, D. (eds.) 1998. *al-Ḥālah al-dīnīyah fī Miṣr. al-adad al-thānī*. al-Qāhirah: Markaz al-Dirāsāt al-Siyāsīyah wa-al-Istirātījīyah bi-al-Ahrām.

Abd Al-Fattah N., & Rashdan, D. (eds.) 1995. *Taqrīr al-ḥālah al-dīnīyah fī Miṣr*. Markaz al-dirāsāt al-siyāsīyah wa-al-istirātījīyah. al-Qāhirah: al-Markaz

Bailey, B.J., & Bailey, J.M. 2003. *Who are the Christians in the Middle East?* Grand Rapids, Mich: W.B. Eerdmans.

Bibawi, N.L. 2001. *Mashākil al-Aqbāṭ fī Miṣr wa-ḥulūluhā*. Cairo: s.n.

Bishri, T. 1988. *al-Muslimūn wa-al-Aqbāt fī iṭār al-jamāah al-waṭanīyah*. al-Qāhirah: al-Hay'ah al-Miṣriyah al-Āmah lil-Kitab.

Bowman, A.K. 1990. *Egypt after the Pharaohs: 332 BC-AD 642*. Oxford, New York: Oxford University Press.

Brewster, D.R. 1979. Dialogue: Relevancy to Evangelism in North American Conference on Muslim Evangelisation. *The Gospel and Islam: A 1978 Compendium*, edited by D.M. McCurry. Monrovia, Calif: Missions Advanced Research and Communication Centre.

Butcher, E.L. 1897. *The Story of the Church of Egypt: Being an Outline of the History of the Egyptians Under Their Successive Masters from the Roman Conquest Until Now*. London: Smith, Elder, & Co.

Etteldorf, R. 1959. *The Catholic Church in the Middle East*. New York: Macmillan.

Habib, S.L. 2010. *Contemporary Situation in the Egyptian Presbyterian Church*. Master's Theses, Pittsburgh Theological Seminary.

Hassan, S. 2003. *Christians versus Muslims in Modern Egypt: The Century-long Struggle for Coptic Equality*. Oxford: Oxford University Press.

Hoffman, V.J. 1995. *Sufism, Mystics, and Saints in Modern Egypt*. Columbia, S.C.: University of South Carolina Press.

Ibrahim Sad Al-Den. 1996. *The Copts of Egypt*. London: The Khaldoun Centre for Development Studies.

Johnson, T.M., Ross, K.R., & Lee, S.S.K. 2009. *Atlas of Global Christianity 1910–2010*. Edinburgh: Edinburgh University Press.

Kamil, J. 2002. *Christianity in the Land of the Pharaohs: The Coptic Orthodox Church*. London: Routledge.

Makari, P.E. 2007. *Conflict & Cooperation: Christian-Muslim Relations in Contemporary Egypt*. Syracuse, N.Y.: Syracuse University Press.

Markos, A. 1969. The Coptic Church in Egypt, in *Religion in the Middle East: Three Religions in Concord and Conflict*, edited by A.J. Arberry. London: Cambridge U.P.

Markos, A. 1994. *Come Across—and Help Us: The Story of the Coptic Church in Africa at the Present Time*. Meinardus, O.F.A.

Meinardus, O.F.A. 2002. *Two Thousand Years of Coptic Christianity*. Cairo: American University in Cairo Press.

Memoir from Africa. Cairo: Coptic Bishopric of African Affairs.

Nazir-Ali, M. 1991. *From Everywhere to Everywhere: A World View of Christian Witness*. London: Collins/Flame.

Oden, T.C. 2007. *How Africa Shaped the Christian Mind: Rediscovering the African Seedbed of Western Christianity*. Downers Grove, Ill: IVP Books.

Roberts, C.H. 1979. *Manuscript, Society and Belief in Early Christian Egypt*. London: Oxford University Press (The Schweich lectures of the British Academy, 1977).

Salama, A.N. 1982. *Tārīkh al-Kanīsah al-Injīlīyah fī Miṣr (1854–1980)*. al-Qāhirah: Dār al-Thaqāfah.

Sullivan, D.J., & Abed-Kotob, S. 1999. *Islam in Contemporary Egypt: Civil Society vs. the State*. Boulder: L. Reinner.

Wahba, T. 2008. *The Practise of Mission in Egypt: A Historical Study of the Integration between the American Mission and the Evangelical Church of Egypt, 1854–1970,* PhD Thesis, Brunel University, U.K.

Watterson, B. 1988. *Coptic Egypt.* Edinburgh: Scottish Academic Press.

CHAPTER 13

Ethiopia

F. Peter Ford, Jr.

The particulars of Christian-Muslim relations in Africa, both historical and current, vary considerably from country to country. Ethiopia especially presents a unique case. Unlike most of sub-Saharan Africa where Islam had long been present when Christianity began to take root, the opposite is true of Ethiopia where a recently established Islam arrived to find a centuries-old Christian church. The same could be said of Egypt and, to a lesser extent, northern Sudan. Unlike them, Islam in Ethiopia became dominated by a powerful Christian state and remained a minority religion.

Early History: A Concord-Conflict Dichotomy

The historical development of Islam in Ethiopia has been very much intertwined with its relationship to Ethiopian Christianity. At times, mutual tolerance and peaceful co-existence have been the norm. More often, issues of power, control of resources and fears of subjugation have led to conflicts between Muslims and Christians. Thus, a dichotomy between concord and conflict developed between the Muslim and the Christian.

Arabia had long engaged in trade with Abyssinia (what is today the northwest area of Ethiopia). Abyssinian traditions report that Christianity was first introduced in the fourth century by Frumentius, a Syrian monk who had been shipwrecked on the Red Sea coast as a boy. Following the conversion of the king (locally known as the Negus) and of the royal court in Axum, Frumentius sought assistance from the church in Alexandria and was appointed a bishop by St. Athanasius. More than a century later, Monophysite Christianity spread among the people through the translation of the Bible into the local language, Ge'ez, and the evangelistic work of a group of Syrian monks known as the 'nine saints' (Marcus 2002: 7–9; Tamrat 1972: 21–30).

According to Muslim sources, during the sixth century the Abyssinians became militarily involved in southern Arabia to assist the Christians of Najran who were facing persecution by a fanatical Jewish king. Shortly thereafter, a renegade Abyssinian officer named Abrahah marched north with a sizeable army that included elephants and led an attack on Mecca. The Muslim sources claim that he intended to destroy the then pagan Ka'bah so Arab traders would instead be attracted to his Christian sanctuary in San'a'. In any case, the failure of his excursion has been enshrined in the Qur'an itself, the Sura of the Elephant (105). By the end of the sixth century, the Persians had conquered the area and eliminated all Abyssinian control (Trimingham 1979: 297–305).

Nevertheless, individual Abyssinian Christians continued to live in Arabia, and Muslim sources mention several who had important contact with Muhammad during his early years in Mecca. These include Barakah, Muhammad's childhood nurse, from whom he might have learned some Ge'ez words (Erlich 2002: 23); Jabr, who apparently used to read his Ge'ez Bible at his trading booth while Muhammad listened (Parrinder 1965: 160–161); and Bilal, a slave who became an early convert to Islam and also the first *mu'adhdhin* to give the call to prayer (Erlich 2002: 27). Such contacts apparently led Muhammad to have a positive view of the Christian Abyssinian Negus, despite the legacy of Abrahah's earlier aggression.

Thus, when the early Muslims faced intense persecution from the pagan Quraysh (the leading tribe in Mecca), Muhammad sent most of them to Abyssinia for refuge under the Christian king. Apparently, around 615 AD they crossed the Red Sea in at least two groups comprising more than eighty people, while Muhammad remained in Mecca under the protection of his uncle, Abu Talib. The Muslims found a friendly reception with the Negus in Axum, but the Quraysh also sent two emissaries there to demand the return of the Muslims. The Negus, portrayed as a man of fair judgment, held two hearings and allowed the Muslims to explain their religion. When their spokesman, Muhammad's cousin, Ja'far, recounted the story of the annunciation and birth of Jesus from sura *Maryam* (19), the king wept, saying, 'This and what Jesus brought have come from the same niche'. He was convinced that their religion was not so different from his own, and he sent the Quraysh emissaries back to Mecca empty-handed. After some years, when the persecution in Arabia had subsided, the Muslims returned home. This incident became known as the 'First Hijra' since it occurred before the main hijra to Medina in 622. Muslim traditions claim that the Negus later converted to Islam and that the prophet prayed for the Negus when he heard of the king's death.[1]

These traditions about the Negus led to dichotomous views among Muslims towards Abyssinia (Erlich 2002: 23–30). In the early period, a positive view prevailed because of the king's hospitality to the Muslim refugees and conversion to Islam. A hadith has Muhammad saying, 'Leave the Abyssinians alone as long as they leave you alone', While the authenticity of this statement might be disputed,[2] it nevertheless represents the primary Muslim position in the classical period. As a result, Abyssinia was not considered to be a part of either the 'Realm of Islam' (*dar al-islam*), or the 'Realm of War' (*dar al-harb*). Rather, Muslims considered Abyssinia to be in the 'Realm of Neutrality' (*dar al-hiyad*), and did not conquer it during the early spread of Islam (Erlich 2002: 24–25; Robinson 2004: 111–112).

Instead, over several centuries Islam entered the Horn of Africa by peaceful means, through trade, intermarriage and settlement. Coming first to the Red Sea coast, Muslims gradually penetrated inland and established several Islamic sultanates south and east of Abyssinia. Contact with the Christian kingdom was mostly of a commercial nature, and although it

---

1. The full story is related in the earliest Muslim biography of Muhammad by Ibn Ishaq, as preserved and edited by Ibn Hisham, translated into English by Guillaume 1955: 146–155. An excellent analysis is provided by Ahmed 1997. Abyssinian chronicles for this period do not mention this event; Ahmed believes this is 'probably because the king had kept his conversion secret' (Ahmed 1997: 57).

2. Among the canonical hadith collections, it is found only in that of Abu Dawud (Trimingham 1965: 46); its absence from the collections of al-Bukhari and Muslim accords it with less than *sahih* (fully sound) status.

included the slave trade, relations between Christians and Muslims were primarily peaceful (Trimingham 1965: 50–69; Braukämper 2002: 19–23).

Beginning with the thirteenth century, conflict began to emerge. Muslim traders started to settle in Abyssinian lands and cross-border skirmishes arose over trade and land disputes. The discord came to a head in 1328 when the Abyssinian king invaded Muslim territory, set up puppet rulers and enforced tribute while the Muslim sultanates succumbed due to their lack of unity (Trimingham 1965: 69–76). In the meantime, Muslim scholars, drawing on the traditions about the conversion of the Negus, concluded that Abyssinia should have been incorporated within the Realm of Islam. To them the reversion of subsequent kings to Christianity pointed to its infidel status and inclusion in the Land of War (Erlich 2002: 27–28). This doctrine became personified in a charismatic Muslim leader named Ahmad bin Ibrahim, known among the Abyssinians as Ahmad Granj, the 'left-handed'. After Abyssinia's control declined in the fifteenth century, Granj unified the Muslim states and in 1529 embarked on a military jihad against the Christian kingdom. The result was devastating: a great number of churches and monasteries were destroyed and the masses were forced to convert to Islam. Granj's forces would have completely conquered Abyssinia had not the Portuguese intervened to turn the tide of the war. Granj was killed in battle and his army disintegrated, while the Christian kingdom barely survived (Trimingham 1965: 76–90).

Later History: A Reverse Dhimma

The Granj episode was 'a major watershed in the development of Islam and its relationship to Christian Ethiopia' (Østebø 2008: 75). Although Islam never again became a strong political force, large segments of the Abyssinian population were now Muslim, and the percentage increased dramatically in the nineteenth century when the borders of Ethiopia were expanded to their current position. The result has been called 'the Ahmad Granj trauma', an anti-Muslim orientation that persists to the present (Erlich 2002: 48–50). Christian Ethiopians vowed to never again allow Muslim aggression to overtake their sacred territory. Royal policies and public sentiment combined to subjugate Muslims to a second-class standing. It became a kind of reverse *dhimmi*, comparable to the so-called 'protected status' that Jews and Christians experienced under medieval Muslim rule (Østebø 1998: 425).

The subsequent history of Christian-Muslim relations in Ethiopia bears this out. Christian kings, in conjunction with the Orthodox Church, enacted policies which discriminated against Ethiopian Muslims. In 1668 a decree was issued which forced Muslims to live in segregated ghettos. In the mid-nineteenth century, Emperor Tewodros II sought to eliminate Islam from the country. His successor, Yohannes IV, issued the edict of Boru Meda, requiring all Muslim subjects to convert or be killed (Trimingham 1965: 102–103, 117–123). Although these measures did not last, they instilled resentment toward their Christian overlords in the Muslim population. One scholar argues that official policies against Muslim segments of the Oromo tribe prompted a 'resistance ideology', which led to increased conversion to Islam (Hassan 1992).

In the twentieth century, three brief episodes gave hope to Muslim aspirations for greater recognition and entitlement, but each was short-lived. The emperor Lij Iyasu (1909–1917) apparently converted to Islam, but was deposed as a result (Trimingham 1965: 129–131). The Italian occupation (1935–1941) provided for the Muslims over against the Christian elite, but after the Italians were ousted, Muslims were punished for supporting them. In 1974 Emperor Haile Selassie was deposed and a Marxist military regime called the 'Derg' ('Committee') ruled Ethiopia for seventeen years. Though favourably disposed to the Muslims, their socialist agenda led to severe repression of all religion including Islam. In general, most of the twentieth century in Ethiopia witnessed continued discrimination against Muslims from both government and Christians (Ahmed 1994: 775–791).

In 1991, the Derg was overthrown by the Ethiopian People's Revolutionary Democratic Front (EPRDF), which has remained in power since. Its detachment from the church and official policy of religious freedom means that Ethiopian Muslims have finally received a measure of equality as full citizens, which was enshrined in the constitution of 1994. This has dramatically changed the dynamics of Christian-Muslim relations in Ethiopia. Although it is doubtful that Muslims have become more numerous, they have certainly become more visible and more assertive of their rights. They have established organisations, published literature and become involved in politics. There is a new surge of religious expression in the form of mosques and the Meccan *hajj*. What is probably most important is a new connection with global Islam and the recent influx of funds, personnel and ideas coming from neighbouring Muslim countries, especially Saudi Arabia (Ahmed 1994: 791–793; Østebø 1998: 427–431; Erlich 2007: 175–183). Yet in the midst of these remarkable changes, the themes of concord/conflict dichotomy and reverse dhimma have continued.

The Faces of Islam in Ethiopia Today

Before exploring the current concord-conflict dichotomy and reverse dhimmi, it is important to examine various dimensions of Islam today.[3] There is no agreement on the size of the Muslim population in Ethiopia. Because of Ethiopia's historic connection with Christianity, the significant number of Muslims in Ethiopia tends to be downplayed. According to the U.S. State Department (2004), Muslims constitute 45 per cent of the population, but according to the 2007 official Ethiopian census (2008: 17) it is only 33.9 per cent. Christians favour the smaller figure, while Muslims insist that the larger figure is more accurate and even that they form as much as half the population. Contemporary scholars are not able to be more precise (Lapidus 2002: 832; Østebø 2008: 71).

Muslims form the majority in regions along the eastern and southern areas of the country, reflecting their original pattern of settlement. They are also found in almost every part of the country, where they often live alongside Christians, both Orthodox and Protestant. Ethiopian Muslims are virtually all Sunni, and historically represent three of the four Sunni schools of law (*madhahib*): Shafi'i (the most common), Maliki and Hanafi (Trimingham 1965: 231–233). More recently Muslims have established various organisations, the most important being the Ethiopian Islamic

---

[3]. Although supporting references from the literature are often provided, much of this section is based on the author's experience during seven years of residence in Ethiopia.

Affairs Supreme Council. However, when Muslim demonstrations in 1995 turned violent, the government began to curb the growth of Islamic organisations (Østebø 1998: 428–430; 2008: 80).

Many of the dozens of ethnic groups within Ethiopia identify closely with either Christianity or Islam. For example, only a small percentage of Muslims are found among the sizeable Amhara and Tigray groups, which have historically adhered to Orthodox Christianity. Some groups are almost completely Muslim, the largest being the Somali in the east (Lewis 1986) and the Afar in the northeast (Kalb 2000: 123–131). The Harari are a small unique group located especially in the ancient Muslim city of Harar in the east (Waldron 1978). During the sixteenth century the Oromo, Ethiopia's largest ethnic group, had migrated into the southeastern and western regions in the aftermath of the Granj invasion; today they entertain nationalistic aspirations in the form of the Oromo Liberation Front (OLF). More than half of the Oromo are Muslims, and for them Islam and ethnicity are very closely intertwined (Østebø 1998: 437–438; 2008: 85–86).

Most Muslims in Ethiopia have found ways to merge religious persuasion with traditional culture so as to include 'a pragmatic incorporation of indigenous religious elements' (Østebø 2008: 71). This came about especially through the diffusion of Sufi teaching during the eighteenth and nineteenth centuries, and Sufi orders such as the Qadiriya, Tijaniya, Ahmadiya and Salihiya extended through various parts of Ethiopia (Trimingham 1964: 233–247; Kapteijns 2000: 233–235; Robinson 2004: 116). This gave rise to the establishment of hundreds of shrines honouring saints and Sufi masters, which have become the objects of pilgrimage and popular devotion (Trimingham 1964: 247–256). The most famous of these is the shrine of Shaykh Hussein in Bali (southeast Ethiopia), where thousands of pilgrims visit each year, seeking miracles, giving alms and fulfilling religious vows (Cole 1997). The traditional Muslim city of Harar encompasses about thirty simple tombs, which pilgrims regularly visit (Foucher 1994; Zekaria 1998).

Beginning in 1991, increased contact with foreign groups has led to an influx of conservative Islamic reform movements. The most important is usually identified as Wahhabi Islam because of its strong link to Saudi

Arabia, where Wahhabism is the dominant form of Islam. However, to Ethiopian Muslims who follow this movement, the term 'Wahhabi' has negative connotations and they prefer such labels as 'Salafi', 'tawhidi' or 'ahl al-sunnah'. Based primarily among Oromo Muslims who are equipped with Saudi education and finances, their main aim is to reform the beliefs and practises of traditional Muslims throughout Ethiopia. Additionally, many Wahhabis are engaged in da'wah activities (Islamic mission) such as the spread of Islamic literature and the Arabic language. A few are involved in the political process, but have not said that they want to establish an Islamic state in Ethiopia. Though mainstream traditional Muslims often resist the efforts of Wahhabis, intra-Muslim clashes are rare (Erlich 2007: 175–192; Østebø 2007: 4–5; 2008: 81–82).

A second foreign-influenced group is the Tablighi Jama'at, from the large missionary movement that originated in Indo-Pakistan. Although the group is well organized in Ethiopia, it has rejected politicization of Islam and has focused on unpretentious outreach among traditional Muslims. Their success has been rather limited because they have largely been shunned by the Oromo Muslim community (Østebø 2007: 5–6; 2008: 82). Muslims in Ethiopia are also involved in sorting out their relationship with their Christian neighbours. It is to this theme that we now turn.

Current Relations between Muslims and Christians[4]

Today, the concord-conflict dichotomy between Muslims and Christians in Ethiopia falls mostly on the concord side. Muslims deal peacefully with neighbouring Christians and violent conflicts are few. Nevertheless, significant tension lies beneath the surface, primarily due to the 'asymmetric relationship' between the two groups (Østebø 2008: 73, 87). Despite the large percentage of Muslims in Ethiopia—or perhaps because of it—the 'reverse dhimma' mentality among Christians remains strong. Christians,

---

4. Much of the information in this section is not available in the literature. I am indebted to several Ethiopian colleagues for providing details of specific incidents and trends: Abdi Tadesse, Anwar Mehammed, Masresha Mengiste and Samuel Yonas.

especially the Orthodox, want to re-assert their heritage within the country, while Muslims want to stress their right to equal citizenship and religious expression. This tension expresses itself in the public arena in various ways. For example, Muslims and Christians alike will almost never eat meat that has been slaughtered and prepared by the other group (Østebø 2008: 72).

Polemical literature only exacerbates the tension. For example, in 1985 the Orthodox Church fiercely resisted an attempt by local Muslims to build a mosque in the ancient city of Axum. The patriarch wrote a magazine article comparing Christian Axum to Muslim Mecca—no one would think of building a church in sight of the Ka'bah! Muslims responded by claiming Axum for themselves, based on the first hijra and the hospitality of the Negus who had converted to Islam. To date there is still no mosque in Axum (Ahmed 1994: 793; Erlich 2007: 187–189).

Muslims frequently publish translations of polemical works against Christians, such as pamphlets by Ahmad Deedat. In 2006 an Amharic version of the *Gospel of Barnabas* was produced; the government soon stepped in to forbid its dissemination, but not before several copies were distributed. In an effort to curb such activity, the government recently enacted a law which severely restricts the writing or publication of any material that might lead to religious conflict.

Occasionally, violent clashes have erupted between Muslims and Christians. The most serious incidents that have occurred in recent years are:

- January 2006, in Kamisse (a predominantly Muslim town in the Oromia region of northern Ethiopia). A Muslim mob burned down three Protestant churches and several Christians were seriously injured. This was, perhaps, a rekindling of violence that took place fourteen years earlier. It is said that Muslim fundamentalists were angered that a cartoon film about Muhammad was being sold there.
- September-October 2006, in three western towns—Chello, Jimma and Beghi (all Oromia Muslim majority). In a widespread incident, Muslim groups calling themselves Kawarya (Amharic for *khawārij* or Kharijites) attacked Christian churches and homes, both Orthodox and Protestant. The assault, which began in three separate locations and spread into surrounding areas,

lasted three weeks. In some cases Christians fought back. About two dozen people, mostly Christians, were killed and many more were injured. Dozens were forced to convert to Islam and hundreds were displaced. The value of the property destroyed amounted to thousands of dollars. Ostensibly, the cause was a personal dispute between a Muslim and Christian, but this seems to have been a pretext for a coordinated planned attack.

- March 2008, in Bale (southeast Ethiopia, Oromia Muslim majority). Two congregations of the Kale Hewet Church (Protestant) were attacked in their churches during Sunday morning worship. One person was killed and sixteen were seriously injured. Again, the attack seems to have been premeditated.
- January 2009, in Gondar (a major Orthodox city of the north where Muslims are a tiny minority). Amhara Orthodox Christians marching in a traditional Epiphany ceremony confronted Muslims at a location previously used by the Christians but where the Muslims had been granted permission to build a mosque. Many were wounded on both sides, and the disagreement has not yet been settled.
- June 2009, in Dessie (a major city in the north, about 70 per cent Muslim and 30 per cent Orthodox Christian). In a similar land dispute, Amhara Orthodox Christians tried to build a structure on property claimed by Muslims. A confrontation occurred mostly between Christians and the police, leaving two dead and six seriously injured.

Numerous reasons could be given for incidents such as these. In addition to the prevailing attitudes of Christian supremacy and Muslim aspirations, other complicating factors come into play. As is typical with many religious conflicts in Africa, ethnicity can never be ruled out. In particular, the historic Amhara-Oromo struggle is often manifested in Christian-Muslim conflicts. At other times, religion does seem to be the dominant issue, for example in cases where Oromo Muslims have attacked Oromo Protestant Christians. Another factor is the militant component of modern Islamic resurgence, though it does not seem to be engendered by the contemporary

Wahhabi movement. Rather, Muslim extremists from Sudan and Somalia have often played a key role in stirring up hatred and violence. Some of the tension can also be attributed to provocative mission activities. Muslims often use foreign investment for their building programmes and encourage Muslim men to marry Christian girls, while Christians respond with noisy 'crusades'[5] and accusations of satanic activity within Islam.

There is also a positive dimension to Christian-Muslim relations in Ethiopia. In this regard, credit should be given to the current national government for seeking to maintain a concord between the two groups. The authorities usually intervene to quickly end such incidents of conflict. Furthermore, the government has initiated local peace and reconciliation committees in the areas of conflict, bringing community Muslim and Christian leaders together to search for ways in which past wrongs can be healed and future hostilities forestalled. The government also sponsored a national convention in 2008, in which Christians and Muslims together explored 'The Role of Religion in Peace and Development Building.' A similar forum was planned for 2010.

Individual Christian denominations have also taken steps to teach their members about Islam and to build relationships with Muslims. Protestant groups, which came into being in the nineteenth and twentieth centuries, seem to be able to move in this direction more easily than the Ethiopian Orthodox Church, with its legacy of confrontation with Islam. The Ethiopian Evangelical Church Mekane Yesus (EECMY) has led the way through its involvement in training workshops, development projects and peace initiatives.[6] In addition, the Mekane Yesus Seminary instituted a bachelor's-level programme in Christian-Muslim Relations in 2003, where church leaders and evangelists cultivate positive attitudes and respectful approaches towards Muslims (Klein 2005: 144–147). EECMY has also hosted the Programme for Christian-Muslim Relations in Africa (PROCMURA)[7] Area Committee for Ethiopia, but unfortunately its

---

5. In other words, large public evangelistic rallies in which Islamic beliefs and practises are often disparaged.
6. A full account of EECMY's recent involvement with Islam in Ethiopia, drawn especially from church archives, is presented in Klein 2005.
7. PROCMURA was formerly known as the 'Islam in Africa Project'.

activities have been limited, and it has not reached its goal of becoming an ecumenical entity (Klein 2005: 191–216). More recently, the Kale Hewet Church (KHC) embarked on a substantial programme of training for evangelism and peaceful cooperation among Muslims. Smaller denominations have initiated similar ventures, but these have been limited. One recent development worth noting is a new NGO called 'Foundation for Academic Excellence Ministry', in which both Muslims and Christians engage in promoting positive Christian-Muslim relations throughout the country.

Prospects for the Future

In light of Ethiopia's legacy of dichotomy between concord and conflict and the realities facing Christians and Muslims today, most analysts are cautious about the future of Christian-Muslim relations in Ethiopia (Erlich 2007: 226; Østebø 2008: 87–88). Although current efforts by the government and some churches are to be welcomed, more will be needed to foster more positive attitudes and relationships between the two groups. I believe especially that Muslims and Christians must work *together* at achieving the following goals:

- education at the grass-roots level about each other's beliefs and practises,
- cooperation in matters of community interest, such as the effective use of local resources for the prevention of HIV/AIDS,
- reformation of religious beliefs and practises without succumbing to religious extremism, and
- engagement in dialogue and outreach which promote common ground along with mutual respect for each other's differences, and recognize freedom of conscience (adapted from Ford 2008: 61–65; 2009: 64–68).

If Ethiopian Muslims and Christians can, in some measure, implement such goals in partnership, I believe Ethiopia can become a model to Africa and the rest of the world regarding the genuine possibility for constructive Christian-Muslim relations.

References

Ahmed, H. 1994. Islam and Islamic Discourse in Ethiopia (1973–1993). *New Trends in Ethiopian Studies: Papers of the 12th International Conference of Ethiopian Studies, Michigan State University, 5–10 September 1994: Humanities and Human Resources*, edited by H.G. Marcus. Lawrenceville, New Jersey: Red Sea Press: 775–801.

Ahmed, H. 1997. Aksum in Muslim Historical Tradition. *Journal of Ethiopian Studies* (Addis Ababa) 29(2), December: 47–65.

Braukämper, U. 2002. *Islamic History and Culture in Southern Ethiopia: Collected Essays*. Hamburg: Lit.

Cole, B.C. 1997. The Pilgrims of Sheikh Hussein. *Selamta* 14(3), July–September: 27–32.

Erlich, H. 2002. *The Cross and the River: Ethiopia, Egypt, and the Nile*. Boulder, Colorado: Lynne Rienner.

Erlich, H. 2007. *Saudi Arabia and Ethiopia: Islam, Christianity, and Politics Entwined*. Boulder, Colorado: Lynne Rienner.

Federal Democratic Republic of Ethiopia Population Census Commission. 2008. *Summary and Statistical Report of the 2007 Population and Housing Census*. http://www.csa.gov.et/pdf/Cen2007_firstdraft.pdf

Ford, Jr., F.P. 2008. Christian-Muslim Relations in Ethiopia: A Checkered Past, a Challenging Future. *The Reformed Review* 61(2), Spring: 52–70. http://www.westernsem.edu/media/rreview/spring2008.

Ford, Jr., F.P. 2009. Christian-Muslim Relations in Ethiopia: Lessons from the Past, Opportunities for the Future. *World Christianity in Muslim encounter: essays in Memory of David A. Kerr*, edited by S.R. Goodwin. London: Continuum: 54–70.

Foucher, E. 1994. The Cult of Muslim Saints in Harar: Religious Dimension. *Proceedings of the Eleventh International Conference of Ethiopian Studies, Vol. 2*, edited by B. Zewde, R. Pankhurst and T. Beyene. Addis Ababa: Institute of Ethiopian Studies: 71–83.

Guillaume, A. 1955. *The Life of Muhammad: A Translation of Isḥāq's Sīrat rasūl Allāh with Introduction and Notes.* London: Oxford University Press.

Hassan, M. 1992. Islam as a Resistance Ideology among the Oromo of Ethiopia: The Wallo Case, 1700–1900. *In the Shadow of Conquest: Islam in Colonial Northeast Africa*, edited by S.S. Samatar. Trenton, New Jersey: Red Sea Press: 75–101.

Kalb, J. 2000. *Adventures in the Bone Trade: The Race to Discover Human Ancestors in Ethiopia's Afar Depression*. New York: Copernicus.

Kapteijns, L. 2000. Ethiopia and the Horn of Africa. *The History of Islam in Africa*, edited by N. Levtzion and R.L. Pouwels. Athens, Ohio: Ohio University Press: 227–250.

Klein, J. 2005. The Ethiopian Evangelical Church Mekane Yesus and Its Understanding of Islam and Approaches to Muslims in Ethiopia from 1969–2004. MPhil. thesis, Missionsseminar Hermannsburg, Hermannsburg.

Lapidus, I.M. 2002. *A History of Islamic Societies*. 2nd edition. Cambridge: Cambridge University Press.

Lewis, I.M. 1986. Islam in Somalia. *Somalia in Word and Image*, edited by K. Loughuan. Bloomington: Indiana University Press: 139–142.

Marcus, H.G. 2002. *A History of Ethiopia*. 2nd edition. Berkeley: University of California Press.

Østebø, T. 1998. Creating a New Identity: The Position of Ethiopian Muslims in Contemporary Perspective. *Swedish Missiological Themes* 86(3): 423–454.

Østebø, T. 2007. *The Question of Becoming: Islamic Reform-movements in Contemporary Ethiopia*. Bergen: Chr. Michelsen Institute (CMI working papers). (No. 2007:8).

Østebø, T. 2008. Christian-Muslim Relations in Ethiopia. *Striving in Faith: Christians and Muslims in Africa*, edited by A.N. Kubai and T. Adebo. Uppsala: Life and Peace Institute: 71–89.

Parrinder, G. 1965. *Jesus in the Qur'ān*. London: Sheldon Press.

Robinson, D. 2004. *Muslim Societies in African History*. Cambridge: Cambridge University Press.

Tamrat, T. 1972. *Church and State in Ethiopia: 1270–1527*. Oxford: Clarendon Press.

Trimingham, J.S. 1965. *Islam in Ethiopia*. London: Frank Cass.

Trimingham, J.S. 1979. *Christianity among the Arabs in Pre-Islamic Times*. London: Longman.

Waldron, S.R. 1978. Harar: The Muslim City in Ethiopia. *Proceedings of the Fifth International Conference of Ethiopian Studies, Session B, April 13–16, 1978, Chicago, U.S.A.*, edited by R.L. Hess. Chicago: University of Chicago Press: 239–257.

Zekaria, A. 1998. Harar: The Land of Ziyara, Pilgrimage. *Papers of the First Interdisciplinary Seminar of the Institute of Ethiopian Studies*. Addis Ababa: Institute of Ethiopian Studies: 1–9.

CHAPTER 14

Ghana

Rahman Yakubu

Ghana, like most sub-Saharan African countries, is multi-ethnic and pluralistic and, therefore, pluralism prevails in the religious sphere. With an estimated population of 23 million, Ghana is ethnically diverse. Ghana has more than seventy-five different languages, and they can be grouped into four language families: the Akan constituting 49.1 per cent of Ghanaians, the Mole-Dagomba (16.5 per cent), the Ewe (12.7 per cent), and Ga-Dangme (8 per cent) (Dakubu 1988). In terms of religious composition, Christians constitute about 69 per cent of the population, African Traditional Religions (ATR) about 8.5 per cent, Islam about 15.6 per cent and other religions about 6.7 per cent (*2000 Census* 2002: 26).

The relations between adherents of the various religious bodies could generally be seen as one of peaceful co-existence, although there have been incidents of tension and mistrust.[1] Despite the fact the number of Muslims is comparatively lower than the number of Christians, Islam is considered as a national religion on a par with Christianity and African Traditional Religion. There is also a perception that Islam is the religion of the north and Christianity the religion of the south.

---

1. Two such incidents are: a case in 1995 where a preacher is alleged to have desecrated the Qur'an in a public preaching resulting in clashes between Christians and Muslims in Sekondi, Kumasi and Tamale (Cf. Yakubu 2006: 106); another case was the refusal of some charismatic/Pentecostal churches to observe the 'ban on drumming and noise making' at certain time of the cerebration of the Ga religious festival in 1999, 2000 (Addo 2009: 95–97).

In what follows, I hope to show how Ghanaian Christians respond to the presence of Islam and engage with Muslims. The primary focus of this chapter is a case study of the Protestant and Catholic response to Islam through the work of the Christian Council of Ghana and the Catholic Bishops' Conference, respectively. These two bodies represent over two-thirds of the Christian population. It is my hope that some conclusions can be drawn and lessons learned from their approach, which will be of use to other Christians in Africa and beyond. In order to see the full picture, let us first take a brief look at Muslims in Ghana and other Christian engagement with Muslims, specifically Pentecostal-charismatic groups and evangelical missionary organisations.

Islam and Muslims in Ghana

Islam came to Ghana from the north by land and spread down to the south around the fourteenth century through Angara Muslim traders also known as Doula and Yare (Clarke 1982: 58–59; Ryan 1996: 71). The total population of Muslims in Ghana today is not certain because the official 2000 population census report was challenged by the Coalition of Muslims Association. They estimate their population to be between 30 per cent to 45 per cent rather than the 15.6 per cent reported in the census. They accused the statistical council of conspiracy to deny the reality of the growing population of Muslims in the country (Dole and Ashanti 2003: 216). The majority of Muslims are originally from the northern part of the country; additionally, immigrants from mostly Muslim people groups from neighbouring countries are also found in the *Zongos*[2] of the south. There are also converts among the Faints, Gas and Ashanti's.

Islam's impact in Ghana was felt as far back as the 1750s when Muslims served as scribes in local courts and helped traditional rulers with administration (Clarke 1983). There were two stages to the Islamization

---

2. *Zongo* is a Hausa word, which means 'strangers' quarters'. In Ghana it is generally use to describe a part of town of city where there are immigrants' settlements. In the south of Ghana this includes the settlements of people from the north.

process; the first was confined to immigrants, a process that may be termed the dispersion of Muslims rather than the spread of Islam, and the second stage was the building up of communication between hospitable chiefs and their guests (Levtzion 1968, xxv). The openness of the chieftaincy institution towards Islam and the cultural adaptability of the early Muslims were instrumental in the spread of Islam in Ghana, as was the British colonial policy of protecting Muslims, which restricted Christian missionary activity to non-Muslim areas. This is evident from the high presence of Muslims among some northern kingdoms, such as Dagombas, Honjas and Wales.

In Ghana today there are three main Muslims groups; the Sunni, *Ahmadian* and Shia. Among the Sunni are the *Tijaniya* and the Hauls Sunna Wall Jama'at (ASWJ), also known as the Wahhabi, although they prefer to be called ASWJs. The Tijaniya is the oldest and most predominant form of Islam in Ghana and represents the mystical and folk face of Islam. They see themselves as a Muslim brotherhood and are mostly peaceful, accommodating, and contextual, if not syncretistic. Although ASWJ is a latecomer, its presence is felt throughout the country particularly in the cities and big towns. They see themselves as reformist (although others consider them to be more fundamentalist or radical), believing in the strict adherence to the Holy Qur'an and the hadith as the only sources of authority.

The Ahmadiyyas are the missionary, and to a larger extent, the polemical face of Islam. The Ahmadiyya Muslim Mission, the main body representing Ahmadiyya Muslims in Ghana, focuses on mission and education. In the past, the mission was noted for its anti-Christian as well as anti-mainline Muslim polemics in public preaching (Azumah 2001). Presently relations between the hierarchy of the group and the church (particularly the Catholic and the Protestant churches) can be described as one of cooperation on social action. They have a separate educational unit recognized by the government, with schools ranging from primary schools to a teacher training college.

Shia Islam, which is the latest arrival on the Ghanaian scene, makes its presence felt in development projects.[3]

---

3. They have a number of projects in the Ghana one of which is the first Islamic University

In term of ethnic distribution, the Tijaniya is very strong among the northern tribes such as the Dagombas, Gonjas and Mamprusis. Likewise, predominant among the Fantis and Ashantis of the south is the Ahmadiya Muslim Mission. The ASWJ attracts the urban populace and therefore is common in the towns and cities.

Tensions and divisions exist between the various Muslim communities. From the 1950s until recently, there have been verbal and physical confrontations not just between the Sunnis and Ahmadiyyas, but also within the Sunni community between Ahlus, Sunna, Wal Jama'a and Tijaniyas (cf. Samwini 2006). This lack of unity has resulted in each group celebrating the two *idds* on different dates most of the time. It is also expressed in the little regard the ASWJs have for the Tijaniya national chief *imam* as the national leader of the Muslim *umma*.

Over the past two decades or so, Islam has been elevated to a level equal with Christianity and African Traditional Religion, and so is not seen as a religion of the minority or of northerners but as a national religion. The government now provides personnel and school materials and even pays the teachers in the Arabic/English schools. The two festivals of *idd-ul-fitr and idd-ul-adha* are celebrated as official national holidays.

Christianity and Christians in Ghana

Ghana's first contact with Christianity happened around 1482 with the arrival of Portuguese merchants and explorers. However, effective Christian witness was not started until around the early 1800s with the arrival of the Basel missionaries (Debrunner 1967: 223). Having arrived from the coast, Christianity was slow in spreading to the north. As noted, this was partly due to the British colonial restrictions of missionary activity to non-Muslim areas until after World War II (Clarke 1982: 191). The upper north of the country had its first contact with Christianity from Burkina

---

College. Other projects include three clinics (two in Accra and one in the Jana, Tamale) and an NGO known as Agriculture and Rural Development, based in Tamale in the Northern region and Kasoa in the Central region.

Faso in 1906 through the 'White Fathers'. However, Muslim areas did not have contact with Christian ministry until 1912, which was through the Basel mission, and in the 1930s through the Assemblies of God Mission (Debrunner 1967: 224, 326).

As a result of over two hundred years of active mission work, Christianity has spread through the length and breadth of Ghana. With 69 per cent of the total population of Ghana, it is the largest religion with hundreds of denominations. With this large number, it is impossible to give a clear picture of the denominational breakdown. The 2000 census put Catholics at 15.1 per cent of the population, Protestants at 18.6 per cent, Pentecostal/charismatics at 24.1 per cent and other denominations at 11.0 per cent (2002: 26).[4] Now there is an increasing awareness of the presence of Pentecostal/charismatic churches because of their radio and television preaching, which usually focuses on healing and prosperity and is to some extent a motivational talk.

One of the main areas in which Christianity makes an impact in Ghana is education. Up until 1850, education was mainly limited to the mercantile class for learning bookkeeping. Starting in the 1860s Christian missions led the way in providing Western education. By 1950 the Christian missions together accounted for more than two-thirds of Ghana's schools, all situated in the south (Samwini 2006: 71). Presently most denominations are setting up private schools, ranging from the elementary to the tertiary level.

Christians Engagement with Muslims in Ghana

Before coming to the main focus of this paper, let us first take a brief look at other Christian engagement with Muslims. A number of church groups, mission agencies and para-church organisations are doing ministry among Muslims in Ghana today. One of the organisations devoted to converting Muslims is the Converted Muslims Christian Association (CMCA) which came to prominence in the 1980s and 1990s. Though some mission

---

4. There was a more recent census in 2010, but those figures have not yet been published. I cannot be sure that the denominational distribution is still the same.

organisations such as Serving In Mission (SIM), World Evangelisation for Christ (WEC) and others have ministry among Muslims, it is not specifically to reach Muslims, but as part of their effort to reach Ghana as a whole. As a result, they view Muslims as 'objects of conversion', not as people to build relationships with, which makes their approach very polemic. I have found that most of these groups, with the exception of the CMCA, do not have policies on Christian-Muslim engagement, only on conversion. Similarly, the Ghana Pentecostal Council (GPC), which most of the Pentecostal and charismatic churches come under, does not have policies or training for member churches on issues relating to Islam and Christian-Muslim relations. As a result, member churches have little understanding of Islam and Christian-Muslim relations.[5] Some of their approaches to Muslims are polemic and confrontational, sometimes resulting in bitter clashes between their members and Muslims.

The Ghanaian Protestant churches, which form the Christian Council of Ghana (CCG), and the Bishops' Conference of the Catholic Church, approach Muslims differently because of their understanding of Islam and motives for engaging with them. The case study that follows is an attempt to show how the two Christian bodies have taken a relational approach in responding to the presence of Islam and approach Muslims.

Mainline Protestants—Christian Council of Ghana

The Christian Council of Ghana was founded in 1929 as an ecumenical body as a result of the union of five churches, which later came to be known as the mainline churches.[6] The Council was formed to strengthen member

---

5. In an email to the Ghana Pentecostal Council requesting information on their policies and approach to Muslims, Dr. M. Tawia-Ransford (the administrator) emailed back that there were no policies and each member decides how they engage with Muslims (email correspondence with author, 8th May 2010).

6. Omenyo refers to mainline churches as those older and generally larger churches instituted as a result of European missionary activity in Ghana in the 19th Century (Omenyo 2002: 36–37). The old Pentecostal churches such as the Assemblies of God and the Church of Pentecost are often considered mainline churches also, although they have never been part of the CCG.

churches for fellowship, service, and witness, to co-operate for the common interest of the churches, and to promote certain fundamental human values such as peace, justice, unity and reconciliation (*Constitution* 2000). Presently the membership consists of sixteen churches and two Christian organisations.[7] Membership is open to all autonomous Christian churches and ecumenical organisations operating within Ghana that confess Jesus as Lord and Saviour. However, Pentecostals and the African Initiated Churches (AICs) chose not to be members mostly due to doctrinal disagreement on the issue relating to the Holy Spirit.

The Christian Council has been engaged with Muslims through the work of the Programme for Christian-Muslim Relations in Africa (PROCMURA). The Council was founded in 1959 as the Islam in Africa Project (IAP), of which Ghana is a founding member. It was established to help the church in Africa understand its mission in the midst of Muslims. It works as a department of the council whose goal, among others, is to understand Islam and interpret the gospel in the midst of Muslims. Since its formation, it has worked to educate the church in Africa by informing it through authentic research into Islam (*PROCMURA Constitution* 1995: 1). It also educates the church by equipping it to understand Islam and offer appropriate Christian witness to Muslims.

PROCMURA uses a number of activities to achieve its purpose; chief among them is the study of Islam. Because of the high level of ignorance about Islam among Christians and the reality of the potential for inter-religious conflicts, PROCMURA saw the need to equip co-ordinators of its programmes to properly educate the church to understand Islam and to constructively engage with Muslims. To achieve this it has been instrumental in helping resource people with the programme to acquire the

---

7. The member churches are: African Methodist Episcopal (AME) Zion Church, English Church Mission (Anglican), Ewe Presbyterian Church (now Evangelical Presbyterian Church of Ghana and Evangelical Presbyterian Church, Ghana), Presbyterian Church of Gold Coast (now Presbyterian Church of Ghana), and Wesleyan Methodist Church (now Methodist Church of Ghana), Salvation Army, African Methodist Episcopal Church, Ghana Baptist Convention, Greek Orthodox Church, Evangelical Church of Ghana, Christ Evangelical Mission, Ghana Mennonite Church, Religious Society of Friends, Evangelical Lutheran Church, F'Eden Mission Church, Christian Methodist Episcopal Church. The two Christian organisations are: Young Women's Christian Association and Young Men's Christian Association.

relevant academic qualification by granting scholarships to study Islam in programmes ranging the certificate to the doctoral level.

One of the main activities of the Council is organizing and running seminars and workshops for churches on Islam, Christian witness and interfaith relations. These run from three days to one week and participants are usually pastors, lay workers, women and youth workers. The seminars consist of two courses: the basic course deals with an introduction to Islam and Christian-Muslim relations and the advanced course deals with issues relating to Islamic theology and Christian witness to Muslims.

PROCMURA also produces literature publications to carry out its educational mandate, including a quarterly newsletter, which seeks to inform churches of its programmes and report on activities. In Ghana, it published a women's newsletter known as *Breakthrough*. This was intended to be an annual newsletter to serve as a forum for dissemination of information and sharing of ideas among members, but it was never published again. The results of the earliest research were published in *Questions Muslims Ask*; it was first printed in pamphlet form and now is in book form. It is intended to help Christians explain their faith to their Muslim friends and be able to give credible witness to their faith.

Based on the above-mentioned activities, one may suggest that the approach of the CCG and the mainline Protestant church to Muslims is non-confrontational (cf. Dovlo and Asante 2003: 219). This is reflected in the work of early consultants to PROCMURA, such as James Dretke, who published a book entitled *A Christian Approach to Muslims: Reflections from West Africa* with the view of promoting the non-polemic approach. This attitude is reflected in their reports, as the following shows:

> To have good news but not know how to deliver that good news could make it bad news. And for that matter Christians who have such good news, and who are commissioned to bear the message of reconciliation to all men on earth need to know how to present this news to all men *without offending anyone* (Samwini 1996: 1, italics mine).

This approach seems to engage Muslims in a holistic way, rather than focusing only on their conversion. It takes into account the Christian responsibility to witness to Muslims and to do this responsibly without inviting conflicts. In so doing, it has tried to keep a balance between its missiological and existential responsibilities. Through research and education on Islam, Christians are equipped to witness in a constructive way. The goal is to work toward peace, mutual understanding and tolerance to create the environment necessary for Christian witness. Any method that does not conform to this is unacceptable, as in the case of a CCG worker in 1984, whose aggressive and confrontational approach, particularly in using public debates to witness to Muslims, eventually resulted in his departure.

Roman Catholic Church

The Ghana Catholic Bishops' Conference, also known as the Bishops' Conference (BC), is the central body of the Catholic Church in Ghana and its main purpose is to deal with issues of concern to the Catholic Church and to encourage activities in accordance with the need of the times. The Association of Episcopal Conferences of Anglophone West Africa – Inter-Religious Dialogue Commission (AECAWA-IRDC)[8] is responsible for inter-religious affairs of the bishops' conferences. The commission is regionally based, which is concerned with Anglophone West Africa. All their policies and activities are geared towards this region.

In a broader sense, AECAWA-IRDC was founded to foster dialogue between Catholics and other religions. It was established in response to Pope John Paul II's address to the Secretariat for Non-Christians (now Pontifical Council for Inter-religious Dialogue, PCID) on 3 March 1984, in which he stressed the importance and necessity of inter-religious dialogue (*Constitution* nd: 1). This address has been the key motivation for Catholic engagement with people of other faiths.

---

8. As of 2010 the AECAWA and its Francophone sister organisation (the Association of Episcopal Conferences of Francophone West Africa) merged to form the Regional Episcopal Conferences of West Africa (RECOWA).

Over the years, the Catholic Church has been engaged with Muslims mainly through joint study sessions and research into Islam. The joint study session is its primary activity of engagement with people of other faiths. It is an annual event and usually a three-day study session during which Muslims, Christians and ATR practitioners present and discuss study papers on issues of common concern.

The first joint study session was organised in 1996 in Nigeria and subsequently others were held alternately in Nigeria and in Ghana. The papers and the discussion of participants and the communiqué are published in booklet form. Most of the topics cover broad areas such as peace, development, social justice and inter-religious dialogue. Additionally, studies on Islam are done and subsequently published to inform Catholics on issues of inter-faith dialogue.

The content of the sessions shows the motivation of the Catholic Church in engaging with Islam is based on existential reasons and on collaboration for development.[9]

The Catholic Church's approach to Muslims is not unique to Ghana but follows Vatican's policy. The approach to Muslims is through dialogue, understood as both a theological and practical engagement. Dialogue of this nature is grounded on love for each human person, the bond connecting cultural and religious confessions of people, giving dialogue an ethical basis and the common roots Christians and Muslims have in Abraham, which calls for a collaborative responsibility (*Constitution*: 1; cf. *Communiqué* 1997: 88 and *Communiqué* 1998: 27).

The manner in which dialogue is engaged in is of particular importance to the commission. Its engagement with Muslims has been termed by some as an institutionalised form of dialogue of life.[10] Witnessing with the sole purpose of converting the other is not part of the agenda. In this dialogue, the participant retains his or her religious identity and respects the religious identity of the dialogue partner. This kind of dialogue is conceptual in

---

9. From 1996 to 2004, seven themes were dealt with and edited by Joseph Kenny O.P.

10. The Vatican distinguishes four types of dialogue: dialogue of life, dialogue of mind, dialogue of heart and dialogue of social action. This institutionalized form of dialogue of life as it is practised by the commission is sometimes seen by Catholics as dialogue of social action.

its approach. The goal is primarily a theological and a practical exchange, aiming at changes in attitude and perception (cf. *Communiqué* 2002: 97). It combines mutual enrichment and practical action as its focus. Although the commission assumes that the mutual enrichment realised (*Communiqué* 2000: 7, *Communiqué* 2004: 2) will translate into dialogue of life for its followers, the truth is, this is far from the reality. For one thing, the target audience of its activities has been the elite or the hierarchy of the Muslim *umma*. In my experience, this has never translated into good neighbourly relationships between Catholics and Muslims.

Assessments and Impacts

In conclusion, one has to say that the approaches of the CCG and of the Catholic Bishops' Conference have made considerable progress in meeting their goals and objectives. Five things have become apparent to me in doing this assessment.

First, as CCG has set out to do, it has raised the level of the awareness of the presence of Islam and the challenge it poses to Christianity. Reports from the CCG show high levels of interest in understanding Islam and engaging with Muslims. According to Samwini, 'the motives for the participants may vary but the important thing detected there was that Christians no longer see Islam as a non-entity but a force to reckon with' (1998: 1).

Second, the approach has contributed to changing Ghanaian Christians' mentality towards Muslims. For instance, in the PROCMURA archives are reports of both change in attitude and perception about Islam and Muslims because of the seminars and workshops. One participant is reported to have said, 'Actually the course has been very helpful to me. Prior to this programme I had a different view of Muslims, but now I have seen that they are not violent people' (Samwini 1996: 3).

Third, in relative terms there is religious tolerance and peaceful co-existence between Christian and Muslims. This is the goal which both the CCG and the Catholic Bishops' Conference sought to achieve.

Fourth, a question that may need to be asked is, 'To what extent has the Protestant Church in Ghana made an impact on Islam and Muslims? Has the programme carried out by PROCMURA increased Christian witness among Muslims?' In other words, is there visible and authentic Christian witness by member churches of the CCG resulting in the formation of churches in majority Muslim areas in the north? There is the need for more research to ascertain the impact of this approach on Muslim conversion to Christianity.

Fifth, a lesson to be learnt and an approach to Muslims to work towards is that of relationship building. As is evident from the approach of both the Protestants and the Catholics, the key seems to be studying Islam to understand Muslims, and thereby build better relationships. This is not necessarily new in Ghana. Christians and Muslims have had shared lives in families and communities. The Christian community should promote this concept and take it into all spheres of society. This should be the Christian witness. Christians seem, in my experience, to be talking to each other about Muslims and Islam, without talking and sharing with Muslims about their experiences of Christ.

References

2000 Population and Housing Census: Summary of Report of Final Results. 2002. Ghana Statistical Service: Accra.
Addo, E.I. 2009. *Worldview, Way of Life and Worship: The Continuing Encounter between the Christian Faith and Ga Religion and Culture*. Zoetermeer: Boekencentrum.
AECAWA-DERIRD Communiqués, 1997, 1998, 2000, 2002, 2004.
Archives of Christian Council of Ghana and Association of Episcopal Conference of Anglophone West Africa-Inter Religious Dialogue Commission (AECAWA-DERIRD).
Azumah, J. 2001. *The Legacy of Arab-Islam in Africa: A Quest for Inter-religious Dialogue*. Oxford: One World.
Christian Council of Ghana. 2002. Constitution of Christian Council of Ghana.
Clarke, P. 1982. *West Africa and Islam: A Study of Religious Development from the 18th to 20th Century*. London: Edward Arnold.
Dakubu, M.E.K. (ed.)1988. *The Languages of Ghana*. London: Kegan Paul International.

Debrunner, H.W. 1967. *History of Christianity in Ghana*. Accra: Waterville Publishing Houses.
Dovlo, E., and Ashanti, A.O. 2003. Reinterpreting the Straight Path: Ghanaian Muslim Converts in Mission to Muslims. *Exchange* 32(3): 214–238.
Dretke, J.P. 1979. *A Christian Approach to Muslims: Reflections from West Africa*. Pasadena: William Carey Library.
Kenny, J. (ed.) 1996. *African Traditional Religious Movements*. Lagos, Nigeria.
Kenny, J. (ed.) 1997. *Islam and Christianity on Human Development in West Africa*. Nsawam, Ghana.
Kenny, J. (ed.) 1998. *Religion and the Pursuit of Peace and Social Justice*. Lagos, Nigeria.
Kenny, J. (ed.) 1999. *Christians, Muslims and Believers of African Traditional Religion and the Great Jubilee*. Accra, Ghana.
Kenny, J. (ed.) 2000. *Inter-religious Dialogue and Nation Building*. Ibadan, Nigeria.
Kenny, J. (ed.) 2002. *Religion, Violence and Peace in West Africa*. Accra, Ghana.
Kenny, J. (ed.) 2003. *Offer Forgiveness and Receive Peace: A Challenge to Multi-religious Society*. Kaduna, Nigeria.
Kenny, J. (ed.) 2004. *Peace: Preachers and Politicians*. Tamale, Ghana.
Levtzion, N. 1968. *Muslims and Chiefs in West Africa. A Study of Islam in the Middle Volta Basin in the Pre-colonial Period*. Oxford: Clarendon Press.
Levtzion, N., and Randall, L. (eds.) 2000. *The History of Islam in Africa*. Athens: Ohio University Press.
National Catholic Secretariats. *Constitution of AECAWA-DERIRD*, nd.
Omenyo, C. 2002. *Pentecost Outside Pentecostalism: A Study of the Development of the Charismatic Renewal in the Mainline Churches in Ghana*. Zoetermeer: Boekencentrum.
Programme for Christian-Muslim Relations in Africa. *Constitution of PROCMURA*, Amended 1995.
Ryan, P. 1996. Islam in Ghana: Its Major Influence and the Situation Today. *Orita*, 28(1–2).
Samwini, N. 1996. *Report on Lay Facilitators School,* Sunyani, November 3–14 (unpublished report).
Samwini, N. 2006. *The Muslim Resurgence in Ghana Since the 1950 and Its Effects upon Muslims and Muslim-Christian Relations*. Berlin: LIT.
Yakubu, A.R. 2006. Christian Eegagement with Muslims in Ghana. *Ghana Bulletin of Theology* 1(1) July: 102–117.

———. 1998. *Inter Faith Programme Report for First Quarter*, January–March (unpublished report).

CHAPTER 15

Kenya

Stephen Mutuku Sesi

In sub-Saharan Africa, the East African coast has a unique experience with Islam and Christianity. Although Islam preceded Christianity in Kenya by almost 500 years, its impact upon the peoples of East Africa and specifically Kenya has been significantly weak. Islam came to Kenya through traders from Arabia. It developed along the coast in three phases: early Arab trade and settlement, establishment of Shirazi city-states and the rule by Omani imams. Between 1498 and 1698 Portuguese colonial rule interrupted Islamic growth.

Arrival and Spread of Islam Along the Swahili Coast of Kenya

The arrival of Islam in Kenya probably dates back to the year 950, when an Arabic population came to Kenya and settled in Manda Island (Allen 1993: 24). As Arabs settled along the East Coast of Africa, people groups slowly became Muslims by being absorbed into the culture of the Muslim Arabs while Islam was absorbed into the culture of the Bantu people. Islamization occurred because of assimilation, political organisation and colonisation.

Early Arab Settlement: Islamization by Assimilation

The assimilation process was influenced by three sociological factors: economics, marriage and slavery. African traders were encouraged by their

Muslim friends to become Muslims as a condition of continuing to trade together. The Muslim traders settled in town centres along the coast and established contact with people who could supply them with ivory, leather, rhinoceros horns, gold and slaves (Sperling 2000: 283).

Intermarriage between Arab traders and Bantu women from the Swahili tribes cemented the affiliation and developed a long-term relationship that helped maintain peace between Islam and other religions along the coast of Kenya. Islam's adoption of a local language, Swahili, which had emerged in the ninth century, contributed to assimilation (Spear 2000: 258–259; Pouwels 2000: 253).[1] Swahili was to become the *lingua franca* of the East Coast of Africa and the liturgical language of Islam.

Slavery was also used to introduce Islam to African tribes, who were captured and sold to slavery as early as the tenth century. Slaves were exported to the gulf nations from north coast ports like Malindi, Mombasa and Lamu (Allen 1993: 167). Many Arabs and Asians in Kenya took Mijikenda land and owned slaves from local tribes like the Digo and Giryama, who cultivated the land[2] and looked after their livestock. The slaves were always forced to become Muslims in order to get better treatment.

After a long trade relationship between the Cushite tribes at the horn of Africa and Arabs from Hadramat in the Arabian Peninsula, the African tribes became Muslims early in the history of the religion. In the ninth century, coastal traders brought Islam to Harar on the Ethiopian plateau and propagated Islam as they traded (Lapidus 2002: 435). This long relationship led to the Islamization of the tribes like the Somali, Rendille, Oromo and Orma, which live in North Eastern Province and the northern part of Eastern Province. Although the populations of these tribes are not

---

1. Swahili is believed to be a Bantu language with a conventional linguistic history. It is closely related with other Bantu languages of the coastal area with its roots from Sabaki languages including Mijikenda, Pokomo, Comorian and Ilwana. However, it borrowed from Arabic in the areas of religion, law, administration, trade, sailing, measurement, and kinship (Spear 2000: 272). An alternative view exists which believes that Swahili is an Arab-African language with its roots from the intermarriages between Bantu women and Arab merchants along the coast of East Africa.
2. 'In 1860 about 700 slaves were annually re-exported from Zanzibar to Mombasa and Malindi' (Sheriff 1987: 70–71).

large, their conversion to Islam changed the demographic distribution of settlement in modern Kenya significantly.

The Shirazian Period: Islamization by Political Organisation

Between 1050 and 1150, Shirazi Muslims, who claimed their origin was Shiraz in Persia, appeared in East Africa and used political organisation to further Islamization. As merchants and landowners, they organized the trade of the Swahili Coast and possessed estates, which were cultivated by their slaves (Nicholls 1971: 25). They were responsible more than any other traders who preceded them for the conversion of the Swahili communities into Islam.

The Shirazi settled in Malindi, Mombasa and Vanga and organized the Coastal Strip politically. Evidence of Shirazi city-state settlements such as the Gedi remains near Malindi is found in the remains of fortified towns along the coast. Abu Abd Allah Ibn Battuta (b. 1304) recorded that when he visited Mombasa he found the organized city-states were wealthy and inhabited by very Black people who followed Shafi'ite School of Islamic Law (Robinson 2004: 33–34).

The Omani Period: Islamization by Colonisation

In 1698 Omani Sultan's forces captured Fort Jesus in Mombasa and colonised East Africa up to the mid-twentieth century (Nicholls 1971: 21). These Arabs comprised several groups, including Sunnis from Muscat, Ibadites and Shafi'is. Only a small number of Muslims who follow the Ibadi School of *fiqh* (Islamic jurisprudence) remain in Zanzibar (An-Na'im 2002: 58).

When Sayyid Said Bin Sultan Al-Busaidy (1787–1856) became the Sultan of Oman in 1830, he transferred his seat of power to Zanzibar in 1837 in order to colonise East Africa from close range. The Omanis did not establish a deep relationship with native Africans and clung to their Arabian identity. They exploited and subjected Africans to servitude and slavery (Middleton 1992: 13). Under the leadership of Saiyid Sa'id, Islam spread into the heart of Kenya and Tanzania through the trade routes (Robinson 2004: 37). Today the symbol of Islamic presence, the mosque, is found along all the main roads and in towns and in high schools. On Mombasa Nairobi highway there is a mosque roughly every fifty kilometres.

Arrival and Spread of Christianity in Kenya

The earliest arrival of Christianity in Kenya was the fifteenth century when the Portuguese introduced Roman Catholicism. In the mid-nineteenth century, Protestant missionaries arrived.

Jesus of Mombasa Fort

In 1497 Portuguese explorers led by Vasco da Gama docked in the town of Malindi and after going to India and back in 1498, constructed the Portuguese chapel and the Vasco da Gama pillar. Both are still standing and maintained by the National Museums of Kenya. Malindi was the headquarters of the Portuguese traders until the Portuguese conquered Mombasa and set up their headquarters in their new fort. The fort was built in 1593 and named 'Jesus of Mombasa'. Building the fort was important on many levels for the Portuguese. 'Trade required the establishment of forts but it was also seen as a religious, and even a missionary, activity. It was part of an anti-Islamic crusade', and needed papal sanction and ecclesiastical authorization (Hastings 1994: 71). Jonathan Hildebrandt records that the Augustinian Friars who accompanied the explorers built a monastery in 1567 and a church in 1598 in Mombasa (1981: 65). In most places where the Portuguese traded, they watched for the opportunities to start Christian work.[3]

Christian Dominicans, who were in Kenya to serve the expatriates who were involved in slave trade, reported that some indigenous Africans had become Christians. The martyr of Christians in Mombasa in 1631 by the Muslim king of Mombasa included expatriates and indigenous Africans (Hastings 1994: 122). As the influence of the Portuguese declined in

---

3. At Ghana, Benin (probably in modern Nigeria) and the Congo Kingdom, the Portuguese sent missionaries along with traders and baptized many people, including members of the royal families (King 1971: 31).

1698 after they were forced out of East Africa by the Omani Imams, the converts relapsed to Islam, and those who resisted were massacred (Groves 1948: 138).

Arrival of Missionaries in Mombasa

On 5 May 1844, Ludwig Krapf (b. 1810), a German, arrived in Mombasa to begin missionary work under the London-based Church Missionary Society (CMS). A linguist, he learned Swahili and translated nearly the entire New Testament into Swahili by 1846 and created a dictionary of about 4,000 words (Groves 1954: 98). This was the first attempt by Christian missionaries to contextualize the gospel for the Swahili tribes of Kenya. With his colleague Johannes Rebmann, he made many trips inland from Mombasa, and they founded their first mission station among the Nyika (*Mijikenda*) in Rabai Mpia (New Rabai) in 1846, fifteen miles north of Mombasa. Later four Methodist missionaries, brought to Mombasa by Krapf in 1862, founded the first Methodist mission station in Ribe.

By 1848 when Ludwig Krapf visited *Udigoni* and his company arrived in the Wadigo village of Kusi, chief Muhensano received him in a friendly manner. Krapf had the chance to preach the gospel to the villagers. When the Muslims challenged him on the issue of dietary laws, he spoke boldly against Muhammad.

In his response to criticism from a Muslim he refers to as 'Bana Kheri', who called him *mkafiri* (infidel) because he ate pork and meat slaughtered by the *wanika* (bush people), Krapf said Muhammad was an 'impostor who stole from the Bible and Christianity everything good taught in the Koran' and spread his religion by sword' (1968: 273–274). This kind of religious confrontation marked the early contact between Christian missionaries and Muslims in Kenya.

Church Missionary Society (1875–1914)

Between 1875 and 1914 the operations of CMS from the Mombasa Diocese were concentrated on three Mijikenda tribes who live around the city of Mombasa, namely the Rabai, Giriama and Digo (Strayer 1978: 31). Within that period CMS expanded its stations from the original two in Rabai and Freetown to sixteen dispersed throughout eastern and central

Kenya. In addition to establishing stations among the Mijikenda, CMS started them mainly among the Taita, Kamba and Kikuyu.

In the 1890s the Church of Scotland Mission, Church Missionary Society, Africa Inland Mission and the Roman Catholic Church moved to inland Kenya. In 1891 the Church of Scotland Mission set up its first mission station at Kibwezi among the Akamba; later they moved to Kikuyu near Nairobi to set up their headquarters. In 1895 the Africa Inland Mission arrived in Kenya and set up its first mission station at Nzaui among the Akamba; later they moved to Kijabe to set up their headquarters. In 1891 the Holy Ghost Fathers pioneered work at Voi and moved to Nairobi in 1899; they also introduced arabica coffee to Kenya at their St. Austin's station in Nairobi. In 1901 CMS and Methodists who had work on the coast, began working in Kikuyuland (Shaw 1996: 191–192).

Demographics of Tribal Distribution and Religious Affiliation in Kenya

Historically the religious beliefs have been divided along tribal lines, with certain tribes being the dominant believers in particular denominations. The latest survey carried by the Pew Foundation on Islam and Christianity in sub-Saharan Africa identified that 88 per cent of Kenyans are Christians and 11 per cent are Muslims (*Pew Forum* April 2010: 20).

Muslim Distribution

Some tribes are officially considered Muslim. Tribes that were Muslims had been left alone until after independence when Christians were allowed to preach the gospel everywhere. To avoid competition among the different Protestant denominations, a comity agreement was reached to divide the country into different spheres of influence (Shaw 1996: 191). The tribes that were Muslims were left alone; therefore, the Digo, Somali, Bajun, Arabs, Rendille, Oromo and other small tribes officially became Muslim tribes.

Kenyan Tribes

Map 1 demonstrates demographically how Kenyan tribes are religiously affiliated. The Coast Province has majority Muslim population south of Mombasa because the Digo tribe, which lives between Mombasa and Tanga in Tanzania, are Muslims. The northern part of the Coast Province is inhabited mainly by the Giryama and Pokomo, who are mainly traditional in their religious beliefs. A few Somalis, Aweer, Bajun, and Arabs near Lamu, are Muslims. In the North Eastern Province Muslim tribes like Somali and the Oromo dominate. Smaller tribes like Munyoyaya, Borana, Gabra, Rendille, Samburu, Burji, and Sekuye are Muslims.

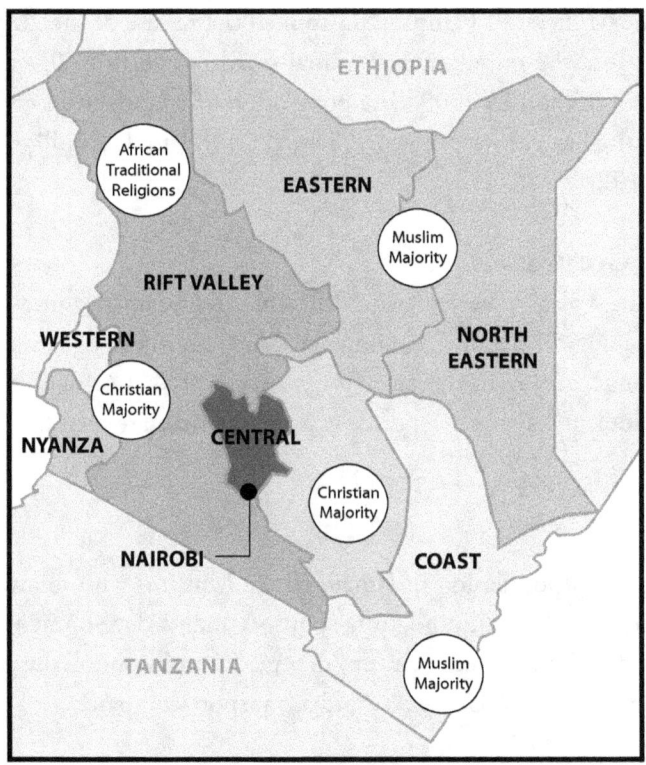

MAP 1: Tribal Distribution and Religious Affiliation in Kenya
(Adapted from Githii 2008:1)

Somali Refugees

The majority of the Somalis live in Somalia and Somaliland, but following the civil war, which has lasted two decades, more than one million Somalis have fled the country with many of them residing in Kenya (Mutuli 2007). It was reported in the *Daily Nation* Newspaper on 16 February 2010 that some of the Somali refugees in Kenya have illegally acquired Kenyan identity cards and passports, something that has significantly increased the current population of Kenyan Somalis (Mayoyo 2010: 17). On 9 January 2010 Andrew Teyie wrote the article 'Kenya: 2009 Census Delayed over Somali Numbers' in the *Nairobi Star*, in which he said that 'the number of Somalis had risen by 140 per cent over the last twenty years' (Teyie 2010). The Minister of Planning postponed the release of the 2009 census results because the population of Somalis had grown from 0.9 million in 1989 to 2.3 million in 2009. The population of Mandera District, which borders Somalia, grew from 0.4 million in 1989 to 1.1 million in 2009 (Teyie 2010).

Muslim Groups

The Muslim tribes have remained Muslim, and Islam has grown mainly through biological means.[4] Among the Muslims, the majority are Sunni (8 per cent according to the *Pew Forum*, April 2010: 143) who follow the Shafii School of Law and 1 per cent is Shia. There are also Ismails, Sufis and Whabis.

Ismailis

There is a small population of Ismaili Khoja Muslims who follow the Aga Khan. The Aga Khan foundation sponsors many development projects including the Nation Media Group, the Aga Khan Hospital, the Aga Khan schools, the Aga Khan University and a transport company.

---

4. A recent survey on Islam and Christianity in sub-Saharan Africa revealed that most of the people who were adherents of African Traditional Religion in 1900 have converted to Christianity, but the tribes that were Muslims have remained Muslims with a small growth that may be attributed to biological growth. In Kenya the situation is not different (*Pew Forum* 2010).

Sufis

The *Shadhiliya*[5] and *Qadiriya* Orders of Sufism are found in Kenya. Shadhiliya is popular in the North Eastern Province and the northern Coast Province among the Somali and Swahili. The Qadiriya order is found in the suburb of Eastleigh in Nairobi, where many Somali immigrants live today. Although the population of Sufi Muslims is not large in Kenya, the annual celebration of *Maulidi al-Nabi* (celebration of Muhammad's birthday) in Lamu every year gives them significant popularity. The event, which is organized by *Riyadha* Mosque and Islamic Centre in Lamu Island, has been held for 120 years. During the festival, Lamu is the centre of attraction receiving up to fifty thousand visitors from various parts of Kenya and other Muslim countries. In 2009 Maulidi was celebrated from 24 to 27 March. The celebrations began with the recitation and memorization of the Qur'an in the Islamic centre of Lamu and were followed by lectures by Islamic scholars on the theme of 'Education and Development' (Sheriff 5 March 2009). Men perform Sufi dances in the open space. The celebrations include visiting the tomb of Habib Swaleh Jamalilayld, the founder of Riyadha mosque, and for some, the visiting of the tomb of prominent scholar Sayyid Mohammad Adnan at the Langoni Muslim Cemetery in Lamu (Sheriff 5 March 2009).

Wahhabi

The Sunni, who form the majority of Muslims in Kenya, are largely moderate; however, there is a small group of *Wahhabiya*, who practise strict dressing and grooming codes with the men wearing a long beard and pants that are above the ankles. The women cover their faces completely and stay away from strangers. Though small in number, the Wahhabi have attracted the interest of Al Qaeda insurgents into the region and have been a cause of concern to Kenyan internal security systems at the borders and in the cities. On 7 August 1998, Al Qaeda operatives in the East African region

---

5. This order was 'named after Abu 'l-Hasan Shadhili (d. 1258) and it is particularly strong in Egypt and North Africa, where their emphasis on sobriety earns them the label the Protestants of Islam' (Baldick 1989: 158).

were responsible for the bombing of two U.S. Embassies in Nairobi, Kenya and Dar es Salaam, Tanzania.

Later on 28 November 2002, a Lebanese terror group known as 'The Army of Palestine' claimed responsibility for the bombing of the Paradise Hotel in Mombasa, Kenya and attempted to shoot down an Israeli charter plane by surface-to-air missiles but missed. The motive was to let the world hear the voice of refugees in Palestine on the fifty-fifth anniversary of the U.N. partition of Palestine (29 November 1947), which Palestinians and Arabs rejected. Recently the group invited a Jamaican Muslim cleric, Sheikh Abdullah el-Faisal, who had been arrested and jailed in Britain for preaching hatred to Jews, Hindus and Westerners.

On 6 December 2009, an email was sent purportedly from *Harakatul-Al-shabab-Al Mujahidin*[6] threatening to destabilize the state if Kenya continued to hunt them in Eastleigh estate in Nairobi. The email claimed to be coming from people based in Kenya and connected to Al Qaeda and Al Shabab in Somalia.

They described themselves thus:

> We are proud to be an Islamic revolutionary group and we are honoured to be affiliated with Al-Qaeda a group of honest Muslims in which we share long-term goals and the broad outlines of our ideologies, while focusing on our efforts on attacking secular and moderate governments in the Muslim world, American and Western targets of opportunity and of course Uganda, Ethiopia, Burundi and Kenya if they do not stop their assistance to the Somali fragile and apostate government (harakatul al-shabab 2009).

---

6. *Ḥarakat ash-Shabāb al-Mujāhidīn*, translated 'Movement of Striving Youth', is a group of Islamist militants fighting to overthrow the government of Somalia. The group is an offshoot of Islamic Courts Union, which was overthrown by Ethiopian forces in 2006 to allow the elected government to establish itself in Mogadishu (http://en.wikipedia.org/wiki/Al-Shabaab, accessed 15 August 2011).

Traditional Religion

The majority of the Sunni Muslims in Kenya practise folk Islam. In research I conducted between 2000 and 2001, imams in Kwale and Msambweni districts said that more than 75 per cent of Digo Muslims mix their Islamic faith with their Digo Traditional Religion (Sesi 2003: 166). Later research projects also allude to this fact concerning other Muslim tribes. Judy Wang'ombe in her study on 'Spirit Possession among the Munyoyayas' (2007: 30–32) and Pauline Murumba in her study on conversion from Islam to Christianity among the Borana (2008: 13), both affirm that Islam is a veneer under which traditional practises continue to uphold.

Christian Denominations

The other areas of Kenya such as the southern part of the Eastern Province, Central Province, Rift Valley Province, Western Province, Nyanza Province and Nairobi are predominantly Christian areas. The Christians have various denominational strengths.

In addition to the mainline Protestant churches and the Roman Catholics, there are African-initiated churches. These churches, which started in the early 1920s and 1930s, have various emphases:

a) *Nationalistic* (AIPC-African Independent Pentecostal Church)
b) *Secessionist* like the African Brotherhood Church and African Christian Churches and Schools
c) *Revival-Pentecostal* churches like Redeemed Gospel Church, Deliverance Church, Pentecostal Assemblies of God
d) *Spirit* churches like the Akurinu, African Israel Church Nineveh
e) *Messianic* like Maria Legio (Barrett 1973: 128–137)
f) *Prosperity gospel* churches like Jesus is Alive Ministries and Winners Chapel

Evangelism and Da'wah in Kenya

Christian evangelism and Muslim da'wah has been going on since Christianity was planted in Kenya. As mentioned, the Portuguese missionaries in the fifteenth and sixteenth centuries used the establishment of forts as means of evangelism and crusades against Islam. Fort Jesus was established with the view of claiming Mombasa for Jesus and reversing the effects of Islam along the Coast.

Since the beginning of the modern mission enterprise in Kenya in 1844, Christians have targeted Muslim tribes like the Arabs, Bajun, Somali, Digo, Gabra, Rendille, Orma, Oromo and Swahili with small success. Christian churches use different methods to evangelize Muslims. The most common one is evangelistic crusade, following the examples of international world-class preachers who have visited Kenya in the past like T.L. Osborne, (1957), Billy Graham (1961), Oral Roberts (1968) and Reinhard Bonnke (late 1980s to early 1990s) (Chesworth 2006: 163–165).

I have attended some evangelistic crusades in Nairobi, Mombasa and Machakos. Initially, evangelistic crusades targeted people who were already churched but not living out their faith. The emphasis in the sermons was on salvation of the soul and healing of the body. In the mid-seventies many local Kenyans became crusade preachers.

In 1989, Reinhard Bonnke preached in a six-day evangelistic crusade in Mama Ngina Drive in Mombasa. I observed many church members in attendance and heard a message directed to people who were Muslims. In Bonnke's message, the central theme was forgiveness of sin through Jesus Christ 'the Son of God'. He called people to leave 'dead religion' and come to Jesus.

Pastor Maisha of Ushindi Baptist Church, a Digo preacher, was also conducting crusades in Mombasa to reach the Muslim population. His message was about the power of Jesus Christ over *mapepo* (evil spirits). In his congregation are Digo converts who came to believe in Jesus Christ through some form of miracle or deliverance from the torment of mapepo.

Christian missionaries who live among the Muslims learn their language and culture, translate the Christian scriptures into local languages and teach those who convert to become faithful followers of Jesus. Successful witness of this kind has been registered among the Digo, Rendille and Borana people. Bible Translation and Literacy, a Kenyan organisation, has been doing the important work of translating the Bible for small tribes in Kenya since 1981. 'Currently, BTL is working with fourteen language groups: Aweer (Boni), Borana, Daasanach, Digo, Ilchamus, Ilwana (Malakote),

Giryama, Marakwet (Endo), Orma, Pokomo, Sabaot, Samburu, Scuba and Tarawa' (http://www.btlkenya.org/).

The church also reaches out to Muslims by establishing Christian schools, hospitals and dispensaries, medical camps, food aid, and children's homes (Muchilwa 2010).

The Muslims have responded in a similar manner in their attempt to convert people from the Christian tribes into Islam, with significant success. They hold public meetings, *mihadhara,* where their preachers also preach to the attentive crowds. In Mombasa, Nairobi, Eldoret, Kisumu and Garissa, Muslim preachers use both the Qur'an and the Bible, pointing out the corruptions in the Bible and showing how the Qur'an is the best and final revelation to humankind. Following the arguments used by the late Ahmed Deedat, the Muslims point out that some passages were added to the Bible.

The rural *madrasas* (educational institutions) have contributed to the resilience of Islam in the villages and provided the younger generation of Muslims with deeper religious training (Sperling 1993: 209). More people now practise Islam among the rural areas of Kenya but only as an addition to their primal religion.

Another powerful influence in Islamizing the Swahili tribes along the coast has been the use of Swahili for religious instruction in addition to its use for business and socialization. Many publications in the Swahili language are used to communicate Islam to the public. Among these are the *Utenzi*,[7] which are expressed in poetic genre (*mashairi*) and distributed through the school system. Other regular publications are the two main Swahili journals published for the African Muslims in East, Central and South Africa: *Sauti ya Umma* (*The Voice of the Community*) is printed in the Islamic Republic of Iran by *Taasisi ya Fikra za Kiislamu* (The Foundation of Islamic Thought), and *Mizani* (literally translated as *Scale*) published by *Umoja wa Wahubiri wa Kiislamu wa Mlingano wa Dini* (Union of Muslim Preachers of Related Religions) based in Tanzania (Balda 1993: 226–228).

---

7. Jan Knappert has discussed at length how the Muslims have used poems to teach Islamic theology and practise. The singing or reciting of poems is very effective in reaching oral societies (1967).

The Ahmaddiya, a group of Muslims who are considered heretics by Sunni Muslims, began the process of translating the Qur'an into local languages in which they translate the name 'Allah' into local names of God just as translations of the Bible do. The Qur'an is now available in the Swahili, Kamba, Kikuyu and Luo languages. This new tool of da'wah is helping Muslims make inroads in predominantly Christian tribes.

Another method the Muslims use to evangelize Christians is economic programmes. Barclays Bank, Kenya Commercial Bank, Diamond Trust and Middle Eastern Bank are now offering Islamic banking facilities to Muslims, which allows them to borrow money without being charged interest rates. Although the bank does not share the profit and loss with the borrower, the Muslim has an advantage over other borrowers because they are allowed to pay only what the Central Bank is asking as the lending interest. The Muslim is charged this as a service charge.

Kadhi's Courts in Kenya and the Christian Response

Kenya has *kadhi's* courts, which enforce Islamic law and are applicable only to Muslims. Their protection in the constitution has been a source of contention for Christians in Kenya. The establishment of kadhi's courts in East Africa dates back to the time of the Shirazi rule. The kadhi's courts were part of their ruling system in their city-states and they applied to the Muslim populations in those cities. When the Omani sultans took over the colonisation of East Africa in 1698, they expanded the jurisdiction of the kadhi's courts to the African tribes who lived within the colonised territory and used them to Islamize the tribes. In 1895, when the Sultan of Zanzibar allowed the British to administer a ten-mile strip along the Kenyan coast that had been part of his territory, one of the conditions was that kadhi's courts should continue to exist. The British administered it as a protectorate.

Establishment of Kadhi's Courts within Kenya's Court System

Kenya has two classes of courts: subordinate courts and courts of appeal. The subordinate courts are further divided into three categories: resident magistrate's courts, district magistrate's courts and kadhi's courts

A strict interpretation of both the constitution and the Kadhi's Court Act of 1967 (chapter 11 of the Laws of Kenya), reveals kadhi's courts are to be established for the ten-mile coastal strip under Section 66 (4) of the constitution and for the rest of Kenya under Section 66(3) of the constitution.

It is to be noted that the Islamic courts did not merely cover the ten-mile coastal strip as negotiated between the Sultan of Zanzibar and the incoming government of Kenya. The kadhi's courts territorially covered the entire Republic of Kenya although for areas with a minimal Muslim population one kadhi court would exercise jurisdiction over a large area. Currently the number of kadhi's courts has been extended to twelve. Kadhi's courts are an integral part of the judicial system in Kenya and are therefore funded by the taxes of all Kenyans be they Muslims or non-Muslim.

Christian Response to Muslims' Claim that They Need Kadhi's Courts Entrenched in the Kenyan Constitution

For both Christian and Muslim religious leadership, the controversy over kadhi's courts was fuelled by the provisions relating to kadhi's courts in the initial Constitution of Kenya Review Commission's draft bill to amend the Constitution (2002–2003) (henceforth CKRC Draft). Muslim clergy and politicians mobilized their faithful to successfully present their position to the CKRC, namely that Muslims preferred to see change regarding Islamic law and the old constitution. Christians, on the other hand, witnessed the extent to which Muslims wanted to expand Islamic law and kadhi's courts in the country's constitution.

The CKRC Draft proposed a parallel judicial system of kadhi's courts from district level to the court of appeal. Hence, from twelve kadhi's courts at the subordinate courts level, a nationwide structure of kadhi's courts similar to the national secular court system was to be created. The minimum number of kadhi's was to be increased from three to thirty

(Section 199 CKRC Draft). This draft was strongly opposed by Christians and a revised draft was produced following a constitutional conference held at the Bomas of Kenya grounds in Nairobi. However, the provisions for kadhi's courts in the draft were not acceptable to the Christian leaders and they opposed it.

The Bomas draft was presented to Attorney General Amos Wako to publish for a referendum. The attorney general changed the Bomas draft by adding Christian courts and Hindu courts to the proposed constitution. The attorney general then published his version of the constitution draft, now referred to as the 'Wako Draft'.

However, Christians had not made any representations for the establishment of Christian courts. They were being imposed on Christians so that the continued constitutionalization of kadhi's courts could be accepted. Christians saw that as a way of dividing the country along religious lines and voted against the Wako Draft on 21 November 2005, and it was defeated.

Christian Dhallenge of Kadhi's Court Through Litigation

In 2004 during an earlier constitutional review, Christians in Kenya had gone to court in order to oppose the entrenchment of kadhi's courts in the current constitution. Twenty-six church leaders submitted an application on 12 July 2004, amended on 30 November 2004, and further amended on 1 February 2005, against the attorney general and the CKRC arguing that:

> Kenya being a multi-religious and multi-cultural State, Section 66 of the current Constitution of Kenya which established and entrenched the office of the Chief Kadhi, and the Kadhis' Court, and the retention of a similar Section in the draft Constitution referred to as the 'Bomas' or 'Zero Draft' and the support thereof from public coffers amounts to segregation, is sectarian, discriminatory as against the Applicants and others and amounts to separate development of one religion and religious practise and is therefore unconstitutional (Jesse Kamau and 25 others v Attorney General [2010] e KLR: 11).

The applicants, through their counsel, submitted to the court that section 66(1), which established the office of the Chief Kadhi and kadhi's courts, and section 66(3), which provided legal framework to enact kadhi's courts Act, were inconsistent with sections 78(2)[8] and 82[9], because entrenchment of kadhi's courts in the constitution elevated the Islamic religion above all other religions. It was discriminatory and sectarian. In addition, they argued that entrenching kadhi's courts means that state is not separate from religion and that the state does not treat all religions equally.

The hearings took almost six years. In a judgment entitled *Miscellaneous Civil Application 890 of 2004* in the Republic of Kenya High Court of Kenya at Nairobi (Nairobi Law Courts), three judges of the high court ruled that section 66 of the constitution was inconsistent with sections of the constitution that separated the state and religion. In their own words, they argued that:

> The financial maintenance and support of the kadhi's courts from public coffers amounts to segregation, is sectarian, discriminatory and unjust as against the Applicants and others and amounts to separate development of one religion and religious practise contrary to the principle of separation of state and religion (secularism) and is therefore contrary to the universal norms and principles of liberty and freedom of religion . . . (Jesse Kamau & 25 others v Attorney General [2010] eKLR: 88–89).

The judges further ruled that:
(1) It was unconstitutional to extend the kadhi's courts outside the former protectorate areas to cover the whole country.

---

8. 'Every religious community shall be entitled, at its own expense, to establish and maintain places of education which it wholly maintains . . .' therefore Muslims should establish kadhi's courts without the interference of the state and fund them privately if they need them to enhance their religion.

9. Section 82 provides that no law shall make any provision, which is discriminatory in itself or in its effect, therefore entrenching a religious court of one religion in the constitution would be discriminatory against other religions.

(2) Any form of religious courts should not form part of the judiciary in the constitution because it offends the doctrine of separation of state and religion.

(3) Entrenchment of the kadhi's courts in the constitution elevates and uplifts the Islamic religion over and above the other religions in Kenya which is inconsistent with the sections of the constitution which say that the state will treat all religions equally and therefore discriminatory in its effect against the applicants and Kenyans of other religions.

In 2008 a new review process was started, and it has produced a new draft to be subjected to a referendum on 4 August 2010. A Committee of Experts (CoE) led the review. The new draft has maintained status quo leaving the kadhi's courts as they are in the current constitution. Article 170 of the proposed constitution said:

(1) There shall be a Chief Kadhi and such number, being not fewer than three, of other Kadhis as may be prescribed under an Act of Parliament.

(2) A person shall not be qualified to be appointed to hold or act in the office of Kadhi unless the person—(a) professes the Muslim religion; and (b) possesses such knowledge of the Muslim law applicable to any sects of Muslims as qualifies the person, in the opinion of the Judicial Service Commission, to hold a kadhi'scourt.

(3) Parliament shall establish kadhi's courts, each of which shall have the jurisdiction and powers conferred on it by legislation, subject to clause (5).

(4) The Chief Kadhi and the other Kadhis, or the Chief Kadhi and such of the other Kadhis (not being fewer than three in number) as may be prescribed under an Act of Parliament, shall each be empowered to hold a kadhi'scourt having jurisdiction within Kenya.

(5) The jurisdiction of a Kadhi's court shall be limited to the determination of questions of Muslim law relating to personal status, marriage, divorce or inheritance in proceedings in which all the parties profess the Muslim religion and submit to the

jurisdiction of the kadhi's courts (6 May 2010).

In addition, the proposed constitution of 2010 exempted the Muslims from the Bill of Rights:

> The provisions of this Chapter on equality shall be qualified to the extent strictly necessary for the application of Muslim law before kadhi's courts, to persons who profess the Muslim religion in matters relating to personal status, marriage, divorce and inheritance (6 May 2010: 24[4]).

Such an exemption of Muslims from rights and fundamental freedoms implies an application of the principle of 'abrogation' in Islamic Sharia. Abrogation (*naskh*) usually involved the suppression of a ruling without the suppression of the wording. In this case the wording in the constitution about rights and fundamental freedoms remains, but the ruling is suppressed to allow Muslims to apply Islamic family law to Muslims.

From the beginning, the relationship between humans and God was based on the freedom of humans to obey God's commandments out of their own choice. Adam and Eve were given the freedom to obey or disobey God in the Garden of Eden (Genesis 2:17). Moses in Deuteronomy 30:15–20 set before the Israelites the way of life and the way of death and exhorted the people to love God and obey his commandments out of their free will and choice. In Joshua 24:15 Joshua said to the leaders of Israel, 'choose for yourselves this day whom you will serve' (NKJV).

In Matthew 11:28 Jesus calls people to make the choice to come to him to get rest from their labour and burdens. In their preaching and ministry, Jesus and the apostles appealed to and persuaded people without coercion to make their choice to join the followers of Jesus. When Muslims have any part of their religious laws entrenched in the constitution of a country to use government organisations and institutions to enforce Islamic law (personal or otherwise), it works against the doctrine of freedom of choice in matters of faith.

The provision of freedom of worship is sufficient, and the freedom of the worshiper to choose where and when to worship God is the only thing the constitution can seek to protect for all citizens. Additional religious courts to regulate personal and family lives of worshipers would subject them to unnecessary legal burden.

Conclusion

The story of Christianity and Islam in Kenya is typical of many countries in sub-Saharan Africa. Islam preceded Christianity but confined itself in small city-states along the coast with minimal influence on the tribal populations around them. In many cases, Muslim merchants were the local imams and had to close their shops to go and lead prayers especially on Friday afternoons.

The emphasis on learning Arabic for adherents of Islam as a requirement to participate in salat did not help in the efforts of da'wah. The majority of Muslims in Kenya are not able to follow the ritual prayers that are supposed to be performed five times daily, thus Islam is mainly used for identity purposes. While the rural *madrassas* have helped to educate the young generations on Islamic education, the conflict with regular schooling in Kenya remains a challenge due to the emphasis on English rather than Arabic as the medium of instruction.

The arrival of Christianity through Portuguese explorers made little impact on local populations. The main impact was through the modern missionary movement beginning with Ludwig Krapf in 1844. Christian missionaries were willing to venture inland, and, with their emphasis on translating the Word of God into local languages, they were able to evangelize vast areas effectively within a short time. In cases where tribes had converted to Islam as a group, Christian evangelists have not been readily successful in winning converts from the tribes. With the proliferation of Christian groups and denominations in Kenya, the churches are on many occasions concerned with maintaining their membership rather than reaching out to Islamic groups. However, significant efforts are being made to bring the gospel to Muslim tribes like the Digo, Somali, Borana, Rendille, Bajun, Swahili, Burji, Aweer, Munyoyaya and Arabs. Bible translations are being done to bring the scriptures and other Christian materials to these tribes in their mother tongues. In spite of a few times of terror attacks by Islamist insurgents, the relationship between Christians and Muslims in Kenya has been one of moderate tolerance.

References

1998 United States Embassy Bombings. Wikipedia, The Free Encyclopaedia, viewed August 17, 2011. http://en.wikipedia.org/wiki/1998_United_States_ embassy_bombings.
2002 Mombasa Attacks. Wikipedia, The Free Encyclopaedia, viewed August 17, 2011. http://en.wikipedia.org/wiki/2002_Mombasa_attacks.
Allen, J.D.V. 1993. *Swahili Origins.* Athens: Ohio University Press.
Al-Shabaab, Wikipedia, The Free Encyclopedia. Viewed August 15, 2011. http://en.wikipedia.org/wiki/Al-Shabaab.
An Nai'm, A.A. 2002. *Islamic Family Law in a Changing World.* London: Zed Books.
Baldick, Julian. 1989. *Mystical Islam: An Introduction to Sufism.* New York: New York University Press.
Barrett, David B., Mambo, G.K., McLaughlin, J., McVeigh M.J. 1974. *Kenya Churches Handbook: The Development of Kenyan Christianity 1498–1973.* Kisumu: Evangel Publishing House.
Chesworth, John A. Fundamentalism and Outreach Strategies in East Africa: Christian Evangelism and Muslim Da'wa. *Muslim-Christian Encounter in Africa.* Edited by Benjamin F. Soares. Leiden: Brill: 159–186.
Githii, David. 2008. Hope for Kenya: Kikuyu Challenges—Backgrounder on East African Tribal Conflicts. Nairobi: Presbyterian Church of East Africa. (Unpublished Paper.)
Groves, C.P. 1948. *The Planting of Christianity in Africa,* Vol. 1: To 1840. London: Lutterworth Press.
Groves, C.P. 1954. *The Planting of Christianity in Africa,* Vol. 2: 1840–1878. London, U.K.: Lutterworth Press.
Hastings, A. 1994. *The Church in Africa: 1450–1950.* Oxford: Oxford University Press.
Hildebrandt, J. 1981. *History of the Church in Africa: A Survey.* Achimota, Ghana: Africa Christian Press.
King, N.Q. 1971. *Christian and Muslim in Africa.* New York: Harper and Row, Publishers.

Krapf, J.L. 1968. *Travels, Researches, and Missionary Labours.* London, U.K.: Frank Cass.

Lapidus, Ira M. 2002. *A History of Islamic Societies.* Second Edition. Cambridge: Cambridge University Press.

Mayoyo, Patrick. 16 February 2010. Porous Borders Raise Security Fears in Spite of Crackdown. *Daily Nation,* Tuesday :17

Middleton, J. 1992. *The World of the Swahili: An African Mercantile Civilization.* New Haven: Yale University Press.

Muchilwa, Bernard Amianda. 2010. A Critical Exploration of Mission Practises of Selected Kenyan Churches among the Unreached Peoples of Northern Kenya between 1960 and 2008: A Case Study of ACK, AIC, CITAM, and KAG Ministries in Marsabit.

Murumba, Pauline Cherop. 2008. A Study on Conversion from Islam to Christianity among the Borana Women in Nairobi, Kenya with Implications for Christian Witness. MTh. thesis, Nairobi Evangelical Graduate School of Theology. Nairobi. Mutuli, M, 2007. Number of Displaced in Somalia Tops One Million Mark. *Daily Nation,* Tuesday 20 November 2007, viewed June 28, 2010. <www.nation.co.ke/News>.

Nicholls, C.S. 1971. *The Swahili Coast.* New York: Africana Publishing Corporation.

Pew Forum on Religion and Public Life. 2010. Tolerance and Tension: Islam and Christianity in Sub-Saharan Africa. Washington D.C., Pew Research Centre, viewed on April 26, 2010. <www.pewforum.org>.

Pouwels, Randall L. 2000. The East African Coast, ca. 780 to 1900 C.E. *The History of Islam in Africa,* edited by Nehemia Levtzion and Randall L. Pouwels. Athens, Ohio: Ohio University Press: 251–271

Robinson, D. 2004. *Muslim Societies in African History.* Cambridge: Cambridge University Press.

Sesi, Stephen M. 2003. Prayer among the Digo Muslims of Kenya and Its Implications for Christian Witness. PhD. thesis. Fuller Theological Seminary, School of World Mission. U.S.A.: Pasadena.

Shaw, Mark. 1996. *The Kingdom of God in Africa: A Short History of African Christianity.* Grand Rapids, MI: Baker Books.

Sheriff, Abdulrahman. March 5, 2009. Lamu Braces for the 120th Maulidi. *Daily Nation.* Thursday, viewed June 28, 2010. <www.nation.co.ke/News.>

Sheriff, A. 1987. *Slaves, Spices and Ivory in Zanzibar.* London: James Currey Ltd.

Sperling, D.C. 1993. Rural Madrasas of the Southern Kenya Coast, 1971–1992. *Muslim Identity and Social Change in Sub-Saharan Africa*. Edited by Louis Brenner Indianapolis: Indiana University Press: 198–209

Sperling, D.C. 2000. The Coastal Hinterland and Interior of East Africa. *The History of Islam in Africa*. Edited by Nehemia Levtzion and Randall L. Pouwels. Athens: Ohio University Press: 273–302.

Spear, 2000. Early Swahili History Reconsidered. *The International Journal of African Historical Studies* 33(2): 257–290.

Strayer, R.W. 1978. *The Making of Mission Communities in East Africa*. London: Heinemann Educational Books, Ltd.

Teyie, Andrew. 9 January 2010. Kenya: 2009 Census Delayed over Somali Numbers. *Nairobi Star*, viewed July 1, 2010. http://allafrica.com/stories/201001120871.html accessed.

Wang'ombe, Judy Wanjiru. 2007. A Missiological Study of the Phenomenon of Spirit Possession among the Munyoyaya, Women in the Madogo Location, Tana River District. *Kenya: A Response to I.M. Lewis' Theory of Deprivation*. MTh. thesis, Nairobi Evangelical Graduate School of Theology. Nairobi.

Welcome to Bible Translation and Literacy, viewed August 17, 2011. http://www.btlkenya.org/.

CHAPTER 16

Nigeria

Matthew Hassan Kukah

Many commentators within and outside Nigeria continue to speak with some degree of impatience about what has come to be known as the 'religious problem' in Nigeria. Within Nigeria, the feelings of frustration with death and destruction resulting from the many crises are palpable. The inexplicable ubiquity and persistence of tension, violence and acrimony among members of the two universal religions, Islam and Christianity, has become unacceptable. Unfortunately, little attention has been paid to how and why this so-called religious problem persists or to how and why so many attempts at its resolution by federal and state governments in Nigeria seem to fail (Falola 2001).

My chapter will attempt to examine some of these issues by revisiting and, hopefully, identifying some of the weaknesses in popular assumptions. Although there are problems with issues of religion, I fear that we have tended to narrow them by not examining the political and social causes that create the conditions for these tensions and violence. To examine the issues, I will divide this chapter into five sections: the first summarizes the historical development of Islam and Christianity in Nigeria; the second examines the role that religion has played in the evolution of the modern nation state; the third identifies some key areas of the manifestation of the tensions between Islam and Christianity and their implications for the Nigerian state; the fourth section looks at the new role of religion in the years following the nation's return to democracy; and finally, the fifth tries to point the way forward.

Historical Overview of the Development of Islam and Christianity in Nigeria

In dealing with the problems of Islam and Christianity in Nigeria, we have tended to think more of present realities and not paid much attention to how aspects of our history still haunt us. Some have argued that after fifty years of independence, Nigeria should have overcome divisions caused by religions. Sadly, although these sentiments are understandable, they do not address all the issues. While this may not be the place to address these issues, it is important to note that a distinction exists between religious factors that shape and affect our lives and the beliefs of the religions themselves.

Islam

The first mistake we make is to speak of Islam or Muslims as a cohesive unit in Nigeria, instead of understanding that they comprise different groups, some of which are at odds with each other. A cursory examination of pre-colonial literature shows that deep-seated ideological and cultural differences existed within the different communities many centuries before the emergence of modern Nigeria. For example, the origins of the Muslims of the Borno Empire in northeastern Nigeria and what would become major parts of the Sokoto caliphate, differ substantially in history and culture (Hogben & Kirk-Greene 1960). The latter involved conquests and subjugation, while the former did not. Consequently, in large parts of Hausa land, the invading colonial state enjoyed tremendous support in the overthrow of the caliphate, which the Hausa and non-Muslim communities had come to see as the oppressive rule of the Fulani aristocracy.[1]

Before and after independence, affiliations to the major Sufi brotherhoods (*Tijaniya* and *Qadiriya*) became the major driving forces for political affiliations among many Muslims in Northern Nigeria (Paden 1973). In the mid 1980s, a movement known as *Jama'at Izalat al Bidia wa Iaqmat al Sunna* (Society for the Prevention of Innovations and the Establishment of

---

1. For a trenchant account of some of these experiences through the eyes of an ordinary Hausa woman, see Mary Smith 1955. *Baba of Karo: A Woman of the Muslim Hausa*; Bala Usman 1982. *The Overthrow of the Sarauta System*.

the Sunna) emerged as a counterforce to the ideology of the brotherhoods. The members became popularly known as *Yan Izala*, and were occasionally referred to as Shiites. Much of the explosion of intra-sect violence in the northern states in the 1980s was associated with the emergence of the Yan Izala and its attack on Sufi Islam and the state. Its members claimed they wanted to establish an Islamic state.[2] The interplay of these forces was responsible for much of the violence in this period. More often than not, the issues had nothing to do with non-Muslims or Christianity, and yet they were often referred to as religious riots.

Although the history of Islam in Northern Nigeria had been characterized by violence, the same is not true of Islam in most parts of southwestern Nigeria, namely Yorubaland. There, with the exception of such areas like Ilorin where the Fulani jihad conquest was halted, Islam enjoyed a relatively peaceful entrance into Yorubaland (Ggabadamosi 1987). Many other factors account for the tolerance and accommodation associated with Islam in the southwest. The first reason is the pre-eminent place that the Yoruba place on their ethnic identity and culture. For the Yoruba, ethnic and cultural identity comes before any other identity such as Islam or Christianity. Second, the Yoruba culture has a more flexible attitude towards religion, believing that the issues of what gods individuals worship are not subject to human judgment. Third, with intermarriages among Christians and Muslims, many families in Yorubaland have members of both faiths in their households, something that is unthinkable and an anathema among Northern Muslims. Fourth, Yoruba Muslims have acquired Western education and achieved a level of modernization that has enabled them to become more accommodating. A combination of these factors may account for the reason why Yoruba Islam has been relatively free of the rancour and violence that has become associated with Islam in the northern parts of Nigeria (Ggabadamosi 1987).

Islam in Northern Nigeria has often been associated with violence from its origins in the history of the Sokoto caliphate (Last 1968). It spread among many distinct ethnic and cultural communities, thus exposing it to

---

2. For a comprehensive analysis and study of this movement, see Roman Loimeier 1997. *Islamic Reform and Political Change in Northern Nigeria.*

disparate cultures and histories. For example, it is possible to identify levels of differentiation between the Muslim communities in some parts of the Middle Belt and those of the Hausa and Fulani communities in the north. Most Muslim children in the northern states are likely to acquire Qur'anic education as opposed to Western education, which is the opposite in the southern parts of Nigeria. This is further explained by the fact that products of Qur'anic education have continued to account for most of the riots in the northern states. I believe that a proper understanding of these underlying factors can help us appreciate the complexity of the Muslim community itself and how this relates to the larger issues of politics, economics and social relations in Nigeria. This is why I believe that to speak of conflicts between Christians and Muslims broadly continues to overstate the issues of religion in conflict.

Christianity

Christianity's perceived connection with the colonial state and Western influences caused Nigerians in various regions to react differently to it. Whereas resistance to colonial rule was marked by violence in many parts of Northern Nigeria, it was not in most of Southern Nigeria. There, a combination of trade and education managed to blunt the excesses of the colonial state, thus creating a more conducive atmosphere of welcome and accommodation. In addition, trade had flourished between the chiefs and foreign traders before the emergence of the colonial state. Subsequently, the provision of Western education and the opportunities it opened up made missionary activities a source of great attraction, especially in eastern Nigeria (Ayandele 1974).

In Northern Nigeria, however, the problem was more complicated. Before colonialism, the relationship between the non-Muslim and the Muslim communities had been marked by war and violence over empire and slavery (Tseayo 1973; Makar 1984). Thus, non-Muslim minorities in the Middle Belt considered missionaries to be a force of redemption and salvation. The missionaries' message of salvation, of liberation from feudal emirate rule and slavery, of prospects of Western education and of a better life, made Christianity an attractive force (Crampton 1975; Ayandele 1966).

The Muslims, and later the nationalists, had difficulties accommodating the missionaries because they believed (wrongly) they were brothers of the colonialists and that deep down their ideological commitments to empire and trade were the same. When the Muslim leaders objected to missionary activities in parts of the north, the colonial response laid the foundation for the tensions that have persisted. Since trade was the primary overriding motive of colonialism, the colonial state was quick to make amends. This was why the colonial state, along with their conquered collaborators, treated missionaries with deep suspicion. The colonial state embarked on what became formally known as the *policy of non-interference*.[3] E. Morel, writing during the colonial period noted, 'Islam is more suitable for the people of the North than Christianity' (Crampton 1975: 48).

In a communication between a local emir and a colonial officer, the former noted that:

> Know that as regards the preaching of Christianity which we discussed here, my opinion is that it is better to stop it altogether, from the first, because if our people are disturbed about their religion, they will become suspicious and afraid. Hence the country will become unsettled. Neither you nor we desire the country to become unsettled for that would be harmful. On the other hand, as regards secular matter and the affairs of the world, we can do anything (quoted in Crampton 1975: 51).

The policy of non-interference sowed seeds of distrust, which has had a lasting effect on Christian-Muslim relations. The Muslims did not trust their non-Muslim brethren because they saw the Christian converts as being agents and collaborators of the colonial state and as having converted to the religion of the White man. Nor did the Muslim community wish to

---

3. The policy of *non-interference* essentially focused on the fact that the British believed that the Muslim community needed to be protected and shielded from the incursions of the beneficiaries of Western education. Their main concern however was to ensure that those with Western education, known as the troublemakers, were not allowed to rouse the sleeping community of Muslims from their illiteracy.

contemplate the prospects of conversions of any Muslims to Christianity. The colonialists, on the other hand, did not trust educated Christians. Based on their experiences in the south, they viewed educated Christians, some of whom had confronted the colonial state, as troublemakers and upstarts. Based on their experience in Southern Nigeria, the newly educated elite had begun to question the legitimacy of the colonial state, an act that threatened the foundations of feudalism on which the colonial state depended in Northern Nigeria. The suspicions sown by these policies found further expression in the building of the strangers' quarters in many northern states. Their purpose was to ensure that non-Muslims lived separately from Muslims so interactions did not lead to deviations and frictions (Lamont 2003). Whatever may have been the good intentions, with hindsight, we might argue that some of these factors deepened mutual suspicions among various groups and its effect have persisted.

Religion and the Modern State

The ethno-regional boundaries drawn by the colonial state in preparation for the independence of Nigeria exacerbated the existing ethnic and religious tensions among communities struggling for power. Leaders of the former caliphate, with whom the colonial state collaborated closely, became the natural inheritors of the apparatus of power in independent Nigeria. Also, by sheer land mass and population, the areas co-terminus with the boundaries of the hegemonic bloc of the Muslim Hausa-Fulani ruling class were far bigger than those of the rest of Nigeria, thereby contributing to the Muslim dominance in an independent Nigeria (Kukah 1993, ch. 2).

The nature of pre- and post-independence political formations and alliances in post-colonial Nigeria reflected the ethno-regional boundaries drawn by the departing colonial state (Sklar 1963). After independence, five dominant themes emerged in the politics of modern Nigeria. Many would later assume regional, ethnic and religious colouration. These were the status of minorities, the status of Islamic law, post-colonial Christian-Muslim relations, the role of the military and the role of religion in the history of dictatorships.

Status of Minorities in the North and South

The critical questions related to the tensions building up over the treatment of minorities, such as the decision of the colonial state to subjugate most of these communities under the authority of the Muslim emirate system of administration. Clearly, in the bureaucracy and politics, non-Muslims in Northern Nigeria, for example, were already beginning to feel excluded from key positions. This led to such formations as the Non-Muslim League (NML) and subsequently, the United Middle Belt Movement (UMBC) (Kukah 1993, ch. 2). In the south, the agitation of the minorities had led to the creation of a Midwest Region.

Status of Islamic Law in a Modern Nigeria

The status of Islamic law became a point of contention. With the emergence of a modern state, Muslims began to express anxiety as to the status and future of Islamic law, while the non-Muslims feared that the influence of Sharia would gradually become part of their lives.

Post-colonial Christian-Muslim Relations

The colonial state did little to safeguard the future of non-Muslim minorities. The colonial administration decided that it would simply leave the future of the non-Muslim minorities in the hands of the Muslims (under the Northern Peoples' Congress Party) and hope for the best.

Role of the Military

Fears for the future after independence were realised in the military coup that took place soon after the departure of the colonial administration. The intervention of the military gradually sucked the country into a civil war, and the effects of that phase of our national life are still playing out in the persistence of military rule, institutionalized violence, corruption, and lack of transparency. Unable to vent their frustrations, Nigerians began to fall back on religion.

Role of Religion

The role of religion in the history of dictatorships does not require repetition. From the story of apartheid in South Africa and of civilian and military dictatorships in the Philippines, Latin America and the former Soviet Union, we can appreciate the historical role of religion as a platform for protest in the face of oppression. The media, civil society and other viable institutions of opposition are often the first to be terrorized. Thus, citizens are often left with the churches or the mosques as the best platforms for protest. In Nigeria, the monopoly of power by the northern military dictators fuelled allegations of favouritism and increased the frustrations of non-Muslims. It also deepened the gulf between the leadership of both religions, creating anxiety and making it difficult for the religions to unite and play their role as a voice for democracy and freedom.

Flashpoints in Christian-Muslim Relations in Nigeria after 1999

If Christian-Muslim relations were frosty and marked by suspicion and fear during colonial state and military dictatorship, what prospects did the return to democracy in 1999 hold for Nigeria? It seemed rather strange that the questions of yesterday would surface immediately after the nation returned to democracy. Let us examine a few of those issues: Sharia law, competition for power, the war against terrorism, da'wah (call), poverty and the failure of politics.

Democracy and the Return of Sharia Law

By 1999, many Nigerians saw in the return to civil rule the prospect of an end to religiously sponsored bickering, rivalry and divisions among politicians. However, the issue of the status of Islamic law, which had been a major factor in the debate about the emerging Nigerian state from the colonial period, continued to divide Nigerian lawmakers trying to fashion a new constitution.[4] Nigeria had hardly settled down to savour the prospects for national integration when suddenly Alhaji Sani Yarima, the newly elected governor of Zamfara State (1999–2007), one of the Muslim-dominated states in the northwestern flank of the country, announced to a stunned nation that his state had officially adopted Sharia law. Naturally, the nation was thrown into confusion. The decision ignited the entire Muslim population in the northern states and in quick succession, one state after the other announced its decision to adopt Sharia law. Within a year, the twelve states with predominantly Muslim populations had adopted Sharia law without clearly debating the issues. However, in Kaduna State, the governor decided to adopt a tripartite arrangement by introducing Customary Courts across the state. This went a long way to calm frayed nerves in a volatile state.[5]

For almost three years, the northern states were rocked by threats of violence or eruptions of outright violence, which reopened the wounds of suspicion and fear on all sides. Indeed, subsequent eruptions of violence can be traced to this unfortunate and ill-timed development. To create the impression of seriousness in the application of Sharia, the governor quickly approved the amputation of a hand of a man alleged to have stolen a goat, after the man had been hastily tried in a Sharia court. The move was seen as a test to frighten citizens. Then alcohol was banned and men and

---

4. For a summary of the issues and the debates, see Matthew Kukah: *Religion, Politics and Power in Northern Nigeria*, ch 5.
5. For details, see: *Kaduna State Committee on the Harmonisation of Drafts of the Sharia Penal Code and Sharia Criminal Procedure Code of Laws* (Officially signed into law on 26 June 2002)

women banned from sharing public transportation. Confusion set in but the climax came with the trial of a divorced woman, Safiyya, for adultery.[6]

This decision to adopt Sharia law turned out to have been ill thought out and an exercise in political adventurism. It created tension within the Muslim community itself and the larger society. Although this decision generated a lot of excitement among the ordinary Muslims across the north, it also exposed the rupture between the ordinary Muslims and their cadre of elites. Ordinary Muslims had hoped that the decision would compel their corrupt elites to live according to the dictates of their faith, such that vices like corruption, gambling and prostitution would end. They had also expected that living under Sharia law would end judicial impunity wherein the Muslim criminal elites had proved to be above the law. There was also the feeling that Muslims would now be compelled to pay their Zakat and thus, create a social safety net for the poor. Sadly, ordinary Muslims soon discovered that only the poor were victims of the Sharia, as seen in the cases of the goat thief and the poor divorced woman. The introduction of Sharia law exposed the ideological dissonance within the Muslim community in Nigeria.

Yarima, who oversaw the implementation of Sharia law was elected a senator; now his political opponents often protest his visits to the state capital, Gusau. Presently, Yarima is being threatened with trial over the allegation of a breach of the Child Rights Act over his marriage to a thirteen-year-old Egyptian child.[7] Some prominent members of the Muslim elite believe that he has done no wrong according to the Muslim religion, since, as they argue, the holy prophet had a six- or seven-year-old bride. This shows we still have a long road to travel in seeking common grounds for relations between citizens in Nigeria. The adoption of Sharia law, which started out with strong support from ordinary Muslims, has now lost much of their support.

---

6. For comprehensive analysis and summary of the developments of this period, see: *Political Sharia? Human Rights and Islamic Law in Northern Nigeria* (Human Rights Watch. Vol 16(9) (A 2003).

7. For a detailed account of the arguments, see Maryam Uwais: *Child Marriage: Yerima Got It Wrong* (Dated 5 May 2010). For an account of the legal and cultural views, see, Onwuka Nzeshi: *Parliament Cannot Annul Islamic Marriage* (This Day, 19 May 2010)

Religion and Elite Competition for Power

The nation continues to suffer under the weight of fear of domination and allegations of domination by competing elites. Almost every administration has been accused of favouring either Muslims or Christians in the area of key appointments. Similar accusations were made about the funding of Muslim pilgrimages until the federal and state governments decided to create pilgrimage bodies for both Christians and Muslims. Today, these initiatives continue to cause discontent while delivering little to ordinary Nigerians, be they Christians or Muslims.

It can be argued that a major factor distorting relations between Christians and Muslims, and a reason why religion has been promoted to the centre of public discussion in Nigeria, is the crisis around competition between elites—a largely corrupt segment of Nigerian society, most of whom use religion to mask their personal, political, economic and social ambitions. Unfortunately, at the level of politics, they are the ones who are quick to use religion as a means of mobilization and use the same religion to allege marginalization. Thus, pressure is constantly put on all sectors of government to guarantee representation of these interests. As a result, a false sense of religious security is manifested when the elites deploy huge resources to service religion in the state bureaucracy and business. Today, a huge chaplaincy business has emerged, spewing out chaplaincies at the levels of the president, state governors and the National Assembly. Prayer warriors are emerging as part of the architecture of governance in Nigeria. Departments of religious affairs dot the federal and state bureaucracies in the north, with a new power elite created around them. Politicians now feel they can carry on with the business of governance while religion plays its role of a supporting cast. In my view, this spells danger for both religion and the state.[8]

---

8. Imams and pastors are now routinely assigned to government houses at federal and state levels, while chapels and mosques are constantly erected in these premises and private homes.

Religion and the War against Terrorism

The war on terrorism has taken its toll on Christian-Muslim relations in Nigeria. All sides have been caught in a web of suspicion. The events of 11 September 2001 added a new dimension to the existing climate of fear and anxiety, thus making for a volatile environment. This anxiety manifested itself in the eruption of violence over issues purported to be in the name of religion. Examples are the violence in Kaduna over the Miss World contest and the Danish cartoons, neither of which had anything to do with Kaduna (Vu 2006).

Islam, Da'wah and Africa

Nigeria has been considered an important and significant platform for world Islam in its Africa da'wah [Islamic missions] project. This may explain why it was made the headquarters of the *Islam in Africa Project* under the auspices of two of Nigeria's richest Muslims, who both wanted to be president of the country soon after the launch of the project. According to the organisers:

> What is commonly known as the 'Abuja Declaration' is officially known as 'Islam in Africa Conference: Communiqué'. This was a communiqué issued at the end of the Islam in Africa conference held in Abuja, Nigeria, on 24–28 November 1989. This conference, organized by the 46-member Organisation of the Islamic Conference (OIC), resolved to create an organisation to be known as Islam in Africa Organisation to spearhead a Muslim initiative to solve the problems facing Africa. This initiative essentially calls for the Islamization of the entire continent of Africa.[9]

Today, Nigeria is often caught in conflicts inherited from the ideology of others. Reactions to crises in the Middle East and the Palestinian question

---

9. The Conference took place in Abuja on 24–28 August 1989.

are often conflated under the vague notion that it is part of a Zionist conspiracy sustained by the United States and that somehow Christians are connected to this plot.

For many years, the United States especially has argued that there are Al Qaeda cells in Nigeria. External influence from the Muslim pilgrimages, academic contacts, the Internet and other Muslim groups serve as contributory factors to the development of cells. Many young people are keen to be associated with Al Qaeda more out of solidarity, expressions of protest, emotions, propaganda and quest for relevance than out of any real affiliation or association with the doctrine of the movement. Over many years, and especially since the end of the Cold War, the unresolved Palestinian question, the United State's quest for global dominance and the war in Afghanistan and Iraq have served to rally many young Muslims to a cause of justice. The case of young Mutallab, who was caught with an undetonated bomb in his underpants in a U.S.-bound flight on 25 December 2009, brought these issues to a climax. The predicament of Mutallab cannot be a measure of what Nigerian Islam is all about, but it is a pointer to the threats we face in a globalized world. It is a wake-up call for us to come to terms with the seriousness that some misguided youth might attach to solidarity and to how some of them view the future of Islam in the world.

Growing Inequalities and Poverty amidst Plenty

The tragedy and persistence of growing inequalities in Nigeria have served to make religious issues a rallying point for the poor to express their frustrations. The frustration that ordinary Muslims have with their elites has driven complex forms of poverty-induced violence in Bauchi, Maiduguri and Plateau states (Christellow 1984; Taiwo & Olugbode 2009). The irony is that northern Muslims have monopolized power for over thirty years and the north is still the most squalid, violent and poverty-stricken part of the county. Today, more than fifteen million young Muslims in the northern states have no access to Western education. Known as Almajirci, this culture has bred young children who are products of a tradition of

Qur'anic recitation, which places them under the tutelage of a teacher. Unfortunately, they have become a threat to society, because they graduate with no marketable skills and roam the streets with an uncertain future. This is why they have become the cannon fodder that feeds riots in the northern parts of Nigeria (Purefoy 2010).

Poverty-induced violence is not only found in the northern states. Elsewhere, deprivation has produced perhaps far more destructive violence. However, since religion is not such a dominant instrument for reform in these areas, communal identities have been invented as metaphors for expressing discontent. This is what produced the culture of militancy that drove protest in the Niger Delta. This is the story of the violence, kidnapping and the breakdown of law and order that characterized the Niger Delta. The amnesty deal arrived at by Umaru Musa Yar'adua, the late president, has led to some significant reprieve and peace in the area (Abide 2009; Baldauf 2010). This is why it is pointless to continue to argue that the violence in the northern states has been a battle of faith between Christians and Muslims. In my view, much of what drives urban violence in Northern Nigeria has little to do with religion and everything to do with social conditions and the decay that surround the poor whether they are Muslims or Christians.

The Failure of Politics

Finally, there is the growing concern about the lack of restraint by the Nigerian elite and their seeming inability to organize the public square in a way that it ensures rationality even for their competition. The military was corrupt and ran a system that did not allow for collaboration among the competing elites. Democracy was supposed to provide for this. Unfortunately, the quality of leadership that the political elite has offered has left much to be desired. Sadly, the culture of corruption, violence and manipulation of power persists. Thus, violence, whether sparked by elections, work conditions or so-called religion is largely an expression of this frustration. We can argue therefore that as long as the political class does not subscribe to a culture of rule of law, and good governance, violence will remain a major part of national life.

From Belligerence to Accommodation: The Nigerian-Interreligious Council

As can be seen from the preceding, since colonial times Nigerian Christians and Muslims have viewed each other at best as rivals and at worst as enemies. Christians and Muslims in Nigeria each have a national body that started out as regional umbrella bodies to deal with the issues of religion and conflict in the north. For decades, the national bodies were rivals and did not work together even on issues of mutual concern. That is beginning to change with the founding of the Nigeria Inter-religious Council.

The Muslims have the Jama'atu Nasril Islam (JNI), a northern organisation founded in the 1960s, and the Supreme Council for Islamic Affairs (SCIA), a national umbrella body founded in the 1980s. Although both are under the leadership of the sultan, they are independent of one another and sometimes espouse different ideas.

In the late 1960s, the Northern Christian Association, now known as CAN, Northern States, was founded to address issues considered peculiar to the northern Christian community. At a national level, Christians have the Christian Association of Nigeria (CAN), which came into being in the 1980s. Each body has different leaders and espouse ideas particular to their environments. The stories of their trials and travails have been well documented (Enwerem 1995).

Until recently, but especially under the military, these organisations and their leaders were engaged in a gladiatorial battle to protect the interests of their adherents, locally and nationally. Beyond the occasional polite talk, the leaders of both faiths made little effort to speak with one voice. They often spoke at cross-purposes, accusing one another of conspiracy, especially in moments of crisis. CAN popularized and amplified a cloud of fear over the successive plots by Muslims to Islamize Nigeria.[10] Muslims

---

10. Some of these sentiments were expressed in two memos written by the Catholic

accused their Christian brethren of jealousy, intolerance, outright hatred for Islam, and conspiracy with the West.[11]

As a result, both religious bodies lost their moral authority to speak truth to power with one voice. In moments of national crisis and tension, they could never agree to speak together as they merely traded accusations. On such key issues as national pilgrimages, involvement of the church in education, Nigeria's purported membership of the Organisation of Islamic Conference (OIC), the status of the Nigerian state (as enshrined in section 10 of the Nigerian Constitution), and teaching of religion in schools, not much genuine dialogue has taken place. Both sides remain suspicious of the role of the state.

Since 1999, when the nation returned to democracy, changes have taken place and, I would say, for the better. One significant development was the emergence of General Olusegun Obasanjo, Nigeria's former head of state, as an international statesman after he willingly surrendered power in 1979 and had become a 'born again' Christian. My intention here is not to assess his controversial tenure as the president of Nigeria (1999–2007). My interest is in the way he changed the face of the national image of the SCIA and CAN. First, the excitement of the Christian community in his inauguration found expression in the Thanksgiving Prayer Service, which the leadership of CAN organized a day after his inauguration.[12] The importance of the Obasanjo administration for the Christian community in Nigeria makes an interesting study. However, some key developments took place in the course of his eight-year administration that are of great significance for Christians and Muslims.

- He successfully completed the construction of the Ecumenical Centre after over 20 years.

Bishops Conference of Nigeria, and submitted to the President on 11 September 1980 and 25 February 1983.

11. Similar sentiments echoed in a statement by Current Affairs Committee of the Jama'atu Nasril Islam (Dated 6 January 1987).

12. This event took place at the International Conference Centre, ICC, Abuja on 30 May 1999 and was well attended by the leadership of CAN, senior clergymen and diplomats. The author was in attendance.

- He built a Christian chapel and appointed a chaplain to the presidential villa.
- He set up the Nigeria Inter-religious Council, NIREC.
- He strengthened the National Christian Pilgrims Board.

In the case of Islam, the Muslim community enjoyed patronage from the president. Among other things:

- He organized the fund raising for the renovation of the National Mosque.
- He openly participated in the Muslim Ramadan and broke his fast with Muslim leaders.
- He developed close ties with the then sultan, Alhaji Maccido.
- He maintained the tempo of support for the Muslim pilgrimage.
- He ensured transfer of power to the Muslim north.

The most important issue was the setting up of NIREC. The details of its emergence are vague, but Archbishop John Onaiyekan, its co-chairman, has sought to clarify some of the facts of its origins (Onaiyekan 2010).

After NIREC's inauguration, the late sultan of Sokoto, Alhaji Maccido, and Rev. Sunday Mbang, the president of CAN at the time and the prelate of the Methodist Church, emerged as co-chairmen of the body. Their tenure was not eventful as it was marked by routine quarterly meetings held at the Transcorp Hilton Hotel in Abuja. However, there has been noticeable change in the last five years, since the emergence of both Alhaji Sa'ad Abubakar, the new sultan of Sokoto and president of SCIA, and Archbishop John Onaiyekan, archbishop of Abuja and president of the CAN, as co-chairmen.

NIREC has changed the face of Christian-Muslim relations significantly and has come into national and international prominence. Under the leadership of both men, ordinary Nigerians have begun to feel somewhat positive about the prospects of religion being a force for good and not being associated with violence. Both men have appeared publicly in such national initiatives as health campaigns (malaria, HIV/AIDS, polio), travelled together for international conferences, signed statements together in moments of national crisis, and so on. Now, it seems both federal and state governments feel more confident in terms of how they can relate to both faiths. Indeed, many positive things are starting to happen, and although we are still far from our destination, the prospects are bright if this momentum continues.

Two significant events have occurred recently, which, if taken further, will help calm frayed nerves and reduce the association of religion as negatives in Nigeria. We might be seeing the end of the religious problem in Nigeria.

On 20 April 2010, CAN took a prophetic step when it organized a one-day seminar in Abuja under the theme 'My Muslim Neighbour'. Both the Sultan and Archbishop Onaiyekan presented insightful papers that spoke closely to the issues of collaboration and cooperation in an unprecedented manner. Both men, in separate statements, focused on issues of religious freedom, love, tolerance, evangelism and good governance. About a month later, the SCIA, at one of its annual meetings in Kaduna, devoted a session to addressing the issues raised by the CAN initiative. For the first time in their history, they extended invitations to the leadership of CAN along with other religious leaders to participate at a special session of their historic meeting. At the session, Bishop Josiah Idowu-Fearon, Anglican Bishop of Kaduna, presented an excellent paper, *Islam in the Eyes of a Non-Muslim*. After the presentation, the Sultan formally asked three other Christian leaders, including myself, to speak for five to ten minutes. This epoch making event has offered a major platform of hope for the future of Christian-Muslim relations in Nigeria.

It is of note that in its over forty years of existence, the Kaduna meeting was the first of the SCIA hosted by a governor who is a Christian. This was a sequel to the twist in the political developments of the country after the death of President Yar'adua.[13] It was also the first time that non-Muslims were invited to the meeting of SCIA. A combination of these factors indicates that Nigeria is on the verge of a new phase in securing a new place for religion in national life, and, hopefully, reducing the tensions that have come to characterize Christian-Muslim relations. It depends on

---

13. Mr. Patrick Yakowa had been sworn in as the Governor of Kaduna State after the sitting Governor Architect Namadi Sambo was nominated vice-president by the new president, Dr. Goodluck Jonathan.

whether the leadership of both faiths carry through with the same trust and enthusiasm that has been displayed by both men for now.

This is a welcome development in Nigeria because elsewhere, the Catholic Church has been at the forefront of creating these kinds of platforms especially in areas of conflict such as the Philippines, Ghana and South Africa (Viviano 2004).[14] It is therefore important that the Catholic Church, in particular, and CAN move decisively to deal with the issues of dialogue with Muslims, even in the face of seeming provocation and reluctance. We can only hope and pray that the excellent working relationship between the two co-chairmen of NIREC will survive their tenure. It is important that NIREC, a voluntary organisation, go beyond mere goodwill as the basis for membership and find a legal basis for its existence. It is also important that it remain prophetically critical in addressing the issues of members or of their adherents. If this happens, we can successfully take religion out of the manipulative and potentially corrupting stranglehold of the state. We will be on the way to building a democratic and secular society.

Summary and Conclusion

As noted, our country's return to democracy has been a troubled journey. However, we must insist that our citizens across the continent understand that despite its difficulties, building a democratic state is a challenge we must face squarely. Unlike dictatorship, which closed the political space, the openness of democracy holds out the best prospects for our country to build on the positive aspects of its multi-culturalism and pluralism. Dialogue at any level is endangered by any form of dictatorship.

Our nation is wracked with myriad problems. However, they are not caused purely by religion, and it is wrong to continue to argue that they are driven by religion. I believe that many factors account for what has been wrongly referred to as the religious problem. These include a poorly designed

---

14. Vivano notes that: 'The Bishops-Ulama Forum in the Philippines came into being as a means of helping to provide a spiritual basis for negotiating and end to the conflict' (2004: 400).

infrastructure of governance in the hands of a corrupt and thoroughly incompetent elite, inability to manage diversity and pluralism, corruption and poor vision. The lack of a culture of human rights, respect for women and for weaker members of society, and growing inequalities and poverty, among a host of other factors, account for our prolonged suffering.

Although the situation remains delicate, NIREC, along with other organisations of a civil society, does have a chance to lay a foundation for the improvement of the quality of governance in Nigeria. Too many issues of poor administration have been given a religious face when they have nothing to do with religion. Many of the issues that have led to violence have been the product of poor vision and bad decisions undertaken by governments that often leave citizens vulnerable. Lack of clear government policies have created the basis for allegations of favouritism. With proper debate and co-operation, NIREC can help the government think through such issues as common citizenship (we are all God's children), pilgrimages (how should government participate?) and procurement of lands for building of places of worship. NIREC should seek out common projects independent of government. Some of this could include collaborating in monitoring elections, implementation of government projects, fight against corruption and so on.

NIREC can also position itself as the gatekeeper of public morality, and in the process, become truly a voice of the voiceless men and women of all faiths or even of no faith. It could remove the ambiguity over who controls the public space and morality (Linden 2004: 48). This development would have a salutary effect on politics and other facets of life in Nigeria. It would free religion and religious leaders to serve as a moral compass while also freeing political leaders from the dubious spell and manipulation of modern-day Rasputins. If we succeed in this project, we will be on the road to freeing the moral force of the adherents of the two universal religions in Africa's most populous nation. We will have justified the findings of the researchers who concluded that Nigerians are both 'the happiest people on earth and also the most religious' (Tablet 2010).

References

Abide, S. 7 September 2009. After the Niger Delta Amnesty Programme: What Next? *Village Square*, Monday.

Ayandele, E.A. 1966. The Missionary Factor in Northern Nigeria, 1870–1913. *Journal of the Historical Society of Nigeria*, 3(3), December: 502–522.

Ayandele, E.A. 1974. *The Missionary Impact on Modern Nigeria, 1882–1914*. Ibadan: University Press.

Baldauf, S. 31 January 2010. Nigerian Militants Call of Truce in Oil Rich Niger Delta. *Christian Science Monitor*. http://www.csmonitor.com/World/Africa/2010/0131/Nigeria-militants-call-off-truce-in-oil-rich-Niger-Delta.

Christellow, A. 1984. *Religious Protest and Dissent in Northern Nigeria: From Mahdism to Quranic Integralism*. Paper presented at the Annual Spring Symposium, University of Illinois. 2–3 April 1984.

Crampton, E.P.T. 1975. *Christianity in Northern Nigeria*. Zaria: Northern Nigeria Publishing Co.

Enwerem, I. 1995. *A Dangerous Awakening: The Politicisation of Religion in Nigeria*. Ibadan. IFRA.

Falola, Toyin. 2001. *Violence in Nigeria: The Crisis of Religious Politics and Secular Ideologies*. Rochester, NY: University of Rochester Press.

Gbadamosi, T.G. 1987. *The Growth of Islam among the Yoruba, 1841–1908*. Ibadan: University Press.

Al-Hajj, A. 1973. *The Mahdist Tradition in Northern Nigeria*. PhD. Thesis, Ahmadu Bello University, Zaria.

Hogben, S.J., and Kirk-Greene, Anthony. 1960. *The Emirates of Northern Nigeria: A Preliminary Survey*. London: Oxford University Press.

Human Rights Watch. 2004. Political Sharia? Human Rights and Islamic Law in Northern Nigeria. *Human Rights Watch* 16(9A), September.

Idowu-Fearon, J. 2010. *Mohammed in the Eyes of a Christian*. Paper presented at the SCIA meeting in Kaduna on 31 May 2010.

Kaduna State Government Committee on the Harmonisation of Drafts of the Sharia Penal Code and Sharia Criminal Procedure Code of Laws.

King, Lamont. 2003. From Caliphate to Protectorate: Ethnicity and the Colonial Sabon Gari System in Northern Nigeria. *Journal of Colonialism and Colonial History* 4(2), Fall.

Kukah, M. 1993. *Religion, Politics and Power in Northern Nigeria*. Ibadan: Spectrum Books.

Last, M. 1968. *The Sokoto Caliphate*. London: Longmans.

Linden, Ian. 2004. Who Controls the Political Space? *World Christianity: Politics, Theology, Dialogues*, edited by Anthony O'Mahony and Michael Kirwan. London: Melisende.

Loimeier, R. 1997. *Islamic Reform and Political Change in Northern Nigeria*. Evanston, IL: Northwestern University Press.

Makar, T. 1984. The Relationship between the Sokoto Caliphate and the Non-Muslim Peoples of the Middle Belt Region. *History of the Sokoto Caliphate*, edited by Bala Usman. Zaria: Ahmadu Bello University Press.

Nzeshi, O. 19 May 2010. Parliament Cannot Annul Islamic Marriage. *This Day*, Wednesday.

Onaiyekan, J. 2010. *The Dividends of Religion in Nigeria*. Lecture delivered at the University of Ilorin. Ilorin, on 12 May 2010.

Paden, J. 1973. *Religion and Political Culture in Kano*. Berkeley: University of California Press.

Purefoy, C. 8 January 2010. *Nigeria's Almajiri Children Learning a Life of Poverty and Violence*. Transcripts of CNN Report.

Sklar, R. 1963. *Nigerian Political Parties*. Princeton, NJ: Princeton University Press.

Smith, M. 1955. *Baba of Karo: A Woman of the Muslim Hausa*. London.

Taiwo, J., and Olugbode, M. 31 July 2009. Boko Haram Leader killed. *This Day*, Friday.

Tseayo, J. 1973. *Conflict and Incorporation in Northern Nigeria: The Incorporation of Tiv*. Zaria: Gaskiya Corporation.

Usman, B. 1982. *The Overthrow of the Sarauta System*. Zaria: Ahmadu Bello University Press.

Usman, Bala & Nur Alkali (Eds). 1983. *Studies in the History of Pre-colonial Borno*. Zaria: New Nigerian Publishing Company.

Uwais, M. 5 May 2010. Child Marriage: Yerima Got It Wrong. *The Voice*, Wednesday.

Viviano, R. 2004. Responses of the Catholic Church to Islam in the Philippines from the Second Vatican Council to the Present Day. *World Christianity: Politics, Theology, Dialogues*, edited by Anthony O'Mahony & Michael Kirwan, Melisende: London.

Vu, M. 27 February 2006. Death Toll Rises to 96 in Cartoon Sparked Violence. *Christian Today*, Monday.

CHAPTER 17

Senegal

Daniel Gomis

The country of Senegal is in the most western part of Africa and serves as a bridge between North Africa, or *Maghreb,* and sub-Saharan Africa. This strategic geographical location explains why Senegal was the gateway for Islam in sub-Saharan Africa, which came through Mauritania in the tenth century.

Historical Survey of Islam in Senegal

Islam was introduced to Senegal in the tenth century by the Berber tribes from Tagant (Mauritania), who were supported by the local authorities in spreading the new religion in North Africa.

Upon the arrival of the Europeans in the fifteenth century and the introduction of the slave trade with the help of the local elite, the economic, political and social structures of Senegambia (present day Senegal and Gambia) were shattered. As the local aristocracy distanced itself from Islam and used more and more violent methods against the population, thousands of people started to convert to Islam and serve as soldiers in the jihad that happened in the region during the eighteenth and nineteenth centuries.

French Colonial Conquest

The French conquered the area by the nineteenth century. Islamic resistance to the French was symbolized by figures like El Hadj Umar Tall (1797–1864) in the north, Maba Diakhou Ba in the Saloum and the Gambia, Mamadou Lamine Drame in the Soninke land and Ahmadou Cheikhou in the Fouta and the Jolof and Fode Kaba Doumbouya in the South (Casamance). After they were all defeated, Islam was under colonial domination and the Sufi brotherhoods emerged as an important influence in society.

The colonial conquest, the political domination of the European powers, the social crisis and the cultural oppression of the populations had serious effects on the religious practises of the Senegalese. In the twentieth century, Islam grew exponentially in the northern part of Senegal and the circumstances gave an impetus to the religious brotherhoods.

The Religious Brotherhoods (Tariqa) in Senegal

In Senegal, the overwhelming majority of the Muslim population is from the Sunni tradition; however, they are characterized by the strong attachment to a number of Sufi brotherhoods or tariqa.[1] In effect, the majority of Senegal's 94 per cent Muslim population consider adherence to a brotherhood, a tariqa, to be a religious obligation, in keeping with the Sufi maxim 'He who does not have a *shaykh* (sheikh) will have Satan for a guide' (Mbacké 2005: 9). In Senegal, followers of Sufism are known as *talibes* and their leaders are called *marabus*. The highest-level leader of a branch of a brotherhood is called the *khalif general* or *grand marabu*.

Four major Sufi brotherhoods have spread through Senegal in the past century and a half. These are in chronological order: the *Qadiriya tariqa*, the *Tijaniya tariqa* (both of which are of Arab origin), the *Mouridiya tariqa* and the *Layenne tariqa* (both of which are of local origin).

---

1. *Tariqa* is the correct singular form and *turuq* is the plural form.

The Qadiriya tariqa is one of the oldest brotherhoods and one of the first to appear in West Africa. It was founded by the *Sharif*[2] 'Abdu'l-Qadir al-Jilani, who was born in Jilan, Iran, and learned Arabic and Sufism in Baghdad. The order spread all over the Middle East and was introduced into the Sahel region in the fifteen century by Muhammad Abd Al-Karim al-Maghrib. One of his disciples, Al-Mukhtar ibn Ahmad of the Arab Kunta tribe founded the motherhouse of Timbuktu, which became the centre for the order in West Africa (Behrman 1999: 18). General diffusion of the Qadiriya tariqa was the work of Mauritanian *shaykhs* (sheikhs), who served as Sufi guides to many Senegalese disciples. The city of Ndiassane (Thiès) is the religious and pilgrimage centre of the Qadiriya tariqa.

The Tijaniya tariqa emerged in the Maghrib during the last decades of the eighteenth century. It was founded by the Sharif Ahmad Ibn Muhammad al-Tijani in 'Ayn Madi in Morocco following a revelation by the prophet. 'Al-Tijani's brotherhood eventually became known, in contrast to the Qadiriya and others, for its relatively uncomplicated prayers, litanies and exercises, the simplicity of which facilitated the understanding of its teaching and practises by uneducated followers' (Behrman 1999: 19). After 1815, large-scale Tijani missionary ventures associated with commercial activities were conducted throughout West Africa. The most important conversion of the period was that of Umar Tall, a Tukulor from the Senegal River area. He was named *muqaddam* of the tariqa while in Mecca and upon his return to the western Sudan launched a holy war with his army of volunteers. At the death of Umar Tall, the Tijaniya had taken firm root in Futa Toro before spreading elsewhere in Senegal through the efforts of the Tijani Shaykh Maba Diakhou. Later, it spread mainly through the efforts of the educator shaykhs, who were not connected to the warfare endemic at the time.

> We can cite as examples al-Hajj Abd Allah Niasse and his children who did much to spread the tariqa in Salum, in the Gambia, and further east in Ghana and Nigeria for instance.

---

2. A *sharif* is a person who claims descent from Muhammad and is understood to have a special gift of grace because of this.

Based in Kaolack, they are still very active in the fields of Quranic teaching and the Islamic sciences, however, of all the Tijani teachers in Senegal, the most active was al-hajj Malik Sy (Mbacké 2005: 35).

The descendants of al-hajj Malick Sy are currently leading the Tijanya tariqa in Senegal. The city of Tivaouane is the religious and pilgrimage centre of the Tijanya tariqa.

The Mouridiya tariqa was founded at the end of the nineteenth century by Shaykh Muhammad Bamba Mbacké in Baol, Senegal. He had been initiated to the Qadiri *wird*[3] by his father and undertook a number of journeys through Senegal and Mauritania and learned Sufi masters' writings such as those of Al-Ghazali. In 1895, French authorities deported him to Gabon, on false charges; this increased his prestige. Upon his return, he was deported to Mauritania in 1903 and finally returning to Diourbel, Senegal, in 1907, where he died in 1927.

One of the main focuses of the Mouridiya tariqa (or Mouridism) was the rejection of the Qadiriya and Tijani wird as foreign and Ahmadu Bamba's refusal to entertain any form of collaboration with the colonisers. The focus on work and discipline and total submission to the marabu is one of the main differences with the other tariqa. Ahmadu Bamba is frequently quoted as saying, 'work is a part of religion' or 'work as if you would never die and pray as if you were to die tomorrow'. The Mouridiya tariqa is the most aggressive, most dynamic and fastest growing brotherhood in Senegal. The city of Touba (Diourbel) is the religious and pilgrimage centre of the Mouridiya tariqa.

The name of the Layenne tariqa is derived from the Arabic term *ilahyyin*, which means 'people of God', or 'deists', this comes from the Quranic verse 46:31. The founder of the tariqa, Libasse Thiaw, who is better known as Limamoulaye, was born in 1843 in the fishing village of Yoff, now a suburb of Dakar. In reply to the French authorities who were convinced he was recruiting soldiers and collecting arms to start a jihad against them, he declared, 'For our part, we have no need to make jihad, I recommend to

---

3. *Wird* is a Sufi spiritual exercise practised during dhikr.

you jihad against the passions of the soul' (Mbacké 2005: 68). The Layenne are mostly from the Lebou ethnic group (a sub-group of the Wolof) and are concentrated on the Cape Verde peninsula where the sanctuaries of Yoff and Camberene are located. Limamoulaye told his disciples that he was a prophet sent by God to the Black race, that he was a saint, master of creatures and the incarnation of the Muhammad. His son, Seydina Issa Rohou Lahi was declared to be the Black incarnation of Jesus Christ the Messiah. The city of Camberene (Dakar) is the religious and pilgrimage centre of the Layenne tariqa.

A Historical Survey of Christianity in Senegal

The Roman Catholic Church in Senegal

The Roman Catholic Church's first contact with Senegalese soil was in the 1440s when a voyage of exploration along the West African coast, sent by Prince Henry the Navigator of Portugal, first reached Senegal. The Holy See gave the King of Portugal charge of the political, economic and spiritual enterprise (Benoist 2007: 16). The first Catholic Church was built in 1444 on Gorée Island. However, confusion between the slave trade and the evangelistic efforts impeded the advance of the gospel.

The arrival of the French missionaries resulted in many changes. Among those who came were the Saint Vincent de Paulm the Société des Missions Etrangères de Paris, the Lazaristes and the Saint-Joseph de Cluny congregation. This latter mission arrived in Saint Louis (North Senegal) and was involved in education, medical care, and agriculture. The Spiritans (Congregation of the Holy Spirit), with Father Aloys Kobés, can be considered the builders of the Senegalese Roman Catholic Church with their missionary and economic work.

In 1962 Hyacynthe Thiandoum, a member of the Spiritans, became the first Senegalese bishop. The Catholic Church contributed to the education of the first political elites in Senegal and Father Kobés and Father Lebret contributed to the writing of the first economic plan of the Senegalese nation.

The Protestant and Evangelical Churches in Senegal

The Protestant church started in 1862 in Sedhiou (South Senegal) with the Mission Evangélique de Paris (Evangelical Mission of Paris), which settled in Dakar in 1913. In 1936 the Worldwide Evangelisation for Christ (WEC) mission arrived in Kolda (South Senegal), New Tribes Mission (NTM) in Ziguinchor (South Senegal) in 1954, and the Assemblies of God in Tambacounda (East Senegal) in 1956. The missionaries translated the Bible in local languages and opened health centres and schools.

From 1960 to 1980, many missionaries worked in Senegal and people converted through the reading of Christian literature, the work among the youth and the establishment of Bible centres in Dakar. In 1963, the Assemblies of God built the first evangelical church in Dakar and started the Senegal Bible Institute. In 1962, Eric Church started work on the translation of the New Testament in Wolof. In 1968, the Fraternité Evangélique du Sénégal (Fellowship of Evangelical Churches of Senegal) was founded. Between 1960 and 1980, numerous missions started working in Senegal including the Lutheran Mission, International Baptist Mission, United World Mission, Southern Baptist Mission, Norway Evangelical Mission and Summer Institute of Linguistics (SIL). They became involved in radio ministry, translation and schools. Currently, African, Asian and South American missions are involved in street-children ministries and holistic ministries. Most churches are led by Senegalese pastors and there is a growing collaboration between the denominations.

Demographics

Today the country is ethnically and religiously diverse. Although there is significant integration of all groups, Christians are concentrated in the west and south, while groups who practise indigenous religious beliefs live mainly in the east and south. Muslims form 94 per cent of the Senegalese population, and the major parts of the country belong to one of the Muslim brotherhoods.

Most ethnic groups in the northern, eastern, western and central parts of Senegal are Muslims: Fulas (99 per cent), Tukulors (99 per cent), Wolof (98 per cent) and Sereer (65 per cent). The majority of Muslim ethnic groups are spread in the main Sufi brotherhoods: Wolofs are mostly Mourides,

Tukulors and Fulas are mostly Tijani, while Lebus are mostly Layennes. The groups in the southern part of Senegal are mostly Christians and from the African Traditional Religions, including Joolas, Manjaks, Balantas and Bainuks.

Encounter and Engagement between Christians and Muslims

Peaceful Relationships

The long tradition of *teranga* (hospitality) in Senegal and early contacts with Westerners and the use of the Wolof language as a trade language have facilitated the relationships between Christians and Muslims. During the colonial era and the existence of the Four Communes,[4] there were many mixed marriages and a peaceful cohabitation between the faiths, which is a unique trait of the Senegalese.

The involvement of the Catholic Church in the education of the Muslim elite also favoured the rise of sympathy and tolerance towards Christians. This is exemplified by the election of Leopold Sedar Senghor, a Catholic, as the first president of the Republic of Senegal. In the city of Saint Louis, in the north of Senegal, the Christian and Muslim cemetery is in the same location. In the southern and western parts of Senegal, one can often find Muslims and Christians from the same family and living in harmony. Even in areas with a strong Muslim presence (like the northeast) Christians live and practise their faith peacefully.

Despite some recent disturbances between the Catholic bishop and the Senegalese head of state—comments on the economic and social situation in the country and death threats from an anonymous group—the relationship between the Christian and Muslims has not been affected.

There is a 'natural' tradition of peaceful relationships between Christians and Muslims in Senegal, and it is visible during the religious festivals like the Mouride pilgrimage (*Maggal*) or Tijani pilgrimage (*Gamu*) and Catholic

---

4. The 'Four Communes' of Senegal were the four oldest colonial towns in French controlled West Africa.

pilgrimage (*Popenguine*) at which officials from each group participate. It is also visible in the everyday interrelations on the Christian and Muslim holidays where meals and celebration are shared.

Christian Attitudes towards Engagement with Muslims

The Roman Catholic Church, which is the largest Christian tradition in Senegal, is involved in education, health and social action and has numerous schools, health care centres and Caritas offices throughout the country. They are constantly in contact with the population but are not involved in active evangelism. The Roman Catholic Church has good relationships with, and is well respected within, the Muslim community. It has a rather collaborative approach towards Islam, as it approves marriages between people of the two faiths and encourages dialogue.

The Evangelical churches take two different approaches to Muslims. One group is confrontational and focuses mainly on outreach. Most of those groups do not have a long tradition of relationship with Muslims, and most of their outreach materials address the polemics between the two faiths. Another leans towards a 'bridge' approach and uses discussion, friendship, chronological stories and common ethical grounds.

There is a holistic approach to the gospel with the building of hospitals, schools and training centres. Organisations like the *Mission Inter Senegal*, the active branch of the Senegalese Evangelical Fellowship, a non-profit organisation recognized by the government, is sending out national missionaries to the towns and villages in the interior that are without any Christian witness. Mission Inter Senegal's main role is to announce the message of Jesus Christ by means of national projects, development and evangelism.

Efforts were made by Evangelicals and Protestants to participate in the preparation of the Muslim and Christian Summit in 2006. A conference of Evangelical and Protestant churches of Senegal is organized every two years to study the trends of evangelism among the Muslims, share statistics and hear lectures by Senegalese and non-Senegalese speakers. There is, however, a strong need to create forums of discussion between both faiths and to encourage Christians to do research on the Senegalese types of Islam.

Muslim Groups

Most Senegalese Muslims tend to be moderate and open to modern democracy and to the Western world while retaining their religious values and practises. A growing group from the Tijaniya branch known as '*Mustarchidina wal mustarchidaty*' advocates a 'return' to the Islamic faith, but it is still hindered by the significant size of the Muslim brotherhoods.

The biggest challenge to Christians is the Muslim brotherhoods and especially Mouridism with its Africanized Islam. The majority of Muslims in Senegal practise a folk-type of Islam, which has a mixture of Islamic and African Traditional Religion beliefs. Mouridism is the fastest growing Muslim brotherhood and its popularity has much to do with 'their assimilation of traditional African customs and elements, such as the transmission of spiritual power through genealogy, the excessive importance accorded to a person's birth, the equation of spiritual guides with traditional chiefs, extended polygamy, etc.' (Mbacké 1976: 14). Today, Mouridism has expanded all over Senegal and in Senegalese communities in the largest cities of the Western world because most of its disciples come from the Wolof ethnic group known as traders and travellers.

Within less than thirty years, the Mourides have gained control of the economic, social and political aspects of the country. The city of Touba, where the founder of Mouridism is buried, has become a pilgrimage centre attracting millions of pilgrims every year.

Some Mouride religious leaders have founded their own political parties, allied with the ruling political party and become members of parliament. Mouride disciples do not specifically adhere to a given political party but follow the *ndigel* or recommendation of their shaykh for electoral voting.

Mouridism is a top-down, male type of leadership that is transmitted through the lineage of Sheikh Ahmadu Bamba.

One *khalif* general supervises hundreds of other sheikhs who each have their own disciples. His authority is based upon the Islamic concept of *barakah* (favour, grace, virtue), which Sanneh depicts in these terms:

> Wrapping themselves in the mantle of *barakah*, the Mouride leaders' claim over the bodies of their disciples came to be complete and total, so much so, that after a point, religious

instruction, with its accompanying initiation into grades of spiritual enlightenment, was almost entirely missing in the otherwise close relationship between the postulant and his spiritual axis (1997: 111).

There is a patron-client relationship between the wealthy and influential disciples and their shaykhs, while the poorest disciples take sometimes the 'crumbs falling from the table'. Mouridism is a brotherhood proudly affirming its roots in the Wolof culture and traditions and trying intentionally to build a Dar al-Murid (Land of Mouride) throughout Senegal.

On the spiritual and cultural grounds, one of the greatest strengths of the Mourid brotherhood is its answers to the 'middle zone or middle level which deals with the *transempirical realities of this world*—with magic, evil eye, earthly spirits, ancestors, witchcraft, divination, and the like' (Hiebert 2008: 49).

Classical ways of sharing the gospel (distributing tracts, door-to-door, *Jesus* film showings, Evangelism Explosion, etc.) will not always answer to the deep needs of the Mouride people and present the message of the cross in all its fullness. As an answer to this challenge, the following biblical, theological and missiological reflections are suggested:

- Studying and understanding the Mouride worldview. A worldview as described by Hiebert as 'what people in a community take as given realities, the maps they have of reality that they use for living' (Hiebert 2008: 15).
- Having a 'shame' rather than a 'guilt' perspective and approach as Kraus argued 'the role of the cross in reconciling us to God must be seen in broader terms as an answer to both shame and guilt' (Green and Baker 2000: 157).
- Approaching Mourides with the grace of God as the Apostle Paul did with the Athenians in Acts 17:2: 'Men of Athens! I see that in every way you are very religious.' This means exploring the bridges through relationships and open discussion.
- Having a holistic (the affirmation of God's presence in all things) and inclusive approach in our sharing of the gospel message.

- Taking into account that the majority of the Mourides are animists in their inner being, we can ask questions about their fears, dreams and directions for their life.
- Giving a proper explanation of the holy life and the work of the Holy Spirit through the example of our own lives and testimonies.
- Reading, teaching and explaining the life of Christ in Wolof and with their own cultural illustrations.
- Focusing on the relationship rather than results and, most importantly, creating a new community for the Mouride background believer, focusing on the different dynamics of the relationships between a disciple and his master.
- Helping develop a theology of worship and submission 'that emphasizes God's volition and human response rather than searching for and trying to manipulate God' (Hiebert, Shaw and Tiénou 1999: 371).

References

Barrett, D.B. 1986. *Schism and Renewal in Africa: An Analysis of Six Thousand Contemporary Religious Movements.* Nairobi: Oxford University Press.

Behrman, L.C. 1970. *Muslim Brotherhoods and Politics in Senegal.* Harvard: Harvard University Press.

De Benoit, J.R. 2007. *Histoire de l'église Catholique au Sénégal: Sur les Traces de l'évangélisation.* Paris: Editions Karthala.

Green, J.B. and Baker, M.D. 2000. *Recovering the Scandal of the Cross.* Downers Grove: Intervarsity Press.

Hiebert, P.G. 2008. *Transforming Worldviews.* Grand Rapids: Baker Academic.

Hiebert, P.G., Shaw, D., and Tiénou, T. 1999. *Understanding Folk Religions.* Grand Rapids: Baker Books.

Mbacké, K. 2005. *Sufism and Religious Brotherhoods in Senegal.* Princeton: Markus Wiener Publishers

Sanneh, L. 1997. *The Crown and the Turban: Muslims and West African Pluralism.* Boulder: Westview Press.

CHAPTER 18

South Africa

Manfred Jung

South Africa is a leading country on the African continent as evidenced by the 2010 FIFA World Cup and in South Africa's gross national product, achievements in education, and invitations from other African nations to be involved with them politically and in peacekeeping. In addition, South Africa is a melting pot of cultures and features, where a host of different religions peacefully co-exist. The South Africa Christian-Muslim encounter, especially in apologetics, has influenced and is still influencing Christians and Muslims throughout the continent. This influence is felt all the way to villages where Muslims raise the age-old objections learned from the South African debates, objections which have long been adequately refuted by Christians in South Africa and elsewhere. This study of the history and current situation in Christian-Muslim relations in South Africa will provide valuable insights to allow people to better understand the southern-most country on the continent and will present valuable insights into Christian-Muslim encounters throughout the continent.

Brief History of the Development of Islam

Early Muslim Arrivals

The written history of Islam in South Africa focuses on the Muslims who were brought from Southeast Asia and much less on native South African Muslims and Muslims from other African countries. This is understandable as the Cape Malay[1] and Indian Muslim communities (Lubbe 1987: 117) constitute the majority of Muslims in South Africa (Dangor 1991: 65–67).

Muslims arrived in South Africa primarily in two waves. The first was about 300 years ago, during the rule of the Dutch East India Trading Company; they were brought from Malaysia, Indonesia and India as slaves and political prisoners and settled in the Cape Town region. The second arrived about 150 years ago and came mainly from India. They consisted of traders and many labourers for the sugar cane fields in KwaZulu-Natal. Their descendants still live mainly in the Durban area and in Johannesburg.

What is sometimes overlooked in the history of South African Muslims is that a number of Muslims of African origin arrived early in South Africa. According to Suleman Essop Dangor, slaves were brought from African nations such as Guinea and Dahomey as well as from Madagascar (1991: 65–66). Yusuf da Costa provides support for this by listing Angola, Cape Verde Islands, East Africa, Guinea, Madagascar and Mauritius as places of origin of African slaves who were brought to the Cape Colony between 1652–1818 (da Costa & Davids 1994: 2).

Prize Negroes of Cape Town

The so-called Prize Negroes were also brought to South Africa. Robert C.H. Shell explains in an article about Islam in southern Africa that after the abolition of slavery, the British Navy intercepted ships at sea and freed slaves from different parts of Africa. Instead of returning them to where they had come from, the Navy brought them to Freetown and Cape Town because they were concerned that the former slaves might be re-enslaved. About five thousand such slaves were brought to Cape Town between 1808 and 1856. They did not become Christians but became Muslims in great numbers contributing to a large increase in the Muslim population. These African Muslims did not form their own Muslim community but integrated into the Cape Malay culture (Shell 2000: 332–334).

---

1. The terms 'Black', 'coloured', 'Indian, 'Malay' and 'White' are used merely in a technical and descriptive sense for lack of better or neutral terms and are in no way meant to be derogatory.

Zanzibaris of Natal

Another group of African Muslims, the Zanzibaris, were brought by the British to Natal from Malawi, Mozambique, Somalia, Zambia and Zanzibar as contract labourers employed in public works between 1873 and 1880 (Dangor 1991: 67). Gerhardus C. Oosthuizen, in *The Muslim Zanzibaris of South Africa*, provides an explanation for why no indigenous Black Muslim community developed:

> Muslim ex-slaves formed their own separate community. They developed closer links with the Indian labourers which is one reason why they feel nearer to the Indians then the local Africans, to whom they refer as 'them' and 'they'. This implies that they are also psychologically separate from the indigenous Blacks [sic] (p. 11).

Only the Zanzibaris became a distinct Black Muslim community, and they did not reach out to other Black South Africans.

Converts

In the 1960s the situation started to change: Muslims became more active in da'wah[2] efforts, and Islam started to make inroads into Black townships and began to grow through conversions. Michael Mumisa states, 'While the South African Muslims are mainly immigrants, the Black and White Muslims are converts to Islam' (2002: 279). Although he does not provide an exact date for when 'Africans began to accept Islam first in the townships surrounding Durban', from the context of his writing it must have been mid-1900 (2002: 285).

Sheik Abbas Phiri was an influential leader in the outreach efforts. Shahid Vawda introduces him as one who 'stands out as an important figure in the emergence of sustained da'wah work and the subsequent spread of Islam in Inanda and then in Ntuzuma and KwaMashu'.[3] Having

---

2. Da'wah is the term used for propagating Islam, literally it means to 'call' others to Islam.
3. Inanda and KwaMashu are districts in KwaZulu-Natal on of the provinces in South Africa.

received Islamic training in his homeland Malawi, Abbas Phiri came to South Africa in the 1940s to work in the coal mines. In the 1970s he started to do da'wah work full-time. After introducing himself to the local Black chiefs, he obtained a house in Ntuzuma and turned a section into a Jama'at Khana[4] in order to hold a madrassa and reach the local young people. Vawda records that Abbas Phiri 'claimed he converted well over a hundred people'. He even used karate and soccer to attract Muslims and non-Muslims, thus it is understandable that the youth especially embraced Islam (Vawda 1994: 537–540).

At about the same time, da'wah-efforts started in earnest in the Western Cape where a news report of the Masakahane Muslim Community says, 'the presence of an organized body of Muslims in the African Townships can be traced back as far as the sixties' (Masakhane 2002). Ebrahim Fakude puts the date as being even later by saying: 'Islam in the townships emerged in the late seventies' (Fakude 2002: 47).

The reason this chapter pays so much attention to the development of Islam among Black people is that the Black Muslim population has the highest growth rate of any Muslim group in South Africa. This is reflected in the government statistics of 2001 and is evident in the growing number of mosques being built in Black townships. In addition, Muslim da'wah organisations claim to have many converts through their social actions and feeding schemes in Black townships. The resulting Muslim communities are a new challenge to the church, especially in the Black townships; yet by-and-large the church is doing little to reach Muslims.

History of Christian-Muslim Encounters

Christians in South Africa

With the settlement of Europeans at the Cape of Good Hope, Christianity also came to South Africa. Protestant Christianity was dominant, with the Dutch Reformed Church (DRC) being the biggest and most influential

---

4. Jama'at Khana, a temporary place for prayers. It can be privately owned unlike a mosque, which falls under the laws of *waqf*.

denomination. The encounter between Christianity and Islam in South Africa goes back to the arrival of the Muslims as slaves in the Cape colony. The Muslims were tolerated, and even Sheikh Yousuf, a prominent Muslim imam who was under arrest in what is today called Macassar, near Cape Town, was allowed to practise his religion and thus influence many (da Costa & Davids 1994: 22–23).

From 1900 until today, the history of encounter is interwoven with the rise, establishment, struggle against and fall of apartheid. The reason is the close relationship of the DRC with the government on the one side and the Muslim identification with the oppressed and the 'struggle'[5] on the other side. Dr Muhammad Haron rightly asserts:

> The Muslims, despite their minority status as a religious group and being part of the larger majority of oppressed, also added their voices against the apartheid policies of the South African state (2004a: 8).

Over time, Christians moved from an exclusivist theological position to an inclusivist position and finally a pluralistic theological position (Haron 2004: 5). This resulted in moves from greater animosity between Muslim and Christians to less animosity, from intolerance to greater tolerance.

Christian Missionary Efforts

The last hundred-plus years have seen many missionary efforts to reach Muslims with the gospel. Although the efforts were backed by the big denominations of the DRC as well as the Anglicans, just a handful of people would labour among Muslims. What follows is a table of the missionaries or pastors[6] who engaged with Islam and Muslim writing (Haron 2004a: 5–8).

---

5. The term 'struggle' was a label for opposing the apartheid regime.
6. The pastors in the Dutch Reformed Church are called 'Dominis,' abbreviated 'Ds.'

Person	Writing	Comment
Ds G.B.A. Gerdener	Onder de Slamsen in de Kaapstad: Afval en Strijd	Appointed by the DRC General commission, he was active from 1913–1917
Ds A.J. Liebenberg	Mohammedanisme in Zuid-Afrika (1925) Die Slams (1926)	Appointed by the DRC General commission in 1919
A.W. Blaxall	An outpost of Islam (1927)	Anglican parishioner
A.R. Hampson	The Mission to Moslems in Cape Town (1934)	Ministered in Cape Town
Dr Izak du Plessies	Die bydraes van die Kaapse Maleier tot die Afrikaanse volklied (1935) Die Maleise samelewing aan die Kaap (1939) The Cape Malays (1944)	Studied the culture of Cape Malays
Ds Lukas Haasbroek	Die Sending onder Mohammedane in Kaapstad (1955)	MA student at Stellenbosch

Since the DRC was seen by many as collaborating with the apartheid government, it was not easy for Muslims to accept a gospel message from what they saw as an oppressing force. Instead, Muslims started to speak out and resist the oppressive government of the day. In March 1961, the *Call of Islam* pamphlet was published in which apartheid policies were condemned (Haron 2004a: 9). Members of the Muslim Youth Movement also became involved in the political arena.

In 1960 the Anglican diocese was involved in mission work among Muslims. The old pamphlet *Hadjie Abdoellah* [sic] from the 1870s, which is a conversion story from Islam to Christianity, was republished and caused a stir among Muslims. The Shayky Ahmad Behardien (Muslim Judicial Council) responded critically in an established Muslim newspaper *Muslim Views* (Haron 2004a: 10). The Evangelical Mission Press produced a series of pamphlets called *Al-Hidayah: Right Guidance*, which were widely distributed in Muslim areas (McComb nd).

Literature and Apologetics

Both Christians and Muslims use apologetics and literature to disseminate their beliefs and refute the other's. In 1958 Ahmed Deedat and Goolam Hussein Vanker established the Islamic Propagation Centre International (IPCI) in Durban. Ahmed Deedat became the most outspoken South African Muslim propagandist, writing twenty booklets and distributing them by the hundreds of thousands in South Africa and beyond. He conducted public lectures and public debates in South Africa and overseas. His approach was polemical, rather than scholarly. Many Muslims in South Africa adored Deedat, not realizing that a greater alienation between Christian and Muslims resulted from his propaganda. Some Muslims, however, spoke out against Deedat. Macki, the editor of the *Muslim Digest* in Durban, criticised Deedat's theology, actions and integrity in almost every issue of his publication (Makki 1990; 1991). Deedat died 8 August 2005, but the IPCI is still publishing and distributing his written material.

John Gilchrist, a Christian lawyer, and Gerhard Nehls, a missionary, responded to every argument made by Deedat and the IPCI. They also reached out to Muslims in a personal way and, although critical of the teachings of Islam and the way that some Muslims put forth arguments, they treated Muslims with respect and dignity. A host of Christian literature was produced and disseminated and is still available from CCM's website (ccm.org.za) and from Life Challenge Africa (www.lifechallenge.de). John Gilchrist was also involved in a number of debates and won a court case against Deedat (interview Gilchrist 2010).

Starting in the years of Deedat, Gilchrist and Nehls, Christian publications increased not only in number but also in quality. They have been reprinted, translated and distributed the world over and form part of a significant resource of Christian apologetics today (http://www.answering-islam.org). South African Christians increasingly research Islam and Christian-Muslim encounters and have started to write about them. Muslims seem to be largely unaware of these more recent academic works, as they do not feature in academic Muslim writings (Maurer 1997; Jung 2005; Scheepers 2005; Sauer 2006).

Expansion and Trends of Islam in South Africa Today

The 2001 South African government lists the total number of South African Muslims as 654,064 and they make up 1.5 per cent of the population (Omar 2004: 1).[7] Although their numbers are low, Muslims in South Africa make a strong impact on South Africa as a whole. Abdulkander Tayob, professor of the department of Islamic Studies, Religion and Public Life at the University of Cape Town, explained that the statistics do not reflect the qualitative experience people actually have (Tayob 1998). This influence is seen primarily in the political arena.

Political Influences of Muslims

A few years before the first democratic election in South Africa (1994) Muslims already found themselves in a position to engage in politics freely. They embraced the democratic process but not without bringing their Islamic agenda to the table. One example is the effort to introduce Muslim Personal Law into the South African legal system (Omar 2004: 3).

The two Muslim parties, the African Muslim Party (AMP, founded in 1994) and the Islamic Party (IP), participated in the first democratic elections but neither secured any seats in parliament. In subsequent elections, only the AMP had candidates, although unsuccessfully (www.africamuslimparty.org). Muslim political involvement instead became a part of the influential majority party, the African National Congress. In 2007 the *Al-Jamaah* party was formed, and its manifesto included topics

---

[7]. Some Muslims are contesting this figure trying to substantiate higher numbers like Muhammed Haron (Haron 2003) although they fail to substantiate their claims and it is all based on assumptions. Both Christians and Muslims anticipated the planned 2011 census with great interest.

such as Muslim personal law, working condition for mosque workers, refugees, etc. The party claims not to be a Muslim party but a party with Muslim values yet open to all people (Mall 2009).

According to Rashid Omar, the former imam of the controversial Claremont Main Road Mosque,[8] the percentage of Muslims involved in parliament is between 5–7 per cent (2004: 3). This figure does not include Muslims working as employees in the government and in ministerial departments. The appointment of Ebrahim Rasool as premier of the Western Cape is a good example the huge influence Muslims have in South Africa (Ismail 2005: 1; Omar 2004: 4).

Islamic Influences through Organisations

Muslims are quite organized and constantly pursue their agenda at all levels of society. Their organisations include welfare groups, Islamic banks and financial institutions, da'wah organisations, and a multitude of small, medium and large businesses. A quick glance at websites like the *Muslim Directory*, the *Muslim Business Directory South Africa* and the *Muslim Pages* confirm the diversity of Islamic organisations and the social, educational, economic and political impact Muslims have in South Africa.[9]

In the realm of education, Muslims have established many institutions and places for training and learning. In local communities, children are sent to *madrasa* at the local mosque. Muslim private schools flourish at primary and secondary levels. *Dar ul Ulums*, Islamic universities and Islamic departments at secular universities allow Muslims to propagate Islam (*Muslim Directory*). An update on the current research conducted and

---

8. See Gamieldien, Gahimi 2004. *The History of the Claremont Main Road Mosque, its People and Their Contribution to Islam in South Africa*. Claremont Main Road Mosque: Cape Town, South Africa. This publication discusses the socio-historical and religio-educational development of this mosque. The mosque is attractive to so-called progressive Muslims, and the Muslim Youth Movement used it as a stable base for years for their political agendas.

9. http://www.muslim.co.za/education/colleges_universities, http://www.muslimpages.co.za/, http://www.mbdsa.co.za/

new developments in Islamic higher education is in Muhammed Haron's academic research paper (2004b).

Expansion in Black Townships and Da'wah Activities

The number of Black Muslims in townships is growing faster than numbers in the coloured and Indian Muslim communities (Jung 2005: 22). Shamil Jeppie and Goolam Vahed believe that this is due to conversions based on factors such as conscious decisions influenced by political motivation; contacts with Muslims outside South Africa; effects of da'wah work as conducted by the Islamic Propagation Centre International (IPCI); and the partial translation of the Qur'an into Zulu (Jeppie & Vahed 2004: 4). Furthermore, recent migrants from Islamic backgrounds have not only boosted the number of Black African Muslims but also led to conversions of Black South Africans to Islam.

In addition to making efforts to win Black people for Islam, the IPCI in Durban organizes debates and symposia as a means of spreading Islam. Other organisations such as the Islamic Information Centre in Lenaisa and the Institute for Islamic Services in Laudium also are involved in proselytizing and engaging with Christians in debates. Christians like John Gilchrist, David Seccombe, Bob Benjamin, to name a few, have responded to these challenges successfully and in the process shared the gospel message (see IPCI website). Nevertheless, the IPCI is also organizing lecture events on topics offensive to Christians with the aim of luring Christians into becoming Muslims. Recent topics were: Finding true salvation: What they did not tell you in church? How much blood is needed for salvation? Easter, what's it all about?

Challenges for Christians Emanating from Islamic Activities

The organized church is doing little to respond to the increasing influence of Islam; however, individual Christians are taking some initiative. Not much material can be found in academic writings concerning Christian initiatives in response to Islam. Because of the ideal of separating church and state, Christians, unlike Muslims, do not get involved in politics with faith driven agendas.

Response from Established Churches

The major denominations issue only occasional and usually non-confrontational statements that comment on Islamic issues. One case in point was the joint statement issued by the South African Council of Churches (SACC) and the United Ulama Council of South Africa commenting on the contested quotation that Pope Benedict XVI had made in 2006 (SACC 2006).

Instead of responding to Islam directly, the major denominations as well as most local churches, seem to go on with their own programmes, proclaiming the gospel, getting involved in projects and making a positive contribution to society in general.

One exception occurred when a number of pastors gathered in Durban to pray and study. They eventually released a public letter challenging Deedat to withdraw his publication entitled *The Combat Kit*. This breathtaking story is on the Answering Islam website (Foster 2005).

Response from Individual Christians

A movement of individuals are working together in bringing the gospel message to Muslims. I have been privileged to be part of this loose network in a leadership capacity for more than twenty years. Although there are no written records available to be quoted, these efforts could be seen as a continuation of the ministry of people like Gerhard Nehls and John Gilchrist.

Christians' understanding of Muslims and the religion of Islam has increased in recent years. Publications like *Facing the Muslim Challenge* (2002) and *Sharing the Gospel with Muslims* (2003), both by John

Gilchrist, as well as *Ask your Muslim Friend* (Andreas Maurer 2008) and other publications have provided Christians with information. They speak of an educated, yet passionate, approach to giving Muslims unambiguous information so that they are able to make an informed choice when considering a faith that is otherwise not part of their experience.

A number of people in South Africa network with one another and sometimes share resources. Practitioners in Muslim evangelism who have sufficient academic qualifications hold annual training events at some Bible schools. Only on a few occasions has their work drawn the attention of the Muslim community and when this happens, it is usually sporadic. Not even the academic works of Christians on Christian-Muslim topics have come to the attention of Muslim academics in the same field. For example, the doctoral theses of Phillip Scheepers and Andreas Maurer, up to this point, have not been quoted in any academic work of Muslims.

Some Christians have worked in Muslim evangelism for years, yet the number of conversions are few. Conversions from Islam to Christianity have never been counted, and it would probably be difficult to do so because instead of forming their own churches, converts have been integrated into existing churches. This shows the close relationship between such efforts and the local churches.

Those in the South African network might be critiqued for their silence and low profile because it may hinder other Christians from joining. Further, this approach may give the impression of practitioners hiding something and not being open, thus leaving the Muslim evangelistic initiatives open to unnecessary criticism. Proclaiming Actively Christ Together (PACT), an organisation that is part of this movement, has decided to step out and operate in the public space. PACT has risen to the challenges from the IPCI and the Islamic information centre and has been instrumental in jointly organizing Christian-Muslim debates. PACT stood its ground in a Christian manner.

Need in Black Townships

Local churches are making no significant response to the Muslim da'wah efforts in Black townships. This is aggravated by Muslims explaining to the uneducated that they are just another church and the Qur'an is just another Bible. The modest Kaifa project is a soup kitchen and community-building project aimed at stemming the Islamic tide by empowering and educating people.

Challenges

The church should not and cannot withdraw into its own space and ignore the challenges from Islam. Resources are available in the literature, media and other materials for training and evangelism and apologetic ministry within the church and without. The current converts who have integrated into many local churches should be seen as a resource with great expertise to inform and possibly lead the evangelistic efforts to reach Muslims. Churches should do the work in a spirit of respect for people and their opinions and beliefs.

In the new South Africa, Muslims and Christians should bring challenges and questions of religious tenets to the discussion table. Muslims, Christians and others must be given the opportunity to listen and understand each other's standpoint and message so a free choice of belief and religion will be possible.

It has also become evident that in the realm of politics, economics and education, Muslims have brought their agenda to bear. Christians should also seize the opportunities to be the salt and light in these spheres of society, though not to create a Christian state, which has never existed and will never exist. The kingdom of God is ultimately not of this world. But living under the rule of the risen Christ will lead to consequences in how we live, namely with integrity, high moral standards, good ethics and compassion, while helping the oppressed and the needy to a life of dignity, just to name a few points. This will include encounters with Muslims for the sake of proclaiming, being and living the witness of our risen Lord Jesus Christ.

References

Africa Muslim Party. *About Us*. http://africamuslimparty.org/Index_files/Page631.htm.
Answering Islam. www.answering-islam.org. Accessed 10 June 2010.
Christian Concern for Muslims (CCM). http://www.ccm.org.za.
da Costa, Yousuf, and Achmat Davids. 1994. *Pages from Cape Muslim History*. Pietermaritzburg, SA: Shuter & Shooter.
Dangor, S.E. 1991. The Muslim Community in South Africa. *Al-Ilm Journal of the Centre for Research in Islamic Studies* 11(1): 65–74.
Fakude, E. 2002. *Annual Review of Islam in South Africa, Vol 5: Muslims in the Townships of South Africa*: 47–49.
Foster, D. 2005. *Deedat's Downfall*. http://www.answering-islam.org/responses/deedat/downfall.htm.
Gilchrist, J. 2002. Facing the Muslim Challenge. Cape Town: Life Challenge Africa.
Gilchrist, J. 2003. Sharing the Gospel with Muslims. Cape Town: Life Challenge Africa.
Haron, M. 2004a. *The Dynamics of Christian-Muslim Relations in South Africa (circa 1960–2000): From Exclusivism to Pluralism*. http://www.uga.edu/islam/christians_muslims_sa.html. Accessed 2 June 2010.
Haron, M. 2004b. *Academic Research on Islam and Muslims in South Africa within a Democratic Environment*. http://www.islamicpopulation.com/africa/South%20Africa/Southafrica_academic%20research.pdf.
Haron, M. 2005. Undercounting or Overcounting South Africa's Muslims: The Era of Democracy (Census of 1996 and 2001). *Journal for Islamic Studies* 23: 1
Islamic Propagation Centre International (IPCI). http:ahmed-deedat.co.za.
Islamic Propagation Centre International (IPCI). n.d. *Brief Biography of Sheikh Deedat*. http://www.ipci.co.za/about/ahmed-deedat. Accessed 29 June 2010.
Islamic Colleges and Universities in South Africa. http://www.muslim.co.za/education/colleges_universities. Accessed 1 July 2010.
Jaffer, I.E. 2005. *Annual Review of Muslims in South Africa, Vol 8: Review of Fahmi Gamieldien's The History of the Claremont Main Road Mosque*.
Jeppie, S., and G. Vahed 2004. *Annual Review of Islam in South Africa, Vol 7: Multiple Communities? Muslims in Post-apartheid South Africa*.
Jung, M. Theological Reflections on the Spread of Islam and Attitudes in Churches: A Case Study on Three Black Townships in Cape Town. MTh Thesis, Stellenbosch.

Levtzion, N., and Pouwels, R.L.. (Eds). 2000. *The History of Islam in Africa*. Athens: Ohio University Press.

Lubbe, G. 1987. *IslamoChristiania, Vol 13: Muslims and Christians in South Africa*: 113–129.

McComb, E. [nd]. *Al Hidaya: Right Guidance for Muslim Friends: Did Jesus Christ Die on the Cross on Behalf of Sinners?* Belville, South Africa: Evangelical Mission Press.

Makki, M. 1990. Dr Shorosh's Controversial and Ill-advised Lecture Tour Once Again Focussed Attention on Deedat's Objectionable Method of Propagating Islam. *The Muslim Digest* 41: 1&2, 23–24.

Makki, M. 1991. Does Deedat Represent the Muslims of South Africa? *The Muslim Digest* 41: 12, 2–5.

Mall, N. 2009. *Muslims' Politics in South African 2009 Elections*. http://www.islamonline.net/servlet/Satellite?c=Article_C&cid=1239888321066&pagename=Zone-English-Muslim_Affairs%2FMAELayout#. Accessed 2 July 2010.

Masakhane Muslim Community. 2002. *Annual Review of Islam in South Africa, Vol 5: Islam in the African Townships of the Cape*: 50–51.

Maurer, A., The Islamic Missionary Society: Johannesburg: A Descriptive Study of Da'wah Activities in Gauteng During 1958–1996. DTh. Thesis. Unisa.

Maurer, A. 2008. *Ask Your Muslim Friend: An Introduction to Islam and a Christian's Guide for Interaction with Muslims*. Kempton Park: AcadSA.

Mumisa, M. 2002. Islam and Proselytism in South Africa and Malawi. *Journal of Muslim Minority Affairs* 22(2): 275–299.

Omar, R.A. 2004. *Annual Review of Islam in South Africa, Vol 7: Democracy and Multiple Muslim Identities in Post-apartheid South Africa*.

Oosthuizen, G.C. 1982. *The Muslim Zanzibaris of South Africa: The Religious Expression of a Minority Group, Descendants of Freed Slaves*. Durban: Research Institute, Dept. Science of Religion, University of Durban-Westville.

Sauer, C. 2006. Where Do Muslims Live in South Africa? An Interpretation of Religious Demography According to Census 1996 and 2001. *Missionalia* 34(1): 137–144.

Scheepers, P. 2005. Islamities Geïnspireerde Terreur—Wat Staan jou te Doen? http://www.phillipscheepers.info/Islam%20Arikel%20Afrikaans.pdf. Accessed 30 June 2010.

Shell, R.C.-H. 2000. Islam in Southern Africa, 1652–1998, in *The History of Islam in Africa*, edited by N. Levtzion & R.L. Pouwels. Athens: Ohio University Press: 327–348.

South African Council of Churches. 2006. *Joint Statement by the SACC and the United Ulama Council of South Africa*. http://www.sacc.org.za/news06/uucsa.html.

Tayob, A. 1998. *Annual Review of Islam in South Africa, Vol 1: Counting Muslims in South Africa*.

Vawda, S. 1994. The Emerging of Islam in an African Township. *American Journal of Islamic Social Sciences* 4: 532–547.

CHAPTER 19

Sudan

James B. Obwonyo

Because of conflicts between Christians and Muslims, Sudan has experienced the longest civil war on the African continent. The politicization of religion and the mingling of it with state affairs exacerbated this civil war. However, during the course of the conflicts, there have also been good relations between the Muslims and Christians. Hence, the purpose of this chapter is to identify the good areas of Christian-Muslim relations in Sudan and identify ways to capitalize on them in evangelisation for peace.

This chapter starts with a historical survey of the entry and spread of Christianity and Islam in Sudan with consideration of Islamic orders and movements. It looks at the ideological face of Islam, Christian denominations' attitudes towards Islam and Christian-Muslim engagement based on some contemporary and lively experiences.

Religious Demographics

Sudan has a total land area of 1,556,108 square miles (Polito 2003). The latest National Census (2008) estimates Sudan has 39,154,000 people with 30,894,000 in Northern Sudan and 8,260,490 in Southern Sudan, with the exception of Darfur region which is undergoing its own census. However, because no data was recorded on religion and tribes for political reasons, there is no accurate and updated data collected to know an approximate number of Christians and Muslims in the country. The latest data estimates Muslims form 62 per cent of the population, practitioners of African Traditional Religion, 22 per cent, and Christians, 16 per cent (Polito 2003).

In Northern Sudan, the Muslim population is estimated at 80 per cent to 85 per cent, Traditionalists at 10 per cent, and Christians at 5 per cent

In Southern Sudan, Christians claimed 48.4 per cent of population: 5 to 7 million people are Catholic, 4 to 5 million are Episcopalians. Presbyterians, Evangelicals, Pentecostals, Sudan Interior Church, African Inland Church, Lutheran Church and African instituted Churches have smaller numbers of followers. Three major Christian denominations (Catholic, Episcopal and Presbyterian) are found in the three regions of South Sudan of Greater Upper Nile (Upper Nile, Unity and Jonglei States), Equatoria (Central Equatoria, Eastern Equatoria and Western Equatoria States) and Bahr el Ghazal (Northern Bahr el Ghazal, Warrap, Western Bahr el Ghazal and Lakes States). Christianity in the Sudan is often adhered to by Black Africans of Southern Sudan and the Nuba Mountains. These figures show the reality of Islam's rapid spread in the country, which likely occurred because of Muslims' commitment to da'wah propagation.

Entry and Spread of Christianity and Islam

Christianity
The existence of Christianity in Sudan goes back to the early contact of Christians from Egypt with Sudanese Nubians, a few years after the crucifixion and resurrection of Jesus Christ (i.e., before the year 40 AD). A Meroitic Sudanese court official, who is called an Ethiopian eunuch in the Bible, is said to be the first convert who introduced Christianity into Sudan. It is also said that after Roman Emperor Decius in 250 and Emperor Diocletian in 297 persecuted the Coptic Church in Egypt, the monks and hermits fled to Sudan in pursuit of peace and solitude (Werner, Anderson & Wheeler 2000: 24–28).

In the second decade of the fourth century, the Emperor Constantine, the first Christian Roman emperor, ascended the throne, stopped the persecutions of the Christians and put Christianity on an equal footing with the other religions of the Empire. In the fourth and fifth centuries, cross trade between Egyptian Christian merchants and Sudanese traders is said to have been an excellent opportunity for spreading Christian faith. In the sixth century, the Emperor Justinian and his wife, Theodora, sent Christian missionaries to Sudan to spread Christianity. A hundred years later, the ethnic Sudanese kingdoms (Nobadia, Makuria and Alwa or Alodia) officially became Christian.

Christianity grew in Sudan leading to the formation of Dongola, the capital of the Christian kingdom in Sudan. The kingdom survived Muslim attacks until the fourteenth century (see the following section on Islam for more). Small groups of Nubian Christians continued to exist in today's Nuba Mountains in the southern Kordofan region.

Muslim conquest was only one factor in the downfall of the Christian kingdom in Sudan. Socio-political, economic and religious factors had weakened the kingdom and the churches.

Socio-political
- Increase of Nomadic Arab tribes in Sudan: Christians were overwhelmed by the Arabs.
- Natural and human-made disasters: Agricultural resources were destroyed by drought and floods that brought about a depopulation of certain parts of Sudan; and Christians were attacked and raided by anonymous raiders.
- Economic changes: River trade was no longer used; people used camel caravans' trade through the desert. Consequently, Nubians became impoverished.
- Islamic rule: Imposition of *jizya* (head tax) on all Christian citizens forced many Christians to convert to Islam so that they could be exempted.
- Restrictions and aggressive policy towards Christians: The Sudanese church was isolated from Egyptian, Syrian, Palestinian and worldwide churches.
- Lack of solidarity with Christians in other countries: Sudanese Christians were almost forgotten and there was no communication between them even from the neighbouring

Abyssinia, which was struggling for its survival and could not go out to help others.

Religious
- Lack of indigenous theological training: Sudanese Christians had never built a theological school of their own.
- Dependency on Patriarchate: Sudan was dependent on the Coptic patriarchate for the ordination of its bishops. When Muslim rulers in Egypt seized power, they prevented Copts from visiting Sudanese churches and did not allow the Christian Sudanese to go to Egypt.
- Relating church to state: in the Sudanese Christian kingdom, church had been related to the state. Thus, when Muslim rulers took power, the church could not stand on its own.
- Exclusion of laity from participation in Church worship: In the late medieval times, when an esoteric type of church service was the order of the worship, the laity was increasingly excluded from direct participation. While their number was increasing, the church building remained small and so could not accommodate them.
- Lack of catechism and evangelists: this weakened the faith of the local laity.
- Increase of magical practises: belief in angels and their powers, superstitious and magical thinking was fashionable.

In the nineteenth century, other Christian denominations began to enter Sudan. A Roman Catholic mission reached Khartoum on 11 February 1848. Protestant missions like the Church Missionary Society, Episcopal Church, the American Mission (Presbyterian Church), Sudan United Mission SUM and Sudan Interior Church arrived in Sudan in 1900 via Egypt. Christianity flourished in Sudan, particularly in Southern Sudan during the colonial rule of the Anglo-Egyptian condominium government and after Sudan's independence.

Islam

After the Islamic religion was founded in the Middle East, Muslim conquerors started to perceive Sudan as a gateway for entering and spreading Islam into Africa. In 641–642, Muslim General Amru endeavoured to conquer the land south of Egypt. His half-brother Uqba ibn Nafi marched with an army to subdue Dongola, the capital of the Christian kingdom in Sudan. However, the Nubians proved to be tougher defenders of their kingdom than expected; they rebuffed the Muslims' army. In 652, a Muslim army general called Abd Allah ibn Saad ibn Abi Sarh led a second attempt at conquest (Werner, Anderson & Wheeler 2000: 41–43). His army reached but did not conquer Dongola because the town was heavily fortified with strong walls and towers. The Muslim army used catapults to hurl large rocks at the beautiful cathedral. The Nubian Christians stood firm. The Nubian bowmen aimed directly for the eyes of the Muslim attackers in the battle with about 150 men being seriously wounded and blinded. This became so terrifying that the Muslim army admitted defeat and proposed a treaty of non-aggression called *Baqt*.[1] The two parties agreed on a ceasefire and co-existence, accompanied by a mutual exchange. For instance, the Nubian Christians had to provide slaves, frankincense, ivory, perfumes and elephant tusks while the Muslims had to provide wheat, lentils, horses and cloth in return. In addition, the *Baqt* ensured the safety of the border of southern Egypt and northern Nubia because the agreement prohibited Muslims from buying land in, or settling in, Nubia permanently. In return, the Nubians were prohibited from settling in Egypt. Despite the treaty, many nomadic Arabs and Muslim traders crossed into Sudan, using marriage ties with Nubian women so they could settle in Sudan (Werner, Anderson & Wheeler 2000: 42). Some Muslim historians call the battle a decisive one because the conquerors had never been defeated before.

Then in 1276 the army of Sultan Baybars destroyed the Dongola kingdom. The first year of the fourteenth century saw the final downfall of Nubian kingdom. In 1317, Abdalla Barshambo was crowned as the first

---

1. *Baqt* comes from the Latin *pactum* (in Greek *pakton*), which means a unique treaty of non-aggression between two sovereign States. However, some later Arab authors tried to portray this as a surrender of the Nubians to Muslims, but this is not justified by the contemporary sources, including Arab ones (Werner, Anderson & Wheeler 2000: 42).

Muslim Nubian king. On 2 May 1317, he turned a room in the royal palace of Dongola into a mosque, which marked the end of Christian kingdoms in Sudan. However, some ordinary Nubian Christians managed to maintain their churches under the new Islamic kingdom (Werner, Anderson & Wheeler 2000: 90–98). The defeat in Dongola had given the Muslim world the impression that a mighty Christian empire existed to the south of Egypt, one comparable to the Islamic empire, a factor that saved the early Sudanese Christian culture from total destruction (Werner, Anderson & Wheeler 2000: 42–43, 124).

Notwithstanding, the mighty Sudanese Christian empire had almost completely faded out when Muhammad Ali Pasha (the Ottoman Turkish ruler of Egypt) invaded Sudan in 1820, overthrowing the Funj Sultanate and establishing a new Islamic capital at Khartoum. His aim in conquering the Sudan was not religious evangelism but to establish a powerful government in Egypt through advancement of economy and formation of a powerful army, using Sudan resources (gold, ivory and other valuable minerals) and strong men. His successors (Abbas Pasha, Muhammad Saeed Pasha and Ismail Pasha) subdued more kingdoms and sultanates like the Fur and the southern part of Sudan with help of some Christian army generals and administrators from European countries such as England, Austria and Italy.

Muslim-Christian relationships were spoiled by the rise of Mahdiya in the Sudan beginning in 1881 and the injustices committed by Turko-Egyptian rulers against the Sudanese (El Mahdi 1965: 61–144).

Islamic Orders and Movements in Sudan

Sudan has a number of different Muslim groups with the largest being the Sunni, which is divided into two major Sufi brotherhoods: Ansar and the Khatimia that is associated with Democratic Unionist Party, while Khatimia followers are based in Khartoum, Northern and Eastern part of Sudan.

The Sufi orders came in existence in Sudan in the sixteenth century. The Muslims who practise these orders seek a closer personal relationship with God in a mystical manner. They perform dhikr-spiritual and physical practise by reciting prayers, reading passages from the Qur'an, repeating the names or attributes of God (*Allah*) and singing or dancing with religious rhythm. Dhikr often lasts for longer hours than normal prayers; it is a state of ecstatic abandon.

The Sufi orders are divided into *turuq*—ways of practise—in accordance to the leaders' lineage. In Sudan, the majority of the turuq are *Qadiriya* founded by Abdal Qadir al Jilani in Bagdad in the twelfth century. There is also *Tijaniya*, founded by Ahmed Ibn At-Tijani in Morocco, which came to Sudan through his followers like Saayyid Ahmed Idris in about 1810; he settled in Darfur and northern Kurdufan. Idris established sub-orders, examples of which are the *Majdhubiya*, *Idrisiya*, *Ismailiya* and *Khatimiya*. The Khatimiya means the 'seal of the path' and is also known as Mirghaniya. The Mirghaniya tariqa-path was established by Muhammad Uthman Al-Mirghani, a student of sayyid Ahmed ibn Idris, in the early nineteenth century. Most of the Mirghani followers are based in eastern Sudan, especially Kasala. Sufi leaders are reluctant to assume political roles because they want to retain their spiritual life.

Khatimia, one of the two majority Sunni groups in Sudan, is associated with Democratic Unionist Party. Khatimia followers are based in Khartoum and northern and eastern parts of Sudan.

There are the *Ansar* or the followers of Al-Mahdi. Though not a tariqa, it has links to the mystical orders. The Ansar, one of the major Sufi brotherhoods in Sudan, was founded by Muhammad Ahmad ibn as Sayyid Abd Allah al Mahdi, who drove the Turko-Egyptian administration out from Sudan in 1885. Adherents of Ansar are found in Khartoum and Western Sudan. Ansar is associated with Umma Party.

There are also minor orders that have less influence on Sudanese Muslim community because they are looked on as traditional and local.

Some movements such as Mahdism, Marganiya and *Ikwan al Muslimun* (Muslim Brotherhood) have been heavily involved in state affairs and shaped Sudanese politics. The Mahdist and Mirganiya orders played a great rule in establishing today's Sudan. The reluctance of Sufi leaders to assume political roles gave primacy to secular and modernizing nationalists within the National Unionist Party (NUP) while the Mahdism ensured the primacy of traditionalist *Ansar* leadership within Umma Party (UP) (Weituor 2007: 40–41).

Mahdist adherents (or the Ansar, meaning 'followers') in Sudan had called for regeneration of Islam. Abd Allah, the founder of Mahdism in the country, proclaimed himself to be *Al-Mahdi al muntazer* (the awaited guide) of the right path of Islam, the messenger of God and representative of the prophet Muhammad. He claimed that he was sent by God to prepare the way for the second coming of the prophet *Issa* (Jesus) and the apocalyptic end of the world.

The idea of the coming of Al-Mahdi is rooted in *Sunni* Islamic tradition. The Mahdi ideology is mostly supported by western Sudanese groups of *Baqqara* (cattle nomads) and some tribes residing on the White Nile in northern Sudan. The leadership is fully controlled by the Mahdi's successors with direct blood links to Abd Allah Al-Mahdi's family. Today, the movement is known as a political party though it split up into more than five political parties headed by different leaders. It lost its religious mission as the adherents become more loyal to the political descendant of the Mahdi than to the religious message of Mahdism. This happened because the emergence of a revivalist movement, the Muslim Brotherhood, sought to return to the fundamentals of Islam vis-a-vis globalization from the West (Religion in Sudan: 1, 2).

Muslim-Christian Relations

Beginning with Mahdism (1881–1898), Sudan has been shaped by the ideological face of Islam. Muhammad Ahmed B. Abdalla (the Mahdi) formed a theocratic Islamic State governed by the Qur'an and Sunna of the prophet Muhammad. President Ibrahim Aboud (1958–1964), President Jaffar Muhammad Numeiry (1969–1985) and President Omer Hassan Ahmad El Bashir (1989 to date), have consecutively declared the Sudan as an Islamic State and introduced Sharia law into the country.

After the independence of the country in 1956, the Sudanese government tried to block southern rejection of Sharia law. Southern Sudanese tried in two civil wars to gain equal rights for citizens, regardless of their racial, ethnic, cultural, religious or political affiliations. The first began in 1955.

On 27 February 1964, the government issued a decree ordering the expulsion of all missionaries from Southern Sudan. The government accused the missionaries of discrediting Southern policy and introducing a new civilization and culture into the country, one alien to Islamic fundamentals. The Sudanese churches opposed the decree. The Catholic Church, in particular, responded calling the government memorandum the 'Black Book' because the government was defending its action against missionaries. The churches were affected badly because the foreign priests, pastors and nuns had to leave the country but had not left enough natives to take over the management of the missions. The Episcopal Church tried to adjust, and the Presbyterian Church in Malakal also tried to do the same but never succeeded. African Inland Church members in Equatoria went into exile in Uganda, and the Sudan Interior Church in the Northern Upper Nile region left behind one nationalist pastor.

The government thought that with the missionaries expelled, the churches would collapse together with the opposition politicians, particularly the Christians from the southern part of the country. Instead, the expulsion developed into political conflicts between Northern and Southern Sudan. The civil war ended with the signing of Addis Ababa Peace Agreement between the North and the South on 27 February 1972, with the mediation of the World Church Conference. In 1973 Christianity was officially recognized in the Sudanese constitution (Weituor 2007: 110–118).

However, on 5 June 1983, President Jafar Muhammad Numeiry abrogated the Addis Ababa Agreement and divided the Southern Sudan into three regions. Numeiry introduced Sharia law in the country without exception. This resulted in forced military recruitment, Arabization and Islamization of the education curriculum, prohibitions on non-Muslims from serving as governors and commissioners, especially in the North, forced displacement of Christians, restriction of alcohol consumption, confiscation of church properties, prohibition of open-air preaching, restriction of clergies' travels internally and internationally, and punishment of Muslim apostates. Christians found no alternative apart from military resistance to Islamic governance. Christian southerners found themselves voiceless and powerless in the unlimited ocean of Islamic ideological streams (Ador 2004: 50–60).

This change marked the beginning of the second devastating civil war, which lasted for more than two decades before it was ended with the signing, in Nairobi-Kenya, of the Comprehensive Peace Agreement (CPA) 9 January 2005. The National Congress Party (NCP) and the Sudan People's Liberation Movement/Army signed the CPA. Throughout the war, Christians were living in a state of Islamic rule. Forced conversion to Islam, demolition of physical infrastructure, abduction of children, national disasters, injustice, racial discrimination, just but a few to mention, became the order of the day. The relationship between Muslims and Christians soured on many occasions. The churches became divided into those at the side of the SPLM/A rebels and those on the side of the Sudan Government, making interaction difficult except in neutral countries abroad.

Despite the end of the second war, Islamic ideology remains imposed on the people, especially in Northern Sudan. It was, however, a blessing to the church. Many souls were saved by accepting Jesus Christ as their personal Saviour. Christian churches grew rapidly to the far northern, western and eastern parts of Sudan via displacement and immigration of Southern Christians to the North. In one way or another, the civil war contributed to acculturation of two communities, Christians and Muslims, and opened many doors for engagement and self-understanding. Biblically, this situation concurs with what is written in the epistle of Romans: 'And we know that in all things God works for the good of those who love him, who have been called according to his purpose' (Romans 8:28).

The Roman Catholic Church, the Presbyterian Church of Sudan, the Evangelical Presbyterian Church and the Episcopal Church, among others, are flourishing today in the capital cities of Sudan. However, with the signing of the CPA, many Christians withdrew to the South.

Christian Attitudes toward Islam

Christian attitudes toward Muslims tend to be negative. Research in the form of informal oral consultation, face-to-face talks and phone calls with some Christian and traditional leaders in parts of Sudan revealed a common attitude towards Islam and engagement with Muslims. The questions were:

What is your personal, church or Christian community attitude towards Islam in Sudan? The answers given were:
1) Islam is the religion of Arabs not Africans; Africans profess Christianity and traditional religions.
2) Arab Muslims are foes of African Christians and traditionalists.

One respondent posed these questions: Do you know why the South is backward in term of development? Do you know where inter- and intra-tribal fighting comes from? Do you know why we fought for 38 years? He answered: *Jallaba* (Arab Muslims) are the cause.

Christians' attitudes are infested with emotions rather than objectivity and shaped by political, religious, economic and racial factors resulting from centuries of Islamic governance. One issue that creates problems is the uneven interpretations of Sharia law; it might vary from one Muslim scholar to another according to their subjective interests, which has contributed to deterioration of Christian-Muslim relations in Sudan. In addition, the Islamic ideology that favours Muslims over Christians and other non-Muslims, especially regarding them as second class, and prohibits them from presiding over institutions, has hindered Christian-Muslims relations in the country. This leads many Christians and Muslims to see any engagement as merely a relationship between superior and inferior, stronger and weaker, and wealthier and poorer.

However, there are good aspects to Muslim-Christian relations that Christians often undervalue. In the Addis Abba negotiations in 1972, the Islamic regime of President Numeiry appointed a Christian Southerner Mr. Abel Aleir, as head of the delegation. The same regime accepted a Christian clergy, Rev. Canon Burgess Carr, Secretary General of AACC, to act as the moderator for the historic reconciliatory conference that put to an end the seventeen-year war and brought peace to the country. During the Naivasha peace talks, another remarkable example for Muslims' good relations with Christians occurred when the Islamic government of Al Bashir accepted Christian General Lazarus S. of Kenya to moderate the Sudan peace talks. These tangible events should never be taken for granted by a Christian or Muslim; this reconciliatory approach should be encouraged even in the smallest issues of everyday relations. Unfortunately, the majority Christian Southerners pay little attention to them because they strongly believe in having an independent state with Christian domain where human freedom at all levels of life is assumed to be preserved.

Thus, the Christians, especially in Southern Sudan, are looking beyond the old Sudan and eagerly waiting for a new Sudan, a new independent nation of their own and a new phase of Christian-Muslim relations.

Christian-Muslim Engagement in Sudan

Sudan's civil wars of 1955–1972 and 1983–2005 had both a negative and positive effect on Christian-Muslim relations. Christian and Muslim communities suffered religious, economic, political and social injustices and mistrust, antagonism, misunderstanding, marginalization and discrimination became order of the day (Weituor 2007: 151–196). But surprisingly, this situation drew together the two faiths and prepared the ground for Christian-Muslim engagement.

Three organisations have been working towards peace and reconciliation through Christian-Muslim engagement in Sudan. They are the Sudan Inter-religious Council (SIRC), which is politicized, Programme for Christian-Muslim Relations in Africa (PROCMURA) and the Sudan Council of Churches (SCC), which is composed of twelve Christian denominations (Catholic, Orthodox and Protestant). The bodies have been bringing together Christians and Muslims in workshops and seminars at national and regional forums. Sub-offices for SIRC and SCC were formed in Khartoum (the capital of Sudan), Juba the capital of Southern Sudan, Nuba Mountains, and the Upper Nile State that borders Northern Sudan to the southeast.

The engagement exists at formal and informal levels. The formal engagement is mostly organized at scholarly levels, and Christian and Muslim scholars dialogue on common theological and political issues relating to Christian-Muslim relations in Sudan. Some of the key themes of their dialogue are Sharia law, non-Muslims' rights and apostasy. In addition, the church and mosque leaders usually meet at regional levels through workshops, seminars or conferences. Further, Christian and Muslim youth meet at the grass-roots level to build intimacy and self-understanding in their daily lives. They discuss social issues like HIV/AIDS programmes and primary health education awareness. Here, theological contentions related to biblical or *Qur'anic* faiths are kept aside.

The informal engagement of Sudanese cultural and social structure occurs during social and spiritual occasions—marriages, funerals, Christmas and Ramadan—when Christians and Muslims always exchange visits. They eat and drink together and wish each other happy feasts. In such occasions, basic cultural and social lives of both faith communities always supersede religious and political loyalties.

The formal and informal engagements create a spirit of neighbourliness, peaceful co-existence and self-acceptance between the two faiths. This form of Christian-Muslim engagement is unique compared to that of other Muslim-majority countries in Africa. In the Nuba Mountains, for instance, intermarriage among Christian and Muslim communities is very common. Muslim women are normally married to Christian men either in the church or through a traditional wedding, as resolved in the Religious Tolerance Conference held in the Nuba Mountains between 10–15 December 1994, as follows:

> Intermarriages between Muslims and Christians are permitted and anyone who preaches or agitates to prohibit it shall be disciplined (Werner, Anderson & Wheeler 2000: 615).

This has proven that cultural solidarity is much stronger than religious affiliation in these communities; it should encourage all parts of Sudan to maintain unity and Christian-Muslim tolerance.

While there is protection for non-Muslims' rights in predominantly Muslim areas, the same is not true for non-Christians' rights in predominantly Christian areas. The CPA obliged the Sudanese government to establish a Commission for Protection of Non-Muslims Rights in Khartoum. This Commission is headed by a Christian official. Its mission is to preserve non-Muslims' rights in the Sudanese capital; these include rights to Christian education and Christian activities, including the acquisition of plots of land for building churches in Khartoum. However, the same type of commission doesn't exist in Southern Sudan for protecting non-Christians' rights. The Christian majority in Southern Sudan does not preserve non-Christians' rights. After the signing of the CPA, the Government of Southern Sudan (GoSS) confiscated some Muslims' properties and closed down Islamic banks because the CPA brought in two banking systems in the country: Islamic in the North and secular in the South. Both religious communities should have been granted equal rights to practise their faiths without discrimination. Equal treatment would pave better ways for realistic and fruitful engagement between Christians and Muslims in the country.

Conclusion

History indisputably asserts the existence of Christianity in Sudan for centuries before the entry and spread of Islam. Regardless of different proportions in the number of members and the spread of two faiths, both Muslims and Christians have remained determined and committed to preserving their beliefs and cultures. Northern politicians have used the Islamic religion to subjugate minorities and form religious monotype under Sharia law. However, the result of this politicized usage was never in favour of both Christians and Muslims; it has exacerbated the civil war and pushed Southerners to call for their own independent state at the expense of dividing the biggest country in Africa. Hence, engagement could be the route for reconciliation, restoration of trust and self-understanding between the Christians and Muslims of Sudan.

The attempt to Islamize and Arabize the country and annex it to Islamic countries shall never succeed. It shall always be met with bloody resistance by the Christians and other non-Muslims. Similarly, the negative attitudes of Christian denominations towards Islam shall never help because it will lead to isolation and other unnecessary setbacks from enmities. Concluding that Arab Muslims are foes of African Christians and Traditionalists is misplaced because there are countries in Africa with a majority of African Muslims that have proven successful in their co-existence. These misunderstandings and false conclusions could be corrected if both Christian and Muslim communities in the Sudan made collective efforts through interactive forums of objective engagement.

References

Ador, Samuel N. 2004. Sharia: Historical and Contemporary Perspectives in the Sudan, in *From the Cross to the Crescent*, edited by Johnson Mbillah and John Chesworth. Nairobi: *PROCMURA Occasional Paper* 1(1), January.

El Mahdi, Mandour. 1995. *A Short History of the Sudan*. Oxford: Oxford University Press.

Polito, Nicholas Lo. 2003. *The Christian Muslim Digest*. West Midland, U.K.: Solihull.

Religion in Sudan: Islamic Movements. http://atheism.about.com/library/FAQS/Islam/countries/bl_SudanIslamicMovement.htm?p=1 Accessed 23 January 2010.

Sudan: International Religious freedom Report 2005. Bureau of Democracy, Human Rights, and Labour. http:wnow.state.goo/9/drl/rls/irf/2005/5/497.htm. Accessed 23 January 2010.

Sudan: International Religious freedom Report 2005. *Sudan: Intro. Religion Free. Rep.* Sudan: Bureau of Democracy, H.R&L.

Trimingham, J.S. (ed.). 1980. *The Influence of Islam upon Africa*. 2nd ed. London: Longman London.

Weituor, G.G. Riam. 2007. *Christian-Muslim Relations in Sudan: A Study of the Relationship between Church and State (1898–2005)*. Amman: Fatafata Printing Service.

Werner, R., Anderson, W., and Wheeler, A. 2000. *Day of Devastation, Day of Contentment: The History of the Sudanese Church across 2000 Years*. Nairobi: Pauline Publications Africa.

CHAPTER 20

Tanzania

William Andrew Kopwe

In his valedictory address in 1985, Julius Kambarage Nyerere, the founding father of the nation of Tanzania, warned of possible religious conflicts in the country. He regarded this danger as greater than any threat of ethnic conflict (Ludwig 1999: 206). Nyerere's prediction was based on his pre- and post-independence experience of Christian-Muslim relations in the country. Although Tanzania[1] has earned fame internationally for its peace and quasi-tranquillity, there have been indications of latent fears influencing the relationship between Christians and Muslims in the country. Today, the relationship is degenerating and growing more volatile. Is this a fulfilment of Nyerere's prediction? Are the political and religious leaders aware of the signs of the times in the country?

This chapter examines Christian-Muslim relationships and factors that have contributed to their deterioration. It looks at the impact of both the latent tensions between the two groups and of growing fundamentalism among Christians and Muslims. This chapter is not intended to fan the fires of conflict; rather it seeks to encourage leaders and the guardians of peace to analyse and take action on Christian-Muslim latent tensions in Tanzania.

In theory, religious discussion has been traditionally treated as anathema in the political sphere of the country. A famous Tanzanian slogan is, 'Do

---

1. The United Republic of Tanzania is a country made up of two formally autonomous countries, Tanganyika and Zanzibar. Tanganyika is what now known as Tanzania Mainland and Zanzibar is currently known as Tanzania Islands. Tanganyika and Zanzibar were united to form Tanzania on 26 April 1964.

not mix politics and religion'. However, in practise, the religious factor has had a strong influence in charting the country's social-political direction. Although Tanzania is secular, it citizens are religious. Political leaders are no exception, even in the case of those who claim to have no religious interests. In fact, religious bias manifests itself clearly in politics as was clearly seen in the debate on the reintroduction of the kadhi's Courts and on Tanzania joining the Organisation of the Islamic Conference (OIC). These matters were unconstitutionally brought for discussion before parliament.[2]

In addition to being an infringement on the secular constitution, these events sent the message to Tanzanian society that religious concerns transcend political ideologies and patriotism. For the first time since multi-party rule was introduced in 1992, parliament was explicitly divided along religious lines rather than party lines. This division among the parliamentary representatives was a microcosm of division among the rest of the citizens. The debates were also a good way for the government to test the sensitivity of religious issues in the country. This state of affairs needs to be analysed in terms of Christian-Muslim relations.

Christians and Muslims in Tanzania

Tanzania, like most African countries, has a threefold religio-cultural heritage: African religion, Islam, and Christianity. Due to the Arab colonial influence in Zanzibar, the Muslims are the majority there. However, there are no official statistics on which religion is predominant on the Tanzanian mainland. The last census that identified the religious affiliation of citizens in the country was in 1967. Since then, it has been government policy to allocate the population as being 30 per cent Muslims, 30 per cent Christians and 30 per cent followers of African Traditional Religions. This can be seen as the background for the political assertion that Christian and Muslims in the country are equal in number.

---

2. Articles 3 and 19 of Tanzania's Constitution state that the country is secular and religious matters are personal issues. See the United Republic of Tanzania of 1977, 1998: 23 (Amendments made in the Constitution since its enactment by the Constituent Assembly in 1977 up to 30 June 1995).

Muslims

Islam is the second oldest religion in Tanzania, the first being African Traditional Religions. Islam was first brought to this country by people from Arabia.[3] Most scholars agree that Islam came to Tanzania within its first century (Ssekamwa 1976: 83; Were & Wilson 1970: 10ff; Palmer 1987: 28). Three major circumstances contributed to the advent of Islam in Tanzania. The political upheaval in Persia and Arabia in the seventh century resulted in Muslim political refugees seeking asylum on the East African coast. Muslim traders settled on the East African coast and later in the interior of the mainland. They controlled the existing trade routes and, in the process, disseminated Islam both intentionally and unintentionally. Some Muslims came from Islamic countries with the express purpose of spreading Islam (Rukyaa 2007). In each circumstance, Islam came to Tanzania in a peaceful way through infiltration.

In Tanzania, Muslims practise various forms of Islam. Lodhi and Westerlund characterize Tanzanian Islam saying:

> The great majority of the Moslems in Tanzania are Sunni. The Shiite minority, mostly of Asian origin, are Imami, Ismaili, and the Bohra/Wohra. The Moslems of Omani origin constitute a special case, most of them being Ibadiyya, which is a moderate branch of the Khariji movement. A small but active Ahmadiyya group is also present in the country (1999).

Sufi Muslims contributed to a great extent to the dissemination of Islam in Tanzania, first in the coast and later in the interior of the mainland.[4] They did so through preaching, teaching in the *madrasa* and establishing different *turuq* (orders) (Becker 2008: 176–206).[5]

---

3. N. Chittick says that 'Some historians have suggested that Egyptians, Phoenicians, Persians and others may have come to the East African coast centuries before the birth of Christ. There is, however, no real evidence that this was so' 1968: 100).
4. Interview with Hamis Mattaka, 3 March 2007 Dar es Salaam.
5. It is said that the famous Majimaji war of 1905–1907 in Tanganyika was inspired by a Sufi Muslim Kinjeketire Ngware who guaranteed people that through mystic ways the

The majority of Tanzanian Muslims are moderates. But currently, Tanzanian Islam is undergoing a strong revival and fundamentalism is growing. This has been fuelled by the interaction of factors ranging from religious, social-economic to political aspects within and without the country. Revivalism in Tanzania is mostly an influence of the *Wahhabi* movement, popularly known as *Ansar Sunna* or *Ansar Muslim*. The most significant feature of Ansar Muslim is its emphasis on returning to a strict Islamic Sharia.[6]

The Wahhabi movement has gained a following composed largely of youths in Tanzania. The Ansar Muslims want to improve the social-economic, political and religious positions of Muslims in the country[7] and agitate for the positions for Muslims in private and public spheres. Because of their revival character, they sometimes introduce new ideas to Muslims. A good example is the earlier timing of moonsighting than those used by the mainline Sunni Muslims to begin important Muslim festivals, like fasts and Idd days. Because of this characteristic, they are branded as sectarians (Chande 1994: 49).

Another important feature of revivalism is the prevalence of polemical preaching, commonly known as *Mihadhara*. In this preaching, Muslims mainly use the Bible and Qur'an to refute certain aspects of the Christian faith. This kind of preaching has caused much discord between Christians and Muslims.

German bullets would turn into water when they shot them. Hence people courageously plunged into the war. However, this was not the case. The war claimed many African lives.

6. In this case, the Ansar Muslims lay emphasis on following all the Muslim precepts as presented by the grand sources of Islam. Sometimes they do not openly say that what they want is a strict Sharia, but from their sermons and behaviour one can easily deduce their zeal for public and private Sharia implementation in the country.

7. My interview with Shembilu of Tanga in 25.08.2008 showed that Ansar Muslims are trying to remove the ignorance of Islam and Arabic language among the Muslims. Shembilu, who is mainstream Muslim Sunni, praises them for their efforts of understanding Islam and the Qur'an instead of reciting it without understanding what it says.

Christianity

There were three main phases to the introduction of Christianity in Tanzania. The first advent of Christianity was in 1498 when the Portuguese came to the East African coast and defeated the Arabs from Somalia down to Mozambique. Franciscan missionaries, who had come with the Portuguese merchants, brought Christianity. However, this phase did not last long because the Portuguese could not survive the opposition from Arabs, who defeated them in 1652 (Sahlberg 1987: 4). The lasting establishment of Christianity in this area resulted from the second advent of Christianity through the strong nineteenth-century missionary zeal in Europe, which was fuelled by the reports of European explorers.

The third advent of Christianity to Tanzania resulted from fundamentalist movements and Pentecostal revivalism in the U.S.A., which occurred in the twentieth century. This movement introduced Pentecostalism and revivalism in Africa and Tanzania in the 1950s and 1960s. This version of Christianity brought a new paradigm of evangelism and missionary campaigns that were given names, such as crusades, open air evangelistic meetings, gospel rallies and gospel festivals.

Christian polemical preaching is prevalent in Tanzania and several small Christian apologetic groups adopt the above Muslim-*mihadhara* philosophy of preaching. The most well known group is the *Biblia ni Jibu* (The Bible is the Answer), which is based in Dar es Salaam. During a personal conversation with me, the leader of the group, Cecil Simbaulanga revealed that he founded the group as a counter measure to the Muslim *Mihadhara*.[8] The group is now divided into several small groups with the goal of expanding their campaign in the country and in the countries bordering Tanzania.[9]

Tanzanian Christianity, like Christianity in the rest of the world, is divided into numerous denominations. 'It is estimated that there are about 150 churches in Tanzania that claim to be followers of Christ' (Rukyaa

---

8. See also John Chesworth (2008: 202).
9. Cecil Simbaulanga and some members have recently been conducting open-air meetings in the Democratic Republic of Congo and Kenya.

2007). The denominations range from the historical groups to new revivalist groups. The Roman Catholic Church is the largest, followed by the Evangelical Lutheran Church in Tanzania and the Anglican Church of Tanzania. There are also Seventh Day Adventist and Pentecostal churches. The denominations are represented by their umbrella bodies with the major ones being the Tanzania Episcopal Conference (TEC), the Christian Council of Tanzania (CCT) and the Pentecostal Council of Tanzania (PCT). Because of its missionary background, the version of Christianity found in Tanzania is a mixture of European, African and American cultures.

Christian-Muslim Relations in History

The history of Christian-Muslim relations in Tanzania is marked by tensions caused by suspicions, accusations and prejudices.

Early Clashes

The first Christian-Muslim encounter occurred during the advent of Christianity on the coast of East Africa in the sixteenth century when relations were hostile. Christian Portuguese and Arab Muslims killed each other *en masse*. First the Christian Portuguese killed the Arab Muslims in the name of a crusade and occupied their territory. Later, with the aid of the Sultan of Oman, the Arab Muslims killed the Portuguese Christians in the name of jihad.[10] They drove the Portuguese from the East African coast and managed to reclaim their territory, which laid a shaky foundation for later Christian-Muslim relations in the region. In the nineteenth century, Christians and Muslims clashed again when Muslims fought against German and British colonial rule (Mbogoni 2004) as well as against Christianity and its domination.[11]

---

10. Usually Jihad is called upon by Muslims when the Muslim community is threatened, because a threat of Muslim *umma* is tantamount to threatening Islam it self. Certainly at that time Muslims called Jihad. However, Mbogoni mentions only the Portuguese-Christian crusade but omits the Jihad aspect of the relationship, which was certainly a reality.

11. Interview with Mohammed Said, 22.05.2007 Tanga.

Christian-Muslim relations were not harmonious in the interior either and some major conflicts occurred. For instance, in 1933 Muslims and Christians fought in Morogoro. A group of Muslims was passing a Roman Catholic mission station while chanting loudly, *allahu akbar* ('Allah is great'). The missionaries were irritated and regarded this action as derogatory because the group had been silent in other areas. One Muslim lost an eye in the fight, which caused the Muslims to circulate a letter to mobilize Muslims in Tanganyika for jihad against those Christians; this created tension in the Tanganyika colonial territory. The colonial government stopped the situation by appeasing Muslims. They charged Father Superior, the instigator of the fight, to pay sh.600 to the Muslim who had lost his eye (TNA 1933, 21715).

Differences in Politics

Christian-Muslim tensions entered the political arena during the country's struggle for independence. Tanganyika African National Union (TANU), the party that managed to bring about the nation's independence in 1961, was Muslim-dominated. The incorporation of Julius Nyerere into the party in 1953 had been taken by some founders, commonly known as elders of the party, as an abomination of desolation. Those elders vehemently repudiated the Christian element. Muslims suspected that Christians would be the ones to form the first independent government because they were more educated than Muslims and some claimed they 'would use Church influence to suppress Islam as a political force' (Said 1998). This threatened the party with schism. However, through its internal mechanisms TANU managed to settle the issue. Nevertheless, some elders like Sheikh Takdir seceded.

In 1959 Muslims outside TANU formed a Muslim political party, the All Muslim National Union of Tanganyika (AMNUT). Its aim was to oppose TANU (Imtiyaz 1990: 104). AMNUT went so far as to call for a postponement of independence until enough Muslims were educated to hold important positions in the government of independent Tanganyika. This party and several others were abolished after independence when the country adopted a single party system.

After independence, Christians regarded Islam as a threat to Christianity. Roman Catholic priests in Bukoba town campaigned against a Muslim candidate based on religion. This caused President Nyerere to write a fierce letter on 8 May 1963 to warn those Roman Catholic priests who had divided people on the basis of religion (Sivalon 1992: 31). Father Robinson, then secretary of the Tanzania Episcopal Council (TEC), met with Nyerere to respond to the letter. Robinson said that the Roman Catholic priests were ready to co-operate with Muslims. But their fear was the announcement made by the Muslims that they wanted to turn Tanganyika into a Muslim nation. Nyerere responded that he suspected that this merely reflected the opinions of a minority of Muslims (Sivalon 1992: 31).

Colonialism in Tanzania had contributed to Christian-Muslim tensions because it left a legacy that resulted in socio-political disparity between Christians and Muslims, a state of affairs seen in the levels of education. Christians had more access to education during colonialism because they felt free to go to the missionary schools, whereas Muslims were reluctant to do so. Parents had feared that their children would be converted to Christianity if they sent them to a Christian school. Instead, Muslims put more emphasis on *Madrasa* than on Western schools.[12] As a result, by the time of independence more Christians than Muslims had acquired a Western education, which more or less determined Christian-Muslim socio-political positions in the post-colonial governments. In those governments, the number of Muslims with government portfolios was relatively smaller than that of their Christian counterparts.

Ignoring the historical aspect of Muslims' levels of education in Tanzania, some Muslims have accused Christians in government positions of conspiring to keep the educational level of Muslims low. The late Kigoma Ali Malima, who was first minister of education after independence, is a good example of such a person. Malima wrote a secret letter to President Ali Hassan Mwinyi stating that after he assumed the position, he had realised that his predecessors who were Christians had purposely barred Muslim children from higher education. Unfortunately, Mwinyi gave in to Malima's allegation without investigating it further. By chance, the letter fell into the hands of the media and was published in the newspapers. The letter caused

---

12. Interview with William Mmbago 18 May 2007, Dar es Salaam.

considerable debate among Christians and Muslims. The issue was quietly settled by the government, resulting in Malima losing his position.

On Good Friday of 1993, latent Christian-Muslim apprehensions in the country came to surface when a group of Muslims attacked pork shops in Dar-es-Salaam under the auspices of Baraza la Uendelezaji wa Kuran Tanzania (Council for the Promotion of the Qur'an in Tanzania BALUKTA).[13] Muslims were complaining of a purposeful defilement of their mosque because Christians were selling pork close to that area. They said they had brought their grievance to the responsible authorities, but no tangible measures were taken. Therefore, they decided to take matters into their own hand by attacking the pork shops. Christians saw that action as breaking the law and being contrary to the country's secular constitution. They had been given legal licences by the government to run the business in the area for several years before that day. This event was yet another important marker for readers of signs of the times (Wijsen & Mfumbusa 2004: 17).

Today two major political parties are in intense competition in the country's politics: the CUF (Civic United Front) and the CCM (Chama Cha Mapinduzi). There are on-going allegations that these parties reflect the dominant influence of Islam and Christianity respectively. There is a perception, although difficult to authenticate, that the presidents show a kind of partiality on the basis of their respective religious affiliation. Some Muslims perceive that the Christian presidents have been biased towards Christians. Hamza Mustafa Njozi (2000), who wrote *Mwembechai Killings and the Political Future of Tanzania*, says that Muslims have been suffering from discrimination within their own country by heads of states who were Christians, referring to Julius Nyerere and Benjamin Mkapa. For him and others like him,[14] Nyerere was there to further the Roman Catholic Church in the country. Nyerere had influenced the ruling party and the government and his influence is still felt. Because of this, Catholic

---

13. This organisation was under the leadership of Sheikh Yahya Hussein, because of its fundamentalist characteristic the organisation was denied registration in the country.
14. Interview with Mohammed Said 22 May 2007, Tanga; Interview with Secretary of DUMT 8 March 2007 Dar es Salaam.

priests had the power to convince President Mkapa to allow the killing of Muslims at Mwembechai mosque in Dar es Salaam on 13 February 1998. The Mwembechai killings were a climax and outward sign of what the government has been secretively doing to the Muslims since independence.

Some Christians suspect that Muslim presidents showed the same attitude towards Muslims.[15] Some Christians complain that the incumbent regime have been appointing more Muslims than Christians to local and international key positions.[16] Christians went further by saying that this is a historical circle. They claim that what is happening today is similar to what Ali Hassan Mwinyi, the former president of Tanzania, did as a Muslim during his regime. During his time, Tanzania nearly joined the Organisation of Islamic Conference (OIC), which showed how partisan he was. During Mwinyi's regime, the country witnessed a mushrooming of mosques, a move toward the Islamization of the country.[17] Christians further said that Muslims' demands and grievances usually come to surface strongly every time a Muslim president is in power in order to manipulate the position of the president.[18] Because of this context, the reintroduction of kadhi's court was attributed to the current president, Jakaya Mrisho Kikwete, a Muslim.[19]

Christian-Muslim accusations and suspicions touch state-religion relations as well. Tensions between Muslims and Christians sandwich the government between the two religious groups. Muslims have numerous grievances, including their perception of being a less-advantaged group. They have gone as far as to call upon the government to carry out 'affirmative action' and 'positive discrimination' for them (Njozi 2000: 237). Christians remark that Muslims are striving for power in order to transform Tanzania into an Islamic state. Christians have become so cautious that they scrutinize

---

15. Interview with Tumaini University Lecturer, 10 May 2007, Arusha. See also Njozi 2000.
16. Interview with Bukuzi, 30 May 07 Arusha.
17. Interview with: Mwaki, Tanga, 22 May 2007; Alfred 12 May 2007, Arusha.
18. An interview carried on 27 August 2007 in Arusha (name withheld).
19. In 11 November 2007, Kikwete publicly made clear that Kadhi's court agenda, which is found in the CCM 2005 general election manifesto, was not engendered by him.

Muslims who become national leaders. This results in more suspicions and accusations between the two communities.

The most recent manifestation of shaky Christian-Muslim relations in the country is the debate regarding the reintroduction of kadhi's courts on the Tanzanian mainland. Currently, Islamic personal law is in operation in the country, dispensed by the Magistrates Courts. However, for several reasons, Muslims are not satisfied by the current practise of the administration of Islamic law by secular courts. Hence, they are demanding a separate kadhi'scourt as it was during colonial times when the courts were not only recognized, but also funded by the government.[20]

Christians feel that re-introducing kadhi's courts as a government institution would introduce Sharia into the domain of the overall administration of justice. This would infringe upon the constitution and remove the secularity of the state. Furthermore, the Christians feel that running the courts at the government cost will cause taxpayers' money to be used by one religious group in the country (*Daily News* 2006). This situation intensifies tensions among Christians and Muslims in the country.

The latent tensions between Christians and Muslims are based mostly on the prejudices, suspicions and ignorance members of both religions have about each other. This is not a good for the country's welfare.

Religious Fundamentalism

Fundamentalism in both religions is escalating in Tanzania in the name of freedom of religion.[21] Because of this, peaceful co-existence between Christians and Muslims is dwindling dramatically. This is yet another sign to be interpreted by the country's stakeholders.

While Islamists speak of *Westoxification*, the non-Muslims and the West speak of *Islamophobia*. Both require keen attention. While they do

---

20. Interview with Sheikh Mataka, 31 January 2007, Dar-es-Salaam and Sheikh Zuberi 14 February 2008, Dodoma. Both are members of the Muslim council of scholars (*ulamaa*).
21. In interview with various religious leaders in Dodoma and Dar es Salaam:
Leonard Mtaita, Einaza Sendoro, and Hamisi Mataka acknowledged the escalation of fundamentalism in the country.

not represent the worldview of the majority of Christians and Muslims in Tanzania, they are dominant among the elite, the religious gurus and socio-political pundits. Experience shows that because of low levels of education, most Tanzanians are prepared to believe what they are told, particularly by reputable religious leaders.

Westoxification and *Islamophobia* harmonise well with Samuel Huntington's (1996) concept of the 'clash of civilizations'. The end of the cold war, says Huntington, brought the world into a new situation of tension. The tension is not so much one of ideology, but rather of civilizations. For him religion is also a civilization. Islam and Christianity are two civilizations contending for space in Africa. Christian-Muslim tensions in Tanzania can be explained along this line of thought. The quasi-democratic Christian West and Sharia Arabic Islam have been constant rivals contending for space in the country.

Perhaps the theory of religious economy by Peter Berger (1963) explains this well. In this theory, religious groups are allegorically taken as commodities in the market place. Propagators of religion are understood as merchants, and society is the market place. Therefore, religion is subject to market competition. Secularism is a free market because the government does not regulate religious activities. Religious groups are free to disseminate their doctrines and practise their various activities. The Tanzanian mainland is a typical case of this kind of religious market system.

Although there were latent tensions before the 1980s, the government was able to contain them through the religious umbrellas bodies TEC, CCT and BAKWATA. Currently some religious groups have broken away from these bodies, which results in these bodies losing their authority. As a result, it is becoming increasingly difficult to control fundamentalism through these institutions.

Islamic Fundamentalism

Islamic fundamentalism in the country is a result of a worldwide Islamic resurgence. The phenomenon is multifaceted. Its expression depends upon the context in which it appears. To understand what is happening in Tanzania today with the various Muslim demands and grievances, it is necessary to gain an overview of the phenomenon and its driving forces. Islamic fundamentalism in Tanzania is similar to the worldwide Islamic militant movements.

The attempt by Zanzibar to join OIC created considerable fear and discontent among non-Muslims, especially Christians in Tanzania. This led the parliament to assign a committee to investigate certain allegations.[22] This kind of statement makes non-Muslims in the country look at the religio-political and socio-economic moves of Muslims with a suspicious eye.

Revivalist Muslims are one of the groups that have broken away from their religious umbrella group. They do not recognize BAKWATA as their sole representative. For them the government's decision to dissolve East African Muslim Welfare Society (EAMWS) in 1968 and replace it with BAKWATA was a Christian conspiracy that aimed at inhibiting Muslim development.[23] These revivalist Muslims say that BAKWATA has been manipulated by the government as its watchdog for controlling Muslims.[24] Two measures were taken by those who are unhappy about the way BAKWATA operates. First they decided to create other organisations outside it as counter measures. But this could not work because the majority of Muslims in the country are loyal to BAKWATA. Its influence is felt in the whole country because BAKWATA follows the CCM philosophy of leadership hierarchy, which has branches in at least every village in the country.

The second measure taken was to transform BAKWATA and its institutions and organisations into fundamentalist ones by replacing the leadership of moderate traditionalist Muslims with the revivalist younger Muslims. This did not entirely succeed. However, the Mufti (the national leader of Muslims) is currently being confronted by a large number of challenges.

---

22. See the Abuja Communiqué in the Kamati ya Mambo ya Katiba na Sheria, (1993) Taarifa ya uchunguzi kuhusu Zanzibar kujiunga na 'Organisation of Islamic Conference' (OIC) na tuhuma kuwa Jamhuri ya Muungano imejiunga wa Tanzania na 'Islam in Africa Organisation' (IAO). This report of the parliamentary probing committee investigated the allegations that Zanzibar had joined OIC and that The United Republic of Tanzania had secretly joined IAO.
23. Interview with Mohammed Said 22 May 2007, Tanga.
24. Interview with secretary of DUMT 08 March 2007, Dar es Salaam.

Some Muslims take the failure of the move as a Christian machination, in particular a Roman Catholic scheme,[25] to weaken Islam. Although the plots were unsuccessful, the message was successfully broadcast that fundamentalism is at the door of BAKWATA. If fundamentalist Muslims manage to take control of the organisation, Tanzania will soon be in trouble because the organisation is deeply rooted in the country through its numerous and widespread branches.

Pentecostalism in Christian Fundamentalism

Though fundamentalism and Pentecostalism are distinct phenomena, in Tanzania the two are not different. When we talk about fundamentalism, we combine both movements to mean radicalism so the terms will be used synonymously.

The fundamentalist groups in Tanzania have not shown much involvement in Tanzanian politics. One party, however, the Democratic Party (DP), is headed by the Reverend Christopher Mtikila who is also the head of the Full Salvation Church. Mtikila has been at odds with the government several times. He is currently accusing the government of suppressing Christianity.

The fundamentalists in Tanzania are also endangering Christian-Muslim relations because of their polemical preaching. This indicates that the majority of Christian fundamentalists in the country are more involved in preaching than in politics. They differ from Muslim fundamentalists in that they do not regard violence as a proper method of attaining one's rights.

Three major factors contribute to the difficulty that the churches have in controlling fundamentalist groups. The powerful mainline churches in Tanzania and the newly founded Pentecostal churches regard at each other with disdain. The Pentecostal churches consider the mainline churches as unspiritual, visionless and traditionalist while the established mainline churches regard the Pentecostal churches as theologically uneducated with emotional people whose Bible interpretation is shallow.

---

25. Interview with Secretary of DUMT 08 March 2007, Dar es Salaam.

Nevertheless, there have been several moves to break down dividing walls and build bridges between the churches. It seems that these moves are showing success. On 25 May 2010 TEC, CCT and PCT, major umbrella bodies, set up a forum called *Jukwaa la Wakristo* Tanzania (Christian Platform in Tanzania). This forum does not interfere with doctrinal issues or the internal affairs of the unit members. Rather it deals with issues pertaining to the Christian community including their rights in the country. It is a new and young forum and there is still much to be done. But its inauguration is vital toward gearing for further development.

In addition, the newly founded Pentecostal umbrella bodies have not been able to incorporate all the mushrooming revivalist churches. Worse still, some churches appoint their own leadership. As a result, the Christian community has witnessed a proliferation of bishops because people establish their own group composed of five to ten members, or sometimes even of one family, and call it a church. The founder calls him or herself a bishop. This person expects to be given the same honour as a Roman Catholic, Lutheran, Moravian or Anglican diocesan bishop. Many Christians of the established churches regard this as ridiculous. For them this downplays the position of bishop, a position highly respected by Christians and even by the government. Because of this, the mainline churches regard the young Pentecostal churches with some disdain.

This matter is further exacerbated by the government's policy on the registration of religious groups in the country. Criteria for registering a church differ slightly from those for registering non-governmental organisations. Even if the government is secular and allows freedom of religion constitutionally, it needs to look at religious groups with a critical eye. Religious convictions have a deep-seated effect mentally and psychologically. One can do anything in the name of religion. It is unwise to leave the 'religious market' unguarded. The way religious groups operate today indicates that the government either does not read the signs of times or has capitulated in the name of the freedom of religion.

Other challenges are facing the mainline churches as far as fundamentalism and fanaticism are concerned. The major challenge is revivalism within their churches, which has acquired different names such as charismatic, revivalism, born again and fellowship. The upsurge of these movements has led to many internal divisions in churches. Some of these groups are interdenominational and sometimes find themselves in conflict with the mainline churches. A typical example of such a group is the New Life in Christ, formerly known as New Life Crusade. It unites revival Christians from churches under the CCT. Such organisations are autonomous and, for this reason, Bishop Dr. Stephen Munga regards them as para-churches. No church can control such groups even if they espouse fundamentalism. Because no one has the courage to say no to them, fundamentalist groups have the opportunity to climb the social ladder.

Conclusion

Christian-Muslim relations in this country are said to be good, but this is only true at a superficial level. More efforts need to be devoted to improving these relations. This needs to take place both at the government level and at the religious group level. Fundamentalism is a reality among both religious groups in the country, and the orthodox religious umbrella organisations are now proving unable to control them because they have no mandate over them. The proliferation of fundamentalist groups further intensifies the latent Christian-Muslim tension. On the other hand, the government seems to be passive on the issue.

The danger is that some organisations are intent on overthrowing the existing religious umbrella bodies and transforming them into fundamentalist organisations. In this respect, both religious groups and the government need to read the signs of times. This situation could explode at any time if the problem is not properly addressed.

References

Becker, F. 2008. *Becoming Muslim in Mainland Tanzania, 1890–2000*. Oxford: Oxford University Press.

Chande, A. 1994. *Islam: Islamic Leadership and Community Development in Tanga, Tanzania:* Doctoral Thesis, Ottawa: Institute of Islamic Studies McGill University.

Chesworth, J. 2008. *The Use of Scripture in Swahili Tracts by Muslims and Christians in East Africa*. DPh. thesis. University of Birmingham. http://etheses.bham.ac.uk/150/.

Chittick, N. 1968. The Coast Before the Arrival of the Portuguese. *Zamani: A Survey of East Africa*, edited by Ogot, B., Nairobi: East African Publishing House.

Huntington, S. 1996. *The Clash of Civilizations and the Remaking of World Order*. London: Simon & Shuster.

Imtiyaz, Y. 1990. *Islam and African Socialism: A Study of the Interactions between Islam and Ujamaa in Tanzania*. (Unpublished dissertation). University Microfilms International (UMI) Ann Arbor, Michigan.

Lodhi, A.Y., and Westerlund, D. 1999. African Islam in Tanzania. *Islam Outside the Arab World*, edited by D. Westerlund, and I. Svanberg. London: Curzon Press.

Ludwig, F. 1999. *Church and State in Tanzania*. Leiden: Brill.

Mbogoni, L.E.Y. 2005. *The Cross Versus the Crescent: Religion and Politics in Tanzania from the 1880s to 1990*. Dar-es-salaam: Mkuki na Nyota.

Njozi, H.M. 2000. *Mwembechai Killings and the Political Future of Tanzania*. Ottawa: Globallink Communications.

Palmer, R. (ed.) 1987. *The Making of Modern Africa Vol.1: The Nineteenth Century*. London: Longman Group Ltd.

Rukyaa, J. 2007. Muslim-Christian Relations in Tanzania with Particular Focus on the Relationship between Religious instruction and Prejudice. *Islam and Christian-Muslim Relations* 18(2): 189–204.

Sahlberg, E. 1987. *Historia ya Kanisa Tanzania 1600–1985*. Nairobi: Scripture Mission.

Said, M. 1998. *Islam and Politics in Tanzania*. Dar es Salaam: Warsha. http://www.gta.igs.net/~kassim/nyaraka/islam_and_politics_in_tz.html.

Sendoro, E. 2001. *Makanisa ndani ya kanisa na kanisa ndani ya Makanisa*. Moshi: New Millennium Books.

Sivalon J, 1992. *Catholic Church and Politics in Tanzania Mainland from 1953 to 1985*. Peramiho: Benedictine Publications Ndanda.

Ssekamwa, J. 1976. *A Sketch Map History of East Africa*. London: Hulton.

Were, G., and Wilson, D. 1971. *East Africa through a Thousand Years: A History of the Years A.D 1000 to the Present Day*. Nairobi: Evans Brothers.

Wijsen, F., and Mfumbusa, B. 2004. *Seeds of Conflict: Religious Tensions in Tanzania*. Nairobi: Paulines Publications Africa.

Part Four: Bible Reflections

CHAPTER 21

Encountering the Other: A Study of Mark 7:24–30 and Matthew 15:21–28[1]

Mercy Amba Oduyoye

When a rich young man asked Jesus, 'Who is my neighbour?' Jesus responded with a story in Luke 10:25–37. In this conference we are reflecting on our relationship with people of other faiths. We Christians share God's world with people of diverse faiths and we struggle with relationships within the human community. We are challenged by factors of diversity, not least of which is that today diversity of faiths threatens to turn us into strangers if not enemies. In consideration of our theme and the challenge posed when believers encounter others who believe differently, I have chosen to highlight one event in the life of Jesus of Nazareth, an event in which a woman challenges the notion of exclusion. It is a familiar story but always worth retelling. And I believe this occasion calls for it.

Ever since I read the book *Hagar, Sarah and Their Children* (Trible & Russell 2006) and read the medieval tale of the combat of Parzival and Fierefiz[2], in connection with a conference on revitalization, an Akan proverb

---

1. This study has benefitted from many commentaries but special acknowledgement needs to be made to Dr. Hisako Kinukawa, *Women and Jesus in Mark* (1994).
2. Middle High German epic poem of thirteenth century by Wolfram von Eschenbach. Parzival a naïve young man pursues the quest of spiritual transformation during the Crusades in what is now part of Islamic Near East. Parzival meets the chivalric battle champion for the Islamic Near East, a person named Fierefiz.
 A battle royal ensues. Parzival's sword breaks on Fierefiz's helmet. The battle stops and conversation begins. They discover that they are kin. Both claim to be related to the French Royal House of Anjou. They remove their helmets and realise they are brothers

has rung in my ears. It is '*Akokoninmaa gyae akuntunkuntun na yen nyinaa ye nkesua mma*', in which the hen says to the cockerel, 'Stop swaggering around, remember we are all children of eggs'.

The passages we are reading constitute the story of a nameless woman as told by two gospel writers, Mark and Matthew.

A nameless woman, a stranger to the Jewish culture and religion but a desperate advocate for the salvation of her daughter who also remains nameless, ignoring all protocol, breaks unobserved into the closed community of chosen people and tells them the good news of God's inclusiveness. God's grace knows no ethnic, social and religious boundaries.

Let us go over some details.

An episode occurred before this event that we should keep in mind as we read the two accounts. Jesus had been disputing the issue of pollution or ritual uncleanness with religious authorities from his own faith community. They had charged his disciples with moving away from the traditions of the elders. Jesus responded by pointing out that they, the religious authorities, broke the commandments of God to adhere to their traditions. Jesus ends up calling them hypocrites. Then Jesus called the people to himself, and taught them what constitutes real uncleanness. Jesus shocked the Pharisees and puzzled his disciples. It was a highly charged encounter by all standards (Mark 7:1–23; Matthew 15:1–20). After the encounter Jesus sought some privacy and went outside Galilee.

Our study begins with his movement from familiar territory, his home base, to other people's domain. Mark says the event took place in a home. In Matthew, we read that he had not even found a refuge when his search for peace and quiet was terminated by the agonizing cries of a woman in distress. Mark says she is a Syro-Phoenician, which may mean Greek.

---

born of different mothers yet fathered by the same man, Ghahmuret of Angevin, who served under the Christian lords in Europe and then the Caliph of Bagdad. 'With kisses Fierefiz and Parzival concluded their enmity and friendship seemed to both better than hearts of hatred against one another. Faith and love rendered battle decision.'

A note in the paper delivered at the conference has this to say. The surname of the Grail family, Mazadan, is Gahmuret's family name. Mazadam means mac. Adam in Middle High German literally means 'Son of Adam' which brings us to the notion of the kinship of all believers—pre-Christian, Muslim, Christian—all descendants of Adam and children of the Most High.

Matthew says she is a Canaanite. This, too, is of some interest as we study the encounter with 'the other', so we shall return to it.

In Mark, the woman simply barges in, falls at the feet of Jesus, and makes her request. In Matthew, she follows the group, shouting and making a scene. Jesus treats her with the disdain expected of a Jewish man. The disciples are embarrassed and ask Jesus to send her away. Jesus responds to his disciples, not to the woman, and states what he sees as his mission: The lost sheep of the house of Israel does not include Canaanites and Greeks. The woman is a stranger, an outsider.

The woman catches up with them and kneels before Jesus, 'Son of David, heal my daughter!' She is saying, 'Okay, I am not a daughter of David, but I am still a human being in need. Help me!' Does that remind you of the story of the Good Samaritan told by Jesus? Note that the request, 'Heal my daughter' in Mark is not preceded with any of Jesus' titles. In other words, the fact that the woman didn't address Jesus by any of his Messianic titles did not stop Jesus from attending to her request.

Jesus now talks directly to her saying, 'It is not right to take the children's bread and toss it to the dogs', which causes the woman to talk back.

Jesus acknowledges her faith and grants her request. (For me the magnitude of her faith is in the fact that she simply got up and went home, taking Jesus at his word).

This, however, is not the focus of our reading, so let us go over the accounts again to see what we can learn from this encounter of strangers as we prepare to look at our own situation of Christian-Muslim relations.

Background

The Venue

Tyre and Sidon, which are often coupled in the Bible, are today part of Lebanon. In the Hebrew Bible, Sidon was the home of Ahab's queen Jezebel (1 Kings 16:29–30), who led him into the worship of the Baalim. It is also the venue of a life-giving miracle, including the cleansing of Naaman in 2 Kings 5:1–19. (See also 2 Kings 4:1–37 and 7:5–24.)

During the time of Jesus, the area had a mixed population of Hellenistic Jews, Romans and Greeks, as well as others said to be the descendants of the peoples that the Israelites displaced when they entered the land. The Jews deemed all these peoples to be unclean, pagans and idolaters. The Canaanites, being a defeated and displaced people, were the lowest of the low.

In Matthew, the event took place in the street because Jesus had not even found a place of rest yet. In Mark, it is in somebody's house, most probably that of a Hellenistic Jew. In which case, this Gentile woman had the audacity to enter uninvited into space that her presence pollutes.

The Characters

Jesus

Jesus is a Jewish rabbi with the reputation of a healer, a prophet like Elijah and Elisha who in ancient times had done miracles in the area of Sidon. This man from Nazareth has a reputation of being the Messiah, Son of David. This was Jesus who had just floored a delegation of religious leaders concerning 'the tradition of the elders' as regards what constitutes a thing being clean and unclean. This was a man who was simply craving quiet but did not ignore people desperately looking for help.

The Disciples

The twelve Jewish men (possibly accompanied by some women) following Jesus were also tired and probably puzzled by the disputation. Not being used to strange women barging into their space and embarrassing them with agonizing cries, these men had taken for themselves the role of 'gatekeepers' around Jesus, their rabbi. The translators of the Jerusalem Bible rendered what the disciples said as, 'Give her what she wants.'[3] Well, doing good so that people can stop bothering or embarrassing you is not exactly noble

---

3. Commentators are embarrassed by the performance of Jesus in this episode (as in the cursing of the fig tree that had no fruits, because it was not the right season to have fruits). Many attempt at explanations, usually concluding with 'Jesus was testing her faith'. One commentator says we need to be realistic and recognize that 'Here he was caught with his compassion down' as many of us are bound to be at one time or the other.

or charitable. It is like doing the right thing for the wrong reason, which is questionable.

The Sick Girl
The sick daughter is not on the scene and is presumably locked in a room at home, raving and ranting. You can feel her presence in the cries of her mother even as she remains nameless like her mother.

The Woman
Matthew gives her the derogatory designation 'Canaanite'. This designation reveals sentiments that have roots in the relationship between the Israelites and the people they displaced when they entered the land. Survivors of the conquest were driven into the north-western hills. Jews looked down upon these people and the relationship was marked by hostility. By the time of Jesus, this term should have sounded anachronistic but was bound to upset the readers of Matthew's version. Being non-Jews, the Canaanites were deemed unclean, and Jesus had just been demolishing the basis of their ancestors' tradition of things being clean and unclear.

Mark says the woman is Syro-Phoenician, which is more contemporary terminology. At the time, the area of Tyre and Sidon had a mixed population, Romans, Greeks and Jews, as well as the descendants of those driven there by the conquest. The Phoenicians who lived there, traded with the Carthaginians, so the area was marked by material wealth. Jews despised these traders for their unfair trading practises. The culture was different and the Israelites considered the Syro-Phoenicians to be pagans. So this woman, whether Canaanite or Syro-Phoenician, Greek or Syrian, was considered unclean by birth and deemed morally depraved. In addition, she has a daughter with a stigma of demon possession. So she too is stigmatized. Noteworthy for that time is that she is a single woman with no male sponsor. Remember the girl of *Talitha Qumi* fame? It was the father who fell at the feet of Jesus seeking help for her.

Gospel translators and commentators have named the Canaanite woman 'amazing woman', a strong woman, a stranger indeed. In the eyes of the disciples and *vis à vis* Jesus of Nazareth, she represents 'the other' while he is the 'norm', so to speak. This woman represents the type of person that the traditions of the Jews excluded but which the community of the early church was to accept and include. She is unclean by birth, a foreign woman with an additional stigma. She could not have been more 'unclean'. She has a triple jeopardy—I count her among the four women whose behaviour was deemed to have defiled Jesus: the anointer (John 12:1–7; Matthew 26:6–13; Mark.14:3–9); the bleeder (Luke 8:40–48; Matthew 9:18–26; Mark 5:21–43); the water carrier (John 4:3–41) and now this shouter. These are women, bold women, who were the occasion for Jesus to breach the purity laws of his Jewish community, to encounter 'the Other', in a way that is healing and humanizing.

This stranger had heard and believed what she had heard about Jesus; that he was the Messiah, who like Elijah and Elisha, had the power to heal her daughter.

The boundaries between the actors in this event may be delineated as race/ethnicity, nationality, religion, culture and upbringing, maybe even gender. (Compare the response to the centurion, Matthew 8:5–13).

Back to the Event

What have we learned that will help our deliberations in this conference?

- Who is a stranger? At one time, Jesus reminded his listeners of God's inclusive care of all humanity by retelling the stories of Elijah and Elisha (Luke 4:25–28). On hearing this, the people of Nazareth were so angered they attempted to kill him.
- 'The Other' ignored. Who are those to whom we give the silent treatment, the cold shoulder, the people we snub? Disdain marks the attitude of Matthew more than that of Mark. In Matthew, Jesus responds to the disciples talking about the priority of the Servant to seek the lost sheep of the house of Israel (Isaiah 49:5–6), but note that he is also to be a light for other nations. Isaiah 56 promises that 'all nations' will be part of God's people.
- The request. In Mark, the woman simply barges in, falls before Jesus and begs him to heal her daughter.

Jesus speaks to her directly, engaging her in a conversation about dogs.[4] Whether it is dogs or puppies (as some commentators claim), the issue is, who gets to sit at the table, and who gets the scraps. In the culture of the woman, house dogs were fed under the table. In the experience of Jesus, stray dogs, fending for themselves in the streets, had food thrown to them.

What is in the story for us? (These points can be used as discussion starters in a Bible study.)

Review our boundaries and the people we exclude and why.

People who desperately need Jesus exist outside our fold. Do we act as gatekeepers, fending them off?

What do we make of the 'Jews first' factor? See Romans 1:16 and the long reflection by Paul in chapters 9–11.

Here the dialogue is about 'children first'. Who are children of God and who are not?

Communication, conversation and conversion: language matters. '*Ano brebre ma adae to*' (The right language removes the threat of execution.)[5] What is our stance when in dialogue with people of other faiths?

Jesus spoke to her directly, not very kind words, indeed a rebuff. However, she did not respond angrily or walk away in a huff. Why?

Her response could be evidence of internalized inferiority; in other words, she is used to being treated that way.

Consider the following and relate them to your experience of encountering 'the other'.

- Evidence of determination to get what she came for.
- Jesus is going along with his traditional upbringing of Jewish superiority over Gentiles.

---

4. About dogs: This harsh response has cultural roots. Jews did not have dogs as pets while Greeks sometimes did. One Rabbi Eliezer is reported to have to have said that, 'He who eats with an idolater is like unto one who eats with a dog'. There are biblical references to dogs that are not complimentary. See Deuteronomy 23:18, Revelation 22:15 and references to unclean persons such as Gentiles and people of Sodom. Some commentators say that by using puppy instead of dog, Jesus softens the blow.

5. The Akan proverb '*anobrebre*' refers to the traditional judicial system in which condemned prisoners were used as human sacrifice during major festivals. A prisoner who knows how to talk, humbly, respectfully, one with 'a soft mouth', might be spared. It is a proverb on respectful communication.

- The exemplary Jesus portrayed as an obstacle to healing.
- How do we respond today to the programme of 'satisfy the Jew first and then the Gentiles second'?[6] Is this evidence of a tension in Jesus' mind about his ministry?

The episode reflects the racial/ethnic, cultural, socio-political, and religious hostilities between neighbours. We may even add men's response to the issues that women raise. The woman does the following:

- She swallows the insult and does not withdraw in anger and disappointment.
- Being no stranger to such attitudes, she had developed her own ways of coping; that is to stand her ground, call upon inner strength and take on the conversation partner.
- Having broken so many taboos to get where she was, she was not going to be deterred by anything, certainly not by insulting language.

Have we encountered people like her?

To conclude let me reiterate a few points.

Here is a woman who knew the cultures and traditions around her and whom God had sent to help resolve the tension of who should hear the good news. Christ, and the salvation he brings, is for all. This was the message of her mission. Her mission statement was simple, taken from the mouth of Jesus and made relevant to the situation: 'Even dogs are fed'. Even people deemed to be nobodies are God's friends. Breaking into the company of a selected closed club cannot be easy, but we are not in mission to do easy things.

The good news according to this desperate woman is that no one is worthy, but God counts us all worthy. Her mission statement resulted in the unexpected revelation that teachers can be learners. She made it possible for Jesus' mission statement to be transparent. I have come to break all chains. I

---

6. There is no second-class membership in the household of God; all who enter by faith are full members. But Jesus, a Jew, started his movement among Jews. Soon it became a sect of Judaism. After the crucifixion, Gentiles hear the gospel, and Mark here wants to make it clear that mission to the Gentiles was already evident in Jesus' earthly ministry. Some of the second wave of oncoming people would be among the people he was writing for. These he wants to assert are full members of the Household of God.

have come for the sinners. I have come that all may have life in abundance. She too has challenged traditional customs and norms and thereby opened the mission of Jesus for all.

Why did the church preserve stories that are not exactly complimentary to Jesus? My sense is that life is like that and truth has to be told to teach us the realities of life. Did this woman change the course of history? Did she contribute to making it possible for you and me to enter the company of Jesus? Does she teach us how we may be in dialogue with people of other faiths?

References

Eschenbach, von W. 2004. *Parzival.* London: Penguin Books.

Kinukawa, H. 1994. *Women and Jesus in Mark: A Japanese Feminist Perspective.* Maryknoll: Orbis Books

Trible, P., and Russell, L. (eds.) 2006. *Hagar, Sarah and Their Children: Jewish, Christian and Muslim Perspectives.* Westminster: John Knox Press.

CHAPTER 22

Bible Reflection: Luke 7:1–10, Healing the Centurion's Slave

Serge Traore

I would like to set my reflection within the context of this conference. I recall that the main idea of the conference is to examine the various ways in which African Christians have encountered, responded to and engaged with Islam and Muslims over the years with the view of gaining insights and learning lessons for much more biblically, theologically and missiologically sound ways of engagement in the contemporary African context. The conference is about *critical African Christian reflections* on Islam and a *biblically and theologically sound* engagement with Muslims in Africa.

Like Christ

For our reflection and meditation, we will look at the encounter between Jesus and the Gentile centurion in Luke 7:1–9. Any Christian reflection on Islam should imitate the attitude of Jesus towards the others, the non-Jews or the non-Jewish. Paul rightly reminds Christians to have the mind of Jesus Christ: 'Let the same mind be in you that was in Christ Jesus' (Philippians 2:5). It is also obvious that this attitude is love. Our mission is to love Muslims, to love any human being. The Master left no room to negotiate it:

> I give you a new commandment, that you love one another. Just as I have loved you, you also should love one another. By this everyone will know that you are my disciples, if you have love for one another (John 13).

In our conference, we are interested in finding 'biblically and theologically sound' ways to approach Islam as a religion and to love Muslims as children of God, taking into consideration the reality of our different social interactions with them. This story of Jesus encountering the Gentile centurion is not about healing, though healing plays a role: 'The point of this story is Jesus' affirmation of the centurion's faith in verse nine, not the report of the healing that concludes the story' (Culpepper 1995: 156).

Truly African

We also want to come up with a specific African approach. It is with this in mind that I chose the encounter of the *Jewish* Jesus with the *Gentile* centurion in Luke. It has something African I believe.

In the Lucan account, Jesus and the centurion speak through intermediaries or delegates.

> The story of the centurion's faith is a brilliant gem in Luke's cluster of scenes from the life of Jesus. Especially when read in a Gentile-Christian context, the scene reflects appealing hues. Because the centurion never actually meets Jesus or speaks with him, in contrast to the Matthean and Johannine parallels, his request is like a prayer mediated to Jesus by others. Thus the story implicitly promises that the Lord hears the prayers of faithful Gentiles and encourages us to believe that when we turn to the Lord in need our requests will be heard also (Culpepper 1995: 156).

It's a dialogue between two persons through a people, through a community. The theological discernment of the centurion's faith is done with the community as active participant. It is finally the faith of the Gentile centurion that is critically assessed by Jesus, the Son of God. Moreover, Jesus affirms the faith of the oppressor, the centurion.

The Text
Let us read the text:

> After Jesus had finished all his sayings in the hearing of the people, he entered Capernaum. A centurion there had a slave whom he valued highly, and who was ill and close to death. When he heard about Jesus, he sent some Jewish elders to him, asking him to come and heal his slave. When they came to Jesus, they appealed to him earnestly, saying, 'He is worthy of having you do this for him, for he loves our people, and it is he who built our synagogue for us.' And Jesus went with them, but when he was not far from the house, the centurion sent friends to say to him, 'Lord, do not trouble yourself, for I am not worthy to have you come under my roof; therefore I did not presume to come to you. But only speak the word, and let my servant be healed. For I also am a man set under authority, with soldiers under me; and I say to one, 'Go', and he goes, and to another, 'Come', and he comes, and to my slave, 'Do this', and the slave does it.' When Jesus heard this he was amazed at him, and turning to the crowd that followed him, he said, 'I tell you, not even in Israel have I found such faith. When those who had been sent returned to the house, they found the slave in good health. (NRSV)

Inspiring Parallels
There are similar stories in the other Gospels: Matthew 8:5–13 (in Matthew, Jesus speaks directly to the centurion); the healing of the nobleman's son in John 4:46–54; the healing of the Syrophoenician woman's daughter in Mark 7:24–30. We find in those accounts:

- the faith of a Gentile,
- an extended dialogue between the Gentile and Jesus, and
- the healing

To Reflect with Compassion

A centurion there had a slave whom he valued highly, and who was ill and close to death (Luke 7:2)

The dialogue between Jesus, a Jew, and the centurion, a Gentile, happened because of and for 'somebody who is ill and close to death.' It is ultimately a life-giving encounter. Compassion drove the Gentile centurion to an encounter with Jesus.

> He is concerned about the well-being of those around him, even his slave. His generosity has extended to the Jewish community as well—he built a synagogue. Although he has not met Jesus, because of what he has heard about Jesus from others he has faith that Jesus can help, and he turns to Jesus with his request. The centurion, therefore, is a model of compassion for weaker persons, goodwill in the midst of divisive tensions between ethnic groups, and faith in Jesus as a result of the testimony of others. He has respect for Jewish sensitivities about entering a Gentile's house, and although he is a man of position and power, he does not want Jesus to be troubled by his problems. Seen in this light, the centurion is one of the unsung and unnoticed heroes of faith in the Gospels (Culpepper 1995: 156).

And yet he was a Gentile. Our critical African reflection on Islam cannot ignore that 'Africans are ill and close to death'. We need, therefore, a reflection that will bring about 'good health' to the African enslaved by so many ills. Our reflection on Islam should take into consideration the Muslim or the Christian who is 'ill and close to death', who is out there. We, sitting here, like Jesus, like the centurion, are not 'ill and close to death',

I hope. We reflect on the religion of the other because we know and they know somebody who is 'ill and close to death'. So our critical reflection should be orientated towards giving life and abundance of life (cf. John 10:10). It is ultimately a discourse on life. We need a Christian theology of other religions that is 'theology of life', not the life of ideas and concepts, but the life of body, soul and spirit.

The Necessity of Good Social Relationship

> *A centurion there had a slave whom he valued highly, and who was ill and close to death* (Luke 7:2).

The picture we get from this text is the existence of good relations between the different parties. This is an important background to any critical reflection.

> When he heard about Jesus, the centurion sent a delegation of Jewish elders to Jesus. The elders would have been the 'town fathers' or distinguished men of Capernaum, leaders in its synagogue. The action of the centurion is consistent with both the elders' testimony to him and his own declaration of unworthiness. He does not approach Jesus directly, but diplomatically sends the Jewish leaders, who could vouch for the merit of his request. The resulting picture is one of good relations among all parties—the centurion has built a synagogue for the Jews; the Jewish leaders speak well of him; and the centurion is deferential toward Jesus (Culpepper 1995: 155).

The work of critically assessing the faith of the centurion can begin in this beautiful context.

A Passion for the Human Person

Our critical Christian reflection on Islam starts with concepts and ideas. However, it is ultimately about human beings. It is about the destiny of human beings, the destiny of Africans. Jesus and the centurion meet because both of them value highly the human person with his or her brokenness. They do not only value, they valued *highly*. This implies a passion for the human person. A slave is valued when he or she works well. When he or she is valued *highly*, it is no longer a question of working well, or of respect.

A critical African Christian reflection on Islam is inspired by the high value given to the African person in spite of his religion, his tribe, etc. The Gentile centurion valued highly his slave. The Jews highly valued the centurion. Jesus highly valued the faith of the Centurion. He also highly valued the person of the centurion. Let us notice the movement from the value given to the person to the value of his faith. Jesus at the end of the story greatly valued the faith of the centurion. He is not only a good person; he is also a good person with a good faith. The dynamics of our critical African reflection can be found in this movement from the person we live with to the faith that inspires him or her.

Living and Reflecting with the Presence of the Other

> *. . . he [the centurion] sent some Jewish elders to him [Jesus]* (Luke 7:3).

> *. . . the centurion sent friends* (Luke 7:6).

The centurion and Jesus never met physically but rather met through people who knew both of them. We can rightly engage in a Christian theological reflection on Islam without Muslims being physically present. Jesus is filled with the presence of the centurion. This is crucial for our reflection. We are filled with the presence of Muslims. We carry within us the presence of Muslims even if we do not have Muslims in our families. We cannot strip ourselves of that presence. The other is near. The other has entered our lives. This is where a critical reflection becomes a necessity and also a difficult task.

We are not alone in our reflection. 'The Jewish elders' and 'the friends' make the encounter between Jesus and the centurion possible. Many people are involved here. Our critical African reflection on Islam should be community oriented. I do think that this is a peculiar African approach:

bearing in mind the faith of the people. Jesus and the centurion listen carefully and attentively to those intermediaries. Their dialogue is based on the words of those people. Jesus' reflection on the centurion's faith was ultimately based on the words of people. What people think and say is the locus of our reflection.

I see a tremendous consequence for Christian theological reflection: to take into consideration what Islam, for example, says about a topic Christians are studying. We do not live in a ghetto. Our Christian message is universal. So our reflection should also be universal and include what the other understands. It means doing theology in a dialogical way. The Islamic *tawhid* may help us articulate relevantly our faith in the unity and unity of God.

The Power of Words

> *But only speak the word, and let my servant be healed* (Luke 7:7).

There is a great deal of speaking in this text. The centurion speaks. Those he sent to Jesus speak. Jesus speaks. And we are going to speak for three days. Thousands of words will be heard. But what is the power of the words we will hear? This story of Jesus and the Gentile centurion puts an emphasis on the power of Jesus' word. The spoken words in this text bring life to all:

> the centurion clarifies that he only expects Jesus to say the word to heal his slave, thereby indicating that he was confident that Jesus could heal at a distance and showing that he acknowledged the power of Jesus' words, a point that Luke has already established for the reader (4:36, 39; 5:13, 24; 6:10) ... The Lord we worship is mighty in word, responsive to our needs, and compassionate to heal (Culpepper 1995: 155–156).

Some words spoken between Christians and Muslims have destroyed our world. We need today to write or voice words that could reconstruct and build. Our African Christian reflection on Islam should be a theology of reconstruction. We assume the past and build something new.

Jesus' Methodology of a Critical Reflection on Other Faith

When Jesus heard this he was amazed at him, and turning to the crowd that followed him, he said, 'I tell you, not even in Israel have I found such faith' (Luke 7:9).

In this verse, we see Jesus' critical reflection. I think Jesus gave us a relevant methodology of reflection: to listen, to search for faith, to be amazed, to announce.

To Listen

First, he *listens*; he hears what people had to say. To listen is a difficult task. We know so much about Islam that most of the time we think that we have nothing to learn from it and that we simply need to criticize. This is a mistake. Islam is an ocean. We cannot pretend to know it too well. We need to listen to Muslims, to what they have to say about Islam. To listen is the first act of love. And it is a religious act: 'Hear, Israel . . .' (Deuteronomy 6:4). We listen above all to God as he wants us to do: '. . . listen to me; be silent, and I will teach you wisdom' (Job 33:33). To listen is to obey. The word 'to obey' comes from the Latin *obaudire*, which means to 'hear or listen to'. In that sense, Jesus obeyed to the crowd. He even went further. He obeyed in faith and 'to obey in faith is to submit freely to the word that has been heard, because its truth is guaranteed by God, who is Truth itself' (*Catechism of the Catholic Church* 1993: 144).

To Search

Jesus *searches* for a particular type of faith that he called 'such faith.' In our critical African reflection on Islam, what is it that we need to be clear about in what we mean by 'faith'? It is not an exclusive faith. It is just a clear faith. It is not a faith in opposition to other faiths. It is just good news or truth that is recognizable as such; 'such faith' is not exclusively 'Christian'. It is complete trust. It is ultimately the will of God that transcends any organized community of believers and any written sacred text; 'such faith' is a complete trust in the will of God. We need to study Islam in search for 'such faith'.

Jesus does not start from the presupposition that 'such faith' is not out there. He searched for it everywhere. He would search for 'such faith' today in Islam. This is a positive way of approaching Islam. It is a journey inside Islam in search for what is true and good because our aim is not to destroy but to build. We can call it 'an *interior* approach' to Islam. This means working from a theological understanding and discernment of religions in the light of faith as we know it through Jesus Christ. The Christian message can reveal, make manifest, and universalize the unique truth that each religion holds. I am not trying to be pluralist or *inclusivist* here. I simply realise that Jesus revealed that unique truth or faith and made it valid for all. This is possible if we have fixed our mind on '. . . whatever is true, whatever is honourable, whatever is just, whatever is pure, whatever is pleasing, and whatever is commendable in the life of others' (Philippians 4:8).

The word *found* means Jesus searched. He did not say he has not *seen*. He said he had not 'found'. It means he looked for it and did not find it. He called for this type of faith. He did not find it among the Jews. He found it in a non-Jew. To approach other religions with the pre-conceived idea that we have a radically opposed view is to close our eyes to God's presence. The worldviews of the centurion and of Jesus may have been different. Despite that, Jesus was capable of seeing a true faith in God in the response of the centurion. In our discernment of other religions, we need such an approach to be able to recognize what is beautiful in it.

To Be Amazed at the faith of Others

The beauty of this text is the fact that Jesus recognizes the truth of the faith of a non-Jew. Jesus is amazed at the faith of the man. We are usually amazed at God's works, but for God to be amazed at us, we really need to be outstanding. To be amazed means also to be surprised. Jesus is surprised at the faith of somebody who is not a Jew. Let us not make out the centurion to be a Christian or an anonymous Christian as some people might want to think. He might have become a Christian later on, but at the time of his request, he was not one.

The centurion was not a disciple of Jesus. The text says that he heard of Jesus. He had not even met him. Where does his incredible faith come from—from his Gentile religion? Where does his deep love for people come from? Did it begin on hearing of Jesus? I strongly believe that the man acquired it from his religion and culture and his personal life experiences because much of our values and convictions are based on our life experiences.

Can we also allow ourselves to be surprised by what we can find in other peoples' religions and cultures, or have we already declared that there is nothing else to be found there? Jesus' remark that he has not found in Israel such faith is important. The expression 'not even' (v. 10) is interesting. It suggests that Israel was the first place he expected to find such faith, because he believes that it is a community God desires. It is a religion that is willed by God. They know God. They know what God expects of them. Do we Christians have 'such faith'?

He is *amazed* at him. He is amazed at the faith he found. He is not amazed to find it in a non-Jew. He knows the unconditional love of God for people. He rightly said in Luke 4:25–27:

> But the truth is, there were many widows in Israel in the time of Elijah, when the heaven was shut up for three years and six months, and there was a severe famine over all the land; yet Elijah was sent to none of them except to a widow at Zarephath in Sidon. There were also many lepers in Israel in the time of the prophet Elisha, and none of them was cleansed except Naaman the Syrian.' When they heard this, all in the synagogue were filled with rage.

Jesus is simply amazed to find it. He is amazed because he has searched for it in vain. He called for it in vain. He desired to see it in his own people in vain. He is pleased to find it now. He is filled with hope that his own people will see it and believe the same way. So Muslims could help us to be better Christians when we are capable of seeing the truth in them.

He Announces What He has Found

A critical African reflection is community oriented. It is destined. It should enlighten the community of believers. Critical theological reflections cannot be confined to the institutes and universities. Nowadays, Muslim and Christian scholars seem to have no impact on the faith of believers. There is a gap and suspicion between critical theological reflections and the faith of people. Jesus destroyed this gap. After his critical reflection, he 'turned to the crowd and said . . . '. The crowd is present at the beginning, during the process, and at the end of the process. Like Jesus, we have to bear in mind the crowd's attitude, mind, and faith in our critical African Christian reflection on Islam. Our reflection should be destined to change deeply Christians' way of approaching Islam. May Jesus Christ enlighten our ways in our search for the truth!

References

Catechism of the Catholic Church. Città del Vaticano: Libreria Editrice Vaticana 1993.

Common Bible: New Revised Standard Version Bible, copyright © 1989 National Council of the Churches of Christ in the United States of America.

Culpepper, R.A. 1996. The Gospel of Luke introduction, Commentary, and Reflections, in *The New Interpreter's Bible, Volume IX, Luke to John*. Nashville: Abingdon Press: 154–156.

CHAPTER 23

Thinking Biblically About Islam and Muslims: Christian Attitudes toward Muslim Women and Seclusion

Josephine Katile Mutuku Sesi

The seclusion of women is mentioned both in the Bible and in Islam. When you think of the seclusion of women in Islam (*purdah*),[1] what comes in your mind? There has been a sharp debate going on among Muslims concerning the practise of *purdah*, that is the veil that serves to screen Muslim women from the sight of not only male strangers but also any male that she can legally marry. In addition, women are also physically separated from men in public places as a way to prevent temptation towards fornication (*zina*). In Qur'anic teaching, '*Purdah* or seclusion of women is believed to be the protector and saviour of the honour, modesty and chastity of the fair sex' (Siddiqi 1982: 1).

Because of the freedom of mixing of men and women in Christianity today, many Christians view seclusion as socially unacceptable and backward. However, in traditional Jewish culture men and women did not mix freely in public; there are cases in the Old and New Testament where only men were counted in crowds where women were obviously present.

The Random House Dictionary of the English Language defines the verb 'to seclude' as 'to remove from social contact and activity'. The adjective 'secluded' is defined as 'sheltered or screened from general activity or view'

---

1. *Purdah* comes from Urdu and Persian languages.

(1973). Seclusion has synonyms like privacy, quiet, shelter or isolation. *Purdah* is defined as a curtain or screen, used mainly in India to keep women separate from men or strangers. It is the Hindu or Muslim system of sex segregation, practised especially by keeping women in seclusion (Answers 2010).

The degree of seclusion of Muslim women in Africa varies from one place to another and sometimes from one group of people to another. Seclusion is practised in homes, at mosques, at work places and in public places. In this chapter 'seclusion' is used in relation to Muslims' practise of isolating women from male strangers and non-Muslim women socially.

In order to discuss seclusion of women in Africa, I have chosen a region and a country that are governed by Sharia, Northern Nigeria and Northern Sudan, and two countries that have freedom when it comes to the practise of Sharia, Tanzania and Kenya. The practises in these areas represent the types of female seclusion observed by Muslims in Africa. I have also chosen four passages from the Bible that support the seclusion of women. In my discussion, I will first give a brief description of female seclusion in the four areas; second, I will discuss Biblical passages that support seclusion; third, I will propose what I think should be Christian attitudes towards females in Islam.

Seclusion of Muslim Women in Africa

Seclusion of Women in Northern Sudan and Northern Nigeria

In the cities of Khartoum, Northern Sudan, and Kano, Northern Nigeria, women are secluded according to age and sect. All women wear dresses which cover their bodies from neck to toe, including their arms to the wrists. However there is a difference is in the how the women cover their faces, depending on whether they belong to one of two general groups, namely the moderate *Sunni* and *al-Wahhabiya*.

Moderate Sunni Women in Khartoum and Kano

The young women in the moderate Sunni group, especially university students, use a *tarha* (veil) that covers their hair leaving most of their faces visible except for their ears. Married women use *khimar* (head scarf), which covers most of their faces except the eyes. The following are descriptions of how seclusion is observed in various settings:

In Learning Institutions: There is a general rule that men and women do not mix in public primary and secondary schools. However, in universities women and men are allowed to learn together. Although there are generally more men than women in university, the number of women is increasing steadily. In Islamic universities, men and women are separated in the lecture halls but in secular public universities some men and women defy the segregation rule and sit together.

In Market Places: In both Khartoum and Kano, the markets have rows of stalls for men only and others for women only. The general practise is for men to buy from male vendors and women to buy from female vendors, except when the buyers cannot find the merchandise they are looking for among vendors of their gender.

Transportation: Up to 1993–1994 buses in Khartoum had two entrance doors. Women used the front door and sat in the front of the bus and men used the back door and sat in the back of the bus. At some point the men complained that the women were sitting next to the driver who was a man and the seating arrangement was changed for about two months. The women, however, complained that the back of the bus was too bumpy and uncomfortable and the seating arrangement was reversed. As the buses were phased out and replaced by smaller passenger service vehicles which have only one door, the rule of seclusion in the buses was gradually not practised.

Northern Nigeria has secluded women more than Northern Sudan on public transportation. In 2004 the state of Kano established a separated transportation system and ruled that men and women could not sit together in the buses. Around the same time, the state bought tricycles known as *adaidaita sahu* as transportation for women alone, and no man is allowed to travel in those vehicles.

Restaurants: In Khartoum, men manage all the restaurants and both sexes can eat in them, but they sit at separate tables unless they are a family. Seldom would men and women sit together to eat in public except again for university students who are trying to challenge the law of seclusion. In Kano, women seldom eat in restaurants except when they are travelling. Very few high class men can take their families to restaurants.

Recreational Public Parks: Public parks are closely supervised by police to enforce the law of seclusion, and only families are allowed to be in mixed groups. However, in Khartoum the police will tolerate university students being a mixed group in public parks. Sports are always played separately, even for fun. Women can play during school tournaments in primary and secondary schools but they must be well covered in long trousers and long-sleeved blouses with the head covering except for their faces.

Cinemas: Families can go to the cinema together only during the day. In the evening only men are allowed in the cinema halls. However, young women may go to cinema as a group during the day. Women are not allowed outside their homes in the dark.

Hotels and Parties: For a man and a woman to book a room together in a hotel they must produce a marriage certificate. At parties women always sit and dance separately from men. It is illegal for men and women to dance together.

It is also illegal for men and women to swim in public swimming pools together. My informant said that for the nineteen years he lived in Khartoum, he has never seen a public swimming pool except in international hotels like the Hilton. However, nationals do not use that pool. Some wealthy families host discrete mixed parties of close friends in their homes, which have tall perimeter walls; however, this goes against the law of segregation, so whenever they are discovered they are arrested. On 25 June 2010 in Khartoum, more than twenty-five people were arrested by the Sudanese authorities after performing the first mixed-gender fashion show (*Sudan Tribune* 2010).

In the work place, women can do office duties but in separate rooms from men. In cases where male and female colleagues are sharing rooms, the desks are arranged in a way to avoid accidental contact between men and women. Some jobs are not open for women, such as driving or waiting on tables in restaurants where they would have to serve men, although women can be flight attendants on Sudan Airways and serve men.

Some women have taken leadership positions as school teachers in girls' schools and lecturers in universities. The government avoids posting female teachers in boys' schools or male teachers in girls' schools, unless the school district lacks enough teachers for particular subjects. In universities women can also be heads of departments and directors of programmes.

Women are allowed by the constitution to contest for parliamentary or civic offices and a few have been elected to official positions. A few women hold administrative posts like commissioners but there has never been a female governor in Sudan.

Females are not allowed to hold any religious offices such as imams, *mu'allims* or kadhis. However there are female religious teachers, *mu'allimat*, who teach girls and other women religious matters.

al-Wahhabiya: Among the *Ansar al-sunna al-Muhammadiya* (followers of the way of Muhammad) in both Khartoum and Kano, seclusion for women is strict. Greeting a man is *haram* (forbidden). Women cover themselves completely and wear the *burqa* to hide their faces from strange men. The concept is that while moderate *sunnis* have specified parts of the woman's body which are considered sexually appealing like the upper part of the arm and upper parts of the legs, as well as the hair, the *al-Wahhabiya* believe that even the eyes are enough to tempt a man to lust after a woman. To remove any form of temptation women must cover themselves completely and avoid all forms of contact with strange men.

Since *al-Wahhabiya* women cannot participate in any form of sports, they are also secluded from other Muslim women in the girls' schools.

Homes: Although in both Khartoum and Kano women are free to relax and remove all forms of veils at home, they still do not sit and converse freely with male members of the family. They have to maintain a level of seclusion even though it is limited compared to that in the public arena. Sometimes a house is divided with an internal wall that separates men from women. If a guest comes to the house, men of the house should welcome them rather than the women. Only the young boys of the house are allowed to go to the women's side; they go through a door in the internal wall. The father eats alone unless he has male guests; boys eat alone, and girls are supposed to eat with their mothers.

The ideal is that women should be chaste and honourable and stay at home and be good mothers to protect themselves from the sensuous life of modern Western women who in their endeavour to be free from motherhood and home have morally debased themselves. The home is a safe haven for the woman and offers her the dignified opportunity to be a mother.

Mosques: Women are given opportunity to pray in the mosque but not to mix with men. They perform ablutions (*wudu*) separately from men. They enter the mosque using different doors than men. They perform their prayers behind the men. This is because the sight of a woman may bring immodest thoughts which would block a man's prayer to Allah and thus block his blessings from Allah. 'Men pray with their eyes open and are therefore cognizant of what is before them. If they are distracted by women they may well be enticed to enter into an act of lust, thereby negating the value of their prayer' (Parshall 1994: 179).

Women are strictly secluded in their practise of ritual prayers by their physical condition that is beyond their control. In addition they cannot keep up with fasting and are thus unable to catch up spiritually with men. Thus women find themselves in an anomalous spiritual position according to Islamic regulations.

Seclusion of Women in Kenya and Tanzania

Islam in Kenya and Tanzania is probably the most moderate in Africa because the majority of Muslims are Sunnis practicing folk Islam. Therefore the degree of female seclusion is moderate except in the mosques, although men and women mix in traditional worship and in ritual dances. With regard to *purdah*, unmarried women cover their hair while married women cover both their hair and ears. The dress standards for Muslim girls in Mombasa are a bit more restrictive than in other places in Kenya. In Tanzania, few girls wear the veil. Some of them wear Western clothes which sometimes expose parts of their bodies.

Girls in school compete with boys in sports while wearing sports clothes. However girls typically from upper-class families in Mombasa do not participate in sports. Also, married women from upper-class families are secluded more than others.

Muslim women eat in the same restaurants with the rest of the people in Kenya and Tanzania; however, Muslims of higher class, and especially Arab-Swahili Muslims, mostly eat as families. Women do most of the types of jobs that men do, although in some cases Muslim women have been denied opportunity to work. They serve as doctors, clerks, teachers, administrative police, ferry controllers and in other jobs; however, it is rare to see a Muslim female working as a public driver. Swahili women along the coast of Tanzania and Kenya run businesses. They sell goods to men, and female seclusion is not strictly observed even though it is present. Men and women do not sit in the same room but eat in separate rooms.

In some of the universities in Kenya, Muslim females disregard the seclusion of women. In a certain university in Nairobi, they may be secluded during the day, but at night they will dress like ordinary university girls and go to Koinange Street for cheap sex.

The Seclusion of Women in the Bible

Just as in Islam, women in ancient cultures used the veil to seclude themselves from men. Women could not sit together with men especially in the presence of male guests. For example, Genesis 18:1–15 presents the story of Abraham, his wife Sarah and the three guests (believed to be God himself and two angels). While Abraham was sitting at the entrance to his tent in the heat of the day, three men visited him. Sarah, his wife, was in the tent. Abraham noticed that the guests did not look like ordinary people. Although he did not know who they were, he asked them to wait for a meal. Immediately he ran to the tent and ordered Sarah to make bread (v. 6). He also ran to his herd, selected a tender calf and gave it to his servant who hurried to prepare it (v. 7). In a short while the meal was ready, and Abraham took some curds and milk and the calf that had been prepared, and set the meal before his guests. He stood near them under the tree as they ate (v. 8).

In the course of the conversation that naturally comes as people enjoy hospitality, the guests asked, 'Where is Sarah your wife?' (v. 9). This question implies that Abraham had not introduced Sarah to the guests. I don't think it was the habit of men at the time to ask about someone's wife when visiting someone's home; however, sometimes a guest's wife could be seen and admired by the host's male friends. But Abraham's guests asked about his wife's whereabouts. Such a question could have communicated to Abraham that Sarah needed to hear the message the guests are about to deliver. Abraham, knowing how beautiful his wife was, simply replied, 'Here, in the tent' (v. 9). This to me indicates that Abraham was not eager to ask his wife to come out and meet the male guests.

A modern person might criticize Abraham for not introducing his beautiful wife to the guests. But in those days there were no international rules to protect women from possible abuse, so men had to protect their women. Probably at this time Abraham remembered an earlier incident in Egypt when an Egyptian pharaoh had noticed Sarah's beauty and wanted to take her to be his wife (Genesis 12:14–16). So this time Abraham did not introduce Sarah his wife to the guests, out of fear of another incident in which guests would be attracted by her and take her away (at this time Abraham had no idea that the guests were divine). God revealed the special message to Abraham concerning the promise of a son saying, 'I will certainly return to you according to the time of life, and behold, Sarah your wife shall have a son' (18:10).

Sarah was listening at the entrance to the tent behind Abraham. She heard that she would give birth to a son and laughed because both she and her husband were well advanced in years, and she was past menopause. She knew she couldn't give birth at her age. God responded to her laughter with these words to Abraham, 'Is anything too hard for the Lord? I will return to you at the appointed time next year and Sarah will have a child'

(v. 18:9–14). Although the guests left without seeing Sarah, they made sure she received the message from God and God fulfilled his promise to Abraham and Sarah (Genesis 21:2).

What was the attitude of Sarah towards the three guests? Again, in these modern times one might think, 'Oh poor Sarah, she never got to be introduced to important guests who had this important message, nor was she given a chance to say 'hello' to them'. But in Sarah's context, she did not want to be exposed to male strangers since, as we have seen above, earlier it had led to serious consequences and almost destroyed her marriage.

Despite Sarah's seclusion, we see her in Genesis influencing Abraham, the father of faith, to take her maidservant in order to get a family for himself. My argument here is that seclusion does not mean the inability to influence change.

Seclusion in Pauline Teaching

In the teaching of Paul, we see another form of female seclusion; in 1 Corinthians 11:3–16 a woman is admonished to cover her head when she is praying or prophesying. The covering of the head is a sign of honour to her husband and to the men in the house. The purpose of covering here is not to prevent men from lusting after her but to protect her honour in society.

In 1 Corinthians 14:34–35 and 1 Timothy 2:12, Paul gives instructions about women speaking in the church and teaching or having authority over men. Although the passage says nothing about the women being secluded from the men, the instructions imply that women and men were mixed in the churches and some women had the spiritual gifts of teaching and prophesying. Perhaps because of cultural reasons it was disgraceful for a woman to speak in the church where men were present.

Seclusion of women is practised in the church today. On the basis of Pauline teaching that women were not allowed to speak in the church, many mainstream dominations including my own do not ordain women into church leadership and to the ministry of the sacraments. Such churches thus seclude women from all church decision-making bodies. This is similar to the practise of Muslims since they do not appoint women to religious posts, for example as imams or kadhis.

Christians Attitude towards the Seclusion of Women

I propose several attitudes Christians should have towards female seclusion in Islam and the Bible.

Christians should not dismiss the idea that women need protection from evil communities. The story of Abraham and Sarah makes a point that women were in danger. Today's women, both Christians and Muslims, need protection. The Western culture that African societies emulate does not protect women. Women are still looked upon as sex objects; this was the fear of woman in ancient times and has continued to be a concern in Muslim communities. The issue of the modern woman presenting herself as something to be admired by men, which can lead them to sin, should change. The Bible teaches that we should present ourselves as the temple of Christ (1 Corinthians 6:19–20). The attitude of looking at women as objects of admiration should change to one of looking at them as the temple of Christ. The issue is not the seclusion of women as in Islam; rather it is the woman set apart as the temple of God.

While the seclusion of women as found in Muslim societies might not be the answer to protecting women, we have to find a way to do it in our societies. We should teach that a woman is a person of enormous worth to God and deserves the highest respect. Women should learn to respect their bodies and to honour God. The basis for covering our bodies as women should not be out of fear that men will lust after us, but rather, so we honour God with our bodies.

Christians should know that being in seclusion does not mean the inability to influence change. The case of Sarah in which she handed over her maidservant to her husband to sleep with her and build a family through her, makes a point. Abraham obeyed; did exactly as Sarah told him to do and received a baby, Ishmael. Muslim women can influence change in their families and communities. Let us give them the gospel of Jesus Christ. Once they receive it and make it part of their lives, though in seclusion, there is a high possibility that they will pass it on to their husbands and family members and thus make Jesus Christ known and accepted in their families.

Christians should know that the issue is not seclusion. The issue here is giving women the dignity, honour and worth that only comes through knowing God in Jesus Christ. Muslim women need to know Jesus Christ, the only one who can give them dignity, honour and worth. How to pass that message to the Muslim woman is the main challenge of the church today.

Christians should know that no seclusion can prevent Muslim women from hearing and responding to the gospel of Jesus Christ. The fact that God asked about the presence of Sarah shows that he has included women in his great plan of salvation. Sarah's laughter shows that she heard God's message in her seclusion. Muslim women can seclude themselves from male strangers and preachers but not from God. God has a way of penetrating through any kind of veil to convey his message to them. Some have responded to the gospel sent straight from God through visions and dreams. They have many questions, and only God can answer them adequately.

Christians need to pray that God will reveal more of himself to Muslim women so that they can hear his voice more clearly and respond more readily to the gospel. Christian women need to take more seriously the commission of Jesus in Matthew 28:18–20 regarding Muslim women and make disciples among them. Christian women need to be better empowered to take the gospel of Jesus Christ to Muslim women.

Conclusion

Christians should make it their purpose to reach out to Muslim women. It is not easy and it will not be easy to take the gospel of Jesus Christ to Muslim women. However, the words of Jesus Christ himself should encourage us as Christians that:

> All authority in heaven and on earth has been given to me. Therefore go and make disciples of all nations, baptizing them in the name of the Father and of the Son and of the Holy Spirit, and teaching them to obey everything I have commanded you. And surely I am with you always, to the very end of the age (Matthew. 28:18b–20).

References

Answers. 2010. Purdah. http://www.answers.com/topic/purdah. (accessed July 4, 2010).

Parshall, P. 1994. *Inside the Community: Understanding Muslims through Their Traditions.* Grand Rapids: Baker Books.

Siddiqi, M.I. 1992. *Islam Forbids Free Mixing of Men and Women.* Dehli: Adam Publishers and Distributors.

Contributors

Rev. Dr. Abraham Akrong is a Ghanaian national and an ordained minister of the Presbyterian Church of Ghana. Dr. Akrong was educated at the University of Ghana and the Trinity Theological Seminary, Ghana and obtained his PhD from the Lutheran School of Theology at Chicago. Currently Dr. Akrong is a senior research fellow and head of Section of Religion and Philosophy at the Institute of African Studies, University of Ghana, Legon, Accra.

John Azumah is an ordained minister of the Presbyterian Church of Ghana. John did his doctoral work with the University of Birmingham, U.K., on Islam in Africa and Christian-Muslim relations. He is currently an associate professor of World Christianity and Islam at Columbia Theological Seminary, U.S.A. Before that, Dr. Azumah served as lecturer in Islamic and Mission studies and director of the Centre for Islamic Studies at the London School of Theology in the United Kingdom. He has taught in theological seminaries in India, South Africa and Ghana and was a research fellow at the Akrofi-Christaller Institute in Ghana. John is author of *The Legacy of Arab-Islam in Africa: A Quest for Inter-Religious Dialogue* (2001) and *My Neighbour's Faith: Islam Explained for Christians* (2008).

Moussa Bongoyok, originally from Cameroon, has had most of his theological education in the Central African Republic and obtained a PhD in Intercultural Studies (with a special focus on Islam) from Fuller Theological Seminary, U.S.A. Dr. Bongoyok served as associate professor of Intercultural and Islamic studies and academic dean of Bangui Evangelical Graduate School of Theology and is currently the director of the Holistic Mission Institute of the Nations and PhD programme director at William Carey International University, Pasadena, CA, U.S.A.

Dr. John Chesworth is lecturer and team member at the Centre for Muslim-Christian Studies in Oxford. Dr. Chesworth did his doctoral work on Christian-Muslim Relations in the East African context with the University of Birmingham, U.K. John has served as senior lecturer and programme director of Postgraduate Courses in Islam and Christian-Muslim Relations at St. Paul's University, Limuru, Kenya.

Rev. Prof. Elom Dovlo is associate professor in the Department for the Study of Religions, University of Ghana. He has been head of department and vice dean of the Faculty of Arts. He pursued his doctoral studies at the University of Lancaster in England. Currently he teaches, researches and publishes in areas of the Comparative History of Religions, Islam in Modern West Africa, New Religious Movements, Religion in the African Diaspora, and Religion in Public Life. He has held fellowships in the U.S., Europe and Asia. Rev. Dovlo is also an ordained Minister of the Global Evangelical Church and the director of Studies.

Rev. Dr. F. Peter Ford, Jr. is an ordained missionary of the Reformed Church in America, having served for twenty-eight years in the Middle East and Africa. He received his PhD from Temple University (Philadelphia, U.S.A.) in the field of Islam and Christian-Muslim Relations. Currently he is Senior Lecturer of the Programme in Islam and Christian-Muslim Relations at St. Paul's University in Limuru, Kenya. Previously he taught ICMR in Ethiopia at Mekane Yesus Seminary and the Ethiopian Graduate School of Theology.

Rev. Daniel Abdou Karim L. Gomis is minister of the Church of the Nazarene of Senegal. Daniel did his Masters in African Literature and Civilizations and presently lectures in Christian Ethics, Homiletics and Spiritual Formation at the Nazarene Theological Institute in Dakar. He also serves as the French editor of Africa Nazarene Publications and a member of the Christian-Muslim Evangelical dialogue committee. Daniel holds a Master of Divinity from Nazarene Theological Seminary in Kansas City, MO, U.S.A.

Bishop Dr. Josiah Atkins Idowu-Fearon did his MA (Islamic Theology) with the University of Birmingham U.K. and completed his doctoral studies (PhD) in Sociology with the Ahmadu Bello University, Zaria, Nigeria. Presently he is the Anglican Bishop of Kaduna, a lecturer in Islamic Studies and director of the Kaduna Anglican Study Centre and a visiting lecturer in Islam and Anglicanism at the Canterbury International Centre, U.K. Bishop Idowu-Fearon also serves as chairperson of the Programme for Christian-Muslim Relations in Africa (PROCMURA) as well as co-president, Network for Interfaith Concerns, Anglican Communion.

Manfred Jung studied in Switzerland, Germany, and the U.S.A., and holds an MTh from Stellenbosch University (2005). He is currently pursuing doctoral studies on the dynamics of the expansion of Islam in South Africa with the University of South Africa. He is heading up Christian Concern for Muslims (CCM) Services and is the managing director of AcadSA Publishing, a Christian Academic publishing house in South Africa. He is a trainer and consultant in the field of Muslim Evangelism.

Rev. William Kopwe is a Lutheran minister, serving in Tanga Region, Tanzania. He studied Theology at Makumira University College, Arusha, and completed an MA in Islam and Christian-Muslim Relations at St. Paul's University, Limuru, Kenya. At present, he is a doctoral candidate at the Open University of Tanzania.

Matthew Hassan Kukah studied Philosophy and Theology at St. Augustine's Major Seminary in Jos, Nigeria. He undertook his PhD at the School of Oriental and African Studies and has a Master's Degree in Public Policy from the Kennedy School of Government, Harvard University. He served as secretary general of the Catholic Bishops' Conference of Nigeria, is a member of the Human Rights Violation Investigation Commission, and was secretary of the National Political Reform Conference. He is currently chairman of the Ogoni Shell Reconciliation Committee and Vicar General of the Catholic Archdiocese of Kaduna, Nigeria.

Rev. James Bol Obwonyo Padiet is an ordained pastor of the Presbyterian Church of Sudan. He holds a Masters degree in Islam and Christian-Muslim Relations from St. Paul's University, Limuru-Kenya. He is currently a pastor in charge of the Good Samaritan Presbyterian congregation in Sudan, Malakal, Dean of Studies for Laa Amoleker Academic Bible School of PCOS-Dolieb Hill Presbytery, and a full-time teacher for the Ministry of Education, Science and Technology of the Government of Southern Sudan, Upper Nile State, Malakal.

Mercy Amba Oduyoye is a Ghanaian Methodist theologian. She is currently the director of the Institute of African Women in Religion and Culture at Trinity Theological Seminary in Ghana. Oduyoye earned a bachelor's degree from the University of Ghana in 1963, a second bachelor's degree from Cambridge University in 1965, and a master's degree from Cambridge in 1969. From 1967–1979, she was youth education secretary for the World Council of Churches; from 1987–1994, she was deputy general secretary for the same organisation. She has taught at Harvard University, Union Theological Seminary, and the University of Ibadan, Nigeria. Oduyoye has written four books and over eighty articles focusing on Christian theology from a feminist and African perspective.

Matthews A. Ojo earned his PhD degree from King's College and the School of Oriental and African Studies (University of London) in 1986, specializing in African Christianity with a special interest in Pentecostal and charismatic movements in Africa and indigenous initiatives in Protestant Missions from Africa. He has published extensively on these and other subjects. His recent book is *End Time Army: Charismatic Movements in Modern Nigeria*. Ojo has served as visiting professor to the University of Edinburgh, Scotland (1993–1994); Northwestern University, Evanston, IL, U.S.A., (1994 & 1995); Harvard University, Cambridge, MA, U.S.A. (2002), and the University of Birmingham, Birmingham, U.K. (2006), among others. Presently, he is a professor of Religious Studies at Obafemi Awolowo University, Nigeria, and an adjunct professor at the Nigerian Baptist Theological Seminary, Ogbomoso, Nigeria.

Dr. John Olorunfemi Onaiyekan, Roman Catholic Archbishop of Abuja in Nigeria, pursued a doctorate programme at the Pontifical Urban University, Rome in Biblical Theology. Currently he is co-president of the Nigerian Inter-religious Council and co-president of the African Council of Religious Leaders (ACR). Archbishop Onaiyekan has been president of the Christian Association of Nigeria (CAN), of the Catholic Bishop's Conference of Nigeria, of the Association of Episcopal Conferences of Anglophone West Africa (AECAWA), and of the Symposium of Episcopal Conferences of Africa and Madagascar. He has been a member of Council of the General Secretariat of the Synod of Bishops in the Vatican and a member of the Standing Committee of the Faith and Order Commission of the World Council of Churches.

Prof. Lamin Sanneh did his PhD in Islamic history at the University of London. Prior to his appointment at Yale University as the D. Willis James Professor of Missions and World Christianity, with a concurrent appointment as Professor of History at Yale College, he was a professor at Harvard University for eight years. Prof. Sanneh is an honorary research professor at the School of Oriental and African Studies in the University of London, and is a life member of Clare Hall, Cambridge University. He serves on the editorial board of several academic journals and has published numerous articles and books including his most recent, *Disciples of All Nations: Pillars of World Christianity*.

Josephine Katile Mutuku has taught at Africa International University (AIU) since 2004 and is currently a full-time lecturer in Missions. She holds a Master of Divinity (MDiv) from Nairobi Evangelical Graduate School of Theology, and a M.Th. and Ph.D. from Fuller Theological Seminary. Josephine is founder of Kyeni International Organisation that takes care of orphans and widows. Her publications include *Social Change Among Digo Muslim Women: Implications for Mission* and a co-author of *African Missiology: Contribution of African Thought*.

Dr. Stephen Mutuku Sesi is an ordained minister of the Africa Inland Church Kenya. He has served as a tutor at Pwani Bible Institute and the national director of the Christian Education Department. Stephen did his doctoral work at Fuller Theological Seminary on worldview change among Digo Muslims of Kenya. Dr. Sesi is now a lecturer in Christian Muslim Relations and Islam in Africa at Africa International University, formerly Nairobi Evangelical Graduate School of Theology.

David W. Shenk is an ordained minister in the Mennonite Church U.S.A. and holds a doctorate in Religious Studies Education from New York University. He served within Muslim communities in Somalia and Kenya and served as academic dean at LCC International University (Lithuania). At present he is adjunct professor at the Lancaster Campus of Eastern Mennonite University and global consultant with Eastern Mennonite Missions with special attention to Islam. An accomplished author, he wrote the well-known *A Muslim and a Christian in Dialogue*, which he co-authored with Badru D. Kateregga, a devout Sunni Muslim scholar.

Serge Moussa Traore is an ordained Roman Catholic priest from Burkina Faso and a member of the Society of the Missionaries of Africa committed to the promotion of Muslim-Christian dialogue in Africa. He holds a Masters from the Institute of Interdisciplinary Studies of Religions and Cultures, of Pontifical Gregorian University, Rome, Italy and a diploma in Arabic and Islamic Studies from the Pontifical Institute of the Study of Arabic and Islamics, Rome, Italy. Serge is author of *The Truth in Islam According to the Official Teaching of the Catholic Church* (Paris: L'Harmattan 2010). He worked in Rwanda as a missionary priest where he collaborated in the Programme for Muslim-Christian Relations in Rwanda. Serge is currently doing a doctoral level research in Islam in Mauritania.

Rev. Dr. Tharwat Wahba is an ordained pastor in the Evangelical (Presbyterian) Church of Egypt. Tharwat did his PhD study with London School of Theology on the history of Presbyterian mission in Egypt and Sudan. Dr. Wahba is currently teacher of mission and evangelism and the chair of mission department in the Evangelical Theological Seminary in Cairo (ETSC), Egypt. He worked as campus director with Campus Crusade for Christ in Egypt for 12 years.

Abdul Rahman Yakubu is an ordained minister in the Bible Church of Africa, Ghana. He holds a Masters degree in Contextual Theology from Kampen University (the Netherlands) in Christian-Muslim relations. Currently he is pursuing a PhD from the same university in contextual theology and interfaith relations in Ghana. Rahman and his family live in a predominantly Muslim area, where he trains pastors and church leaders with a view to enhancing inter-faith relations.

www.ingramcontent.com/pod-product-compliance
Lightning Source LLC
Chambersburg PA
CBHW050524300426
44113CB00012B/1944